When the TRUMPET SOUNDS

Pre-Trib Research Center

THOMAS ICE & TIMOTHY DEMY
General Editors

HARVEST HOUSE PUBLISHERS
Eugene, Oregon 97402

WHEN THE TRUMPET SOUNDS

Copyright © 1995 by Harvest House Publishers
Eugene, Oregon 97402

Library of Congress Cataloging-in-Publication Data

When the trumpet sounds / Thomas Ice & Timothy Demy, general editors.
    p.   cm.
    Includes bibliographical references.
    ISBN 1-56507-313-4
    1. Eschatology. 2. Dispensationalism. 3. Rapture (Christian eschatology) 4. Tribulation (Christian eschatology) I. Ice, Thomas. II. Demy, Timothy J.
    BT821.2W45 1995
    236'.9—dc20

        95-13480
        CIP

95 96 97 98 99 00 01 — 10 9 8 7 6 5 4 3 2 1

*This collection of essays
is affectionately and respectfully
dedicated to
John F. Walvoord,
who, as the greatest defender of the
pretribulation rapture in our century,
has faithfully and daily
preached, taught, and lived
with the blessed hope of His coming.*

Contents

Foreword
Charles C. Ryrie

I used to tell students that I would rather they come to some conclusion concerning what the Bible teaches about the future, even if it were not premillennialism, rather than to be eschatological agnostics. An eschatological agnostic is one who says the biblical teaching about the future is unknown and unknowable and therefore a subject to be avoided.

I think this label could also be applied to the rapture question. There are rapture agnostics as well. They think that we cannot know the relation of the rapture to the Tribulation, so they will not even try to come to some conclusion about that doctrine.

Or sometimes the excuse for ignoring the rapture question is that since there is so much difference of opinion about it, we should play it down. But there is difference of opinion about all biblical doctrines. People differ on their understanding of the authority of the Bible, the concept of God, the person and work of Christ, the person and work of the Holy Spirit, creation, sin, the church, and future things. Should we then avoid all doctrine and be complete doctrinal agnostics?

Here is a book that will help answer questions people have concerning various aspects of eschatology, including the time of the rapture. It deals with the interpretation of relevant passages of Scripture, hermeneutics, imminency, history, and other subjects important to a proper understanding of the rapture. The contributors are a Who's Who of pretribulational premillennialists. They and what they say cannot be ignored.

Studying this book will not only increase the reader's knowledge of this subject, but hopefully will also deepen his or her love for our Lord's appearing.

Introduction

The New Testament clearly teaches that each believer has a hope, a *blessed* hope, which is a grand and glorious destiny. This hope is both personal and a Person. First, it is given to each individual believer and, second, our hope is in the Person of the Lord Jesus Christ. The Bible portrays this hope as pictured in ancient Jewish marriage customs. In biblical times a betrothed maiden would eagerly await the any-moment coming of her groom to take her to his father's house in marriage celebration. During this time of waiting and watching expectantly, the bride's loyalty to the groom was tested. In a similar way, the rapture provides for the church this same sense of expectation and anticipation. The rapture expectation provides believers with a similar daily motivation for a pure and godly life until He comes. Just as the betrothed maiden eagerly waited because of her love for the groom, so also do we await our Lord's any-moment coming. *Though you have not seen Him, you love Him* (1 Pet. 1:8a). Such motives are not "escapism" but, rather, flow from the love and devotion of a sincere believer to our Lord.

Christ's rapture of His bride holds a central place in the New Testament, and it assumes the same in the thought and life of the Christian. The study and implications of God's Word are always important. It is because of this importance that we present the following essays. The rapture is the central future prophetic event for the Christian, and its study is therefore vital in both the individual and corporate lives of Christians. The study of prophecy is not to be undertaken because of its sensational or unique nature, but because of a desire to know the Word of God and the truths found in it. Beginning students of prophecy are frustrated at times by the complexity of prophetic schemes and the divergent views often found among sincere and dedicated Christians. This is unfortunate, for in their discouragement over prophetic complexity they forget prophetic certainty. Our hope is both certain and glorious!

Anyone interested in end-time prophecy and the rapture will benefit greatly from the essays in this book. Some are simple and lift the heart, others are more technical and challenge the mind, but all advance and support the biblical teaching that Christ will rapture His bride before the seven-year Tribulation. Contributors to this book include many of the most well-known spokesmen for pre-tribulationism. This is likely one of the most significant collection of essays relating to the rapture.

The desire to promote greater understanding of this certain and glorious hope led, in 1994, to the establishment of the Pre-Trib Research Center in Washington, D.C. The center grew out of Tim LaHaye's burden for communicating the rapture to the present generation. In 1992, LaHaye and Thomas Ice drew together a group of biblical scholars, communicators, and pastors for a conference known as the Pre-Trib Study Group. This group has expanded and met each year since 1992, and many of the essays found in this work originated in those conferences. There are many materials available from the Center, and anyone desiring to know more about the Center, its resources, and ministries can write to: Pre-Trib Research Center, 370 L'Enfant Promenade, S.W., Suite 801, Washington, D.C. 20024.

The editors wish to thank Dr. Roy Zuck, editor of *Bibliotheca Sacra* for permission to reprint Jeff Townsend's July-September 1980 article on Revelation 3:10. Thanks also goes to Frontier Research Publications for allowing use of material from Grant Jeffrey's book *Rush to Judgment* in his essay. Special thanks also to Harvest House Publishers, especially Bob Hawkins, Jr. and Betty Fletcher. The love, patience, and support of two brides, Janice Ice and Lyn Demy, have been immeasurable.

Thomas Ice and Timothy Demy
Washington, D.C.
February 1995

Thomas Ice

BACK TO THE FUTURE:
Keeping the
Future in the Future

_____*OVERVIEW*

When will Bible prophecy be fulfilled? Why is timing crucial for a proper understanding of biblical prophecy? Major prophetic events such as the Tribulation, millennium, and the second coming will occur in the future, after the current church age is past. Therefore, to try to relate events that will unfold during a future time in the present church age is inconsistent with the original interpretative conclusion that they will happen in the future. This writer argues that we need to be aware of what is future and keep the future in the future.

*T*iming is everything," I recently heard someone say. A good joke can be ruined with bad timing. A car's engine will not run properly without correct timing. Timing for a hitter in baseball makes the difference between a .250 and .350 batting average. Timing is significant if one were to inherit a million dollars. If the inheritance came a few days before the inheritor's death, the money would not mean as much for that person as if it came in the prime of life. Timing is also important in biblical prophecy.

One of the most important, but seemingly little recognized, aspects of the proper interpretation of Bible prophecy is the role of timing. When will a prophecy be fulfilled in history? There are four possibilities, and they reflect the only four possibilities in relation to time: past, present, future, and timeless.

The *preterist* (past) view believes that most, if not all, prophecy has already been fulfilled, usually in relation to the destruction of Jerusalem in A.D. 70. The *historicist* (present) view sees much of the current church age as equal to the Tribulation period. Thus, prophecy has been and will be fulfilled during the current church age. *Futurists* (future) believe that virtually all prophetic events will not occur in the current church age but will take place in the future Tribulation, second coming, or millennium. The *idealist* (timeless) view does not believe that the Bible indicates the timing of events, or that we can determine their timing in advance. Therefore, idealists think that prophetic passages mainly teach that great ideas or truths about God are to be applied regardless of timing.

The Necessity of Futurism
in Support of Pretribulationalism

Of the four views noted above, the only one that logically and historically has supported the pretribulation position is futurism. Why? Because, the timing of the rapture relates to when the Tribulation will occur in history. Preterism declares that the Tribulation has already taken place. Historicism says that the Tribulation started in the fourth century, with events surrounding Constantine's Christianization of the Roman Empire and that it continues until the second coming. Idealism denies that there is a timing of events Thus, only futurism, which sees the Tribulation as a yet future event, could even allow for a rapture before the beginning of that seven-year period. This does not mean, however, that all futurists are pretrib; they are not. But to be a pretribulationist, one must be a futurist.

Historical Development

The early post-apostolic fathers tended to see prophecy as indicating imminent future events. They could best be classified as inconsistent futurists, since they almost always understood prophetic events and personalities as future (e.g., the Antichrist, the rebuilding of the temple, and the mark of the beast). But upon occasion they spoke as if they believed they were in the Great Tribulation (a characteristic of historicism). Since futurism is the product of the most consistent application of a literal interpretation to the text of Scripture, it began to wane as allegorical interpretation rose to dominance when the fourth century passed into the fifth. Because of the merger of church and state under Constantine, many church leaders wanted to suppress the literal interpretation of premillennialism, which cast the Roman Empire in the role of a villain. In fact, Jerome (345-420), Augustine (354-430), and others began to teach that the golden age of Revelation 20 did not have to wait for the second coming of Christ, as taught by premillennialists. Instead, it had already been established through the church's defeat of pagan Rome and the rise of Christianity to virtual dominance within the Empire. Thus, the seeds of preterism, historicism, and idealism were brought forth as allegorical interpretation and replaced literal interpretation of prophecy.

Preterist History

Antimillennialism provided the motive for the non-literal interpretation of preterism, historicism, and idealism. A preterist interpretation of the Olivet discourse began to appear in writers such as Eusebius (263-339) in his *Ecclesiastical History* and *The Proof of the Gospel*. However, he did not apply it with any degree of consistency to the book of Revelation. An A.D. 70 fulfillment of the Olivet discourse is often held by preterists, historicists, and idealists. "The first systematic presentation of the preterist viewpoint originated in the early seventeenth century with Alcazar, a Jesuit friar."[1] Alcazar's work first appeared in 1614 and influenced the first Protestant preterist, Hugo Grotius of Holland, who published his work in 1644. Preterism first appeared in England through a commentary by Henry Hammond in 1653.

These early forms of preterism were mild and undeveloped by today's standards. They saw Revelation as "descriptive of the victory of the early church, as fulfilled in the downfall of the Jewish nation and the overthrow of pagan Rome, and in this way limited their range to the first six centuries of the Christian Era, and making Nero the Antichrist."[2] In contrast, current forms of preterism concentrate the whole fulfillment of the book of Revelation around the A.D. 70 destruction of Jerusalem. Thus, preterist David Chilton writes, "The book of Revelation is not about the second coming of Christ. It is about the destruction of Israel and Christ's victory over His enemies in the establishment of the new covenant temple."[3]

Historicist History

The preterist and historicist interpretations both emphasize historical fulfillment in the present church age, though they are sometimes confused. Preterists usually limit historical fulfillment to the first century, because they believe that prophecy has already been fulfilled. On the other hand, historicists usually view the whole of church history as fulfilling Revelation, leading up to the yet future second advent. Thus, while most of Revelation has already been fulfilled, the historicist believes that a few passages and events are awaiting future fulfillment. They also believe, more than the other viewpoints, that prophecy can be fulfilled in our own day, since they think the church has been in the Tribulation for over 1500 years.

Early forms of historicism arose around the fourth century when some interpreters began to see current events fulfilling biblical prophecy. Later, Joachim of Fiore (1135-1202) accelerated development of the historicist approach by dividing church history into three ages. First, the Old Testament age under the Law and Moses was the age of God the Father. Second came the New Testament age of Christ and the grace of Paul until 1260. The third age of the Holy Spirit (to begin in 1260) would be a time of love until the whole world would be won to Christ. Historicism developed more fully when Joachim's scheme was reworked and associated with fulfillment of the book of Revelation. The Reformers were especially attracted to historicism, as they taught that the Pope was the Antichrist and saw themselves as the godly remnant being persecuted by Rome. Historicism became so dominant during the Reformation and into the nineteenth century that it was accepted as *the* Protestant interpretation.

Shortly after reaching its height of popularity in the early 1800s, historicism began a decline from which it has never recovered. This was the result of a number of factors. As 1800 years of church history elapsed, historicist belief that the second coming was very near reached almost fever pitch. American William Miller set the date of Christ's return on the basis of historicist principles for 1843, and then revised it for 1844. This kind of date-setting helped destroy confidence in the system. Another factor was related to historicism's view that the Roman Catholic Church was the Antichrist because of her departure from the faith. By the mid 1800s, Protestantism was being threatened by the rise of liberalism, which Evangelicals saw as a more pressing threat. Finally, the rise of the more literal approach to prophecy, producing a revival of futurism, made more sense to evangelical premillennialists. Today, if it were not for Seventh-Day Adventists, historicism would virtually have no proponents.

Futurist History

While not as consistently developed as modern futurism, the early church would have to be classified as futurist more than anything else. With a few exceptions, the early church believed that events of the Tribulation, millennium, and second coming were to take place in the future. As antimillennial views begin to arise in the third century, and the Christianization of the Roman Empire through Constantine spread in the fourth century, futurism began to be displaced. As the fourth century turned into the fifth, Jerome's and Augustine's influences against futurism drove it underground during the thousand-year era of medievalism. But there remained during this time pockets of futurism scattered throughout a number of groups who refused to come under Roman Catholic authority. There have also been discoveries of medieval apocalypticism during this time which incorporated varying degrees of futurism.

The Reformation brought a return to a study of the sources. In northern Europe those sources included the early church writers, and they aided in a renewal of prophetic study from a futurist perspective within the Roman Catholic and then the Protestant churches. Jesuit Francisco Ribera (1537-1591) was one of the first to revive an undeveloped form of futurism around 1580. Because of the dominance of historicism, futurism made virtually no headway in Protestantism until the 1820s and Church of England scholar S. R. Maitland in 1826. In the late 1820s, futurism began to gain converts and grow in the British Isles, often motivated by a revived interest in God's plan for Israel, during which time it gained one of its most influential converts in John Nelson Darby. Through Darby and other Brethren expositors, futurism spread to America and throughout the evangelical, and later fundamentalist, world. The last 150 years have seen, for the first time, the full development of consistent futurism. This has led in turn to the formulation of dispensationalism and a clearer understanding of the pretribulational rapture of the church.

Idealist History

Idealism is the least systematic of the four approaches. Therefore, it is more difficult to classify as to specific characteristics. Most likely, it had its beginnings during the fourth and fifth centuries, through those who were anti-premillennial and anti-literal in their understanding of prophecy. From that time until the present, there has been a small minority within the church who have not dealt with the timing of biblical prophecy. The most vigorous debate has been between the three approaches that advocate a specific timing of the fulfillment of Bible prophecy.

Complex Commingling

For many, understanding the differences between premillennialism, postmillennialism, and amillennialism represents a significant challenge. However, it becomes even more complex when the four "timing" approaches to prophecy are added. But, like many complex appearances, it is not too difficult if an effort is put forth to learn the basic characteristics of each aspect. There is then a basis for understanding the commingling of the different aspects. In terms of the logic of the various aspects, what are the possible mixes that can be produced? The following chart summarizes this information.

PROPHETIC TIMING & MILLENNIAL VIEWS

Timing	AMILL	POSTMILL	PREMILL
Preterism	YES	YES	NO
Historicism	YES	YES	YES
Futurism	NO	YES	YES
Idealism	YES	YES	NO

Within premillennialism, there are other possibilities, as charted below.

PREMILLENNIAL TIMING VIEWS

Timing	PRETRIB	MIDTRIB	POSTTRIB
Preterism	NO	NO	NO
Historicism	NO	YES	YES
Futurism	YES	YES	YES
Idealism	NO	NO	NO

This material shows the different viewpoints so that a consistent biblical approach may be developed. Assuming the pretribulational premillennial viewpoint, what would be the most consistently biblical model? I believe it is illustrated in the chart below. The chart of the pretribulational house is composed of three main aspects: 1) the foundation; 2) the body of the house; 3) the roof. The foundation depicts four biblical areas that support pretribulationism. The body of the house represents six major arguments for pretribulationism. The roof illustrates the practical significance of the doctrine that is supported by the foundation and building.

THE PRETRIB RAPTURE DOCTRINE

Practical Motivation for Godly Living

Pretrib Rapture		
• Contrasts Between Comings		
• Interval Needed Between Comings		
• Doctrine of Imminency		
• Nature of the Tribulation		
• Nature of the Church		
• Work of the Holy Spirit		
Premillen-nialism	Futurism	Israel/Church Distinction
Consistent Literal Interpretation		

Consistent Futurism

Once a biblical interpreter reaches a conclusion that determinative persons and events are future (it is beyond the scope of this essay to establish and defend futurism), then he or she must be consistent with such a conclusion. For example, if events and personalities related to the seven-year Tribulation are determined to be future to the current church age, then it is inconsistent to say that events happening today, during the church age, are fulfilling events which are really going to take place during the Tribulation. Historicists equate the church age and the Tribulation, but futurists do not. At least logically they are not supposed to.

The Wacko in Waco

All of us remember the episode of David Koresh, who led a cult on the outskirts of Waco, Texas, a few years ago. Koresh viewed prophecy from a historicist perspective, in keeping with his Seventh-Day Adventist heritage. Consistent with a historicist approach, he did not believe in the pretribulational rapture. He thought that he and his followers were in the Tribulation and that the first six seal judgments had been poured out upon America and the world. Koresh's ministry revolved around his belief that he was the Lamb of Revelation 7:17, and he was ready to open the seventh-seal judgment of

Revelation 8:1-5. He believed that prophecy was being fulfilled in our day. Of course, Koresh was wrong for many reasons, but one included the fact that his view about timing was incorrect. We are not yet in the Tribulation. We are still in the church age. Tribulation events cannot take place in the church age.

The Inconsistency of Futurist Date-Setting

During the last few years we have seen a rash of futurists who have tried to date the rapture. I believe that that is impossible if a futurist is consistent with the principles of futurism. Why? Because, according to pretribulational futurism the date of the rapture is not linked in any way to an earthly event that can serve as a basis for date-setting. The rapture is a sign-less event. Since there are signs related to the second coming, some say that we can calculate the date of the second coming based upon a sign and then subtract seven years to arrive at the date for the rapture. The problem with this is that none of the signs for the second coming are activated until the start of the Tribulation, after the rapture. Then, and only then, does the seven-year countdown commence. The Tribulation cannot begin until after the church age has ended in the rapture; then the seven-year period will be positioned to begin. Until it does begin, none of the signs will aid in date-setting.

Those who are pretribulational futurists have to abandon the futurist method to even speculate on a date for the rapture. The system of futurism precludes date-setting. This is why futurist date-setters actually lapse back into some kind of historicism that equates the current church age with the Tribulation. But if one is operating upon the logic of the historicist approach, then historicism will not support the pretrib rapture doctrine. The futurist, operating upon historicist principles, has just undermined the basis for the pretrib rapture that he is trying to date. Perhaps it is the lack of awareness concerning the timing principles upon which the pretrib rapture is supported that has allowed such inconsistency to occur within the pretribulational traditions.

When Edgar Whisenant came out with his date-setting book *88 Reasons Why the Rapture Will Be in 1988*, I did a thorough and detailed study of it. Whisenant assumed the pretrib rapture (possibly the partial rapture) and then handled the text of Scripture not as a futurist, which he should have done to be consistent with the rapture, but as a historicist, who used passages written to Israel and assumed that they were really speaking of the church. If logical use was made of Whisenant's approach, as found in his book, there would be no basis for supporting the pretrib rapture, the very thing he was trying to date.

Israel's Fall Feasts

Another popular, but inconsistent, date-setting approach involves Israel's Feast of Trumpets. The Bible teaches a cycle of seven feasts, which Israel was to celebrate yearly. The seven feasts are Passover, Unleavened Bread, First Fruits, Feast of Weeks, Feast of Trumpets, Day of Atonement, and the Feast of Tabernacles. The first four feasts are celebrated in Spring, while the remaining three are commemorated in the Fall. A common interpretation concludes that the feasts also are prophetic of the career of the Messiah. The Spring cycle is said to have been fulfilled by Christ at His first coming, while the Fall cycle will be fulfilled in the future through events surrounding the second coming. Up to this point, I have no problem with this scheme. However, I do have a problem with those who teach that the fifth feast (Trumpets) is a reference to the rapture. Since Rosh HaShanah (Hebrew for Feast of Trumpets) is celebrated annually on Tishri 1, according to the Hebrew calendar (usually in September, according to our contemporary calendar), and since it is argued that trumpets are related to the rapture (1 Corinthians 15:52), the conclusion is that the rapture will occur on Tishri 1, as the Spring cycle begins to be fulfilled. This scheme argues that if the year of the rapture can be determined, then we would know that it would occur in the Fall of the year. It seems that many of the more recent and popular date-setting schemes have implemented Israel's feast cycle in some way.

There is, however, one major problem with this approach, which disqualifies any use of it for date-setting. Israel's feasts relate to Israel and Israel alone. True, the fulfillment of Israel's feasts relate to salvation for all humanity, but the precise fulfillment relates exclusively to national Israel. The rapture is a new event related only to the church, and thus it could not have been predicted through Old Testament revelation such as Israel's feasts. Therefore, any use of the feasts of Israel in an attempt to date-set the rapture is invalid.

A Consistent Approach

How does the interpreter of biblical prophecy ensure that he has correct timing? A good interpreter keeps the future in the future. If an event in a passage is to occur during the Tribulation, then it cannot happen during the current church age. It is wrong to say that something is being fulfilled.

In the early 1970s, during my college days, I recall reading Isaiah 24:4-5, which speaks of the earth as "polluted by its inhabitants." The thought popped into my mind that this was a prediction about the pollution of our day, because I had been hearing so much about pollution in the news. Therefore, I approached a number of my friends with the notion that Isaiah 24:5 was being fulfilled in our day. Needless to say, they were not as excited about my interpretive find as was I. Later I found out that I was wrong because the context of the passage refers to the judgments that will take place during the future Tribulation period. Thus, whatever was happening in 1970 with regard to pollution was not related to Isaiah 24:5. I had used a historicist approach to the passage by relating a future event to the present church age.

Having emphasized the point that we are not to commingle the future with the present, it does not mean that current events have no future meaning in the present. The issue is *how* they relate and have meaning. After all, as a futurist, I do expect that God will one day fulfill His plan for the last days in the future, likely the near future. But what is a consistent approach to this matter?

I believe that it is valid to think God is *setting the stage* for His great end-time program. What does that mean? The rapture and the end of the current church age is related to a sign-less event, thus making it impossible to identify any signs that indicate the nearness of the rapture. This is why all attempts to date the rapture have had to wrongly resort to an application of passages relating God's plan for Israel to the church. However, since the Bible outlines a clear scenario of players, events, and nations involved in the end-time Tribulation, we can see God's preparation for the final seven years of Daniel's seventy weeks for Israel. Note the chart on page 22.

National Israel

That ethnic Israel has been reestablished as a nation and now controls Jerusalem is a strong indicator that we are near the end of

INTERPRETING SIGNS OF THE TIME

RAPTURE: is always an "any-moment" possibility and sign-less
SECOND COMING: could be thought to be "near" and has signs

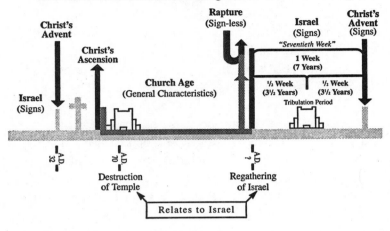

the church age. This can only be a general indication, since no timetable is given for current preparation. Therefore, we cannot know for certain that we are the last generation before the rapture, since God may choose to "stage set" for another 100 years or longer. John F. Walvoord correctly says, "There is no scriptural ground for setting dates for the Lord's return or the end of the world.... As students of the Bible observe proper interpretation principles, they are becoming increasingly aware of a remarkable correspondence between the obvious trend of world events and what the Bible predicted centuries ago."[4] While probably all of the Old Testament passages that predict the restoration and return of Israel to the land in the last days relate to future Tribulation or millennial events, and thus, in a precise, technical sense, are not fulfilling Bible prophecy (Ezekiel 37 is an exception), this does not mean that today's events are unrelated to the fulfillment of Bible prophecy.

Ezekiel 37 teaches that Israel will be restored to the land in phases. These stages are the reverse of what happens in the decaying process of a dead body. Thus, Ezekiel 37:6-8 pictures a valley of dry bones in which the sinews connect the bones, the flesh grows back on the bones, skin re-covers the flesh and bones, and then the last stage occurs: Breath is restored to the body, and life will have been restored to national Israel. Even though the completed, end product, will be finished at some point in the future Tribulation, it is clear that Israel will be regathered in unbelief in preparation for that future point in time when she will be spiritually reconstituted.

Futurist prophecy scholars have long taught that, on the basis of Ezekiel 37, Israel will be regathered to the land in unbelief and will then be converted to Jesus her Messiah. For example, in 1918, the Philadelphia Prophetic Conference adopted a statement of prophetic faith. The fifth article read: "We believe that there will be a gathering of Israel to her land in unbelief, and she will be afterward converted by the appearing of Christ on her behalf."[5] Israel is in the process of fulfilling biblical prophecy because of her current existence and regathering, and because the context of Ezekiel 37 allows for the fulfillment of part of that passage before the Tribulation in the current church age. Thus, the fact that national Israel exists and is being regathered does give meaning to other current "stage-setting" events.

Stage-Setting for the Tribulation

Another point to remember is that just as there was a transition in the early church away from God dealing with Israel as a nation, so it appears that there will be a transition at the end of the church age as God sets the stage to resume His unfinished plan with Israel after the rapture. The church age clearly began on Pentecost, but about 40 years later in the destruction of Jerusalem in A.D. 70, a specific prophecy relating to God's plan for Israel was historically fulfilled. This was the final fulfillment relating to the transition from Israel to the church. During the last 100 years we have seen events occur which are setting the stage for the players to be in place when the rapture brings the church age to an end and God resumes His plan for Israel during the Tribulation.

In addition, there are general predictions about the course of the church age, such as a trend toward apostasy (1 Tim. 4:1-16; 2 Tim. 3:1-17). These do not relate to the timing of the rapture, but are instead general trends about the church age. It is important to realize that when speaking of a general characteristic like apostasy, no matter how bad something may be it can always get a little worse or progress a little further. Thus, it is tenuous to cite general characteristics, apart from clear historical indicators, as signs of the last days. Regardless of how much our own time may look like it fits that trend, we can never be certain that there are not more developments to come.

Some pretribulational futurists understand Matthew 24:3-8 as referring to the end of the church age leading up to the Tribulation (Matt. 14:9-28). They see contemporary significance to recent world wars, famines, and earthquakes (Matt. 24:7-8). Other pretribulational futurists interpret Matthew 24:3-8 as descriptive of events that will take place during the first half of the Tribulation, and thus they do not see contemporary significance to wars, famines, and earthquakes. However, this is a legitimate difference in interpretation, not application.

I think it is consistent with futurism to develop a scenario of players and events that will be in place when God's plan for Israel resumes after the rapture. This scenario views current events as increasingly setting the stage for end-time events, even though they will not commence during the current church age. This model allows a pretribulational futurist to see the rapture as imminent, but at the same time to believe that we could be the last generation of the church age. John Walvoord has noted:

> In the present world scene there are many indications pointing to the conclusion that the end of the age may soon be upon us. These prophecies relating to Israel's coming day of suffering and ultimate restoration may be destined for fulfillment in the present generation. Never before in the history of the world has there been a confluence of major evidences of preparation for the end.[6]

Conclusion

Some stage-setting developments are casting a shadow in our day. They include religious apostasy, preparation for a revived Roman Empire in Europe, Israel's return to the land, revival of Israel's ancient enemies such as Iraq (as Babylon), and the rise of Russia as a military power (Gog and Magog invasion)—all preparing the way for Tribulation events. But before the curtain rises, the church will rise into the air at the rapture. In the meantime, let's get back to the future, by keeping it in the future.

2
Mal Couch

Major Rapture Terms and Passages

_____*OVERVIEW*

What are the major New Testament terms and passages that support the pretribulational rapture? This writer overviews all the New Testament terms relating to the coming of the Lord and shows how they are used. He also examines the major passages that teach the rapture in the New Testament, discovers their meaning, and shows the similarities between the passages. This produces a solid support for the pretribulational rapture as you are impacted by the weight of this collection of New Testament passages. Maranatha!

*B*elievers of every generation have had a longing for Jesus Christ's return. This "coming" of the Lord was considered the blessed anticipation—that Jesus would come back to earth and end all human sorrow. And after a general resurrection and judgment, Christ would initiate a new heaven and a new earth, even eternity itself. Though few could explain the details of how the Lord would come back, this second coming was voiced by nearly all Christians.

With the resurgence of the study of Bible prophecy at the beginning of the nineteenth century, students of the prophetic Word noticed something about 1 Thessalonians 4:13-18. In this passage the apostle Paul first speaks of a resurrection of those who have died "in Christ" and then of those "caught up together to meet the Lord in the air."

How did this Pauline prophecy fit with Jesus coming back to judge the nations here on earth? Where do the scriptural statements about resurrection and judgment fit? And what about the new heaven and earth? How is this passage reconciled with the idea of a so-called millennium, the possible restoration of the Jews, and the church as the kingdom?

Most of the great amillennial scholars ignored the idea that 1 Thessalonians 4 could be any different from other passages that teach about "the coming" (*parousia*) of Christ. In fact, to them the word *parousia* seemed to sum up the doctrine of only one return of Jesus.

Toward the end of the nineteenth century, scholars of prophecy became more keenly aware of studying eschatological passages with greater attention to solid hermeneutics. This led to a better understanding about: 1) how God providentially worked differently in various ages of biblical history; 2) how the end of history had a larger prophetic scheme of things than originally thought; and, 3) how important a role interpreting by context played in comprehending the full scope of prophetic truth.

In time it became more clear to some that, by contextual study, the coming of Christ to "rapture" away the church saints was an entirely different event than was His coming to judge sinners and to rule and reign for a thousand years. As well, many of the great Bible teachers of that period were able to see that both events were to be taken as distinct literal, historic comings and could not simply be spiritualized away. Even today it is appropriate to ask certain questions. How can we be certain of this difference when we read a given prophetic passage that speaks of Christ coming again? How do we know if it is a rapture passage or if the verses are referring to the second coming of our Lord to rule worldwide for a thousand years in Jerusalem?

This chapter will deal with the distinctives of rapture passages, and it will classify the common factors that bind these passages together. There are truths that seem to tie these rapture verses into common units of thinking, though some of the elements may also appear in passages and contexts that deal with the second coming of Christ. Though not all of the similar elements may *prove* the doctrine of the rapture, there are links that carry strong and convincing arguments that cannot be simply overlooked nor dismissed.

By studying contexts, it can be shown that there are *two* distinct resurrections. There is the resurrection for "those in Christ," who will be taken to glory before the terrible Tribulation begins. And there is a raising of the Old Testament saints and the Tribulation martyred believers to enjoy the blessings of the Lord's one-thousand-year literal kingdom reign.

Just what are those common factors which act as indicators and pointers that can be discovered in all rapture verses? Below are 11 categories that help classify the key elements in such passages. While other categories may be found by other scholars, we believe these are the most obvious. And of the verses listed, only one has less than five of the common categories! After listing the categories, we will look at them more in depth.

- RESURRECTION. Though the resurrection is mentioned in second coming passages, these verses and sections of verses reveal certain special elements when they prophesy about those who will be coming forth from the grave. 1 Corinthians 15:23-24,51-52; 1 Thessalonians 4:13-18; 5:1-11.

- HOPE AND COMFORT. These passages tell of a particular hope and comfort, because believers in Christ will be caught away to be at home in heaven with their Lord. John 14:1-3; James 5:7-9; 1 Thessalonians 1:9b-10; 2:17-19; 4:13-18; 5:1-11; 2 Thessalonians 2:1-2; 1 Corinthians 15:23-24; 15:51-52; Philippians 3:20-21; Titus 2:13; 1 John 2:28; 3:2-3.
- THE CHANGE. A new body is given to both those who are resurrected as well as to those who are alive but who will suddenly be transformed so that they can go home to be with the Lord in heaven. 1 Thessalonians 4:13-18; 5:1-11; 1 Corinthians 15:51-52; Philippians 3:20-21; 1 John 3:2-3.
- A RETURN TO HEAVEN. John 14:1-3; 1 Thessalonians 1:9b-10; 3:13; 4:13-18; 5:1-11; 2 Thessalonians 2:1; Philippians 3:20.
- TAKEN DIRECTLY BY THE LORD HIMSELF or, INTIMATELY FACING CHRIST AT HIS COMING. John 14:1-3; James 5:7-9; 1 Thessalonians 1:9b-10; 2:17-19; 4:13-18; 5:1-11; 2 Thessalonians 2:1-2; Philippians 3:20-21; Titus 2:13; 1 John 2:28, 3:2-3.
- LIVING GODLY BECAUSE HE IS COMING. James 5:7-9; 1 Thessalonians 5:1-11; 5:23; 1 Timothy 6:14; Titus 2:12-14; 1 John 2:28; 3:2-3.
- THE PRONOUNS WE, YOU, AND US AS A PROOF THAT THE RAPTURE COULD HAVE HAPPENED TO PAUL'S OWN GENERATION. John 14:1-3; James 5:7-9; 1 Thessalonians 1:9-10; 2:17-19; 3:13; 4:13-18; 5:1-11; 5:23; 2 Thessalonians 2:1-2; 1 Timothy 6:14; 1 Corinthians 15:51-52; Philippians 3:20-21; Titus 2:13; 1 John 2:28; 3:2-3.
- THE USE OF THE TECHNICAL TERM *PAROUSIA* TO DESCRIBE THE RAPTURE. James 5:7-8; 1 Thessalonians 2:17-19; 3:13; 4:13-18; 5:23; 2 Thessalonians 2:1-2; 1 Corinthians 15:23-24; 1 John 2:28; 3:2-3.
- OTHER EXPRESSIONS USED FOR THE COMING. John 14:1-3; James 5:7-9; 1 Thessalonians 4:16; 5:23-24; 2 Thessalonians 2:1-2; Titus 2:13; 1 John 2:8; 3:2-3.
- BEING TAKEN TO THE FATHER. John 14:1-3; 1 Thessalonians 3:13; Titus 2:13.
- THOSE IN CHRIST OR ALLUSIONS TO THE CHURCH. 1 Thessalonians 2:17-19; 4:13-18; 5:1-11; 2 Thessalonians 2:1-2; 1 Corinthians 15:23-24; 15:51-52; Titus 2:13.

The Rapture and Resurrection

The Living and the Resurrected Saints Caught Up Together

What makes the resurrection as mentioned with the rapture any different from the resurrection at Christ's second coming? The resurrection related to the rapture has to do with "the dead in Christ," or "those in Him." This is specifically referring to the church saints, those who have become a part of the spiritual body of Christ in this dispensation.

Four distinct passages link the resurrection of church saints to the rapture. In the most all-inclusive rapture passage, 1 Thessalonians 4:13-18, the apostle Paul addresses the issue of "those who have fallen asleep in Jesus" (4:14). He ties together this "catching away" (*harpazō*), or the rapture of living believers, with the resurrection of church saints, or those "in Christ":

> But we do not want you to be uninformed,... about those who are asleep... (v. 13). God will bring with Him those who have fallen asleep in Jesus (v. 14). The Lord Himself will descend... and the dead in Christ shall rise first (v. 16). Then we who are alive and remain shall be caught up together with them in the clouds to meet the Lord in the air... (v. 17 NASB).

The Thessalonian church seems to have been concerned about the death of those who had accepted Christ as Savior. "Will they live again?" "When will they be raptured?" These questions had not been answered and they were grieving as the pagans who had no guarantees about an afterlife (v. 13). The Thessalonians are answered as they are informed that those believers who have died will in no way miss out on the blessing of the Lord's coming.

And from the Greek text Paul adds: "In no way, not even, should we proceed the ones who have been put to sleep" (v. 15). The word "proceed" (*phthasōmen*) has with it a double negative that carries the force of an extra emphatic, "We should *absolutely not* proceed those who have been put to sleep!" This becomes a Greek idiom which effectively takes away any apprehension about the dead in Christ being left.[1] This idiom has the sense of an emphatic future, i.e. "when the time comes this is the sequence of events."[2] The dead in Christ shall rise first (v. 16).

Those Awake and Asleep Will Live Together With Christ

In 1 Thessalonians 5:1-11 the apostle Paul writes about the coming "day of the Lord" (v. 2) or the "wrath" (v. 9) that will fall on the lost who are proclaiming "peace and safety" (v. 3). In verses 2-7 the apostle pictures the "birth pangs" of trouble and pain that fall suddenly on "them," the lost. They are in [spiritual] darkness, and they will not escape the terror which will overtake them like a thief (vv. 3-4).

In verses 5:9-10 Paul comes back to the issue of the rapture he began writing about in 4:13-17. In verse 10 he summarizes and restates the fact that both those who are asleep (the dead in Christ) and those awake will live together with Jesus:

> Whether we are found among the living or the dead when he comes...This was designed to calm their minds in their trials, and to correct an error which seems to have prevailed in the belief that those who were found alive when he should return would have some priority over those who were dead.[3]

From the Greek text, verse 10 would read:

> [Christ] died for us, in order that whether we should right now be fully awake or whether we should right now be sleeping, we shall in the future, [and] all at once at the same time, be alive together with Him (author's translation).

The expression "in the future...be alive"[4] prophetically sees the resurrected saints in Christ and those raptured believers together someday living with Him. The force of the verb could also mean *"now and forever* we shall live with Him." [5] And the expression "all at once at the same time" sheds even more light on this resurrection and the rapture. Actually, this represents two expressions joined together: "Together with" (*hama*) and "with Him" (*sun autō*). Barnes interprets this: "Those who are alive and those who are dead—meaning that they would be *together* or would be with the Lord *at the same time;* ..."[6] Hendricksen adds: "Those who are *awake* are those who are *alive,* the survivors, the ones who according to 4:15 are 'left until the coming of the Lord'."[7]

Two Resurrections or More?

Even some of the older Bible scholars who would not be accepting of a dispensational rapture see two resurrections in 1 Corinthians 15:23-24. In the full context, Paul promises a resurrection in which "in Christ all shall be made alive" (v. 22). From the Greek text, verses 23-24 might read:

> To explain, each [will be resurrected] in his own order: Christ the first fruits, next after that, those [believers] who belong to Christ at His coming, after this, [will come] the consummation whenever [Christ] [in the future] will be handing over the kingdom to the God and Father, [including] whenever He abolishes all rule and all authority and power (author's translation).

"The whole context is governed by" in Christ...made alive.[8] Dispensationally, verse 23 clearly has the church saints in mind and is not describing Jesus' coming to reign over Israel as the Son of Man nor His coming to judge the world. He is returning to take the church. Since the kingdom is unquestionably separated in verse 24 from verse 23, the rapture resurrection is the only explanation for this passage.

Ellicott's Commentary notes:

> There is to be a sequence in the resurrection of the dead, and St. Paul explains this by the three groups: 1) Christ Himself, the first fruits; 2) the faithful *in Christ* [emphasis mine] at His coming; 3) all the rest of mankind at the end, when the final judgment takes place. The interval between these two as to its duration, or where or how it will be spent, is not spoken of here. The only point the Apostle has to treat of is the order of the resurrection.[9]

Alford writes:

> ...the resurrection of the rest of the dead, here veiled over by the general term *to telos* [the end]—that resurrection not being in this argument specially treated,

but only *that of Christians* [emphasis mine]....It ought to be needless to remind the student of the distinction between this *parousia* [the coming for those in Christ] and the final judgment; it is here peculiarly important to bear in mind.[10]

Robertson and Plummer also believe this passage is open to be interpreted as Christ coming exclusively for His own, the church saints, as separate from another coming in which He raises other dead:

Of these *tagamata* [each in his own order] there are two, clearly marked, in the present passage; Christ, who has already reached the goal of Resurrection; and Christ's Own [the church], who will reach it when He comes again. Perhaps St. Paul is thinking of a third *tagama* [order], some time before the End. But throughout the passage, the unbelievers and the wicked are quite in the background, if they are thought of at all.[11]

Christ's own, the church saints who have died, are still waiting for the resurrection.[12] This passage shows a sequence in the unfolding of the final events concerning that resurrection. Since Paul was addressing the church, he was not concerned with detailing all future resurrections. He concentrated instead on the present church saints who are asleep and their place in the scheme of things.

Hope and Comfort

Almost all of the rapture passages speak of the blessing of the Lord's return for His own, or more specifically, the return of Jesus Christ to take His children home to heaven. This is the hope and comfort! And it is a different scenario than that of Jesus coming back to judge the earth, to reign and rule as Messiah. In fact a key to most rapture passages is this "going home" joy and anticipation!

Going Home!

In John 14:1-3, Jesus made a promise to His disciples of going to prepare a place for them. From the Greek text the passage could read:

Let not the heart of each of you be disturbed. All of you together are believing in God, in the same way, all of you continue to trust in Me. In My Father's house are many dwelling places, but if not, I would have told you; because I go to prepare a room for you [to live in]. And if I am going and prepare a room for you, I will be coming again and take you along [to my own home], that where I am, I and you [together]! (author's translation).

The hope and comfort in this passage is stated in a kind of a negative, "Let not the heart be disturbed." The reason: Christ is going to prepare a place for them, and He will come again for them and receive them to Himself. This is a rapture passage because it is implied that His coming could have taken place while they were alive. Though death could overtake them (as it did), their new bodies would be taken home by the resurrection at the time of the rapture.

The Father's "house" (*oikos*) could not be the location of the earthly kingdom in which Jesus will reign. Jesus would be going soon, in the historical context of His death, to His Father's house. He will come for His own and take them back to a location He has prepared. Thus it is a specific and personal promise concerning the new dispensation of the church that would soon replace the dispensation of law. Jesus is not saying that His disciples will simply die and go to the Father's house (though that would be true of their souls if they died before He came for them). Therefore, His coming for them must refer either to the rapture while they are living or the bodily resurrection that takes place simultaneously. "The dead in Christ shall rise first. Then we who are alive and remain shall be caught up together with them in the clouds to meet the Lord in the air, and thus we shall always be with the Lord" (1 Thess. 4:16b-17 NASB).

Waiting Steadfastly

James 5:7-9 may be one of the earliest references to the rapture, apart from Christ's words in John 14:1-3. Regarding hope and anticipation, verses 7-9 could read from the Greek text:

33

Be waiting steadfastly then, until the time of the visitation *(parousia)* arrives. Behold, the farmer waits for the precious fruit of the ground, waiting patiently concerning it,...You too, be waiting steadfastly, firmly stabilize your emotions, because the visitation of the Lord has progressively been drawing near (author's translation).

The phrase "be waiting steadfastly" refers to patience and forbearance.[13] In the illustration of the farmer, it is said he also "waits." This verb *(ekdechetai)* has the idea of "eager expectation."[14] James urges his readers not only to wait eagerly with expectation for the Lord's coming but also to "firmly stabilize your emotions *(kardia)*."

This rapture passage gives confidence and hope despite persecutions falling on the early church. The farmer waits hopefully for the refreshing rains that herald the coming of new crops. So believers can look for the Lord coming for them. Barnes writes, "In due time, as [the farmer] expects the return of the rain, so you may anticipate deliverance from your trials."[15]

Rescued from the Coming Wrath

First Thessalonians 1:9-10 is a powerful rapture passage that further speaks of an "eagerly waiting" kind of hope. It gives this comfort or hope because it speaks of us being dragged away from the terror of the wrath that is on its way to this world. In regard to this hope the Greek text could read:

You turned...to presently be serving a living and true God, and to presently be eagerly waiting for His Son from the heavens, whom [God] raised from the dead, Jesus, who [will be] dragging (rescuing) us [to Himself] from the wrath which is coming! (author's translation).

The verb "be eagerly waiting" *(anamenō)* is given intensity with the preposition *ana*. And, it has a continual or linear idea, "to keep on waiting."[16] On this hopeful anticipation Hendricksen adds:

The force of the verb *to wait* must not be lost sight of. It means *to look forward to with patience and confidence*....It implies (both in Greek and in English) being *ready* for his return.... The thought of His coming does not spell terror for the believer.... For it is this Jesus *who rescues* (is rescuing) *us from the wrath to come* (the coming wrath).[17]

Barnes says:

The hope of his return to our world to raise the dead, and to convey his ransomed to heaven, is the brightest and most cheering prospect that dawns on man, and we should be ready, whenever it occurs, to hail him as our returning Lord, and to rush to his arms as our glorious Redeemer.[18]

Our Hope When He Comes

Paul writes in 1 Thessalonians 2:17-19: "For what is our anticipation or joy or crown of rejoicing? Is it not even you in the presence of our Lord Jesus Christ at His coming?" (NKJV). This is an unusual way of speaking about hope and comfort. But Paul is telling the believers at Thessalonica how much he rejoices in their stand for the gospel. In fact their suffering and persecution for the name of Christ was almost overwhelming. Thus Paul says that when the rapture occurs, those saints of the Lord will be at that moment his great rejoicing when he stands literally before the face of Jesus. It is with this coming that the Thessalonian believers will be presented as Paul's joy. This is not the coming of Christ to deliver worldwide judgment. This is the Lord taking His own home to be with Himself—clearly the rapture!

Comforting One Another

In the most important central rapture passage (1 Thessalonians 4:13-18) the apostle Paul writes to the Thessalonian church about this great miracle event so that they might "not grieve as do the rest who have no hope" (v. 13). He concludes, "likewise be comforting one another by these words" (v. 18). The word "grieve" should be translated "might [not] be made to grieve." Paul tells believers that if they grieve, it is because they allow grief about their relatives who are asleep to overtake them, thereby acting as the unsaved who look upon death as final destruction.[19] Paul, trying to correct this erroneous thinking, pictures the pagan world as having no hope, and he tells the Christian of the blessed assurance of resurrection to glory with the Lord Jesus Christ.

In verse 18, Paul exhorts the believers to find and give comfort in these words from the Lord about the rapture and the accompanying resurrection. At its root the word "comfort" (*parakaleō*) can mean to "call alongside" or "counsel." "Likewise, be counseling one another by these words." The present tense and active voice in Greek are used to emphasize that they need to be comforting each other right now *and* until the Lord comes. This is an exercise in faith in order to recognize the certainty of ultimate triumph.[20]

After writing about the Day of the Lord (5:2) and the wrath to come (5:9), the apostle again concludes with the same command to comfort one another because God will not put His own through these days of horror that will come on the world. From the Greek text, Paul writes in 5:11:

> Therefore, be continually comforting one another and building up one another, even as [I know] you presently are doing (author's translation).

Some believers had fallen asleep in Jesus (4:14-15). Some will be alive when the rapture takes place (4:17), and they will assuredly miss the terrible Day of the Lord that is coming on the earth (5:9). Thus, the larger hope is that we will be with our Savior whether by the rapture or by resurrection. Comforting words indeed!

The Day of the Lord Has Not Come

Most believe 2 Thessalonians 2:1 is a reference exclusively referring to the rapture. From the Greek it could read:

> Now I am begging you, brothers, concerning the coming of our Lord Jesus Christ even [concerning] our gathering together up to Him ... (author's translation).

A.T. Robertson sees the entire verse as "referring to the rapture, mentioned in 1 Thessalonians 4:15-17,..."[21] Paul then writes, "that you may not be quickly shaken from your composure..."

(2:2). Though the words "hope" or "comfort" are not used here, the apostle is comforting them by saying that the Day of the Lord has not come. He goes on to say that the apostasy must come first and the Antichrist (the man of lawlessness) first be revealed (2:3-4).

Paul gives comfort by using two negatives: "Do not totter or waver" (*saleuō*) in [your] mind, nor "be terrified" (*throeō*), to the effect that the Day of the Lord has come (v. 2). As A.T. Robertson has already noted, Paul is indeed referring back to the rapture in 1 Thessalonians 4:15-17 and amplifying the assurance that believers would escape the wrath.

Christ's Resurrection Gives Hope

In the larger context of 1 Corinthians 15, Paul argues that we have no hope if Jesus was not raised from the dead. "Those also who have fallen asleep in Christ have perished. If we have hoped in Christ in this life only, we are of all men most to be pitied" (15:18-19 NASB). The apostle then gives the great assurance to church saints: "in Christ all shall be made alive" (v. 22 NASB). And following Christ's resurrection comes the resurrection of the believers at the rapture, "after that [the resurrection of Jesus] those who are Christ's at His coming" (v. 23 NASB). "As He promised (John 14:2-3) Christ will return for those who compose the church and the dead in Christ will be raised" (1 Thess. 4:16).[22]

In 15:49, Paul continues his anthem of hope in regard to the resurrection, "as we have borne the image of the earthly, we shall also bear the image of the heavenly." He follows this with the hopeful declaration: "Behold, I am telling you something not before revealed, we shall not all be put to sleep, however, we shall all be changed, in a moment, at a blink of an eye, with the last trumpet; for the trumpet will sound, and the dead ones will be raised imperishable, and we shall all be changed" (15:51-52, author's translation).

These verses truly express a hope and comfort. Saying "behold," the apostle uses a forceful exclamatory to point the reader's attention to a "momentous revelation...to which he calls our earnest attention."[23] This is an "emphatic introduction of information of great moment."[24] Paul twice says "we shall be changed" (*allassō*) at some point in the future. This word has the force of "to alter," or in other contexts, "change the customs."[25] As well, "to take a new position, one thing for another, to alternate."[26]

Because of the unique dispensation of the church, and the fact that living believers in Christ will be changed and translated before the coming wrath, Paul proclaims with great joy this blessed "new" revelation. "That [Paul] did not refer only to those whom he was then addressing, is apparent from the whole discussion. The argument relates to Christians—to the church at large."[27]

A New Citizenship

One of Paul's most hopeful proclamations is found in the Greek of Philippians 3:20-21: "For our citizenship really exists in heaven, out of which we are waiting expectantly [to welcome] a Savior, the Lord Jesus Christ, who will alter the configuration of our body [that has] a limitation" (author's translation).

Here Paul declares our heavenly citizenship and the future transformation of our humble (abased, limited) body. He adds: "we are waiting expectantly (*apekdechomai*) for a Savior." This word can mean "receive, welcome."[28] Paul includes himself in that anticipation. Alford puts it this way: "We wait for, expect, till the event arrives...."[29] "Paul's heart is in heaven. *We wait for*... vividly pictures Paul's eagerness for the... coming of Christ as the normal attitude of the Christian colonist whose home is heaven."[30]

Great Expectations!

Paul almost shouts his excitement about the possibility of the rapture in Titus 2:13. From Greek the passage can read: "[We are] excitedly expecting continually, the joyous prospect, even [the] glorious appearance of our great God, even [our] Savior, Christ Jesus!" (author's translation).

"Excitedly expecting continually" is often translated simply "looking for" (*prosdechomai*) in some versions. And indeed, the present tense makes this "expecting" a continual hope. "This expectation [is] an abiding state and posture."[31] But the word also has the force of "welcome, wait for, expect."[32] The "blessed hope" might be translated "the joyous anticipation." There is no question about this "expectation." It *is* going to come about, and it produces within a great joyousness that looks forward to ultimate redemption. "This describes the great expectancy which is the ruling and prevailing thought in the lives of men looking for their Lord's return."[33]

Having Confidence When He Comes

Christ could reveal Himself by the rapture at any time. The apostle John continues the thoughts of Paul in his personal love letter, 1 John. In two different contexts he speaks of "confidence" and hope in regard to Jesus' coming. From the Greek text he writes:

> However, now [I want you to specifically] keep on sticking with Him, so that whenever He should be revealed, we might have confidence, and not shrink away from Him in shame at His coming (2:28). We shall be like-ones with Him, because we shall see Him as He is. And everyone who is having this antici-pation on Him, is purifying himself, as that One is [existing as] pure! (3:2b).

Sometimes "confidence" (*parousia*) can be translated "joyous-ness," "courage," or "boldness."[34] By using "we" John implies that even he himself may be alive when Jesus comes and that his generation of believers may not have to die. He also encourages them to live the Christian experience close to Jesus, lest they are ashamed at His appearance. John is not referring to a post-resur-rection experience but something that could happen while he is alive

In 3:2, John declares that when a believer "anticipates" or "hopes" for the Lord's return it produces a purifying effect within. "One who sets his hope by faith on the Son of God experiences an inward purification that is as complete as Christ's own purity."[35]

The Change

When the rapture takes place, believers will instantly receive a new, glorified body like Christ's, and the resurrection of those asleep in Jesus takes place. This "change" really affects both the living and the dead, in order that they may be brought into the very presence of the living God and His Son. By implication Paul first addresses this in 1 Thessalonians 4:13-18.

Meeting the Lord in the Air

It is clear the dead in Christ could not be raised (4:16) and that we who are alive could *not* "be caught up together with them in the clouds to meet the Lord in the air" (4:17 NASB) unless we had glorified bodies. The apostle seals this issue with his conclusion, "Thus we shall always be with the Lord" (v. 17 NASB).

We May Live Together with Him

Since believers in Christ are not destined for the wrath (5:9) but are to obtain salvation through His sacrifice, they are raptured to "live together with Him" (5:10b NASB). This thought continues the fact that Christians must be changed in order to exist with the Lord.

Those Who Belong to Christ

After thoroughly explaining the need for the resurrection (1 Cor. 15:12-21), Paul summarizes by saying that "in Christ all shall be made alive" (v. 22 NASB). He then adds (Greek): "To explain, each [will be resurrected] in his own order: Christ the first fruits, next after that, those [resurrected] who belong to Christ at His coming" (v. 23). Again, the change is specifically the resurrection. But in 15:51-54, it also includes a transformation physically of the living believers in Christ:

> We shall not all sleep [physically die], but we shall all
> be changed.... The dead will be raised imperishable,
> and we shall be changed. For this perishable must put
> on the imperishable, and this mortal must put on
> immortality (vv. 51b, 52b-53 NASB).

In Greek the word "change" (*allassō*) can mean "to take a new position, one thing for another, to alternate."[36]

Conforming Our Body

From the Greek, Philippians 3:21 forcefully explains this needed and dramatic change to our bodies: "[Christ] will alter the configuration of our body [that has] a limitation, into a together-forming with the body of His glory." He does this by the "energizing of His power, even [the ability] to subject all things to Himself."

The word "alter," often translated "transform" (*metaschamatizō*) can literally mean to "alter the schematics." Jesus will "turn about" our present body into something *new!* The word can mean to "change the form of a person or thing, to be changed in form, change configuration, change of position or posture."[37] "Limitation" is often translated "humble state" (*tapeinōseōs*). The word can mean "to lower, reduce, to humble, abase, a lessening."[38] Paul is speaking about a body that is now less than "the body of His glory." It is earthly, natural, fleshly, perishable (1 Cor. 15). Sin controls, condemns, and brings about a groaning for release. Thus, we groan "within ourselves, waiting eagerly for our adoption as sons, the redemption of our body" (Rom. 8:23 NASB).

The word "together-forming," often translated "conformity" (*summorphon*), can literally mean "together-formed." Homer Kent writes:

> The present body is described literally as "the body of lowliness"..., a description calling attention to its weakness and susceptibility to persecution, disease, sinful appetites, and death. At Christ's coming, however, the earthly, transient appearance will be changed, whether by resurrection of those dead or by rapture of the living, and believers will be transformed and will receive glorified bodies that will more adequately display their essential character...as children of God and sharers of divine life in Christ.[39]

Being Like Jesus

Though it is hard to fully fathom, John says, "We know with certainty that, whenever He should be revealed, we shall be like-ones with Him, because we shall see Him as He is" (1 John 3:2b, Greek). " 'Whenever' sounds uncertain but the grammar construction implies certainty."[40] The Greek grammar literally says "like-ones with Him we shall be." We shall have a body and constitution just like Him! "It is clearly implied here that there will be an influence in beholding the Savior as he is, which will tend to make us like him, or to transform us into his likeness."[41]

A Return to Heaven

Many of the rapture passages imply or speak directly of a return to heaven. In fact, seven specific contexts let us know our destiny is above. These "catching away" passages are rapture verses.

To My Father's House

Jesus said to His disciples: "In My Father's house are many dwelling places. I go to prepare a room for you [to live in]. I will be coming again...where I am, I and you [together]!" (John 14:2-3, Greek). Christ actually said, "Again I am coming." By context, this should be taken as a future present. "I will be coming again."[42] This event "is regarded as so certain that in thought it may be contemplated as already coming to pass."[43]

Rescued From the Wrath

In 1 Thessalonians 1:9-10, Paul says we wait for God's Son from heaven, who will deliver us from the wrath to come. The implication is that we are taken up so that "we shall always be with the Lord" (4:17 NASB). This has to mean we are taken to heaven. Again, this is not the Son of Man coming to reign on earth but to deliver us out of the way when God afflicts earth's inhabitants with an unparalleled series of physical torments.

Taken Before the Father

In 1 Thessalonians 3:13 the apostle further argues that our hearts be established unblamable in holiness before our God and Father at the coming of our Lord Jesus with all his saints. As in 2:19 (the presence of our Lord Jesus at his coming), "before" is used as a face-to-face encounter! Note the parallel: "Before (the presence of) our Lord Jesus"—2:19, and "before (the presence of) our God and Father"—3:13. This has to be in heaven.

Always With the Lord

Few would argue that when Paul says "thus we shall always be with the Lord" (1 Thess. 4:17 NASB), he must be referring to heaven. Bible scholars of all prophetic persuasions have always held this means going home to heaven. The passage in Greek even more strongly suggests this: "We shall be snatched (raptured) into the clouds into the meeting place of the Lord in the air. Thus, altogether we shall ourselves be together with the Lord." Also, Bible teachers concur that Paul is alluding to heaven when he writes: "whether we are awake or asleep, we may live together with Him" (5:10).

Gathered to Him

Many believe when the apostle writes of "the coming of our Lord Jesus Christ, even our gathering together to Him," he is still speaking of our going home to heaven (2 Thess. 2:1). Some have called this the muster of the saints to heaven! In fact, the phrase "to him" can be translated "up to him."[44]

Our Citizenship in Heaven

There is no question about what Paul is saying in Philippians 3:20. Christians, while living on earth, have their citizenship else-where—in heaven. This contrasts with those who set their minds on earthly things (3:19). "Their mind [the world's] is on earth; our country is in heaven, and to it our affections cling, even during our earthly pilgrimage."[45]

Taken Directly to the Lord Himself
or Intimately Facing Christ at His Coming

This "taking" is not before Jesus as the King of Israel, the Messiah when He begins His earthly rule. All the contexts of the rapture passages either explicitly state or imply "going home to be with the Lord in heaven." But they also indicate believers will see Jesus instantly by the dynamic rapture and change upon those living or by the resurrection of the church saints. The purpose for this "catching away" of the living is so that the wrath may fall on the earth. When He comes to reign in His second coming, church saints return with Him.

Where Jesus Is, We Are

In John 14:3 Christ states it clearly: "I will be coming again and take you along [to my own home], that where I am, I and you [together]" (author's translation). The Lord's disciples could have been raptured while living, but they died and their souls were taken to heaven. So Christ's coming back with their souls will bring about the bodily resurrection whereby their souls will be joined to their bodies. The disciples will then receive their new bodies. But they could have been snatched away while living and suddenly have met Him in the air.

Waiting for God's Son

Believers are to be eagerly waiting for the return of the resurrected Jesus, God's Son from heaven (1 Thess. 1:10). They will see Him face-to-face! The Greek word "wait" (*anamenō*) could be translated "to keep on waiting up for His Son." Hendricksen notes:

> The force of the verb to wait must not be lost sight of. It means to look forward to with patience and confidence, ... being ready for his return.... The thought of his coming does not spell terror for the believer.[46]

The Judge Is Approaching

When the apostle James writes of Christ as an approaching Judge (James 5:9), he is not referring to a judgment of our eternal destiny but of the *bēma* judgment for works. "For we must all appear before the judgment seat (*bēmatos*) of Christ, that each one may be recompensed for his deeds..." (2 Cor. 5:10). From the Greek text James actually says: "The coming of the Lord has progressively been approaching, coming nearer, drawing nearer [at hand]" (5:8). Thus, Christ our Judge is "brought near," He is "at the point of" appearing.[47]

Jesus Who Drags Us Away

Paul writes of "Jesus, who delivers us from the wrath coming" (1 Thess. 1:10). The deponent Greek word *ruomai* has the idea "to deliver, rescue."[48] In some contexts it is translated "*saved* from the jaws of the lion" (2 Tim. 4:17) and "*delivered* from the power of darkness" (Col. 1:13). Being a participle, some see this as a descriptive of Christ's office, "Our Deliverer."[49] Also, it could be a timeless substantive denoting one of Jesus' characteristics, "Jesus who will return as rescuer."[50] In classical Greek the word (*erruō*) can be translated "drag" or "draw away."[51] Vincent translates *ruomai* with the force of the middle voice, "to draw to one's self" with the specification from evil or danger.[52] The word can also have the force of a prophetic future, "The One who will drag us away [to Himself]" from the wrath which is coming.

Snatched Away

First Thessalonians 4:17 reads from the Greek text: "We shall be snatched into the clouds into the meeting place of the Lord in the air." The word "rapture" comes from the Greek *harpazō* which indicates being suddenly swooped away by a force that cannot be opposed.[53] Believers are going to meet the Lord in an appointed place in the air. The term "meeting place" (*apantēsin*) has a technical meaning in the Hellenistic world in relation to the visits of dignitaries. Visitors would be formally met by the citizens, or a deputation of them, who had gone out from the town for this purpose. The dignitary would then be ceremonially escorted back into the city. In the rapture, Christ will rescue us (1:10) and snatch us away to the meeting place in the sky, before the wrath of God falls on the earth (5:1-9).

Other passages speak of that face-to-face encounter *"(in the presence of)"* with the Lord (1 Thess. 2:19). And, "we shall always be with the Lord" (4:17 NASB). Other like phrases make it clear that when the rapture comes, *we are indeed to be with Him!* "Whether we are awake or asleep, we may live together with Him" (5:10). "Our gathering together to Him" (2 Thess. 2:1). "We eagerly wait for a Savior, the Lord Jesus Christ" (Phil. 3:20). "Looking for the blessed hope and the appearing of the glory of our great God and Savior, Christ Jesus" (Titus 2:13). Stay with Him, "so that when He appears, we may have confidence and not shrink away from Him [from His face][54] in shame at His coming" (1 John 2:28). "We shall see Him just as He is" (3:2).

Living Godly Because He Is Coming

In six distinct passages, godly living is tied to the rapture hope. Critics of the rapture often claim this doctrine is but an escape for those who teach it. But the apostles James and Paul both make it an incentive for living because He could appear to take us to Himself at any moment.

Do Not Complain Against Another

James pleads: "Do not complain, brethren, against one another, that you yourselves may not be judged; behold the judge is standing right at the door" (James. 5:9 NASB). James further warns against swearing and being flippant or profane. The Lord could come at any moment: "Above all, . . . do not swear, . . . let your yes be yes, and your no, no; so that you may not fall under judgment [when the judge comes]" (5:12 NASB).

Do Not Sleep, Be Sober

After Paul's great teaching on the rapture and the accompanying resurrection of church saints, he reminds believers in Christ they are not "destined for wrath" (1 Thess. 5:9). The saints will escape the "day of the Lord" (5:2) which will fall with sudden destruction on "them," those who have not trusted in Christ and who are in darkness (5:3-7). But with this reminder, Paul wants the believers to live a godly life. He writes: "We are of the day, let us be sober, having put on the breastplate of faith and love, and as a helmet, the hope of salvation" (5:8 NASB). The apostle says we are sons of light and are not to sleep. We must be sober (5:5-6). Paul clearly is talking about how we are to live in the light of His any-moment return for those in Christ.

Paul further prays that God will sanctify the whole person so that we may be preserved morally intact and undiminished because of Christ's return:

> Now may the God of peace Himself sanctify you entirely; and may your spirit and soul and body be preserved complete, without blame at the coming of our Lord Jesus Christ (5:23 NASB).

The word "entirely" could read "quite complete" or "through and through."[55] "To concentrate, to separate from things profane....Here alone in the New Testament it means the whole of each of you, every part of you 'through and through' (Luther) qualitatively rather than quantitatively."[56]

Living Without Stain

Paul urges those in Christ to "keep the commandment without stain or reproach until the appearing (*epiphaneias*) of our Lord Jesus Christ" (1 Tim. 6:14). The word "stain" can refer to a hidden reef or a soiled blemish.[57] The word "reproach" carries the idea of "irreproachable conduct."[58] In the context, the apostle seems to be referring to the issues of money and wealth. Quite clearly he has in view proper moral living, in regard to the proper use of material things, in order to stand spiritually tall when Jesus comes for us.

The Blessed Hope and Christian Living

The grace of God and its accompanying salvation should cause us to be instructed and to be looking "for the blessed hope...." (Titus 2:12-13). This salvation should assist us in denying ungodliness and worldly desires and help us "live sensibly, righteously and godly in the present age." And it should produce a welcoming and an expectation of the Lord's soon return. On the two participles "instructing" (v. 12) and "looking" (v. 13): together they would read "The grace of God has appeared... *instructing* us [that we might live sensibly]... [as we are] *looking* for the blessed hope..."

Do Not Shrink Back

Like Paul, the apostle John urges believers to "have confidence" and "not shrink away from Him in shame at His coming" (1 John 2:28). As with us, it may have been easy for the early church Christians to forget their Savior. For many, their lives must have been imperfect. John (and Paul) tie the believer's life to the hope of the rapture, so that they might not "shrink away from His face" with guilt when He arrives.[59]

John adds that just fixing our hope on Jesus' return has a purifying effect on the child of God: "Everyone who has this hope fixed on Him purifies himself.... One who sets his hope by faith on the Son of God experiences an inward purification that is as complete as Christ's own purity."[60]

The Pronouns *We, You, Us* as a Proof That the Rapture Could Have Happened to Paul's Own Generation

Without doubt, the early church and the apostles hoped for Christ's soon return. As with some engagements, a wedding date may not have been set, or it may even be uncertain as to the *when*. Yet the bride and groom long for and anticipate their coming union. So the disciples had this longing but were given no hint as to the time of the rapture. Since it did not come upon them, we do not question their hope nor the Lord's revelation about the doctrine itself. It simply means that it is yet to come. We could be that generation!

The phrases and verses below (author's translations) demonstrate this great and eager "going home" taught by the apostles.

Sometimes the *we, you,* and *us* may not be directly translated in all versions. But it is *understood* in the Greek grammar.

John 14:1-3

Let not *your* heart be troubled.

I go to prepare a place for *you.*

And if I prepare a place for *you.*

I will receive *you* to Myself.

Where I am, there *you* may be also.

James 5:7-9

You be patient, therefore, brethren, until the coming of the Lord.

[*You*] behold, the farmer waits for the produce of the soil.

You too be patient.

[*You*] strengthen your hearts, for the coming of the Lord is at hand.

[*You*] do not complain,... that *you* be not judged.

[*You*] behold, the judge is standing right at the door.

1 Thessalonians 1:9-10

You wait for His Son from heaven.

Jesus, who delivers *us* from the wrath to come.

1 Thessalonians 2:17-19

You [our hope], in the presence of *our* Lord Jesus at His coming.

1 Thessalonians 3:13

That [He may] establish *your* hearts...before *our* God and Father at the coming of *our* Lord Jesus with all His saints.

1 Thessalonians 4:13-18

We do not want *you* to be uninformed, brethren, about those who are asleep.

That *you* may not grieve.

If *we* believe that Jesus died ..even so God will

bring with Him [Jesus] *those* who have fallen asleep in Jesus.

We say to *you* by the word of the Lord.

That *we* who are alive, and remain until the coming of the Lord, shall not precede *those* who have fallen asleep.

The dead in Christ shall rise first. Then *we* who are alive and remain shall be caught up *together* with *them* in the clouds to meet the Lord in the air.

We shall always be with the Lord.

[*You*] comfort one another with these words.

1 Thessalonians 5:1-11

You, brethren, are not in darkness, that the day [of the Lord] should overtake *you* like a thief.

You are all sons of light and sons of day.

We are not of night nor of darkness.

But since *we* are of the day, let *us* be sober.

God has not destined *us* for wrath, but for obtaining salvation through *our* Lord Jesus Christ.

[Christ] who died for *us*, that whether *we* are awake or asleep, *we* may live *together* with Him.

[*You*] encourage *one another*, and [*you*] build up *one another*.

1 Thessalonians 5:23

May the Lord sanctify *you*...without blame at the coming of *our* Lord Jesus Christ.

2 Thessalonians 2:1-2

With regard to the coming of *our* Lord Jesus Christ and *our gathering together* to Him.

[*You*] be not quickly shaken...to the effect that the day of the Lord has come.

1 Timothy 6:14

You keep the commandment without stain or reproach until the appearing of our Lord Jesus Christ.

1 Corinthians 15:51-52

> *We* shall not all sleep, but *we* shall all be changed in a moment, in the twinkling of an eye.

> The dead in Christ will be raised imperishable, and *we* shall be changed.

Philippians 3:20-21

> *Our* citizenship is in heaven.

> *We* eagerly wait for a Savior, the Lord Jesus Christ.

> [Christ] will transform the body of *our* humble state.

Titus 2:13

> [*We* are] looking for the blessed hope and the appearing of the glory of *our* great God and Savior, Christ Jesus.

1 John 2:28

> *We* may have confidence and not shrink away from Him in shame at His coming.

1 John 3:2-3

> *We* know that, when He appears, *we* shall be like Him, because *we* shall see Him just as He is.

> *Everyone* who has this hope fixed on Him purifies *himself*, just as He is pure.

The Use of the Technical Term *Parousia* (the Coming) to Specifically Describe the Rapture

It is not the purpose of this section to give a complete study on the word *parousia* except to simply say that the word can be applied to the rapture of the church or to the coming of Christ to establish the millennial kingdom. *Context* is the key issue in determining which coming is in view. It is also important to note that the word does not mean simply "a coming." It may, by context, mean "a presence," "an arrival," "a situation," or simply the coming of a dignitary for an official "visit."[61]

Thus, when the word *parousia* is used in rapture passages, it in no way has to be understood as a "coming to stay." Nor does the word automatically have to relate to the second coming of Christ;

that is, His coming *to* earth to reign on the throne of David. By context then, it may just be translated the "event," the "appearance," or the "visit." In light of this, the passages below are translated from the Greek text (author's translations).

James 5:7-9

> Be waiting steadfastly then, until the time of the *visitation* arrives.
>
> Be waiting steadfastly,...because the *visitation* of the Lord has progressively been drawing near.

1 Thessalonians 2:17-19

> Are not you in fact [our joy] when we face our Lord Jesus at [the time of] His *appearance*.

1 Thessalonians 3:13

> That [He may] firm up the hearts of you faultless,...in the [very] presence of the God and Father of us with the *arrival* of our Lord Jesus.

1 Thessalonians 4:13-18

> We, the ones living and remaining until the *coming* of the Lord.

1 Thessalonians 5:23

> May He preserve your spirit and soul and body with the *arrival* of our Lord Jesus Christ.

2 Thessalonians 2:1-2

> Concerning the *coming* of our Lord Jesus Christ even [concerning] our gathering together *up to* Him.

1 Corinthians 15:23-24

> Christ the first fruits [resurrected], next after that, those who belong to Christ at His *visitation*.

1 John 2:28

> So that when He appears, we may...not shrink away from Him in shame at His *coming*.

Other Expressions Used for the Coming

Besides *parousia,* other words and phrases describe the idea of Christ's rapture return to catch His own away. These words add weight and confirm this doctrine.

I Will Return

Jesus said, "I will come again, and receive you to Myself" (John 14:3). Actually it reads, "Again I am coming" (*palin erchomai*). By context and because of the "again," this should be taken as a future present. "I will be coming again." This should be taken as a definite promise.[62] "This use of the present tense denotes an event which has not yet occurred, but which is regarded as so certain that in thought it may be contemplated as already coming to pass."[63] Christ makes it clear He is coming back for His own. Since He was addressing the apostles, this return could have even taken place while these disciples were alive.

The Lord's Coming Is Imminent

Besides using the word *parousia*, James adds this coming "is at hand" (James 5:8). From the Greek the expression "is at hand" (*engizō*) could read, "The coming of the Lord has progressively been approaching, coming nearer, drawing nearer. The word has the idea 'to be imminent' and can be translated 'to be at the point of."[64] The word *engizō* is related to the noun that has the idea of "in the vicinity of, close by."[65]

James further sees Jesus the Judge *standing right at the door* (5:9). Christ "has come right up to the door." By the perfect tense, the apostle is saying, "He is, as it were, even now approaching the door..."[66]

The Lord Descends From Heaven

In 1 Thessalonians 4:16, the Greek word "descends" means "to come down" (*katabainō*). "He will (future tense) come down *from heaven*." The result is that the dead in Christ shall rise first, then we who are alive and remain shall be caught up. But notice, He does not stay here on earth. In fact, *we*, along with the resurrected, are taken up to Him. This is one of the most important characteristics of the rapture concept.

Gathering Together Up to Him

In 2 Thessalonians 2:1, though the apostle Paul uses the word *parousia* to describe the rapture coming of Christ, he then adds "and our gathering together to him." Several Greek scholars feel the "coming" and the "gathering" are the same event and thus the passage should read "the coming, *even* the gathering together." Ellicott sees this "gathering" the same as the "taking up" in 1 Thessalonians 4:14-17.[67] A.T. Robertson adds: "Paul is referring to the rapture, mentioned in 1 Thess. 4:15-17, and the being forever with the Lord thereafter."[68]

The Blessed Hope and Appearing

Though the noun "appearing" (*epiphaneia*) can refer to the second coming of Jesus (2 Thess. 2:8), twice it refers to the rapture coming of our Lord (1 Tim. 6:14; Titus 2:13). As a verb, "to appear" is used twice in 1 John to refer to the rapture (2:28; 3:2), "when He appears."

In Titus 2:13 Paul says "we" (us) are looking for this "appearing" of the glory of our great God and Savior, Jesus Christ. "The glory" is a descriptive genitive, translated as an adjective.[69] Thus, "the glorious appearance." The "and" between the two phrases "is explanatory, introducing the definition of the character of the thing hoped for. Looking for the object of hope, *even* the appearing" of the glory.[70] "The Greek connects 'the blessed hope and glorious appearing' under one article, suggesting that the reference is to one event viewed from two aspects."[71] The reference to the Lord should read, "the great God *even* Savior, Christ Jesus."[72]

Being Taken to the Father

Three main passages refer directly to our being raptured to the Father. The first is John 14:1-3. "In My Father's house are many dwelling places;...I go to prepare a place for you." This house could not be the location of the earthly kingdom in which Christ will reign. Jesus is going *now*, in the historical context of this passage, and in reference to the near event of His death, to His Father's house. He will come for His own and take them back to a location in heaven He has prepared.

Thus, this is a specific and personal promise concerning the new dispensation of the church. Jesus is not saying His disciples will simply die and go to the Father's house. (Though that would be true of their souls if they perished before He came for them. And indeed, this is what happened.) Thus, His coming for them would either be the bodily resurrection, or the bodily rapture while they would still be alive. We know now, of course, that they died. They now await the resurrection of their new bodies and the joining of their souls to those bodies.

First Thessalonians 3:13 pictures believers in Christ as kept *"in holiness* before (in the very presence of) our God and Father at the coming of our Lord Jesus Christ with all His saints." Paul is arguing for the believer's maturity, spiritually and morally, so that he may stand before God *uncensored* by the way he lived.

In a powerful passage on the Trinity and the deity of Christ, Paul writes about the "appearing of the glory of our great God and Savior, Jesus Christ" (Titus 2:13). Though the Father and the Son are separate Persons in the Godhead, they share the same essence and attributes. We are raptured by God the Son and taken to the very presence of God the Father. In this same epistle, Paul says, "God [is] our Savior" (3:4) and "Christ [is] our Savior" (3:6).

Those in Christ or Allusions to the Church

The rapture has to do with the dispensation of the church or those "in Christ." The church age is a unique period with special promises. Those with Him now by faith will not face the coming wrath (1 Thess. 5:9). There was nothing like the rapture for Old Testament saints, and there will be nothing similar for Tribulation believers.

Most of the rapture passages mention the believer's relationship to Jesus. Paul speaks of "our Lord Jesus at His coming" (1 Thess. 2:19) and of the dead as those "who have fallen asleep in Jesus" (4:14), who are now called "the dead in Christ" and who will rise first (4:17). The reason for the rapture, Paul says, is so we might escape the coming wrath and obtain salvation "through our Lord Jesus Christ" (5:9). Awake or asleep we will live together "with Him" (5:10). The apostle continues to punctuate this relationship with our Redeemer when he reminds the confused Thessalonians of this "coming of our Lord Jesus Christ and our gathering together to Him" (2 Thess. 2:1).

In Paul's great resurrection and rapture section, 1 Corinthians 15:12-28, both events are tightly tied to our spiritual position in Christ. "In Christ all shall be made alive," he says (15:21). Jesus is the first fruits of the resurrection and then those who are Christ's "at

His coming" (15:23). And following the apostle's great description of our "change" at the rapture and the resurrection of the dead, he concludes with this triumphant statement, "thanks be to God, who gives us the victory *because of* our Lord Jesus Christ" (15:57).

In Titus, Paul calls the Lord "our great God and Savior, Jesus Christ" (2:13). He "gave Himself for us," and thus redeems and purifies "a people for His own possession" (2:14).

These statements are important because they reveal the unique position the church now has with its Savior that spares it from the coming wrath. Thomas writes:

> When God vents his anger against earth dwellers (Rev. 6:16, 17), the body of Christ will be in heaven as the result of the series of happenings outlined in [1 Thess.] 4:14-17 (cf. 3:13). This is God's purpose.[73]

Kent concludes:

> At Christ's coming, ... the earthly, transient appearance will be changed, whether by resurrection of those dead or by rapture of the living, and believers will be transformed and will receive glorified bodies that will more adequately display their essential character ... as children of God and sharers of divine life in Christ.[74]

Conclusion

These rapture passages form webs of related themes that can be identified and cataloged. Key verses interface with each other and give patterns that are undeniable. All the accumulated rapture data strengthens the doctrine and gives believers assurance. These verses spell out that the living believers in Christ will be changed and taken home by the Lord before the terrible period of the wrath begins, and they reveal that the dead in Christ will be resurrected to receive a new, eternal body. Together we go home with the Lord and are presented to God our Father.

Too often the rapture is dismissed as an imaginary creation of fanatical dispensationalists. But the patterns defined here reinforce this doctrine. As this author examined various amillennial and post-millennial grammatical commentaries for this study, he found most of the scholars in these persuasions true to the grammar observed in the rapture passages. But too often they were not able to rise above their preconception of the second coming of Christ only. They assumed that all the verses about the return of our Lord fell into just the one category. It is hoped that this overview and correlation of most of the rapture verses will help us see more clearly the full revelation of end-time events. (For those interested in a detailed grammatical analysis of the rapture passages, they may write for the booklet *The Rapture Passages*, Tyndale Seminary, 6800 Brentwood Stair, Suite 100, Fort Worth, TX 76112.)

3

J. Randall Price

Old Testament Tribulation Terms

_____*OVERVIEW*

Where do the New Testament writers get terms like "wrath," "Tribulation," and "Day of the Lord"? This writer shows that they are first revealed by God in the Old Testament, which provides the basis for their use in the New Testament. Therefore, it is important for any student of prophecy to develop an understanding of these terms first from Old Testament usage to better see their significance in the New Testament. Here is a study that will aid anyone interested in biblical prophecy.

*T*he eschatological period of divine judgment that precedes the time of national Jewish redemption and the establishment of God's kingdom on earth is known as the Tribulation period. This concept was part of Jesus' eschatological teaching.[1] It was a frequent theme of the apostles[2] and of the early church.[3]

Where did this concept originate? Was it a new revelation imparted by Jesus or Paul, or an invention of early Christianity to explain their suffering? Though this same teaching occurs in the intertestamental period Jewish apocalyptic literature,[4] which influenced the early rabbinic writings,[5] when we study the New Testament we discover that the primary source for the Tribulation doctrine developed from antecedent Old Testament usage. This is evident from the citations[6] and allusions[7] of the Old Testament in the principal New Testament eschatological texts of the Olivet discourse and the book of Revelation.[8] Since the line of revelation begins in the Old Testament, an investigation of the meaning and usage of its Tribulation terms is essential to an understanding of the New Testament doctrine.

The Identification of Tribulation Terms in the Old Testament

The examination of words, and especially idiomatic phrases, such as those that often characterize prophetic speech, shows their unique theological meaning, which is essential to a correct interpretation.

In the Old Testament the concept of suffering distress or trouble was frequent and expected, whether the scale was personal or corporate. On the personal level, Job records tribulations common to the experience of man in Adam: "Man is born unto trouble as the sparks fly upward" (Job 5:7). On the corporate or national level, the provision for trouble resulting from punishment was inherent within the covenantal contract (cf. Lev. 26:14-39; Deut. 11:26-28; 27:15-68) since violation was inevitable (cf. Deut. 4:25-30a), and even judicially determined (Isa. 6:9-10; cf. John. 12:37-40; Rom. 11:7-10). Nevertheless, such tribulations are only for prescribed periods, and afterward there is the expectation of deliverance and blessing (cf. Job 42:10-17; Deut. 4:30b; Isa. 6:11-13; Rom. 11:11, 25-27).

The Greek term commonly employed in the New Testament as a technical expression for the Tribulation period is *Ithlipsis* (wrath, tribulation).[9] This may be observed in Luke's substitution of the phrase *Ianagke megale* (great distress) in Luke 21:23 for Matthew's *Ithlipsis megale* (great tribulation) in Matthew 24:21, to distinguish the "days of vengeance" (the Roman destruction in A.D. 70) from the eschatological Tribulation.[10] The Greek translation of the Old Testament, the Septuagint (LXX), used *Ithlipsis* to render the Hebrew term *Isar/Isarah* (trouble, tribulation, distress). This Hebrew term was especially used in contexts in which curses based on violations of the Mosaic covenant were threatened or pronounced. It appears in principal Old Testament texts alluded to by the New Testament (e.g., Deut. 4:30; Jer. 30:7; Dan. 12:1). Other terms and texts in the Old Testament that have been adduced as containing the concept of a future tribulation are given on page 61.[11]

Lesser expressions also are used to describe this period as a time when God "arises to shake violently the earth" (Isa. 2:19), to "make the earth utterly emptied and ruined" (Isa. 24:1,3,6), to "break down" and "dissolve" the earth (Isa. 24:19), or to "punish the kings" and "the inhabitants of the earth for their iniquity" (Isa. 24:21; 26:21).

While these terms and expressions would seem to indicate an eschatological time of fulfillment for the events they describe, and Jesus and the New Testament writers certainly understood the Tribulation as a future event, the question to be decided is whether these events were to be fulfilled in an immediate or distant future. Non-futurists have interpreted the New Testament Tribulation texts as being fulfilled at one of several different, but chronologically proximate, times: 1) in the lifetime (especially the passion) of Jesus;[17] 2) at the destruction of the Jerusalem temple by the Romans in A.D. 70;[18] 3) the appropriateness of these terms as eschatological expressions describing a time of tribulation depends in part upon their immediate or remote futurity in the Old Testament contexts.[19]

The Futurity of Tribulation Terms

Old Testament terms for "tribulation," as well as temporal expressions that govern them, reveal both an indefinite and definite sense of futurity. In some cases, the idiomatic nature of prophetic speech allows for an immediate, or a more remote or ultimate, application to a future event (e.g., Assyrian or Babylonian destructions). In this category is the phrase *Iyom YHWH* (the Day of the Lord), which unlike technically eschatological expressions may be used to refer to similar historical judgments in the prophetic plan. The strictly remote application of retributive judgment texts to an eschatological Tribulation appears most clearly in those contexts that contain an eschatological time referent (i.e., an attendant phrase that serves as a *technical* expression of the end time), or by qualifying phrases that imply a climatic "end of days" fulfillment. An example of the former are chronological referents such as *'Iet qetz* (the time of the end) (Dan. 8:17; 11:35,40; 12:4,9). An example of the latter are phrases such as: "that day is great, there is none like it" (cf. Jer. 30:7; Dan. 12:1). Where the chronological referent in the Old Testament is ambiguous, eschatological meaning may be attributed as such by virtue of its citation or allusion in an eschatological context in the New Testament.

The "Day of the Lord"
in the Old Testament

The concept of the "Day of the Lord" may have originally derived from the ancient near Eastern tradition that a mighty warrior-king could consummate an entire military campaign in a single day.[20] Viewing YHWH in this light, the history of divine intervention in Israel's early wars may have also contributed to the later appearance of the concept in the Old Testament prophets.[21] The expression is generally used idiomatically to "emphasize the swift and decisive nature of the Lord's victory over His enemies on any given occasion."[22] It is used more particularly to refer to actual "days" on which specific events or battles took place. These may be occurrences of past history, such as the Assyrian conquest of Israel (Isa. 10:5-15), the Babylonian conquest of Egypt (Jer. 46:10), the Medo-Persian conquest of Babylon (Isa. 13:6; cf. Jer. 27:4-11;

OLD TESTAMENT TRIBULATION TERMS AND EXPRESSIONS

Tribulation Term	Old Testament Reference
Yom YHWH (day of the Lord)	Obad. 15; Joel 1:15; 2:1,11,31; 3:14; Amos 5:18,20; Isa. 2:12; 13:6,9; Zeph. 1:7,14; Ezek. 13:5; 30:3; Zech. 14:1
Yom YHWH hagadol v^{e}hanora' (great and terrible day of the Lord)	Mal. 4:5
Sar/sarah (trouble, tribulation)	Deut. 4:30; Zeph. 1:16
'Et/yom sarah (time/day of trouble)	Dan. 12:1; Zeph. 1:15[12]
'Et sarah hi' l^{e}ya'^{a}cov (day of Jacob's trouble)	Jer. 30:7
Chil (birth pangs)	Isa. 21:3; 26:17-18; 66:7; Jer. 4:31; Mic. 4:10 (cf. Jer. 30:6)
Yom 'edom (the day of calamity)	Deut. 32:35; Obad. 12–14
Zaram (indignation)	Isa. 26:20; Dan. 11:36
Ma'asehu zar (the [Lord's] strange work)	Isa. 28:21[13]
Shot shotef (overflowing scourge)	Isa. 28:15, 18[14]
Yom naqam (day of vengeance)[15]	Isa. 34:8a; 35:4a; 61:2b; 63:4a[16]
Yom '^{e}vrah (day of wrath)	Zeph. 1:15
Yom '^{e}vrat YHWH (day of the Lord's wrath)	Zeph. 1:18
Yom m^{e}suqah (day of distress)	Zeph. 1:15
Yom sho'ah (day of destruction)	Zeph. 1:15
Yom m^{e}sho'ah (day of desolation)	Zeph. 1:15
Yom hoshek u'^{a}pelah (day of darkness and gloom)	Zeph. 1:15; Amos 5:18,20; Joel 2:2
Yom 'anan u'arapel (day of clouds and thick darkness)	Zeph. 1:15; Joel 2:2
Yom shofar ut^{e}ru 'ah (day of trumpet and alarm)	Zeph. 1:16
Yom 'af YHWH (day of the Lord's anger)	Zeph. 2:2,3
[Yom] sod mishaddai ([day of] destruction, ruin, from the Almighty)	Joel 1:15
'Esh qina'to (the fire of His jealousy)	Zeph. 1:18

51:20-25; Hab. 1:5-12), or they may be eschatological events or conflicts of the future "last days." De Vries has pointed out that the traditional use of the "Day of the Lord" clearly "provides the pattern for eschatology, and that there is no sense in trying to assess the meaning of 'the day of Yahweh' or of any other futuristic image except on the model of 'that day' past and 'this day' present."[23]

Three elements are usually associated with this model "Day of the Lord": 1) the judgment of national Israel; 2) the judgment of the Gentile nations; and 3) the restoration of national Israel.[24] For this study, the first element is of primary importance, since this event is a time of punishment for Israel, although its positive purpose is ultimately Israel's repentance and restoration. This negative focus may be seen in relation to the Day of the Lord in Amos 5:18-20: "Alas, you who are longing for the Day of the Lord; for what [good] purpose will the Day of the Lord be to you? It will be darkness and not light." However, in order to identify the scope of this eschatological event, all its elements must be considered.

The Scope of the "Day of the Lord"

To encompass all of these aforementioned elements eschatologically, the "Day of the Lord" must have a broad as well as a narrow focus. However, because the *goal* of the Day of the Lord is the establishment of the Messianic kingdom, it has been debated whether the *terminus a quo* (commencement) of this "day" is at the beginning or end of the Tribulation and/or the millennium,[25] and whether its events include Daniel's entire seventieth week and/or the duration of the millennium.[26] But a broad/narrow eschatological focus follows the pattern of the near (historical)/far (eschatological) focus, and it allows for an extension of the idiom to broader events associated with, or theologically similar to, the ultimate (narrow) event.

An example of this may appear in Joel's use of the phrase in chapter 2. In Joel 1 an actual locust plague is the basis for the prophecy of a near historical invasion (2:1-11)[27] and a call for repentance in view of that day (2:12-17). Joel 2:18-27 is a transition from the near to the far with 2:28–3:21 having exclusively a far future application.[28] While Joel's prophecy increases in intensity and scope, the idiomatic (hyperbolic) language he uses of the "Day of the Lord" is applicable to any day of divine intervention that has these elements, but ideally to that future day which completely fulfills and concludes the literal realities behind his figures. Since the "Day of the Lord" has an ultimate eschatological application, any application of the phrase to earlier historical situations should be viewed in light of that greater day. Therefore, describing a past historical event in eschatological terms does not prevent future application; it confirms it by revealing the eschatological pattern that will require ultimate eschatological fulfillment.

The Eschatological Extent
of the "Day of the Lord"

Having considered the scope of the "Day of the Lord," its eschatological extent should fit this form.[29] Because the eschatological "day" will be its climax, it must include all of the elements of that "day" for complete fulfillment. In the eschatological context, therefore, the "Day of the Lord," as the event that culminates the final period, may represent the *whole* of that period rather than the final event of that period.[30] This would mean that the entire time of the Tribulation should be regarded as the "Day of the Lord," since all of the events of that period both characterize and eventuate in the decisive intervention of YHWH at the second advent. Jesus apparently adopted this principle when He used language descriptive of the "Day of the Lord" (Jer. 30:7; Dan. 12:1; Joel 2:2) in the Olivet discourse (Matt. 24:21) to apply to part of this period—the latter half of Daniel's seventieth week.

That the "Day of the Lord" was not intended to be limited to a specific event within the Tribulation, such as Armageddon (which is a series of battles), may be seen in John's description of the sixth seal (Rev. 6:12-17). His language places the events of the sixth seal in the "Day of the Lord." However, it is clear that the sixth seal is not the climactic event but the preliminary to greater judgment under the seventh seal. The end will not come until the entire period of persecution has run its course (Rev. 6:11). Therefore, in light of the chronology of the Olivet discourse (cf. Matt. 24:29), the events of the sixth seal foreshadow the events which will occur immediately after the seventieth week and immediately before the second advent.[31]

The "Latter Days"
in the Old Testament

Another chronological expression of future time during which the Tribulation is predicted is indicated by the Hebrew phrase b^e'ah^arit $hayyamim$ (the latter days). This expression appears as a fixed form of speech, always in the same construct state with the same preposition—b^e (in). The eschatological connotation of this formula is especially prominent in the prophets (e.g., Isa. 2:2; Jer. 23:20; 34:20; 48:47; 49:39; Ezek. 38:16; Hos. 3:5; Micah 4:1) and in Daniel (2:28; 8:19,23; 10:14; cf. 12:8), although it is by no means limited to them. It is found as early as the Pentateuch (e.g. Gen. 49:1; Num. 24:14; Deut. 4:29-31).[32]

Cognate terms in ancient near Eastern languages reveal a usage that appears to refer to a general future,[33] although the paucity of extant and undisputed eschatological texts does not eliminate the possibility that in such texts it might have such a remote temporal meaning.[34] However, though parallels have been sought as sources for Israelite eschatology, it appears likely that eschatology in Israel was an inner-Israelite development, and that extra-Israelite parallels simply represent concepts common to the entire ancient near East.

In the Old Testament, the phrase "latter days" appears 14 times (Gen. 49:1; Num. 24:14; Deut. 4:30; 31:29; Isa. 2:2; Jer. 23:20; 30:24; 48:47; 49:39; Ezek. 38:16; Hos. 3:5; Micah 4:1; Dan. 2:28 [Aramaic]; 10:14), although the root $zahar$ occurs 1,140 times with denominative meanings in the verb, preposition, and adjective as temporally future.[35] The noun $zaharit$, which is part of the compound expression, is used some 62 times, and usually considered to be abstract. It generally describes that which takes place *after* the speaker's temporal reference (i.e., the future, cf. Deut. 8:16; Job 42:12), as well as what results from a situation or an action (i.e., the end, cf. Prov. 14:12).[36] Only context can determine the specific meaning or time of the future intended. In some texts, the noun means essentially the promise of "future life" (cf. Prov. 23:17-18; 24:14). There is, however, one instance in which it may have an eschatological meaning. In Daniel 8:19 it is paralleled by the expression $qetz$ $hayyamim$ (final or end period). This usage especially strengthens the eschatological meaning of "latter days" because the substitution of $qetz$ (end), which is the proper Hebrew expression for a completion of time, coming from the root *qutz* (cut off), for *z^{a}harit* (last), makes the meaning decisive of the ultimate end.[37]

The Eschatological Sense
of "Latter Days"

When we examine the usage of the compound expression "latter days" in the Old Testament, we find that it is used in the general sense of "days to come" (cf. Gen. 49:1; Num. 24:14; Deut. 31:29), but more often it has the more definite sense of a time in the future. Sometimes this future sense indicates an end of time as contrasted with its beginning (cf. Isa. 46:10). At other times it indicates a time of change or a historical turning point (cf. Hos. 3:5; Ezek. 38:8,16). This definite future sense encompasses both near (historical) and far (eschatological) points of reference; some of an immediate future, others spanning a comprehensive period from the author's vantage point until the Messianic age. In some cases a specific turning point in future Israelite history is eschatological (Deut. 4:30; Isa. 2:2; Jer. 23:20; 30:24; Micah 4:1), while in others it is not (Deut. 31:29; Jer. 48:47; 49:39).

This distinction can be demonstrated by comparing the two similar-sounding texts of Deuteronomy 4:30 and 31:29. In Deuteronomy 31:29, Moses is warning the Israelites in his farewell address against the future apostasy they will suffer as they enter the Promised Land, an imminent event. This apostasy was historically realized during the period of the Judges that immediately followed (cf. Judg. 2:11-16). By contrast, in Deuteronomy 4:30, the setting is Moses' first address. Its literary structure resembles the suzerainty-vassal treaty of the ancient near East, a form upon which the Israelite law code is patterned. What is here, then, is a sermon on the covenant recounting its provisions on the cursings and blessings (verses 26-40). As this covenant forms the basis for God's judicial acts against Israel, culminating in the Tribulation of the end time, its use of "latter days" has a definite sense of future time, especially an eschatological one. The specificity to this eschatological period is reinforced by the prediction of "tribulation" (*sar*), which in context will eventuate in national Israelite repentance and restoration, one of the purposes of the Tribulation.

While commentators in general apply this prophecy to any of Israel's past exilic experiences (cf. "dispersion among the peoples,"

v. 27),[38] more conservative commentators and dispensationalists have recognized its eschatological setting and identified it with the Messianic time of completion,[39] or the end of the age,[40] or the "Great Tribulation of the end-time."[41] Rashi, the leading Jewish biblical commentator, also apparently sees an end-time fulfillment, for he follows the Targum's explanation of the "tribulation" in vv. 28-30 as occurring after the entire period of Gentile domination has ended.[42]

In other cases of eschatological reference, the "latter days" are either comprehensive of a time stretching from the period of the conquest and monarchy until the Messianic age (Gen. 49:1; Num. 24:14)—from the viewpoint of the prophet down to the millennium (Dan. 2:28; 10:14), specific to the Messianic age itself (Isa. 2:2; Micah 4:1; Hosea 3:5)—or to the time preceding the Messianic age whenever the battle of Gog and Magog occurs (Ezek. 38:16).[43]

While the expression "latter days" may refer to the time of future tribulation, it is not a technical term for such, since its contextual settings and varieties of usages allow it to be employed in different ways.[44] Even so, in some cases where the historical application represents the initial fulfillment of the time, typological elements present carry the fulfillment forward to the eschatological period (e.g. Gen. 49:1; Num. 24:14).

The "End-Time" in the Old Testament

Usage of the Hebrew expression 'et qetz (end-time) in the Old Testament is distinct from the term "latter days." While both are eschatological expressions, only 'et qetz refers exclusively to the final eschatological period or event. Its component element is the temporal term 'et (time), which has a basic chronological or quantitative use (cf. Judg. 11:26; 1 Kgs. 6:1), but it is also used to refer specifically to the time of eschatological judgment on national Israel (e.g., Jer. 8:1-3; 18:23; 51:6).

In other texts it refers to the eschatological restoration expected by Israel after judgment was completed (cf. Jer. 3:17; 33:15; Zeph. 3:19-20). Its other component is the term qetz (end). In three texts (Amos 8:2; Lam. 4:18; Ezek. 7:2,3,6), qetz is employed in the context of the "Day of the Lord," with clearly eschatological intent. In Daniel 8:19; 9:26; 11:27,45; 12:6,13, it has eschatological significance or refers to the end of the age.[45] The combined construction *zet qetz*, which appears uniquely only in the latter half of Daniel, is strictly eschatological (cf. Dan. 8:17; 11:35,40; 12:4,9). Here it appears 11 times as a chronological marker of a specific eschatological period (cf. Dan. 9:21,25; 11:6,13,14,24; 12:11). In Daniel 12:1-2, especially, it assumes the character of an apocalyptic *terminus technicus*, denoting the final period that culminates the divine program, including all the events of that time.[46]

The Typology of the Tribulation

Typology is a recognition that an essential unity belongs to Scripture. The events which conclude the divine history (eschatology) were predicted from the beginning (protology). As S. Lewis Johnson has said: "It is the divine purpose that secures the correspondence, the linking of that which precedes to that which follows in the progress of revelation, but the design is no part of the typicalness. All scriptural events are divinely designed."[47] Beginning with Deuteronomy 4:30 and ending with Revelation 19:20, terms for the Tribulation form a line of revelation that progresses from the explication of covenantal curses to the great judicial denouement of history. The general Old Testament terms used to express the general experience or condition of tribulation, when viewed within the covenantal structure, acquire a technical sense, forming a typological pattern by which the doctrine of the eschatological Tribulation is progressively revealed. Judicial desecration is enforced at a definite and announced point in history, and its earlier motif (the cursings prescribed by the legal treaty) sets the precedent for this ultimate and final demonstration of divine wrath in the future.[48] This pattern develops incrementally throughout the history of divine revelation, so that while a term may have an indefinite usage in its initial context, its usage becomes definite by the time it reaches its ultimate context.

An example of this may be found in Deuteronomy 4:30, whose tribulation setting in the "latter days" is seen to be in relation to God's affirmation of His covenant (v. 31). While in the context the covenant has not yet been violated, the prophetic warning is in view of perceived future violations (vv. 25-27), which will culminate in punishment (v. 28) designed to bring covenantal repentance and restoration of blessing (vv. 29,30b). Ultimately the sense is eschatological, for there could be no sure guarantee of successful fulfillment until the final drama is played out. For this reason we read, in several prophetic announcements, of God's judgment against Israel (for covenant violation, usually through idolatry): "In the last days you will understand it" (cf. Jer. 23:20; 30:24).

In other texts, the association between the covenantal violation and the Tribulation judgments on all mankind is expressly stated: "The earth is also polluted by its inhabitants, for they transgressed laws, violated statutes, broke the everlasting covenant. Therefore, a curse devours the earth, and those who live in it are held guilty. Therefore, the inhabitants of the earth are burned, and few are left" (Isa. 24:5-6 NASB; cf. Rev. 8:7-8; 16:8-9; 18:18). This phenomena of escalation or intensification is part of the nature of typological correspondence and may be illustrated by the most common designation for the Tribulation: the "Day of the Lord."

Typological development from type to antitype may be seen in the imagery surrounding figures who oppress or desecrate Israel in its national or religious purpose. While earlier figures, such as the Edenic serpent and Amalek, may be typological oppressors, the Egyptian pharaohs of the oppression and the exodus (unnamed to focus on their role as antagonists to the divine) appear to begin the development, followed by successive oppressors toward an ultimate antitype, the Antichrist. As the divine program develops with respect to Israel nationally, elements such as the central sanctuary are added, since God's presence (the object of the oppression) has now become localized there as well as in identity with His people.[49] This oppression from Gentiles is paralleled by tribulation from God for Israel's own violations of covenant. The Jewish-Roman historian Josephus, for example, saw a divine punishment for Israel behind the judgment on both the first and second temples, since both occurred on the same day (the ninth of the Jewish month of Av). Thus, the past tribulational judgments on Israel, involving the elements of Jerusalem and its temple as the stage for its sin (e.g. Jer. 7:1–8:3; Ezek. 6:1-14; 8:1-18), were typical of the great antitypal day of judgment, the Tribulation.

Tribulation Terms and the Nature of the Tribulation

The nature of the Tribulation is revealed by the characteristic terms we have seen as descriptive of this period. A brief catalog of such expressions gives a clear picture of its severity: wrath

(Zeph. 1:15,18), indignation (Isa. 26:20-21; 34:1-3), trouble, distress (Jer. 30:7; Zeph. 1:14-15; Dan. 12:1), destruction (Joel 1:15), darkness (Joel 2:2; Amos 5:18; Zeph. 1:14-18), desolation (Dan. 9:27; Zeph. 1:14-15), fire, burning (Zeph. 1:18; Isa. 24:6), punishment (Isa. 24:21), overflowing scourge (Isa. 28:15,18), and vengeance (Isa. 34:8; 35:4; 61:2).

The accumulation of such terms dealing with divine judgment is exceptional. It was this characteristic above all that served to highlight and heighten these references and project them onto the eschatological stage. The exceptional nature of the Tribulation is earmarked by such phrases as: "that day is great, there is none like it" (Jer. 30:7), or "such as never occurred since there was a nation until that time" (Dan. 12:1). These expressions emphasize the uniqueness of this specific judgment, while the accompanying contextual descriptions of the effects such judgments have, on both God and Israel, affirm that this is a time unparalleled in Israel's previous history. Understanding the eschatological nature revealed by these Old Testament expressions of final judgment, Jesus likewise qualified the Tribulation of the end time with a language patterned after Daniel 12:1: "such as has not occurred since the beginning of the creation which God created, until now, and never shall" (cf. Matt. 24:21; Mark 13:19). It has been argued that such expressions of severity were repeatedly used of past judgments not only of Israel but of others as well.[50] As such they take the form of proverbial expressions and should not be taken literally.

The Use of the Superlative Statement

If, however, we look at each of these superlative expressions in their respective contexts, they do not represent a fixed form but are appropriate to the event they describe (i.e., they convey the same sense, but have different referents). In Exodus, the plagues of hail burning with fire (Ex. 9:18,24) and the locusts (Ex. 10:6) are comparatively the greatest disasters (in kind) that Egypt had ever experienced. The similar wording in Deuteronomy 4:32 is used of a divine theophany manifested on the national level, certainly an unparalleled event in history to that point. The uses of superlatives in Jeremiah 30:7 and Daniel 12:1 refer to the same period of tribulation and restoration. In the New Testament, the same language is applied to Jesus' miracle healing of a congenitally blind man (John 9:32). Further uses parallel the Old Testament contexts, with Matthew 24:21 and Mark 13:19 citing from Daniel 12:1 (with allusion to Jer. 30:7) and Revelation 16:18 (to the seventh bowl judgment, which bears resemblance to the exodus hail-fire plague). While in general we may recognize that the superlative statement accompanies contexts of divine intervention, each of these is specific to its context, except for the eschatological contexts that refer to the same period.

Nevertheless, there may be an intentional connection in the use of this superlative in the exodus and eschatological contexts. Considering the progressive theological development of the concept of the Tribulation, we find that this expression of incomparability owes its origin to a divinely patterned revelation motif of distress and deliverance introduced at the time of the exodus. The language used to describe the plagues sent against the Egyptians to secure Israelite deliverance is similar: "such as was not seen in Egypt from the day it was founded until now" (Ex. 9:18), or "such as has not been and such as shall never be again" (Ex. 11:6; cf. 9:24; 10:6,14). The prophets' description of the Tribulation period is in terms of the exodus experience (Isa. 51:9-11; Jer. 23:7-8; Ezek. 20:34-38; cf. Micah 7:15-17).

In like manner, the trumpet and bowl judgments of the Tribulation follow the model of exodus plagues (cf. Rev. 8:7–9:21; 16:1-21). Just as the unnamed pharaoh was a prefigurement of the Antichrist, so the divine judgment brought upon him (to demonstrate God's power to the nations and to deliver Israel at the exodus) was a prefigurement of the final Tribulation judgments and their ultimate demonstration of divine sovereignty and Israelite redemption (Isa. 51:5-8; Jer. 23:5-6; cf. Rev. 11:4-9; 15:3-4). Further, God's judgments against His people in the exodus wanderings (to separate out the righteous from the rebels) prefigured the final purging of Israel in the Tribulation (Ezek. 20:35-36; cf. Matt. 24:10-12). The text of Deuteronomy 4:30 concerning the Tribulation of the "latter days" is buttressed with statements of the demonstration of divine intervention at the exodus (vv. 32-40), and it is referred to as so unique that nothing of the like had ever been seen since the creation of man on the earth (v. 32).

The Tribulation "Birth-Pangs"

The nature of the Tribulation is also conveyed in related contexts by the use of a figure of intense suffering and expectation. Specifically, the *experience* of end-time judgment in the Tribulation is depicted by the travail of childbirth, i.e., Hebrew: *kayyoledah*, "as a woman giving birth" (Jer. 30:5-6).[51] The eschatological "Day of the Lord" is often associated with the expression of birth pangs as well (cf. Isa. 13:8; 25:17-18; 66:7-8; Jer. 22:23; 48:41; Hos. 13:13; Zeph. 1:14-18; Micah 4:9-10; 5:1[2]). The New Testament also makes this association (cf. 1 Thess. 5:2-3). The Hebrew expression for these pains is derived from the root *chil*, which has the basic meaning of "being in labor," with the resultant idea of "fear" and "trembling."[52]

On the one hand, the figure is applied to the experience of tribulation because its application to males or to the nation of Israel is tantamount to reducing them to the helpless state of women at the time of birth, something every army hoped their enemy would become (cf. Jer. 50:37). On the other hand, the involuntary and uncontrollable nature of birth pangs, as well as their intensification leading ultimately to a time of deliverance, well pictured the concept of a time of divine judgment that must run its course until the promise of new life could be experienced.

For this reason Israel's eschatological song of salvation, at the outset of the millennium (Isa. 26:1-21), reflects back on the Tribulation from which they have been recently saved and describes their past experience in terms of childbirth: "O Lord, they sought You in tribulation (*sar*)... Your chastening was upon them, as the pregnant woman approaches the time of birth, she writhes [in birth pangs] (*tachil*) and cries out in her birth pangs (*ch^aval^eyah*)—so we were because of You, O Lord, we were pregnant, we were in birth pangs (*chalnu*)..." (vv. 16-18a).[53] The next verse may depict both Israel's national resurrection (cf. Ezek. 37:1-14) and the resurrection of the righteous that occurs at the second advent (Rev. 20:4-6). This same sequence of events (tribulation and resurrection) is also found in Daniel 12:1-2 (cf. Hosea 6:2).

In Daniel's tribulation text (Dan. 12:1), rabbinic commentators interpreted the "time of trouble" as a future eschatological time equivalent with the period known as the *ch^avalim* (birth pangs), or *chevlo shel mashiach* (birth pangs of the Messiah).[54] This identification was based on the signs of the messianic birth pangs described in the Mishnah, which in turn appear to have been drawn from Daniel's text.[55] Typical of those making this connection were the medieval sages Rashi and R' Sh'muel Masnuth. In his commentary on Daniel (c. A.D. 1230) R' Sh'muel Masnuth stated that "this generation will see the pangs of the Messiah—the tribulations of the generation described in tractate *Sanhedrin* 97b."[56] Rashi, in his commentary on Daniel (c. A.D. 1100) interpolated the signs of religious enmity and civil lawlessness among Jews, in "the generation of the Messiah" (from *Kethubot* 112b), to "the sons of your people" in this verse.[57] So frightening was the prospect of encountering this time of tribulation preceding the messianic arrival that some sages hoped it would not come in their lifetimes. Among them was Rabbi Yochanan who exclaimed: "Let [the Messiah] come, but may I not see it!" (*Sanhedrin* 98b).[58]

The birth pangs are significant in the timing of the Tribulation, as revealed by Jesus in the Olivet discourse (Matt. 24:8).[59] Jesus' statement of the "birth pangs" is specifically that the events of the first half of the Tribulation (vv. 4-7) are merely the "beginning," with the expectation of greater birth pangs in the second half (the "Great Tribulation"). Based on this analogy, the entire period of the seventieth week is like birth pangs. As a woman must endure the entire period of labor before giving birth, so Israel must endure the entire seven-year Tribulation. The time divisions of Tribulation are also illustrated by the figure, for just as the natural process intensifies toward delivery after labor ends, so here the Tribulation moves progressively toward the second advent (vv. 30-31), which takes place "immediately after" the Tribulation ends (v. 29). As there are two phases of the birth pangs (beginning labor and full labor), so the seven years of Tribulation are divided between the less severe and more severe experiences of terrestrial and cosmic wrath, as revealed progressively in the Olivet discourse and the judgment section of Revelation 6–19.

In order to strengthen our conviction that the New Testament writers understood the Tribulation to have been taught in the Old Testament, let us examine three of the Old Testament texts most commonly alluded to by them.

The "Day of Jacob's Trouble" (Jer. 30:7)

The reference to "Jacob" is to Israel as a national entity, and therefore the time of distress refers to a period of national trouble unlike any other. To what time of trouble was Jeremiah referring? As to the *time*, some have argued that the use of the Hebrew time marker *'et*, and its translation by the LXX as *chronos*, indicates a reference to a *specific* future time in contrast to a distant future.[60] According to this near fulfillment view, the *trouble* would be identifiable from the historical context, making the reference to Babylon.[61] However, what *event* connected with Babylon is intended—the Babylonian conquest or the captivity? A clue may be provided by the term "yoke" (v. 8), which describes the "trouble" of verse 7. Used figuratively of servitude or bondage under foreign oppressors (cf. Lev. 26:13; 1 Kings 12:9; Isa. 14:25; Jer. 27:8,11,12),[62] this might refer to the king of Babylon and indicate that the captivity, rather than the conquest, was in mind.[63]

Further support for this may be found in the use of the introductory phrase *hayyom hahu'* (*that* day) in vv. 7-8. If Jeremiah had written *hayyom hazeh* (*this* day), it would suggest a reference to Babylon's present capture and destruction *of Jerusalem*. But since he used "*that* day," a future invasion and destruction *of Babylon* better fits the context. If this were the "time of trouble" Jeremiah intended, it could harmonize with the command in verses 2-3 to record the prophecy, of restoration from captivity, in a book. Since Jeremiah had previously spoken of such a future witness, designating it for the time of release at the end of the 70 years (cf. Jer. 25:13; 29:10-14), this witness could also refer to that period.

In addition, verse 4 appears to address the prophecy to both the northern kingdom of Israel and the southern kingdom of Judah. Since Israel had been taken into exile by the Assyrians 136 years earlier, news of a Jerusalem destruction would hardly be a cause of distress for them on the same scale as for the Judeans who experienced it. However, if their descendants formed part of the exilic community in Babylon with the Judeans, then they could share an experience of "trouble," and the only possible historical occasion would be the conquest of Babylon. Therefore, this interpretation understands the "time of trouble," in verses 5-7, as the overthrow of Babylon by Cyrus and the Medo-Persians in 539 B.C. and the "restoration of fortunes," in verses 4,8-9, as the return from exile under

Ezra in 538 B.C. and the intention of reestablishing the Davidic dynasty in Judea.

If we accept this, we could still argue on the pattern of progressive revelation that this *past* Babylonian punishment and Medo-Persian deliverance prefigured the *future* time of Jacob's trouble in the Tribulation and the messianic rescue and restoration which marks its end. In the prophetic scheme each immediate historical incident sets the pattern for the ultimate eschatological end. However, several other contextual factors argue against this interpretation and strongly suggest that Jeremiah's intended reference is primarily eschatological.

First, even if the historical return under the Cyrus edict included remnants of both Israelites and Judeans, verses 2-3 predicts the *union* of these kingdoms as one national entity whose loss of territorial inheritance by captivity would be reversed.[64] This restoration did not occur in the Persian period returns. However, the prophets had predicted such a restoration in eschatological terms at the time of Jewish incorporation within the new covenant (Jer. 31:27-34) and the establishment of the messianic kingdom (Jer. 33:14-18; cf. Ezek. 37:16-28). In the following chart, the elements of restoration in this text are seen in parallel with those in these eschatological restoration passages.

Comparison of Jeremiah 30:1-9
and Restoration Contexts

1) Physical deliverance from distress (vv. 7-8; cf. 31:28; 33:16; Ezek. 37:23b)

2) Return of the united remnant to possess the land of Israel (v. 3; cf. 31:27; 33:14; Ezek. 37:16-22)

3) Condition of permanent settlement and security in the land (v. 8b; cf. 31:40; 33:16a,17-18; Ezek. 37:25-28)

4) National spiritual regeneration (v. 9; cf. 31:33-34; 33:16b; Ezek. 37:23a,24b)

5) Restored theocratic government under a Davidic/messianic regent (v. 9b; cf. 33:15; Ezek. 37:24-25)

Interpreted literally, none of these elements could be fulfilled in these terms except in the future eschatological context (the days concluding and following the Tribulation period, cf. Matt. 24:29ff and Mark 13:24ff). This is especially true of the promise of irreversible peace, as in verse 8: "foreigners (*zarim*, lit. "those who disperse") shall *never again* (*lo'...zod*) hold them in servitude."[65] Although the Jews experienced nearly a century of independence under the Hasmonean state (c. 163–63 B.C.), they were still under Greek hegemony, and Jewish exilic communities continued in Egypt and Babylon. Today, even though an independent Jewish state of Israel has existed since 1948, this condition of worldwide diaspora (dispersion) continues. Only the experience of the Tribulation will be sufficient to reunite world Jewry and bring them to Messiah (Matt. 24:29-31; cf. Zech. 12:1–13:1; 14:1-5).

Second, in verse 7 the time is clearly a time of punishment upon the Jewish people (Jacob), *not* upon the Babylonians. How could the Jews "terror" and "dread" (v. 5), when compared in the extreme to parturition (v. 6), refer to the approaching invasion of Babylon by Cyrus? Would not Cyrus be viewed as the divinely appointed deliverer, as predicted by Isaiah (Isa. 44:28-45:5,13) and therefore be a cause for confidence and rejoicing? How could the Jews be "saved" from this "trouble" if in fact this trouble (the Persian invasion) was what saved them? Furthermore, the aforementioned use of the third-person suffix "his" with "yoke," as a reference to the king of Babylon, cannot be justified by its immediate context. The very next word in the Hebrew text uses the second-person suffix "your" (cf. LXX their) neck, as does the next word "bonds," which is parallel to "yoke."[66] The understanding then must be that "his" refers to "Jacob" (since he appears to be addressed here), and that the "yoke" is that experience of captivity (unspecified) which he has been made to suffer.

It should also be noted that neither Babylon nor the king of Babylon is mentioned anywhere in this passage, but, conversely, *"all"* nations" are stated to be the subject of God's destruction (v. 11). If we then eliminate the possibility of a Babylonian setting, the only remaining future historical occasion when Israel and Judah will suffer in unison and together be delivered is the worldwide persecution of Jews during the last half of the Tribulation and the eschatological regathering at its conclusion (cf. Matt. 24:20-22,31, Rev. 12:6,13-17).[67] This better accords with the picture of universal Jewish anguish and salvation described in verses 6-7

Third, the words which Jeremiah is to write in a book (v. 2) include *all* the message of the restoration prophecy (at least chapters 30–31, as the summary statement in v. 3 indicates). The prophetic message Jeremiah is to preserve is intended for the distant future, when the conditions of the new covenant will be finally implemented by a regenerate national Israel, whose blessings will be fully realized. Therefore, the "time of trouble," from which a united Israel will be "saved" to enjoy restoration, must refer to the end-time tribulation period.

Fourth, the consolation of Jacob in verses 10-11 is repeated with slight variations in chapter 46:27-28. Why is this? The context is an oracle of judgment against Egypt, depicting her punishment through the Babylonians, rather than her destruction (vv. 25-26a), so that her future restoration will be assured (v. 26b). Since Egypt's situation parallels that of the Israelites in exile, Jeremiah repeats his previous word from the Lord, concerning Israel's restoration, to give them assurance.

The words would certainly give hope to the exiles, not because they were addressed to the immediate restoration but because they were a prophecy of the ultimate restoration. The reference to God's destruction of *all* nations where Israel has suffered exile (Jer. 30:11; 46:28) is clearly eschatological. This restatement, then, was an assurance that God, who promised to one day destroy all of Israel's oppressors, could be trusted to deliver Israel from its present oppression. In other words, if Israel was to realize ultimate restoration in the future, she would not be destroyed by her present experience. Because Egypt's restoration was understood to be eschatological (cf. Isa. 19:16-25), the application to Israel's restoration was appropriately taken from the eschatological context of chapter 30.[68]

The "Covenant" and the "Abomination of Desolation" (Dan. 9:27)

The premiere tribulation text, cited by Jesus in the Olivet discourse (Matt. 24:15; Mark 13:14), and alluded to by Paul in his Day of the Lord discourse (2 Thess. 2:4), is Daniel 9:27.[69] Detailing the events of the seven-year Tribulation, this passage uniquely set off the beginning, midpoint, and end of the Tribulation. The beginning (v. 27a) is designated as the time Israel enters into a covenant[70] with the figure known as "the prince" (Hebrew *nagid*, leader) that was predicted to come, and whose "people" (i.e., Gentiles [Romans]) destroyed the [second] temple (v. 26).[71]

While this covenant is not mentioned in the Olivet discourse or the Apocalypse, it is implied in the events that flow from its violation (especially in relation to Jerusalem and the temple).[72] The midpoint (v. 27b) is the act of temple desecration (implying the rebuilding of the temple in the first division of the seventieth week) by a foreign intrusion into sacred space (the basic idea of the "desolating abomination"). This act forces the cessation of the sacrificial system, thereby violating the terms of the covenant which had included the institution of the temple (v. 27c). It was this act that Jesus earmarked as the signal for the Jewish people by which they could determine the end (cf. Dan. 12:11). The end itself is given as the decreed destruction of the temple desolator, the Antichrist (v. 27d), an event which corresponds to the second advent of Jesus Christ and the Antichrist's defeat at Armageddon (cf. 2 Thess. 1:7-10; Rev. 19:11-21).

The Entire Seventieth Week as a Time of Wrath

Daniel views the entire seventieth week as a time of wrath (cf. Dan. 12:7). The exilic condition he suffers is understood as a punishment for transgression, sin, and iniquity (Dan. 9:24b-c), and this condition will continue as a decree of divine wrath against Israel until the end, when everlasting righteousness and the messianic consecration of the temple can take place (v. 24d-f). The resolution of Daniel's concerns for his city and people (Dan. 9:2,24a) will not be realized until *after* the seventieth week has concluded and its events of deception and desecration have passed (Dan. 9:27; 12:1).

Some of the Jewish commentators (e.g., Rashi and Metzudos) understood the "transgression," "sin," and "iniquity" of verse 24 to be that of the Jewish nation. Interpreting the 70 weeks as 490 years, including the exile following the destruction of the second temple, they believed that the transgression would only be ended after this period. Rabbi Hersh Goldwurm, in his commentary anthologized from rabbinic sources, summarizes their view: "Thus, seventy weeks have been decreed upon your people and your city [for relative well-being] after which the Jews will receive the remainder of their punishment in the last exile whose purpose will be to terminate [i.e., atone for] transgression."[73]

Daniel understood that the desolation from the middle of the seventieth week is connected with the covenant that also commenced this period. Therefore, the entire seventieth week must be of a desolating character. Furthermore, the image of "the prince that will come" is informed by the previously mentioned "prince," whose acts were consonant with those of the Babylonians, whose desolating activity was judicially decreed by God (2 Kings 25; 1 Chron.; cf. Hab.). Daniel would have seen the seventieth week not only as an extension of this program of Gentile domination (the 70 weeks), but especially as an appointed time of decreed desolation ("a determined decree," v. 27; cf. 12:9), following the pattern of divine wrath judicially inflicted as a result of a covenantal breech by the Israelite nation.

The Jewish Context
of the Tribulation in Daniel 9:27

It is quite significant that Tribulation terms deal exclusively with a national Jewish context. This context includes both the climax of the punishment of national Israel for violating the covenant (which unbelief resulted in the rejection of the Messiah, John 12:39; Rom. 11:20), and the judgment of Israel's national Gentile oppressors. This is evident in the seventieth week prophecy, which, as the 70 weeks' prophecy, concerns the Gentile domination of national Israel and the time of the fulfillment of the promised restoration. The phrase "your people," i.e., Daniel's nation (v. 24), emphasizes this exclusivity. Even though the historicists may argue that the church is somehow included in the messianic or christological section of Daniel 9:24-26a, the remaining section of verses 26b-27 are *not* messianic; it revolves around the figure of the non-messianic prince (v. 26b), whose actions are both desecrating and destructive, and who will be destroyed (v. 27). While posttribulationalists wish to see the church also in this context, the events deal *only* with Jewish concerns: the covenant made with Israel; the rebuilding of the temple and reinstitution of the sacrificial system; the desecration of the temple by the desolating abomination; the divine vindication evidenced in retributive judgment on the desolater.

Furthermore, Tribulation texts include the elements of judgment, repentance, and blessing, which in context are always in relation to the land of Israel. For example, Revelation 11:18 states one reason that divine wrath falls is to "destroy those who destroy the land [of Israel]" (taking Greek *gēs*, "earth," as equivalent to Hebrew *ha-ᵃretz*, i.e., the promised land). This agrees with the final clause of Daniel 9:27 and the decreed purpose "to destroy the desolater [of Jerusalem, and by extension, all Israel]." This limits the application of Tribulation terms to a period of national Jewish residency in the land and to the people who represent that resident population. This would, again, eliminate the church, to whom the territorial promises of the Abrahamic covenant are not applied. This would also argue that uniquely Jewish events, such as Israel's signing of the covenant with Antichrist at the beginning of the seventieth week, or the resumption of temple worship during the first half of the seventieth week, are part of the period described by Tribulation terms. Therefore on this basis, the entire seventieth week ought to be regarded as the time of the Tribulation.

The Temple and the Tribulation in Daniel 9:27

Since the rebuilding of the temple, through the covenant with Antichrist (Dan. 9:27a; Rev. 11:1), and the cessation of the sacrificial program, as a result of the abomination of desolation (Dan. 9:27b; Rev. 11:2), are signal events of the Tribulation (marking its beginning and midpoint), the expression of temple desecration must also be considered as additional Tribulation terminology. The primary text for these terms in the Old Testament is Daniel 9:27, since it is this text which our Lord gives as having its fulfillment in the eschatological Tribulation (Matt. 24:15; Mark 13:14; cf. 2 Thess. 2:4).

The phrase used to describe this act of desecration is *shiqqutz meshomem* (abomination that makes desolate), a combination of terms that were used to describe the condition of exilic punishment inflicted on Israel for covenant violation. These terms portray the nature of the Tribulation as a time of desolation or ruin (literally resulting from the seal, trumpet, and bowl judgments), and abomination or idolatry (resulting from the worship system imposed by Antichrist and the false prophet, Revelation 13:4-18). As the temple is the central chronological focus of the Olivet discourse, the events surrounding it may be taken as informative of the Tribulation as a whole. With this understanding, the Tribulation temple characterizes the two divisions of the Tribulation with its erection and the resumption of its institutions (in unbelief)—the probable consequence of the covenant of Daniel 9:27a—as corresponding to the opening of the first seal at the beginning of the Tribulation (cf. the time of delusion of 1 Thess. 5:3) and its desecration with the interruption of sacrifices and the abomination of desolation as corresponding to the last 42 months (cf. Rev. 11:2). This division was employed in Jesus' Olivet discourse, which was arranged according to a chiastic structure,[74] reveals the escalation of events leading, on the one side, to the desecration at the midpoint of the Tribulation, and, on the other, to the restoration that accompanies the second advent of Christ and which ends the Tribulation. The focal point is the desecration event of the "abomination of desolation," because from this comes the *need* for the restoration event, and the new focal point of the second advent. The following chart presents this arrangement.

Midpoint—Seventieth Week **Desecration Event** E. "Abomination of Desolation" (Matt. 24:15; Mk. 13:15)	
▲	▼
First Half—Seventieth Week	*Second Half—Seventieth Week*
D. Preliminary Tribulation (Matt. 24:9-13; Mk. 13:9-13) C. *Signs on Earth* (Matt 24:6-8; Mk. 13:7-8) B. False Messiahs (Matt 24:25; Mk. 13:5-6) A. Prediction of Destruction of Temple & Jerusalem (desolation: A.D. 70—end of 70th Week) (Matt. 23:37–24:3; Mk. 13:2)	D'. Great Tribulation (Matt. 24:16-22; Mk. 13:15-20) C'. False Messiahs (Matt. 24:23-28; Mk. 13:21-23) B'. *Signs in Heaven* (Matt. 24:29; Mk. 13:24-25) A'. Final Destruction of Temple's desolator (i.e., *Roman* *Antichrist*) at 2nd Advent (Matt. 24:30-33; Mk. 13:26-27) **Restoration Event** (Matt. 24:30-31; Mk. 13:26-27; Lk. 21:27-28)
Desecration Series	*Restoration Series*

The "Time of Tribulation" (Dan. 12:1)

The phrase employed by Daniel to refer to the future period of Israelite Tribulation and deliverance is *zet sarah* (time of trouble), modified by the clause *zasher lo nihyetah miheyot goi* (such as never occurred since there was a nation until that time). That a future period is in view is understood by the opening phrase *ba'et hahi* (at that time), which has its antecedent the eschatological *terminus technicus zet qetz* (the end time) in 11:40. This same eschatological referent appears in this context, in verses 4 and 9, as the time of the revelation of these prophecies, specifically the seven-year Tribulation (cf. v. 7). Furthermore, the eschatological context is indisputable in view of the prophetic events it describes; namely, the resurrections of the righteous (at the second advent, Rev. 20:4) and the wicked (at the end of the millennium, Rev. 20:5). Incidentally, Daniel is told that he, as one of the righteous, will miss the Tribulation, and will be resurrected to enjoy the promised millennial blessings (vv. 10-13).

The principal Tribulation term in this phrase is the Hebrew word *sarah*, derived from the root *sarr*, which has meanings ranging from "tight," or "binding," to "being narrow, constricted, in straits," and therefore it expresses a condition or experience of "suffering distress or trouble."[75] The nominative forms *sar* and *sarah* are used to express intense inner turmoil (cf. Psa. 25:17), the terror of war (cf. Jer. 6:24), and, especially, the severe punishments inflicted upon Israel for violating the covenant (cf. Jer. 30:6-7; cf. Isa. 8:22; 30:6; Ps. 78:49). It is also associated with the birth pangs in Jeremiah 4:31.

Daniel's use of the phrase *'et sarah* (time of tribulation) is evidently borrowed from Jeremiah 30:7 (cf. 14:8; 15:11), since that book had been informing Daniel's interpretation of the 70 weeks (Dan. 9:2) and his prayers for restoration (Dan. 9:3-19). Similar uses of this term for unprecedented times of distress precede Daniel (cf. Judg. 10:14; Ps. 37:39), and other prophets also use the same idea (cf. Isa. 32:3). While Daniel may have been familiar with such usage, the historical scope is raised to its eschatological dimension in Daniel's context; its chronological setting being the same as that of Daniel 11:40-45, which immediately precedes it. The conflict of Antichrist at Armageddon, climaxed by the advent of Christ, is particularly in view. However, it is not the battles between the Gentile powers that require protection for the Jewish people; it is Antichrist's activity in relation to the land of Israel (Dan. 11:41). This concern has been described in Daniel 9:27, in which the events of the first half of the Tribulation lead up to the abomination of desolation and the invasion of Israel. The whole of the seventieth week, therefore, should be included in Daniel's concept of the unprecedented "distress."

Jeremiah 30:7 contains the same qualification of unprecedented time, and the presence of Michael, Israel's archangelic protector (cf. Dan. 10:13-21; Jude 9), is further evidence that this tribulation is unparalleled by any previous period. Jesus and the Gospel writers apparently recognized both Daniel's text and Jeremiah's (upon which Daniel depended) as eschatological. In Matthew 24:21 (cf. Mark 13:19), the citation text from the LXX renders Daniel's crucial clause *'et sarah* by *kairos thlipseos* (a time of tribulation). For Jesus, this was certainly not a time of past trouble experienced in the Babylonian destruction of Jerusalem and the captivity; it was future to His day. His further delineation of this time based on Daniel 9:27

COMPARISON OF TRIBULATION TEXTS
IN THE OLD AND NEW TESTAMENTS

Biblical Text	Deut. 4	Jer. 30	Dan. 9	Dan. 12	Matt. 24/ Mk. 13	2 Thess. 2	Rev. 6–19
Event	Tribulation *(sar)* (v. 30)	Tribulation *(sar)* (v. 7)	seven-year covenant (v. 27a)	Tribulation *(sar)* (v. 1b)	Tribulation *(thlipsis)* (24:21; 13:19)	revealing of Antichrist (vv. 3,8)	Great Tribulation (7:14)
Time Reference	after previous exiles, latter days (v. 30)	great day, that day vv. 7,8	70th week (v. 27)	end time (11:40)	those days, immediately prior to Second advent (vv. 22,29)	Day of the Lord (v. 2), in his time [i.e. day of Antichrist] (v. 6)	great day of wrath (6:17), hour of judgment (14:7), great day of God (16:14)
Scope	has anything been done like this [ref. to Exodus] (v. 32)	none like it (v. 7), complete destruction (v. 11)	complete destruction (v. 27c)	such as never occurred (v.1)	such as never occurred nor ever shall (24:21; 13:19)		such as had not been since man came on earth (16:18)
Religious Context	idolatry (vv. 25, 28)	false prophets (29:24-32)	prince that will come (Antichrist), abomination of desolation (v. 27)	Antichrist (11:36-45), wicked (12:10)	false prophets' signs & wonders (24:24; 13:22)	Antichrist, false signs & wonders (vv. 4-9)	Antichrist, false prophets' signs & wonders (13:1-10)
Temple Activity	promise of spiritual restoration (v. 30)	promise of spiritual restoration & theocracy (v. 9)	temple desecrated (v. 27)	temple desecrated (v. 11)	temple desecrated (24:15; 13:14)	temple desecrated (v. 4)	temple desecrated (11:1,2)
Salvation Message	you will return (v. 30)	saved from time (v. 7)	implied in destruction of desolator (v. 27)	[elect] rescued (v. 1)	elect saved (24:22; 13:20)	day will not come [upon you], elect saved (v. 3,13)	bond-servants of God saved (19:1,2)

(Matt. 24:15; Mark 13:14) excludes the Roman destruction of Jerusalem and the captivity, since the diaspora Jews escaped this experience, although they were gravely affected by the loss of Jerusalem as the center of their faith. Of course, by the very fact that Daniel had predicted these events for the "end time," and time did not end (for either Jews or Gentiles) at A.D. 70, these events in all their details still await future fulfillment.

The Old Testament Tribulation Motif

The Tribulation texts in the Old Testament contain characteristics (or motifs) that are reflected in the New Testament texts which refer to this period. The chart on page 82 compares several of these Old Testament and New Testament texts to reveal their shared elements.

This chart shows that the Old Testament references to the Tribulation, in every case, expected fulfillment at a time corresponding to the end time. The scope of the judgment is in most cases unparalleled, and it required salvation (physical deliverance) as a sign of the severity of the event. That these contexts involved idolatry in some form, whether generally as false prophets, or specifically as the Antichrist and the abomination of desolation, agrees with the frequent inclusion of the temple, or the promise of restoration to a theocracy. While we have not sought within the scope of this study to examine linguistic parallels between the Old and New Testament texts, it should be apparent from these motifs and semantic parallels that the New Testament doctrine of the tribulation was dependent upon these Old Testament tribulation passages.

Larry V. Crutchfield

The Blessed Hope and the Tribulation in the Apostolic Fathers

_____*OVERVIEW*

What did the early Christians, who lived just after the apostles, believe about the Tribulation and the rapture? Did these post-apostolic fathers think that a believer would escape the trials of the Tribulation, or did they teach that the church would be tested through them? This writer examines early church documents and shows that, although not unanimously, many of the early church fathers believed they were living in the last days and were looking daily for the return of Christ. You will gain an understanding and appreciation for the earliest Christians' trust in the blessed hope.

*T*he position of the early church fathers on the time of Christ's return, and its relation to the Tribulation, has been the subject of considerable disagreement among conservative scholars. That the early fathers were predominantly premillennialists cannot be challenged with success. But whether that premillennialism leaned in the direction of pretribulationism or posttribulationism continues to be vigorously debated.

Did the fathers teach that the church could expect to endure severe trial and testing in the Great Tribulation prophesied for the end times, or did they expect believers to be raptured before the Tribulation began? Did they believe that Christ's coming was imminent, or did they look only for a complex of events, including Antichrist's reign of terror during the Tribulation, which would attend and precede the Lord's return? Should the early fathers be identified as pretribulationists, posttribulationists, imminent posttribulationists, or something else?

The answers could hardly be more divergent. One side of the debate is represented by scholars like George Eldon Ladd and Robert H. Gundry. Ladd asserts, "The hope of the church throughout the early centuries was the second coming of Christ, not a pretribulation rapture."[1] Although Ladd does allow that "the early church lived in expectation of Christ's return," he warns that "to deduce from this attitude of expectancy a belief in a pretribulation rapture and an any-moment coming of Christ, as has often been done, is not sound."[2] Ladd concludes that "every church father who deals with the subject expects the church to suffer at the hands of Antichrist." Thus, "the prevailing view is a posttribulation premillennialism."[3] Gundry arrives at the same conclusion.[4]

On the other side of this issue are men like Henry C. Thiessen and John F. Walvoord. While Thiessen and Walvoord agree with Ladd and Gundry that the early fathers were premillennialists, they argue that the fathers held also a consistent belief in the imminent return of Christ, which is the key ingredient in pretribulationism.

For example, Thiessen states, "It is clear...that the Fathers held not only the premillennial view of Christ's coming, but also regarded that coming as imminent. The Lord had taught them to expect His return at any moment, and so they looked for Him to come in their day."[5]

Walvoord agrees that "the early church fathers understood the Scriptures to teach that the coming of the Lord could occur any hour,"[6] and he identifies imminency as the central feature of pre-tribulationism.[7] Yet, while he suggests that the early fathers should "generally speaking...be classified as posttribulational," and that "the historical fact is that [their] view on prophecy did not correspond to what is advanced by pretribulationists today," he nevertheless argues that belief in imminency is an important point of agreement between the early fathers and the pretribulationists of today.[8]

As suggested, Ladd and Gundry agree with Thiessen and Walvoord that the early church was premillennial, but they insist that it was also distinctly posttribulational and harbored no belief in the any-moment return of Christ.[9] Gundry asserts that in ante-Nicene chiliasm, "posttribulationism...formed an integral part of the premillennial outline of coming events."[10] Ladd sums up this position by saying that:

> Every church father who deals with the subject expects the church to suffer at the hands of Antichrist. God would purify the church through suffering, and Christ would save her by His return at the end of the Tribulation when he would destroy Antichrist, deliver his church, and bring the world to an end and inaugurate His millennial kingdom.[11]

Although there is general agreement between Ladd and Gundry here, there are a number of conflicting opinions among premillennial posttribulationists regarding the early church's views on imminency and pretribulationism. For example, while Ladd takes the extreme view that "we can find no trace of pretribulationism in the early church,"[12] Millard J. Erickson, who often follows Ladd, allows for the possibility that "the premillennialism of the church's first centuries may have included belief in a pretribulational rapture of the church."[13] Even though Thomas Lea says, "We cannot use the teaching of the fathers to support the contention that Christ is coming at any moment,"[14] J. Barton Payne does precisely that.[15]

The cause of the confusion among modern scholars on this issue is no mystery. They are confused because the fathers were confused on the subject. Eschatology was in its infancy in the early centuries A.D. If anyone searches the fathers for a fully detailed, systematic presentation about the doctrine of last things, he searches in vain Nevertheless, many early fathers make provocative statements about prophetic events, which are of great interest and importance in any contemporary discussion of the origins and antecedents of views held today.

The Apostolic Fathers

Clement of Rome (fl. ca. A.D. 90–100)

While it has been argued, and not without some justification, that the evidence for Clement's premillennialism is sparse, the same is not true regarding his views on imminency. He says, "Of a truth, soon and suddenly shall His will be accomplished, as the Scripture also bears witness, saying, 'Speedily will He come, and will not tarry;' and, 'The Lord shall suddenly come to His temple, even the Holy One, for whom ye look.'"[16] In view of this any-moment return of Christ, Clement urges watchfulness and obedient service to Him. Of Christ he says, "He forewarns us: 'Behold, the Lord [cometh], and His reward is before His face, to render to every man according to his work.' He exhorts us, therefore, with our whole heart to attend to this, that we be not lazy or slothful in any good work "[17] And, "Let us therefore earnestly strive to be found in the number of those that wait for Him in order that we may share in His promised gifts "[18]

A few words must be said here in response to Robert H. Gundry's assessment of Clement's position on imminency. In referring to the passage in *I Clement*, chapter 33, Gundry notes that it is preceded by an "illustration of a tree budding and putting forth leaves and fruit which finally ripens—an illustration which hardly conveys imminence."[19] Clement has evidently drawn this illustration from a source now unknown to us. In any event, the import of the illustration is self-evident. Clement's point is that just as it takes a short time for a tree to pass from bud to fruit stage, so in reality it takes a short time for the accomplishment of God's will. When Christ does come, and that could be at any moment, it will result in the sudden accomplishment of His will.

Gundry seems to assume that the whole process of budding to ripened fruit must yet take place. But it can be argued that his message to these "old men," who have waited in vain for Christ's coming, is that they have seen and are presently part of the budding and putting forth of leaves stages, while only the appearance of ripened fruit remains. Some time is necessary for the accomplishment of God's plan for mankind, just as it is for a tree to bear fruit. How much time is necessary, no one knows. All of that necessary time could be spent at any moment. Then suddenly, as fruit appears on a tree, Christ will return to accomplish His will.

Gundry also discusses the Malachi 3:1 quotation in connection with Malachi 4:5f.[20] The latter passage he interprets in a posttribulational sense,[21] and then conveniently saddles Clement with it. On this arbitrary basis, Gundry concludes that it is the posttribulational coming of Christ which Clement holds forth as "their [the Christians'] hope and object of watchfulness." Thus, he continues, "This passage can hardly be claimed for the doctrine of imminence (as has been done) when it clearly pertains to the posttribulational advent."[22]

It is another example of the *non sequitur* that one finds in this particular work by Gundry. Clement's sole reason for quoting Malachi 3:1 was to set forth the suddenness of Christ's second coming. The posttribulational interpretation is Gundry's, not Clement's. Therefore, while we can appreciate Gundry's ventriloquistic inventiveness here, in the absence of Clement's own exegesis of the Malachi 4 passage, and in all fairness to him, his silence must be honored.

Ignatius of Antioch (d. ca. A.D. 98/117)

It is evident from the letters of Ignatius that he believed the church was living in the last times and that the coming of the Lord was at hand. He says, "The last times are come upon us. Let us therefore be of a reverent spirit, and fear the long-suffering of God, that it tend not to our condemnation."[23]

In his epistle to the venerable Polycarp, bishop of Smyrna, Ignatius encourages him to "be watchful, possessing a sleepless spirit."[24] Later he says, "Be ever becoming more zealous than what thou art. Weigh carefully the times. Look for Him who is above all time, eternal and invisible, yet who became visible for our sake." Just prior to this admonition, the longer version of the letter to Polycarp adds an exhortation "to bear all things for the sake of God, that He also may bear with us, and bring us into His kingdom."[25]

The Didache (before end of first century A.D.)

Of greatest interest for the present study is the final chapter in *The Didache*. Here we have one of the best early examples of extra-biblical teaching on the second coming of Christ and attendant events. One of its chief eschatological concepts is imminency. In chapter 10 of *The Didache*, we find this conclusion to a Eucharistic prayer: "Let grace come, and let this world pass away. Hosanna to the God (Son) of David! If any one is holy, let him come; if any one is not so, let him repent. Maranatha. Amen."[26]

In the final chapter, the Didachist says, "Watch for your life's sake. Let not your lamps be quenched, nor your loins unloosed; but be ye ready, for ye know not the hour in which our Lord cometh."[27] In light of the imminence of the Lord's return, the Didachist urges frequent fellowship of the saints for the purpose of the mutual up-building, which will lead to perfection in "the last time." This course of action is expedient, the reader is told, because of the proliferation of "false prophets and corrupters" in the last days.[28]

In *The Didache*, we have the fullest outline of things to come up to this point. The reader is told that after the appearance of the many false prophets and corrupters, the "world-deceiver" shall come to bring fiery trial upon all mankind so that "many shall be made to stumble and shall perish; but they that endure in their faith shall be saved from under the curse itself."[29] What is meant by "the curse" is not clear. Perhaps it is the Tribulation.

The time of Antichrist will be followed, says the Didachist, by the revelation of three "signs of the truth." The first of these is "an outspreading [opening, ἐκπετάσεω] in heaven."[30] The second sign is that of the "sound of the trumpet." The third sign is given as the "resurrection of the dead; yet not of all, but as it is said: The Lord shall come and all His saints with Him." Finally, the whole world will witness the coming of the Lord "upon the clouds of heaven."[31] On such sequences of events in the fathers, and their relation to imminency, Ladd says:

> The expectation of the coming of Christ *included the events which would attend and precede His coming.* The early fathers who emphasized an attitude of expectancy believed that this entire complex of events— Antichrist, Tribulation, return of Christ—would soon occur. This is not the same as an any-moment coming of Christ.[32]

The position of these fathers may be described as a type of imminent posttribulationism.[33] We prefer the designation "imminent intratribulationism" as perhaps more descriptive of the fathers' position, and at the same time to avoid confusion with modern posttribulationism. To deny a true belief in imminency to the fathers is not in harmony with the facts. While we freely admit that these church leaders were not fully pretribulational in the contemporary sense, neither is it true, as Gundry suggests, that "Irenaeus... was as forthright a posttribulationist as could be found in the present day."[34]

In the case of the Didachist, it cannot be denied that he taught watchfulness on the basis of the any-moment coming of Christ, in keeping with Matthew 24:42.[35] Why is it, then, that he proceeds to warn of an increase in false prophets and corrupters, the appearance of the "world-deceiver," and the "fire of trial"—all to come in the last days—if Christ is to return first? How is the apparent contradiction to be explained?

The answer, it seems to us, is twofold. First of all, the fathers of the early church lived in the shadow of persecution. Beginning with Nero in A.D. 64, and continuing in various degrees of intensity until just two years short of the Council of Nicea, in A.D. 325, persecutions were a present reality for the believer. As early as the *Epistle of Barnabas*, the Roman Empire itself—the fourth beast of Daniel 7:7-8—was identified as the Antichrist.[36] And while Victorinus of Petau casts the discussion of Antichrist in the context of the Roman emperors,[37] Commodian believes, as do others, according to Lactantius,[38] that a revived Nero will function as the evil one to come in the last days.

In the above reference to *Barnabas*, which appears to be a quotation from *The Didache*, there is an exhortation to watchfulness, lest in the end one's faith profits nothing. But it is an exhortation for "*these* last days," not "*the* last days." For Barnabas, the last days were at the door. Justin Martyr was later to speak of the "man of apostasy," and the persecutions inflicted upon the saints by him, as if they were simply a continuation of persecutions already suffered.[39]

The picture, then, is this. False teachers in abundance are already threatening the church, as Ignatius suggests.[40] The Antichrist, whether the Roman Empire generally, the present emperor, or a revived Nero, may already be here or perhaps soon will be. The church is even now being persecuted by this evil government. "Watch," therefore, "for your life's sake. Let not your lamps be quenched, nor your loins unloosed; but be ye ready, for ye know not the hour in which our Lord cometh."[41] Our conclusion is stated well by Walvoord:

> The fact is, ... in the early church fathers there was no clear agreement that a specific seven-year period as is indicated in Daniel 9:27 had to occur before the Lord could return. Generally speaking, the early church fathers, as well as the Protestant Reformers, tended to identify contemporary events with the events of the Great Tribulation and because of this could look for the imminent return of Christ.[42]

The second response to the seeming contradiction here, between imminency and events yet to take place before Christ's return, concerns the simplistic, unreflective manner in which the subject is treated by the early fathers. Note that the whole earth shall be delivered into the hands of the "world-deceiver," and that it is all "the creation of men" who are to undergo the πύρωσι (fiery trial). That there is a question of maintaining faith during this time is clear, but to whom does this refer?

In chapter 16.2, the Didachist maintains that "the whole time of your faith will not profit you, if ye be not made perfect in the last time." The parallel passage in the *Constitutions of the Holy Apostles* states, "Watch therefore, and pray, that ye do not sleep unto death. For your former good deeds will not profit you, if at *the last part of your life* you go astray from the true faith."[43] The warning is given because of the proliferation of false teachers in the last days. That the faithful, whoever they may be, are admonished to stand firm against false teachings is evident, but their identity is not explicitly stated.

The identification of the faithful in chapter 16.5 poses no smaller problem. Here we are told that of all mankind who undergo the "fire of trial," "many shall be made to stumble and shall perish; but they that endure in their faith [Matt. 10:22] shall be saved from under the curse [Tribulation?] itself."[44] Is this the church or others who become believers during the Tribulation? The church is not mentioned here at all. The reference, rather, is to mankind in general, out of which mass some shall endure in faithfulness.

After giving the "signs of the truth," which are to appear after the fiery trial, the Didachist says, "The Lord shall come and all His saints with Him [Zech. 14:5]."[45] That this number includes saints who have died is certain enough from the reference to the third sign: "the resurrection of the dead; yet not of all...." But this company, of "all His saints," would seem also to include living believers as well, the resurrection and rapture both having taken place. Modern readers are left without a clear understanding of who the participants in these events are.

The bulk of the material from the last chapter of *The Didache* recalls the language of Matthew 24, the Olivet discourse. The writer makes no direct statement that it is the church which is in view here. Rather, in early patristic fashion, he simply repeats the language of the inspired text with little amplification or interpretation. Thus we cannot say with conviction, as Ladd does, that "the many who are to be offended and be lost are professing Christians who do not stand true; for only those who endure in their faith shall be saved." Nor can we say, "The purpose of the Didachist in writing this exhortation was to prepare the Church for the Great Tribulation and the sufferings to be inflicted by the Antichrist...."[46]

Gundry stands on even shakier ground in this matter. He cites the Didachist's references to the "church" in the Eucharistic prayers— which he requests be gathered from the "ends of the earth," "from the four winds," into the kingdom—as substitutions for "the elect" of Matthew 24:31, who are to be gathered together "from the four winds, from one end of the sky to the other" (NASB).[47] Gundry's inference is that the church (equated with the elect on the basis of Matthew 24) must be the subject of the apocalyptic chapter at the conclusion of *The Didache* (also based on Matthew 24).

To begin with, the references to the church in chapters 9 and 10 are not direct quotations from the Matthew 24 passage. Furthermore, as the editors of the *Ancient Christian Writers* series point out, such expressions were common among the early fathers to emphasize the "universality of Christ's kingdom or the church."[48] In essence, Gundry has simply made a quantum leap from two separate passages in *The Didache* (chapters 9 and 10) to a third (chapter 16), as if they were not only contiguous in thought, but textually contiguous as well.

It is useless, however, to pretend that these earliest of the fathers were such precise thinkers. If the Didachist had Matthew 24 in mind when he referred to the gathering "from the four winds," there is no sure way we can know it. Even if this were his intent, it cannot be proved that he had in mind also an equation between the elect and the church on that basis. A father's casual use of phrases, supposed to have been drawn from a certain scriptural context, hardly provides one with the higher ground from which to defend a position.

Epistle of Barnabas (ca. A.D. 70/117-138)[49]

Like his contemporaries, Barnabas employs the language of imminency when speaking of Christ's return. Having just spoken of the kingdom, resurrection, and retribution, Barnabas says, "For the day is at hand on which all things shall perish with the evil [one]. The Lord is near and His reward."[50] Elsewhere he warns, "It therefore behooves us, who inquire much concerning events at hand, to search diligently into those things which are able to save us." Later he says, "The final stumbling-block (or source of danger) approaches, concerning which it is written, as Enoch says, 'For this end the Lord has cut short the times and the days, that His Beloved may hasten; and He will come to the inheritance.'" Finally, Barnabas urges the saints to "take earnest heed in these last days," to be steadfast in faith and the avoidance of evil in order that the "Black One may find no means of entrance...."[51]

In our understanding of the matter, there is nothing in Barnabas' epistle which would preclude the possibility of the any-moment return of Jesus Christ. He speaks about Antichrist in cryptic terms (e.g., "Black One," "wicked prince"), but he seems to identify the fourth beast of Daniel 7:7-8—the Roman Empire—as the Antichrist of the last times. Naturally, then, as patristic scholar J. N. D. Kelly points out, " 'Barnabas' is satisfied that the scandal of the last days is actually upon us...."[52] Again we encounter a type of imminent intratribulationism.

To the contrary, Ladd, Gundry, and Erickson,[53] all argue for a strictly posttribulational interpretation of Barnabas, devoid of imminency. At the outset, these men make certain unwarranted assumptions: First, they arbitrarily interpret Barnabas on Daniel 7:7-8 in a wholly contemporary way as lending support to their view. Both Ladd and Erickson insist that Barnabas looked for a still-future tenfold division of the Roman Empire to precede the return of Christ. But no such interpretation is forthcoming from the passage.

That Barnabas understood the fourth beast to be the Roman Empire as the weight of later patristic literature affirms, is a safe assumption. But what Barnabas thought of the ten-three-one horn scenario, we do not know. The single horn was of course the evil one to come in the end (Roman Empire). And perhaps he held the others to represent minor kingdoms already subdued by Rome. In any case, it is no less valid to say that because he believed the church to be living in the last days and Christ's coming imminent, that he could not have been looking for a tenfold division of Rome, than to say that because he looked for a tenfold division of the Roman Empire to precede Christ's coming, that the second coming could not be imminent. At least we have marshaled several passages from Barnabas to demonstrate his attitude of expectancy, while the posttribulationists have brought forth no clear evidence that Barnabas held to the necessity of a tenfold division of the Roman Empire prior to Christ's return.

Another erroneous assumption made by these posttribulationists is that Barnabas looked forward to a time of Tribulation distinct from that which the church was then experiencing. As we have shown, Barnabas speaks regularly of *"these* last days" and of *"this* wicked time."[54] Note that Barnabas does not even imply that things will get worse before the end. He suggests, rather, that things are already bad, and thus it behooves his readers to be on their guard, for "the day is at hand on which all things shall perish with the evil [one]. The Lord is near, and His reward."[55] For some of these fathers, it seems that the difference between the persecution which they were undergoing and that which was to precede the second advent, was not a difference in kind, and perhaps, not even a difference in degree of severity. Thus our designation "intratribultionism," may not be without merit.

The Shepherd of Hermas (in two parts, ca. A.D. 96/140-150)

For our purposes, the greatest interest generated by Hermas is his teaching on imminency and "the great tribulation that is coming."[56] In chapters 2 and 3 of the fourth vision, we have an intriguing dialogue, the interpretation of which has produced no little controversy. Do we have here a distinctly pretribulational reference, as Thiessen suggests?[57] Or, as Ladd believes,[58] does it present the church with a clearly posttribulational expectation?

Like those we have examined above, Hermas employs the language of expectancy with respect to the Lord's coming. In the ninth similitude, he sets forth the parable of the tower. The tower pictures the church (chapter 13, cf. the third vision, chapter 3) under construction, in preparation for the Lord's return. When Hermas asks the Shepherd why the building has not been completed, he is told that the tower "cannot be finished just yet, until the Lord of it come and examine the building" (chapter 5). Further on, the Shepherd says to Hermas:

> Let us go, and after two days let us come and clean these stones, and cast them into the building; for all things around the tower must be cleaned, lest the Master come suddenly [see Mark 13:36; Matthew 24:46-51], and find the places about the tower dirty, and be displeased, and these stones be not returned for the building of the tower, and I also shall seem to be neglectful towards the Master.[59]

In chapter 26 of this similitude, those who intend to repent are told to "do so quickly, before the tower is completed."

The identity of all of the players in this parable is never completely clear. For example, in chapter 6 of the ninth similitude, a party of men come to the tower, and in their midst is "one man of so remarkable a size as to overtop the tower." Whether this man, who is "the lord of the whole tower" (chapter 7), and who performs what appears to be some type of preliminary inspection, is Christ is unknown. In any event, the whole parable is permeated by an air of urgency in light of an any-moment return of the "Master." But what of Tribulation to come and its relation to the tower (the church), which Hermas is assured "will soon be finished"?[60]

Hermas' thoughts on this question are contained chiefly in the fourth vision. He tells the reader that he was traveling down a country road when he asked for the final installment of revelations, which had been given him "through [the Lord's] holy Church," that he himself might be strengthened, that the wayward might repent, and that the Lord might be glorified. He then saw dust rising more and more as "a mighty beast like a whale," with fiery locusts coming out of its mouth. At the sight of this 100-foot high beast, with its urn-shaped head, Hermas began to weep and called upon the Lord for deliverance. Then Hermas remembered the things he had been taught, and the admonition to those clothed with faith in the Lord not to doubt, and he stood firm in preparation for the beast's fury. But when Hermas drew near the beast, it "stretched itself out on the ground, and showed nothing but its tongue, and did not stir at all until I had passed by it." As he passed, Hermas observed that there were four colors on its head, "black, then fiery and bloody, then golden, and lastly white."[61]

After this harrowing experience, Hermas was met by a virgin whom he recognized, from former visions, to be the church.[62] When questioned about his experience, Hermas explains that he was met by a beast, "but through the power of the Lord and His great mercy I escaped from it." The virgin then replies:

> You have escaped from great tribulation on account of your faith, and because you did not doubt in the presence of such a beast. Go, therefore, and tell the elect of the Lord His mighty deeds, and say to them that this beast is a type of the great tribulation that is coming. If then ye prepare yourselves, and repent with all your heart, and turn to the Lord, it will be possible for you to escape it, if your heart be pure and spotless, and ye spend the rest of the days of your life in serving the Lord blamelessly.[63]

When Hermas asks for an explanation about the four colors on the beast's head, the virgin replies:

The black is *the world* in which we dwell: but the
fiery and bloody points out that *the world must perish
through blood and fire*: but the golden part are *you
who have escaped from this world*. For as gold is
tested by fire, and thus becomes useful, so are you
tested who dwell in it. Those, therefore, who continue
steadfast, and are put through the fire, will be purified
by means of it. For as gold casts away its dross, so
also will ye cast away all sadness and straitness, and
will be made pure so as to fit into the building of the
tower. But the white part is *the age that is to come*, in
which the elect of God will dwell, since those elected
by God to eternal life will be spotless and pure.
Wherefore cease not speaking these things unto the
ears of the saints. This then is the type of the great
tribulation that is to come.[64]

How are we to understand the position here presented by
Hermas? Thiessen maintains, "This surely shows that there was
teaching to the effect that the church would escape the Great Tribulation, and that this is not a doctrine that was unknown, as has been
charged, until it was popularized by the Plymouth Brethren."[65]
Ladd, on the other hand, states that "when one reads the entire
passage, he finds that the exact opposite is taught, for the author is
referring to preservation in and through Tribulation."[66]

Three things are beyond dispute. One, the beast represents the
coming Great Tribulation, and the imagery of blood and fire certainly evokes the language of the book of Revelation (see 6:12;
8:7-8; 9:17-18; 11:5-6; 14:18-20; 16:3-8; 20:9). Two, Hermas escaped
the Tribulation completely unscathed, and he is told that it is possible for any to escape, "if [their] heart be pure and spotless, and
[they] spend the rest of the days of [their lives] serving the Lord
blamelessly."[67] Three, the virgin and the tower both represent the
church; Hermas does not. Hermas represents only an individual, "a
saint under construction" (a stone), being made fit through trial and
testing for inclusion into the tower.

Thiessen's position on Hermas, that the church will be "taken
away before that period of judgment begins,"[68] is difficult to
defend. Hermas is definitely pictured in the presence of the beast,

though fully protected. Elsewhere, we read in the *Shepherd*, "Happy ye who endure the great tribulation that is coming on, and happy they who shall not deny their own life. For the Lord hath sworn by His Son, that those who denied their Lord have abandoned their life in despair, for even now these are to deny Him in the days that are coming."[69] Here, too, the implication seems to be that believers will be present during the coming Tribulation. It must be said, however, that the pretribulational position represented by Thiessen captures the essence of Hermas' position, in its emphasis on the imminency of Christ's return and the believer's escape from the coming Tribulation.

Obviously, if the foregoing is true, Ladd's modern posttribulational position is in for even tougher sledding. The type of preservation that Ladd envisions for the church "in the presence of tribulation" includes her purification by "the fiery trial of persecution." He maintains that "if the church is prepared, it need not fear the sufferings to come; they will be as nothing to those whose faith is fixed in the Lord." Ladd asserts that this "is proven by the interpretation of the four colors."[70]

The first of these colors, black, represents the world. The second color, fiery and bloody (red?), points to the destruction of the world by fire and blood. That this could represent God's wrath on a Christ-rejecting world, as revealed in the Apocalypse, we have already shown. But what of the "golden part," which typifies those "who have escaped from this world," those who will be purified as gold—"tested by fire"? Three things must be said in response to Ladd's insistence upon a modern posttribulational interpretation of Hermas at this point.

First, it should be observed that in Hermas' encounter with the beast, he comes away from the experience totally unmolested. There is not the slightest hint of suffering or torment, with the exception of the initial dread. On the contrary, when approached by Hermas, the beast becomes as docile and unmenacing as a lap dog. This seems to suggest a time of wrath only upon those who lack faith in God.

Second, earlier in the *Shepherd*, Hermas is said to have already "endured great personal tribulations" on account of his own "wicked transactions" and "the transgressions of [his] house...." This indictment is immediately followed by these words of encouragement:

But you are saved, because you did not depart from the living God, and on account of your simplicity and great self-control. These have saved you, if you remain steadfast. And they will save all who act in the same manner, and walk in guilelessness and simplicity. Those who possess such virtues will wax strong against every form of wickedness, and will abide unto eternal life. Blessed are all they who practice righteousness, for they shall never be destroyed. Now you will tell Maximus: Lo! tribulation cometh on.[71]

While Hermas says nothing of the Roman persecutions of the day, he nevertheless seems to see Tribulation as a continuum, culminating in the Great Tribulation at the end of the age. Note that he is pronounced saved, and will yet be saved if he remains steadfast in the faith. Thus the trial and testing at the end is a continuation of that which has gone before.

Third, Hermas sets forth more than one means of purification for the church. He is told that the color white represents the "age that is to come, in which the elect of God will dwell, since those elected by God to eternal life will be spotless and pure." The stones, having been made ready, are fitted into the tower. The means of purification here is said to be the test by fire.[72] Elsewhere, however, it is cast simply in terms of the process of selection and rejection of the different types of stones available for the tower's construction.[73] The context is one of the personal practice of evil or the practice of good. Purification is achieved, it seems, without the instrumentality of fiery testing.

Can this be a type of posttribulationism that precludes imminency, then? We think not. That Hermas presents Tribulation as a continuum, we have already shown. Furthermore, he makes no reference to the chronology of Daniel 9, nor does he in any way posit an estimate of duration for the Great Tribulation. In fact, the whole encounter with the beast is depicted as rather brief and imminent "There was a noise, however, and I turned round in alarm, thinking that that beast was coming."[74]

Any attempt to fully understand this peculiar allegory, and to reconcile it with Scripture, is doomed. We must concede that

Hermas held to a type of condensed, imminent, posttribulationism (or "intratribulationism") unlike that previously encountered. He lives in constant expectation of the Master's sudden return to the tower. But at the same time, he has the sound of the ponderous feet of the fiery, locust-breathing urn-headed, whale-like beast ringing in his ears. Hermas, who represents not the church but an individual saint in the making, escapes the beast and this world, on the one hand; then he must either go through fiery trial for purification, or simply make morally correct choices to the same end, on the other hand. Though on the whole the *Shepherd of Hermas* is an interesting patristic production, it is not with regret that one contemplates God the Holy Spirit eventually convincing the early church that this was indeed an uninspired work and therefore to be excluded from the canon of Scripture.

Conclusions and Implications

The student of patristic literature quickly discovers that the position of the early fathers on the Tribulation and its relation to the saints and Christ's return is impossible to decipher and synthesize completely. Many of them, however, especially in the first century, make explicit statements which indicate a belief in the imminent return of Christ.[75] The doctrine of imminency is especially prominent in the writings of the apostolic fathers. It is on the basis of Christ's impending return (e.g., *Didache*), and on the strength of the literal fulfillment of past prophecy (e.g., *Barnabas*), that they exhort the Christian to live the life of purity and faithfulness.

In actuality, as Walvoord points out,[76] the position of the early fathers was a type of imminent posttribulationism (or, as we have suggested, "imminent intratribulationism"), with an occasional pre-tribulational inference.[77] The reason for this peculiar hybrid is that, on the one hand, Scripture clearly teaches that Christ's coming could occur at any moment, and therefore the believer is to live his life in holiness and with an expectant attitude. On the other hand, until Constantine's Edict of Milan, which granted Christianity full legal toleration (A.D. 313), persecutions of every sort were a present reality for believers in the Roman Empire. For many, this, coupled with the belief that Christians must be tested and purified by fire (i.e., trials in the form of persecutions for Christ's sake), to make them fit for God's kingdom, led to something like the Thessalonian error (2 Thessalonians 2). The church, it was thought, was already in the Tribulation and could therefore expect the any-moment return of the Lord.

In addition to direct statements on imminency, in some fathers, language decidedly associated with the rapture is found.[78] Others maintain that the saints will escape the time of persecution under Antichrist, in a manner reflective of Revelation 3:10.[79] But due to the circumstances of that period of church history, there is no exact correlation between tribulationism as held by the early fathers and views commonly held today.

The Roman Empire of Daniel's prophecies (the fourth beast of Daniel 7), for instance, was naturally understood by these fathers to already exist. The persecution to be suffered at the hands of Antichrist, who was often identified in some way with the Roman Empire, was seen by many early church leaders as merely an extension of the persecution currently being suffered at the hands of Rome. For many of them, all that remained was for Antichrist to appear suddenly to carry out the final stage of hostility against the saints. But coupled with this sense of the impending revelation of Antichrist was the attitude that Christ could come at any moment to raise the righteous dead, rapture the saints, destroy Antichrist's evil regime, and inaugurate the golden kingdom age.

The fathers generally saw all persecutions as serving a purifying purpose.[80] As gold is refined by fire, the saints must be purified by fiery trials. But this purifying process had been underway since at least the time of Nero, beginning in A.D. 64. Any further purifying persecution at the hands of Antichrist was seen within the Roman context.

Concerning the time and duration of Antichrist's reign and the final phase of persecution, as understood by the early fathers, there is much that we cannot say for certain. Several of them associate the time of the end with the tenfold division of the Roman Empire, spoken of in Daniel 7:7-8,23-25 and Revelation 17:12, and Antichrist's rise to power.[81] But the mere fact that this event was to precede Christ's coming does not in itself negate the sense of expectancy among those fathers who held this view. In *Barnabas*, for example, it cannot even be said for certain that the tenfold division of Rome is seen as yet future.[82] And Irenaeus still speaks of Antichrist's "sudden coming," and the church "suddenly" being caught up.[83] Tertullian exults, "But what a spectacle is that fast-approaching advent of our Lord, now owned by all, now highly exalted, now a triumphant One!"[84] And even though Lactantius maintains that signs are to precede the end, he says, "It is permitted us to know respecting the signs, which are spoken by the prophets, for they foretold signs by which the consummation of the times is to be expected by us *from day to day*, and to be feared."[85]

With few exceptions,[86] the premillennial fathers of the early church believed that they were living in the last times. Thus they looked daily for the Lord's return. Even most of those who looked for Antichrist's appearance prior to the second advent, saw that event as occurring suddenly, and just as suddenly being followed by the rescue and rapture of the saints. Furthermore, the fathers who expected the tenfold division of Rome, appear to compress that event into a very short period of time. This belief in the imminent return of Jesus Christ within the context of ongoing persecution has prompted us to broadly label the views of the earliest fathers: "imminent intratribulationism."[87]

It should be noted that dispensationalists today do not say that the early church was clearly pretribulational, or that there are even clear individual statements of pretribulationism in the fathers. As previously noted, Walvoord says, "The historical fact is that the early church fathers' view on prophecy did not correspond to what is advanced by pretribulationists today except for the one important point that both subscribe to the imminency of the rapture."[88] This view of the fathers on imminency, and, in some, references to escaping the time of the Tribulation, constitute what may be termed, to quote Erickson, "seeds from which the doctrine of the pretribulational rapture could be developed...."[89] Had it not been for the drought in sound exegesis, brought on by Alexandrian allegorism and later by Augustine, one wonders what kind of crop those seeds might have yielded—long before J. N. Darby and the nineteenth century.

5

Grant R. Jeffrey

A Pretrib Rapture Statement in the Early Medieval Church

_____*OVERVIEW*

Was the pretribulational rapture first found in 1830 in Scotland, as some have speculated? Or can other statements be found prior to that time? This writer produces several interesting statements which suggest that some people may have divided the rapture and the second coming into two events long before 1830. In fact, Mr. Jeffrey has discovered an amazingly clear pretrib statement from the fourth century in a sermon by someone called "Pseudo-Ephraem." This discovery may revolutionize the evangelical church's understanding of the history of the rapture.

*A*fter more than a decade of research I have found evidence that the doctrine of the pretribulation rapture was taught in the early church almost 1500 years before John Darby issued his revival of this New Testament teaching, which had been ignored

during the medieval period. In this chapter I will discuss two remarkable textual discoveries from my latest book *Final Warning*.[1] These texts conclusively prove that a number of Christian teachers in the centuries before John Darby rediscovered this biblical teaching in A.D. 1830, clearly taught that the rapture would occur before the Tribulation period.

Was the Pretribulation Rapture Taught Before John Darby in A.D. 1830?

Obviously the truth about the timing of the rapture will ultimately be found only in Scripture. The Protestant Reformation was based essentially on a return to the authority of the Bible. The Latin phrase *sola Scriptura,* meaning "Scripture alone," became the rallying cry of Reformers who ignored centuries of tradition and church councils in their insistence that truth could only be discovered in the Word of God. While the ultimate resolution of this discussion must be based on our interpretation of Scripture, it is important to answer the errors of opponents who disparage "the blessed hope" with misinformation about the modern rediscovery of the truth about the pretribulation rapture.

Many of these writers falsely assert that the pretribulation rapture theory first originated around A.D. 1830. They ascribe the theory's initial creation variously to Emmanuel Lacunza (Ben Ezra, 1812), Edward Irving (1826), Margaret Macdonald (1830) and, finally, to John Darby (1830). Many of those who despise the teaching of the pretribulation rapture have dogmatically asserted that the doctrine of the pretribulation rapture is a modern innovation that was taught for the first time in history in approximately 1830 by John Darby of the Plymouth Brethren. Posttribulationist writers have attacked the pretribulation rapture doctrine by claiming that it cannot be true because none of the early church writers and none of the Reformers ever taught it. Obviously, their argument has been quite effective in causing some Christians to abandon their belief in the pretribulation rapture. The question for sincere students of Scripture must be whether or not the Bible truly teaches this doctrine. The argument that no one ever saw this "truth" throughout 1800 years of church history has been somewhat effective. The only problem with their argument is that they are wrong.

False Statements that the Pretribulation Rapture Was Never Taught Before A.D. 1830

Posttribulational teachers have falsely made dogmatic statements for many years that no one ever taught the pretribulation rapture before A.D. 1830. The following statements are just a few examples taken from the books of those who reject the pretribulation rapture. George E. Ladd has said:

> We can find no trace of pretribulationism in the early church; and no modern pretribulationist has successfully proved that this particular doctrine was held by any of the church fathers or students of the Word before the nineteenth century.[2]

Rapture critic John Bray insists:

> People who are teaching the pretribulation rapture teaching today are teaching something that never was taught until 1812....Not one of those early church fathers taught a pretribulation rapture....I make the offer of five hundred dollars to anybody who will find a statement, a sermon, article in a commentary, or anything, prior to 1812 that taught a two-phase coming of Christ separated by a stated period of time, such as the pretribulation rapturists teach.[3]

Perhaps the most vocal of all rapture critics, Dave MacPherson says:

> Margaret Macdonald was the first person to teach a coming of Christ that would precede the days of Antichrist.... Before 1830 Christians had always believed in a single future coming, that the catching up of 1 Thessalonians 4 will take place after the Great Tribulation of Matthew 24 at the glorious coming of the Son of Man when He shall send His angels to gather together all of His Elect.[4]

A number of these authors will have to drastically revise the next edition of their books based on the discovery of new pretribulation rapture texts from the writings of the early church.

The Discovery of Ephraem's Teaching in A.D. 373 on the Pretribulation Rapture

> For all the saints and Elect of God are gathered, prior to the tribulation that is to come, and are taken to the Lord lest they see the confusion that is to overwhelm the world because of our sins.[5]

Over the last decade I came to the conclusion that the pretribulation rapture is taught so clearly in the New Testament that it is virtually impossible that no one ever taught this doctrine in the 18 centuries before 1830. During the summer of 1994, after a decade of searching, I found several fascinating manuscripts that contain clear evidence of pretribulation rapture teaching in the early church. The early Christian writer and poet Ephraem the Syrian (he lived from A.D. 306 to 373) was a major theologian of the early Byzantine Eastern Church. He was born near Nisibis, in the Roman province of Syria, near present-day Edessa, Turkey. Ephraem displayed a profound love of the Scriptures in his writings, as illustrated by several of his written comments quoted in the *Works of Nathaniel Lardner,* Volume Four (A.D. 1788): "I esteem no man more happy than him, who diligently reads the Scriptures delivered to us by the Spirit of God, and thinks how he may order his conversation by the precepts of them.... The truth written in the sacred volume of the gospel is a perfect rule. Nothing can be taken from it, nor added to it, without great guilt." To this day his hymns and homilies are used in the liturgy of the Greek Orthodox and Middle Eastern Nestorian Church.

The 16-volume Post-Nicene Library includes a number of homilies and psalms by Ephraem the Syrian, and the editors noted that he also wrote a large number of commentaries which have never been translated into English. For example, Ephraem's fascinating teaching on the Antichrist has never been published before in English until today. This important prophecy manuscript from the fourth century reveals a literal hermeneutic and a teaching of the premillennial return of Jesus Christ. More importantly, Ephraem's text revealed a clear statement about the pretribulational return of Christ to take His elect saints home to heaven to escape the coming Tribulation.

In addition, Ephraem declares his belief in a personal, Jewish Antichrist, who will rule the Roman Empire during the last days, a rebuilt temple, the two witnesses, and a literal Great Tribulation lasting 1260 days. He also taught that the war of Gog and Magog would occur in the years leading up to the Tribulation period. And a second text by Ephraem reveals he taught that Daniel's seventieth week will be fulfilled in the final seven years at the end of this age, which will conclude with Christ's return at the battle of Armageddon to establish His kingdom.

What Ephraem the Syrian Said

Here is what Ephraem the Syrian wrote about the last times, the Antichrist, and the end of the world (translated by Cameron Rhoades, Tyndale Theological Seminary, Fort Worth, Texas).

1. Most dearly beloved brothers, believe the Holy Spirit who speaks in us. Now we have spoken before, because the end of the world is very near, and the consummation remains. Has not the first faith withered away in men? Which appears in boys...slanderous things among the priests, liars among the priests, false swearing among the Levites, among the ministers evil deeds, adulteries among the older men, dissipation among the youths, false appearance among women, the adulterer is influenced among virgins! And among them all there are the wars of the Persians, and the threatening of

diverse nations and kingdom rising up against kingdom...
and when the kingdom of the Romans begins to be consummated by the sword, the advent of the evil one is near.
Because it is necessary that the age is consummated in the
fulfillment of the Roman kingdom. In those days two brothers
come to the Roman kingdom, and indeed they preside with
one accord, but since one surpasses the other, a division will
take place between them. And so the Adversary is released
and shall provoke hatred between the kingdoms of the Persians and the Romans. In those days many people rise up
against the kingdom of the Romans, and the people of the
Jews will be its adversaries. Because there will be violent
movements of the nations and evil reports, and there will be
plagues and hunger and earthquakes (movements of the
earth) throughout the regions, and captives shall be led
among all nations, and there will be battles and rumors of
battles, and the sword shall consume many things from the
rising to the setting of the sun. And there will be very many
dangerous times, which do not permit the mind to think of
better things because of fear and perturbation, since many
pressures and desolations of regions have come.

2. We ought to understand thoroughly therefore, my
brothers, what is imminent or overhanging. Already there
have been hunger and plagues, violent movements of nations
and signs, which have been predicted by the Lord, they have
already been fulfilled, and there is not other which remains,
except the advent of the wicked one in the completion of the
Roman kingdom. Why therefore are we occupied with worldly
business, and why is our mind held fixed on the lusts of the
world or the anxieties of the ages? Why therefore do we not
reject every care of earthly actions and prepare ourselves for
*the meeting of the Lord Christ, so that He may draw us from
the confusion, which overwhelms the world?* Believe you me,
dearest brothers, because the coming of the Lord is nigh,
believe you me, because the end of the world is at hand,
believe me, because it is the very last time. Or do you not
believe unless you see it with your eyes? See to it that this
sentence be not fulfilled among you of the prophet who
declares: "Woe to those who desire to see the Day of the
Lord!" *Because all saints and the Elect of the Lord are*

gathered together before the tribulation which is to about to come and are taken to the Lord, in order that they may not see at any time the confusion which overwhelms the world because of our sins. And so, brothers, most dear to me, it is the eleventh hour, and the end of this world comes to the harvest, and angels, armed and prepared, hold sickles in their hands, awaiting the empire of the Lord. And we think that the earth exists with blind infidelity, arriving at its downfall early. Commotions are brought forth, wars of diverse peoples and battles and invasions of the barbarians threaten, and our regions shall be desolated, and we neither become very much afraid of the report nor of the appearance, in order that we may at least do penance; because they hurl fear at us, and we do not wish to be changed although we at least stand in need of penance for our actions!

3. When therefore the end of the world comes, there arise diverse wars, commotions on all sides, horrible earthquakes, perturbations of nations, tempests throughout the lands, plagues, famine, drought throughout the thoroughfares, great danger throughout the sea and dry land, constant persecutions, slaughters and massacres everywhere, fear in the homes, panic in the cities, quaking in the thoroughfares, suspicions in the male, anxiety in the streets. In the desert people become senseless, spirits melt in the cities. A friend will not be grieved over a friend, neither a brother for a brother, nor parents for their children, nor a faithful servant for his master, but one inevitably shall overcome them all; neither is anyone able to be recovered in that time, who has not been made completely aware of the coming danger, but all people, who have been constricted by fears, are consumed because of the overhanging evils.

4. Whenever therefore the earth is agitated by the nations, people will hide themselves from the wars in the mountains and rocks, by caves and caverns of the earth, by graves and memorials of the dead, and there, as they waste away gradually by fear, they draw breath, because there is not any place at all to flee, but here will be concession and intolerable pressure. And those who are in the east will flee to the west, and moreover those who are in the west shall flee to the east, and there is not a safer place anywhere, because

the world shall be overwhelmed by worthless nations, whose aspect appears to be of wild animals more than that of men. Because those very much horrible nations, most profane and most defiled, who do not spare lives, and shall destroy the living from the dead, shall consume the dead, they eat dead flesh, they drink the blood of beasts, they pollute the world, contaminate all things, and the one who is able to resist them is not there. In those days people shall not be buried, neither Christian, nor heretic, neither Jew, nor pagan, because of fear and dread there is not one who buries them; because all people ignore them while they are fleeing.

5. Whenever the days of the times of those nations have been fulfilled, after they have destroyed the earth, it shall rest; and now the kingdom of the Romans is removed from everyday life, and the empire of the Christians is handed down by God and Peter; and then the consummation comes, when the kingdom of the Romans begins to be fulfilled, and all dominions and powers have been fulfilled shall appear, he, whom Moses named in Deuteronomy, saying: Dan is a young lion, reclining and leaping from Basan. Because he reclines in order that he may seize and destroy and slay. Indeed he is a young whelp of a lion not as the lion of the tribe of Judah, but roaring because of his wrath that he may devour. And he leaps out from Basan. "Basan" is certainly interpreted "confusion." He shall rise up from the confusion of his iniquity. The one who gathers to himself like a partridge the children of confusion whom he has not brought forth, also shall multiply them in a heap and call them, just as Jeremiah the prophet says. Also in the last day they shall forsake him just as disorderly.

6. When therefore the end of the world comes, that abominable, lying and murderous one is born from the tribe of Dan. He is conceived from the seed of a man and from a most vile virgin, mixed with an evil or worthless spirit. But that abominable corrupter, more of spirits than of bodies, while a youth, the crafty dragon appears under the appearance of righteousness before he takes the kingdom. Because he will be craftily gentle to all people, not receiving gifts, not placed before another person, loving to all people, quiet to everyone, not desiring gifts, appearing friendly among close

friends, so that men may bless him, saying: He is a just man, not knowing that a wolf lies concealed under the appearance of a lamb, and that a greedy man is inside under the skin of a sheep.

7. But when the time of the abomination of his desolation begins to approach, having been made legal, he takes the empire, and, just as it is said in the Psalm: They have been made for the undertaking for the sons of Loth, the Moabites and the Ammanites shall meet him first as their king. Therefore, when he receives the kingdom, he orders the temple of God to be rebuilt for himself, which is in Jerusalem; who, after coming into it, he shall sit as God and order that he be adored by all nations, since he is carnal and filthy and mixed with worthless spirit and flesh. Then that eloquence shall be fulfilled . . . of Daniel the Prophet: And he shall not know the God of their Fathers, and he shall not know the desires of women. Because the very wicked serpent shall direct every worship to himself. Because he shall put forth an edict so that people may be circumcised according to the rite of the old law. Then the Jews shall congratulate him, because he gave them again the practice of the first covenant; then all people from everywhere shall flock together to him at the city of Jerusalem, and the holy city shall be trampled on by the nations for forty-two months just as the holy apostle says in the Apocalypse, which become three and a half years, 1260 days.

8. In these three years and a half the heaven shall suspend its dew; because there will be no rain upon the earth, and the clouds shall cease to pass through the air, and the stars shall be seen with difficulty in the sky because of the excessive dryness, which happens in the time of the very fierce dragon. Because all great rivers and very powerful fountains that overflow with themselves shall be dried up, torrents shall dry up their water-courses because of the intolerable age, and there will be a great tribulation, as there has not been, since people began to be upon the earth, and there will be famine and an insufferable thirst. And children shall waste away in the bosom of their mothers, and wives upon their knees of their husbands, by not having victuals to eat. Because there will be in those days lack of bread and water,

and no one is able to sell or to buy of the grain of the fall harvest, unless he is one who has the serpentine sign on the forehead or the hand. Then gold and silver and precious clothing or precious stones shall lie along the streets, and also even every type of pearls along the thoroughfares and streets of the cities, but there is not one who may extend the hand and take or desire them, but they consider all things as good as nothing because of the extreme lack and famine of bread, because the earth is not protected by the rains of heaven, and there will be neither dew nor moisture of the air upon the earth. But those who wander through the deserts, fleeing from the faces of the serpent, bend their knees to God, just as lambs to the udders of their mothers, being sustained by the salvation of the Lord, and while wandering in states of desertion, they eat herbs.

9. Then, when this inevitability has overwhelmed all people, just and unjust, the just so that they may be found good by their Lord; and indeed the unjust, so that they may be damned forever with their author the Devil, and as God beholds the human race in danger and being tossed about by the breath of the horrible dragon, he sends to them consolatory proclamation by his attendants, the prophets Enoch and Elijah, who, while not yet testing death, are the servants for the heralding of the second coming of Christ, and in order to accuse the enemy. And when those just ones have appeared, they confuse indeed the antagonistic serpent with his cleverness and they call back the faithful witnesses to God, in order to free them from his seduction....

10. And when the three and a half years have been completed, the time of the Antichrist, through which he will have seduced the world, after the resurrection of the two prophets, in the hour which the world does not know, and on the day which the enemy or son of perdition does not know, will come the sign of the Son of Man, and coming forward the Lord shall appear with great power and much majesty, with the sign of the word of salvation going before him, and also even with all the powers of the heavens with the whole chorus of the saints, with those who bear the sign of the holy cross upon their shoulders, as the angelic trumpet precedes him, which shall sound and declare: Arise O sleeping ones,

arise, meet Christ, because his hour of judgment has come! Then Christ shall come and the enemy shall be thrown into confusion, and the Lord shall destroy him by the Spirit of his mouth. And he shall be bound and shall be plunged into the abyss of everlasting fire alive with his father Satan; and all people, who do his wishes, shall perish with him forever; but the righteous ones shall inherit everlasting life with the Lord for ever and ever.

Throughout their books posttribulation authors have made statements such as, " 'The significance in this matter lies in the fact that the origin of the embryo teaching of the pretribulation rapture teaching has been traced back to a book by Emmanuel Lacunza first published in 1812 *and no further back than that.*"[6] They will have to change the next editions of their books to reflect the error of their previous teaching. The teachings of Ephraem the Syrian (or Pseudo-Ephraem) and Dr. John Gill (1748) prove that long before 1830 these writers taught the idea of the rapture occurring as a separate event prior to the Tribulation, which would end with Christ's return to earth.

The Byzantine Apocalyptic Tradition

Paul Alexander, perhaps the most authoritative scholar on the writings of the early Byzantine church, concluded that Pseudo-Ephraem's text on *The Antichrist* differed from other apocalyptic writings of the first centuries in its description of how God would "alleviate the period of tribulation for his saints and for the Elect." While other early church commentators suggested that the Lord would shorten the length of the three-and-a-half-year Tribulation period to protect the saints, Professor Alexander noted that Pseudo-Ephraem interpreted the Scriptures to teach that the Lord would supernaturally remove the church saints from the earth "prior to the tribulation that is to come."[7] Pseudo-Ephraem wrote that the saints will be "taken to the Lord lest they see the confusion that is to overwhelm the world because of our sins." This text was originally a sermon called *On the Last Times, the Antichrist, and the End of the World.* There are four Latin manuscripts of this text ascribed to St. Ephraem or to St. Isidore (the Parisinus, the Augiensis, the Barberini, and the St. Gallen manuscript). In 1890 C. P. Caspari wrote a German commentary on this Latin manuscript.[8]

Dr. Alexander wrote that, "Pseudo-Ephraem does not refer to the shortening of time. This author, however, mentions another measure taken by God in order to alleviate the period of tribulation for his saints and for the Elect." He then quoted this passage from Pseudo-Ephraem's text: "For all the saints and Elect of God are gathered, prior to the tribulation that is to come, and are taken to the Lord lest they see the confusion that is to overwhelm the world because of our sins." Alexander commented, "It is probably no accident that Pseudo-Ephraem does not mention the shortening of the time intervals for the Antichrist's persecution, for if prior to it the Elect are 'taken to the Lord,' i.e., participate at least in some measure in beatitude, there is no need for further mitigating action on their behalf. The Gathering of the Elect according to Pseudo-Ephraem is an alternative to the shortening of the time intervals."[9]

Dr. Paul Alexander believes this text was written by some unknown writer in the sixth century and was derived from an earlier Pseudo-Ephraem manuscript. Other scholars, including the German editor Professor Caspari, believed that Ephraem's mention of wars between Rome and Persia, with two imperial brothers ruling Rome, indicated the book was actually written by Ephraem in A.D. 373 following the joint imperial reign of the brothers Valentinian and Valens.

My friend, Thomas Ice, provided assistance in confirming the significance of this discovery. In addition, Latin instructor Cameron Rhoades of Tyndale Theological Seminary translated the Latin text into English at our request.

A Summary of the Key Points
in Ephraem's Text on the Antichrist

1. Ephraem's manuscript lays out the events of the last days in chronological sequence, beginning with the rapture, then the Great Tribulation of three-and-a-half years' duration under the Antichrist's rule, followed by the second coming of Christ to earth with His saints to defeat the Antichrist.

2. Significantly, at the beginning of his treatise in section 2, Ephraem uses the word "imminent" to describe the rapture occurring before the Tribulation and the coming of the Antichrist. "We ought to understand thoroughly therefore, my brothers, what is imminent or overhanging."

3. He describes the pretribulation rapture: "Because all saints and the Elect of the Lord are gathered together before the tribulation which is about to come and are taken to the Lord, in order that they may not see at any time the confusion which overwhelms the world because of our sins."

4. He then states that God's purpose in rapturing the church "before the tribulation" is so that "they may not see at any time the confusion which overwhelms the world because of our sins."

5. Ephraem says the saints need not fear the coming Tribulation because, "we neither become very much afraid of the report nor of the appearance, "because the rapture will occur prior to the Tribulation.

6. Ephraem describes the duration of the "great tribulation" (the last half of the seven-year Tribulation period) in sections 7, 8, and 10 as follows: "forty-two months" and "three-and-a-half years" and "1260 days."

7. He summarizes: "There will be a great tribulation, as there has not been since people began to be upon the earth," and he describes the mark of the beast system.

8. Significantly, Ephraem states there will be some (Tribulation saints) who reject the Antichrist during the Tribulation and who will "bend their knees to God," and "while not yet testing death, are the servants for the heralding of the second coming of Christ."

9. He declares that Christ will come to the earth after the "three and a half years" great Tribulation period in section 10: "And when the three and a half years have been completed, the time of the Antichrist, through which he will have seduced the world, after the resurrection of the two prophets...will come the sign of the Son of Man, and coming forward the Lord shall appear with great power and much majesty."

Ephraem the Syrian
and the Seventieth Week of Daniel

A question naturally arises about how long Ephraem believed the Tribulation would last. While Ephraem describes the "great tribulation" as three-and-a-half years, his other writings reveal that he believed the whole Tribulation period, "that sore affliction," would last "one week" of seven years. In Ephraem's book *The Book of the Cave of Treasures,* written about A.D. 373, he includes a section about the genealogy of Christ. Ephraem reveals his belief that the sixty-ninth week of Daniel 9:24-27 ended with the rejection and crucifixion of Jesus the Messiah. He wrote, "The Jews have no longer among them a king, or a priest, or a prophet, or a Passover, even as Daniel prophesied concerning them, saying, '*After two and sixty weeks Christ shall be slain,* and the city of holiness shall be laid waste until the completion of things decreed.' (Daniel 9:26). That is to say, for ever and ever" (italics added; page 235, *The Cave of Treasures*).

However, in the section of his book dealing with the future war of Gog and Magog, Ephraem wrote about the final (seventieth) week of Daniel as follows. *"At the end of the world and at the final consummation... suddenly* the gates of the north shall be opened.... They will destroy the earth, and there will be none able to stand before them. *After one week of that sore affliction (Tribulation), they will all be destroyed in the plain of* Joppa.... Then will the son of perdition appear, of the seed and of the tribe of Dan.... He will go into Jerusalem and will sit upon a throne in the Temple saying, 'I am the Christ,' and he will be borne aloft by legions of devils like a king and a lawgiver, naming himself God.... *The time the error of the Anti-Christ will last* two years and a half, but others say *three years and six months"* (italics added). Although there are some curious elements in Ephraem's description of prophetic events, it is clear that he believed that the seventieth remaining week of Daniel's 70 weeks will finally be fulfilled in the final seven years of this age when the Antichrist will appear. This evidence of belief in a "gap" or "parenthesis" between the sixty-ninth and seventieth week of Daniel 9:24-27 from the fourth century of the Christian era is significant.

Requirements for Evidence
of an Early Teaching of the Pretribulation Rapture

Dr. William Everett Bell, Jr.'s doctoral dissertation, *A Critical Evaluation of the Pretribulation Rapture Doctrine in Christian Eschatology,* described criteria required to prove the early teaching of the pretribulation rapture. Bell stated, "No trace of the doctrine is to be found in church history after the Ante-Nicene fathers until the nineteenth century."[10]

In his dissertation he set out the following requirements for definitive proof of the early pretribulation teaching that was taught in the centuries before 1830:

> Any of the following items would be of crucial importance, if found, whether by direct statement or clear inference:
>
> 1. Any mention that Christ's second coming was to consist of more than one phase, separated by an interval of years
>
> 2. Any mention that Christ was to remove the church from the earth before the Tribulation period.
>
> 3. Any reference to the resurrection of the just being in two stages.
>
> 4. Any indication that Israel and the church were to be clearly distinguished, thus providing some rationale for a removal of Christians before God again deals with Israel.[11]

Dr. John Gill Taught
the Pretribulation Rapture in 1748

Dr. John Gill, a famous eighteenth-century Calvinist theologian, published his commentary on the New Testament in 1748. In his commentary on 1 Thessalonians 4:15-17, Dr. Gill points out that Paul is delivering teaching that is "something new and extraordinary." Gill calls the translation of the saints "the rapture," and he calls for watchfulness because "it will be sudden, and unknown before-hand, and when least thought of and expected." This is the clearest detailed teaching on the imminent pretribulation rapture that I have found, following the A.D. 373 Ephraem text just quoted, in the centuries prior to John Darby in 1830. It is significant that Dr. Gill taught an imminent, sudden rapture which could occur at any moment. In his comment on 1 Thessalonians 5:1, he wrote, "It was a well known thing that it would be sudden, and at an unawares, like the coming of a thief in the night."

Dr. Gill commented on 1 Thessalonians 4:15 as follows:

> "For this we say to you by the word of the Lord, that we which are alive and remain unto the coming of the Lord shall not prevent them which are asleep" (1 Thess. 4:15).

Commentary:

The Apostle having something new and extraordinary to deliver, concerning the coming of Christ, the first resurrection, or the resurrection of the saints, the change of the living saints, and the rapture both of the raised, and living in the clouds to meet Christ in the air, expresses itself in this manner. The dead saints will rise before the living ones are changed, and both will be caught up together to meet the Lord.

"Then we which are alive and remain shall be caught up together with them in the clouds, to meet the Lord in the air; and so shall we ever be with the Lord" (1 Thess. 4:17).

Commentary:

Suddenly, in a moment, in the twinkling of an eye, and with force and power; by the power of Christ, and by the ministry and means of the holy angels; and to which rapture will contribute the agility, which the bodies both of the raised and changed saints will have; and this rapture of the living saints will be together with them; with the dead in Christ, that will then be raised; so that the one will not prevent the other, or the one be sooner with Christ than the other; but one being raised and the other changed, they'll be joined in one company and general assembly, and be rapt up together: in the clouds; the same clouds perhaps in which Christ will come will be let down to take them up; these will be the chariots, in which they'll be carried up to Him; and thus, as at our Lord's ascension a cloud received Him, and in it He was carried up out of the sight of men, so at this time will all the saints ride up in the clouds of Heaven: to meet the Lord in the air; whither He'll descend, and will then clear the regions of the air of Satan, and his posse of devils, which now rove about there, watching all opportunities, and taking all advantages to do mischief on earth; these shall then fall like lightning from heaven, and be bound and shut up in the bottomless pit till the thousand years are ended; here Christ will stop and will be visible to all, and as easily discerned by all, good and bad, as the body of the sun at noon-day; as yet He will not descend on earth, because it is not fit to receive Him; but when that and its works are burnt up, and it is purged and purified by fire, and become a new earth, He'll descend upon it, and dwell with His saints in it: and this suggests another reason why He'll stay in the air, and His saints shall meet Him there, and whom He'll take up with Him into the third heaven, till the general conflagration and burning of the world is over, and to preserve them from it: and then shall all the elect of God descend from heaven as a bride adorned for her husband, and He with them...then they shall be with Him, wherever He is; first in the air, where they shall meet Him; then in the third heaven, where they shall go up with Him; then on earth, where they shall descend and reign with Him a thousand years; and then in the ultimate glory to all eternity.

Summary of Dr. Gill's
Pretribulation Rapture Teaching from 1748

While there is a certain ambiguity in Dr. Gill's 1748 teaching of the timing and sequence of prophetic events, it is vital to note what he declared:

1. The Lord will descend in the air.

2. The saints will be raptured in the air to meet Him.

3. In the air Christ will stop and will be visible to all.

4. As yet He will not descend on earth, because it is not fit to receive Him.

5. He will take up [the saints] with Him into the third heaven, till the general conflagration and burning of the world is over.

6. This will preserve them from that conflagration.

7. Then all the elect of God shall descend from heaven.

8. Then they shall be with Him, wherever He is

    a) first in the air, where they shall meet Him

    b) then in the third heaven, where they shall go up with Him

c) then on earth, where they shall descend and
reign with Him for a thousand years.

Therefore, in addition to Ephraem's pretribulation teaching
from the fourth century we have another statement of this doctrine
from Dr. John Gill more than 80 years before John Darby in 1830.
Those who have attacked the pretribulation rapture on the basis that
it is some kind of innovative theory, never taught before throughout
the history of the church, need to become more familiar with these
important texts. The French writer Joubert once wrote, "Nothing
makes men so imprudent and conceited as ignorance of the past and
a scorn for old books."

The Importance of the
Pretribulation Rapture Doctrine

The apostle Peter warned that a characteristic of the last days
would be the rise of voices that would challenge our Lord's promise
of His second coming. "Knowing this first, that there shall come in
the last days scoffers, walking after their own lusts, and saying,
Where is the promise of His coming?" (2 Peter 3:3,4). What does
the Bible teach us about the proper attitude of a Christian to the
subject of Christ's return? In 1 Corinthians 1:7 Paul tells us, "So
that you come behind in no gift; waiting for the coming of our Lord
Jesus Christ." One of the distinguishing characteristics of a true
follower of Jesus will be an attitude of a faithful, waiting, and
watching servant.

Dr. Klink, one of the great students of the early church, wrote,
"This constant expectation of our Lord's Second Coming is one of
the characteristic features of primitive Christianity." Paul also com-
mends a constant expectation of the rapture in Philippians 3:20,
where he said, "For our conversation is in heaven; from whence
also we look for the Saviour, the Lord Jesus Christ." Dr. Klink also
wrote about the centrality of this hope to the Christian's life: "The
right waiting for the Coming of Christ allows us to remain neither
idle nor unfruitful, but inspires us with an earnest zeal constantly to
appropriate and improve every spiritual gift."

Among the Reformers, Calvin wrote of the hope as follows, "It
ought to be the chief concern of believers to fix their minds fully on

His Second Advent." Martin Luther, in his Sermon of Consolation, declared that the hope of Christ's return is an absolute necessity for a Christian: "If thou be not filled with a desire after the Coming of this day, thou canst never pray the Lord's prayer, nor canst thou repeat from thy heart the creed of faith. For with what conscience canst thou say, 'I believe in the resurrection of the body and the life everlasting,' if thou dost not in thy heart desire the same? If thou didst believe it, thou must, of necessity, desire it from thy heart, and long for that day to come; which, if thou dost not desire, thou art not yet a Christian, nor canst thou boast of thy faith." Throughout the New Testament we read continual exhortations to hold the hope of our Lord's soon return as the focus of our spiritual life. Far from being a side issue of importance only to students of prophecy, the blessed hope of the rapture should be a cornerstone of our spiritual life.

The message and hope of the imminent second coming of Christ to rapture the saints has the following purposes:

- It calls us to live in constant watchfulness for His return (1 Thess. 5:4-6).

- It motivates Christians to witness to unbelievers in light of His imminent coming (John 9:4).

- It calls the church to walk in holiness in an immoral world awaiting His return (1 John 3:3).

- It comforts the saints by reminding them of their eternal destiny with Christ (John 14:1-3).

- It warns us of the coming judgment on those who reject Christ's salvation (2 Thess. 1:8-9).

- It calls on Christians to persevere against all opposition in light of His reward (2 Tim. 4:1-8).

- It encourages sinners to repent and accept the Lord while there is still time (Acts 3:19-21).

The promise in the Scriptures of the imminent return of the Messiah Jesus Christ is the last, best hope of mankind. It is the promise of the ultimate vindication of God's plan to redeem mankind and the earth from the curse of sin and death. The final vindication of Jesus Christ's claim to be the promised Messiah and the final fulfillment of the prophecies of the coming kingdom of God will culminate on that day when the heavens open to reveal Christ coming in all His glory at the battle of Armageddon. However, the Scriptures clearly teach that another event occurs separate from and earlier than the moment when Christ will defeat the Antichrist and the armies of the world at the climactic battle of Armageddon at the end of the seven-year Tribulation period. This separate and earlier event is often termed the "rapture." The timing, the participants, and the purpose of the rapture differ in every way from the characteristics of the second event, the revelation of Christ at the battle of Armageddon. Throughout the Bible, the passages that describe the revelation of Christ at the end of the Tribulation period describe a totally different event than those passages that describe the coming of Christ in the air to take the saints home to heaven.

The longing for the rapture and the return of Christ has motivated generations of Bible students to examine the Scriptures in a search for clues as to the exact timing of His glorious appearing. Unfortunately, despite clear Scriptural warnings against date-setting regarding the time of His return, many have indulged in unhelpful speculation about the time of the second coming, including Harold Camping's bestseller, *1994*, which claimed Christ would return on September 17, 1994. Millions of followers of these men's writings were deeply disappointed when their foolish predictions proved false. However, despite these disappointments, we must not abandon our hope for the imminent rapture. We must simply be obedient to Christ's command, "Now when these things begin to happen, look up and lift up your heads, because your redemption draws near" (Luke 21:28).

John Wesley de Fletcher wrote a fascinating letter to Charles Wesley in 1755 that expressed the proper attitude we should have toward the return of Christ: "I know that many have been grossly mistaken as to the year of His return, but, because they were rash, shall we be stupid? Because they say 'Today!'; shall we say, 'Never!' and cry 'Peace, Peace,' when we should look about us with eyes full of expectation?"

Conclusion

I believe Ephraem the Syrian's A.D. 373 manuscript, *On the Last Times, the Antichrist and the End of the World*, fully meets the challenge of Dr. William Bell and Rev. John Bray's $500 challenge. This new evidence clearly refutes the dogmatic declarations of many that there is no evidence that anyone ever taught the pre-tribulation rapture before A.D. 1830. The biblical truth of the glorious rapture of the church prior to the Tribulation was definitely taught in the early church. As I have shared in my earlier books, the truth of the pretribulation rapture is supported by the clear insistence on the imminent return of our Lord found throughout the writings of the Ante-Nicene Fathers. In addition, as I pointed out in my *Apocalypse* book, the apocalyptic fourth vision of *The Shepherd of Hermas* from A.D. 110 declared that the elect will escape the Great Tribulation. This finding of the pretribulation rapture in Ephraem's writings illustrates that the biblical truth of God's blessed hope and deliverance of the saints was upheld by a remnant of the faithful from the beginning of the church until today

Floyd Elmore

J. N. Darby's Early Years

_____*OVERVIEW*

How much do you know about the man who has had the greatest impact upon the study of biblical prophecy in the last 150 years? Find out more about how God has used one of His choice servants to impact His church's understanding of biblical prophecy. The author introduces you to human influences upon the life of J. N. Darby. God used Darby's life and ministry to formulate the system of theology known as dispensationalism and to recover and develop the pretribulational rapture of the church. It has been said of Mr. Darby that he has had the greatest influence upon Evangelicalism, and yet he is virtually unknown. This essay will help you become one of the few who know J. N. Darby.

*J*ohn Nelson Darby (1800-1882) is the acknowledged father of systematized dispensationalism and a key modern developer of the pretribulational rapture. He conceptualized God's revelation in Scripture as a world and life view comprehending all of human history. Within the framework of this worldview, Darby emphasized the uniqueness of the church as a heavenly body, its necessary disjuncture with history, and its prophetic relationship relative to Israel. Moreover, Darby came to his distinction between Israel and the church very early in his Christian ministry, and he later confessed that this opinion never changed throughout his career.[1] Formative ideas and forces which influenced Darby's thinking concerning Israel and the church can be found quite early in his life.

A Biographical Sketch of J. N. Darby

John Nelson Darby was born in London of Irish parents on November 18, 1800. His was an honorable family, relatives and close friends accomplished noteworthy deeds in British history. Darby's uncle was Admiral Sir Henry Darby, who commanded the *Bellerophon* in the Battle of the Nile. He was a close friend of Lord Nelson, who "to the great delight of the parents [J. N. Darby's], consented to be one of the sponsors at the christening of his friend's little nephew."[2] Thus "Nelson" was given to little John as his second Christian name.

In 1815, the family returned to Ireland to live in their ancestral castle. In that year J. N. Darby was admitted to Trinity College, Dublin. While there he won premiums (monetary awards) in science as well as classics, the two streams into which premiums, medals, and scholarships were divided. At the final examination, when a class "answers for a degree," students may choose to compete for the highest honors, a science or a classical gold medal. Darby graduated in 1819 as a Classical Gold Medalist.[3]

Although Darby trained for a career in law for three years, and then entered the Irish Chancery Bar in 1822, he abandoned the profession after only one year. Apparently he was in the grip of a deep spiritual struggle from 1818 to 1825, which led to his conversion.[4] Almost immediately Darby sought to serve Christ. In discussing this time he wrote, "I longed for complete devotedness to the work of the Lord; my chief thought was to get around amongst the poor Catholics of Ireland."[5]

He was ordained as a deacon in 1825, and as a priest (curate) of the Church of England in 1826, by Archbishop Magee, serving the parish of Calary in the county of Wicklow.[6] His devotion to proclaiming the gospel drove him to neglect his own health and appearance. "He spent his patrimony in schools and charity..."[7] and thus he endeared himself to the local people. Moreover, they evidently responded well both to the man and to his message, such that "Roman Catholics were passing over to Protestantism many hundreds in a week."[8] Certainly this man was not a cold, calculating, ruthlessly objective hairsplitter at that time!

After 27 months of labor, the young curate faced another crisis. Goddard observed, "Several things bothered him, chief of which were: the absence of a true catholicity in the Establishment, its unblushing Erastianism [the belief in state supremacy in ecclesiastical causes], and its clericalism."[9] The ecclesiastical crisis Darby was to wrestle with forms the backdrop for the "Great Divide"—his conclusion that the unique calling and nature of the church sets it apart from Israel as far as heaven is from earth.

The Great Divide

Between 1826 and 1828, Darby came to a personally painful decision relative to the established Church of England in which he ministered. Although he did not immediately separate from it, the theological basis for such a separation was in place. His parting of the ways with the established church corresponded with his new understanding of the division between Israel and the true church. The "Great Divide" for Darby is thus true in two senses. The immediate occasion for the divide was provided by the very man who had ordained him: Archbishop Magee of Dublin.

The Ecclesiastical Crisis

The Erastian controversy. Darby loved the church, which for him in 1826 meant the Anglican Church. The established church was a barrier against Popery, and so Darby did not at first despise it. Only after he became convinced that "it [the established church] has ceased to be such a barrier, and, for many, has been the road into it [Popery], and that infidel principles have been judicially pronounced to be fully permissible in it,"[10] did he make the break.

The occasion for Darby's serious doubts about Anglicanism was "The Metropolitan Charge and Clerical Petition." Archbishop Magee denounced the Roman Catholic Church before Parliament, and at the same time claimed special favors and protection for the Anglican Church.[11] Along with the Petition, Archbishop Magee "imposed, within the limits of his jurisdiction, the oaths of allegiance and supremacy"[12] and this caused the evangelistic work Darby maintained to cease.

Darby believed it was the duty of Christ's ministers to keep themselves free of earthly entanglements to minister God's grace. He saw the delivering of souls from Romanism as a way to partially set up the kingdom of God before Christ returned. To counter Rome by adopting its earthly method, of courting the glory of this world, would be contrary to faith. True believers must identify with Jesus Christ in His humiliation while they await His return.

Darby's treatise, "Considerations Addressed to the Archbishop of Dublin and the Clergy who signed the Petition to the House of Commons for Protection,"[13] was written in 1827, but it was not published until years later. Three themes, which became central truths of Christianity for him, are already seen in it: 1) the purity and heavenly nature of the church; 2) the presence of the Holy Spirit in true believers to empower for ministry; 3) the future prospect of the church, i.e., the second coming of Christ. It should be noted that these themes were formulated within the matrix of his evangelistic interests, not because of mere academic pursuits.

Darby's accident and convalescence. An accidental fall from a horse turned out to be another event that propelled Darby toward the "Great Divide" as it related to the church. His horse was frightened and threw him against a doorpost. Darby's leg was injured and required surgery in Dublin. During part of 1827, he was forced into convalescence and relative seclusion. During this extended period

Darby cast himself upon God and His Word alone for support. Out of that time of reduced activity, his thinking concerning the basis for personal assurance of salvation, the authority of the Scripture, the church as the body of Christ, Christ's second coming for His church, and Israel's place in a subsequent dispensation, became clear.[14]

Since he was on crutches, he could not attend corporate worship or immediately make public his developing views. Although he could not then work out the details of his eschatology, he said:

> In my retreat, the 32nd chapter of Isaiah taught me clearly, on God's behalf, that there was still an economy to come, of His ordering; a state of things in no way established as yet. The consciousness of my union with Christ had given me the present heavenly portion of the glory, whereas this chapter clearly sets forth the corresponding earthly part.[15]

Concerning his belief in the restoration of original truths to himself, Darby stated that the "truths themselves were then revealed of God, through the action of His Spirit, by reading His word."[16] The earthly/heavenly distinction between Israel and the church had taken form in Darby's thinking.

Separation from the Establishment. Darby published his first tract in 1828, titled "Considerations on the Nature and Unity of the Church of Christ."[17] Crutchfield aptly noted, "It is important to observe here that Darby's disaffection for the Church of England was not precipitated by prophetic teachings."[18] Darby's eschatology grows out of his ecclesiology. He did not publish his first work on prophecy, "Reflections upon the Prophetic Inquiry and the Views Advanced in It," until 1829.[19]

In his "Considerations" of 1828, Darby expounded his thesis that the real unity of the church is not in outward form but in inward faith in Jesus Christ. Darby reasoned that the Anglican Church had been delivered from the secular dominion of the Roman Church, but that it had not been delivered from the spirit of apostasy that gave rise to Romanism. Instead of rendering a witness of a heavenly Lord and His coming to the earthly system, the established church and the dissenting ones were "using the advocacy of . . . unbelievers . . . to obtain a share in, or keep to themselves the secular advantages and honors of that world out of which the Lord came to redeem us."[20] The only way Christ's church can avoid the world and be united is by a work of the Spirit, following the testimony of the Holy Spirit in the Word, and living with a view to the Lord's return.[21] The centrality of the Lord's table appears in association with this last theme. Darby summarized his belief: "In a word, we find *His* death is the centre of communion till His coming again. . . . Accordingly, the outward symbol and instrument of unity is the partaking of the Lord's supper. . . ."[22] Even in this tract, the church's heavenly character differentiates it from Israel, whose portion is earthly.

The exact time of Darby's renunciation of the Establishment is difficult to determine. Neatby suggested that Darby was not comfortable in breaking entirely with the Church of England as late as November, 1829.[23] Soon thereafter the Brethren at Dublin "broke bread" together and thus broke fellowship with the Establishment. Darby could not stay in a system which would, in his mind, exclude the apostle Paul from preaching because "he had no letters of orders."[24] The system was wrong and had to go.

A spiritual church, joined to a heavenly Christ, indwelt and empowered by the Holy Spirit, and awaiting their Lord's return: This is the heart of Darby's doctrine, resulting from his passing through the ecclesiastical crisis.

The Eschatological Climate

The early Darby. As the details of Darby's new ecclesiological decisions began to take shape in his mind, their impact on his eschatology started to show. The ecclesiological-eschatological synthesis that so characterizes later dispensationalism became clearer as his thinking progressed. Thus Darby before the Powerscourt conferences (1831-33) deserves special attention.

In a letter dated 1863, Darby summarized truths clarified in his mind in the course of his conversion experience. Among them are juxtaposed: "the church as His body; Christ coming to receive us to Himself; and collaterally with that, the setting up of a new earthly dispensation, from Isaiah 32."[25] From his earliest statements, Darby recognized the earthly/heavenly distinction between Israel and the church as the key to his ecclesiological-eschatological synthesis.[26]

From his first tract on prophetic themes, "Reflections upon 'The Prophetic Inquiry' and the Views Advanced in It,"[27] dated

1829, Darby is openly premillennial. What is rarely mentioned is that the early Darby espoused a premillennial historicism *before* the famous Powerscourt prophetic conferences of 1831–33. Years later, he added a footnote to his paper "On 'Days' Signifying 'Years' in Prophetic Language," written in 1830, disclaiming the historicism taught in it, but honestly leaving the paper unedited because it "may serve to shew historically the progress made in the apprehension of truth."[28] Apparently, Darby saw no immediate connection between futurism, the pretribulational rapture of the church, and his new synthesis which so differentiated Israel and the church.

In his "Reflections upon 'The Prophetic Inquiry'" (1829), Darby took to task both the extremists among the premillennial historicists[29] and the postmillennial historicists. Edward Irving received special criticism at this early date. It is difficult to see how Darby would have been influenced by him after making such statements about his work as, "The observations from the Apocalypse are a total misapprehension of its force."[30] For Darby, the extremists refused to submit their own novel ideas to the control of Scripture.[31] He believed that most of the problems for these extremists stemmed from "a confusion of the Jewish and Gentile dispensations—a hinge upon which the subject and the understanding of Scripture turns."[32]

At this time, Darby was looking, as his hope, for the powerful appearing of Jesus Christ to judge the earth, and not for the secret rapture of the church. In light of this, when he did speak of the rapture, he most naturally could be understood as referring to a posttribulational, yet pre-wrath, rapture. Thus he concluded "On 'Days' Signifying 'Years'" with "I am persuaded that this will lead more . . . to the deep conviction that we are within the verge of the end of all, so as to be daily looking for the Lord, i.e., to be caught up to meet Him in the air in order to His judging of the nations."[33] Being posttribulational, he saw the entire "Gentile dispensation" as a time of trial, fitting the historicist approach, with the resurrection and rapture occurring after Christ had in power put down evil.[34] He also understood that, although Israel and the church were distinct, Jewish and Gentile saints would share the kingdom bliss, glorified and natural saints together on earth. In his mind, the Jews could be restored to their land and the church could reign with Christ in the kingdom age without a conflict of concepts.

Powerscourt developments. Millenarian expectations and speculations were rampant at the turn of the century when Darby was born. The French Revolution gave a powerful push to millennial hope, and Napoleon's treatment of Italy and the Pope fueled end-time date-setting fanaticism.[35]

English millenarian traditions from the late eighteenth and early nineteenth centuries are of two varieties, following social class structure. Both varieties accepted the Bible to be divinely inspired and the unquestionable authority. The popular millennial movements among the lower classes, however, were also characterized by the following: 1) a distrust of the paid clergy; 2) a belief that God spoke directly to believers, women as well as men; 3) a use of the Bible as a handbook to contemporary events; 4) a hope for catastrophic social changes soon.[36]

In contrast to this, Hempton described the millenarian ideologies of the upper classes:

> However, the first half of the nineteenth century saw the growth of a different type of millenarianism. This was not a popular movement led by religious psychotics claiming special revelations from God, but a development from within the traditional churches which proceeded through the perfectly sensible channels of theological pamphlets, special periodicals, and conferences in aristocratic homes. Far from being an underground movement, by the 1840s it had attracted the attention of leading Anglican evangelical clergy men like Bickersteth, Marsh, and Wilson, and the parliamentarians, Shaftesbury, Drummond, and Plumptre.[37]

It is in one such "development from within the traditional churches" that the prophecy conferences which were probably most influential on Darby's early thinking took place.

The Albury Park prophetic conferences of 1826–28 in Surry were hosted by Henry Drummond, an ex-member of the House of Commons and a benefactor of the London Society for Promoting Christianity Amongst the Jews.[38] With only a few exceptions, Drummond invited laymen and clergy from the English and Scottish national churches. Concerning the proceedings, Sandeen remarked:

In the conference sessions themselves, the program
was about equally divided between the three chief
concerns of the day—prophetic chronology, the second advent, and the restoration of the Jews. No appeal
to authority or argument was allowed in these sessions except the authority of direct biblical quotation
or an argument designed to reconcile scriptural references.[39]

Darby never attended the Albury conferences, but news of the
prophetic revival in London was brought to him in 1827 by Bellett.[40]

Three important prophetic conferences were held at Powerscourt House on Irish soil in the parish next to the one served by
Darby when he had been a priest. These convened on October 4-7,
1831, September 24-28, 1832, and September 23-28, 1833.[41] (Others
of lesser importance were held until 1838.) These paralleled the
Albury conferences, probably by design of their hostess, Lady
Theodosia Powerscourt.[42] She had attended with delight the Albury
conferences, visited with Drummond, and entertained Irving. Irving
himself never attended the Powerscourt conferences. A few
Irvingites were present at least at the second and third conferences,
but their ideas were not warmly received.[43] Bishop Robert Daly,
rector of the parish, presided over the meetings until 1833. At that
time the anticlericalism and despair over the state of the church was
so great that he feared division.[44] The Brethren dominated the third
conference in 1833.

The topics of discussion at the Powerscourt conferences indicate a shift in some details of Darby's eschatology. In general, the
corrupt state of the church, the 1260 days of Daniel and Revelation,
and the imminent return of Christ were favorite themes. The proceedings of the second conference, however, shed considerable light
on Darby's shift.[45]

Darby, acting as correspondent, gave a detailed agenda of the
second conference to the editor of the *Christian Herald*, who apparently refused to mention it because he was growing disgusted over
controversies occasioned by millenarian disputes.[46] Specific agenda
topics included the use of Old Testament quotations in the New
Testament, the prophetical character of each book of the Bible,
whether a personal Antichrist is to be expected, the connection

between Daniel and Revelation, and what light Scripture gives on present events.

Lacking transcripts of the discussions at the second Powerscourt conference, one can only surmise in what direction the thoughts of the participants were headed. The agenda questions listed by Darby, however, do suggest clues concerning certain points of debate. On September 24, the literalness of the fulfillment of the Old Testament citations in the New Testament was dealt with. Twenty-three pairs of references were examined, "with their connections and explanations," to see if there was " 'accommodation,' or whether they were quoted according to the mind of the Spirit in the Old."[47] This statement suggests that the participants were exploring whether there is a single-intended meaning of Scripture or whether the New Testament authors were giving new and expanded meaning to the Old Testament references.

Day two of the conference got into the prophetic nature of "the three great feasts of the Jews, the blessings pronounced on Jacob's sons, the Parables in the Gospel, and the Epistles to the Seven Churches in Revelation."[48] A possible connection among these topics relates to the historicist approach to prophecy: does the Bible record the present course of world and church history ahead of time?[49] Darby, having been somewhat historicist up to 1830, never completely relented of that approach (at least as to church history), as is seen in his interpretation of Revelation 2 and 3.[50] Since Darby's subsequent futurism is well known, one can only guess that in discussing these topics he began to shift away from his earlier historicism.

On day three, in deliberating on whether to expect a personal Antichrist, the participants discussed finer points of prophetic detail surrounding him:

> Should we expect a personal Antichrist? If so, to whom will he be revealed? Are there to be one or two great evil powers in the world at that time? Is there any uniform sense for the word *Saint* in the Prophetic, or New Testament scripture? By what covenant did the Jews, and shall the Jews, hold the land?[51]

The question over "any uniform sense for the word *Saint*" is suggestive. Prior to 1830, Darby had come to believe that the church was a heavenly body, and that a remnant from Israel would have a future on earth in a dispensation subsequent to the church's. It would be a logical step, as he worked through applying this ecclesiological distinction to the eschatological studies at Powerscourt, to see at least two senses for *saint*: one applies to the church, and one applies to the remnant of Israel. In fact, Darby eventually would see more than two senses of the word.[52]

Day four of the second Powerscourt conference dealt with the relationship between Daniel and Revelation. The wording of Darby's note, "An inquiry into, and a connection between Daniel and the Apocalypse,"[53] suggests that a connection was certainly seen. *How much* of a connection was the battleground between the historicists and futurists. Besides seeing the events of Revelation fulfilled in European history, the historicists "judged that much of Daniel was recapitulated in the book of Revelation and that the two accounts could and should be used to interpret each other."[54]

The futurists interpreted everything after Revelation 3 as yet unfulfilled. They also rejected the day-for-a-year interpretation of the 1260 days of Daniel and Revelation. Sandeen reported that an announced topic at the first Powerscourt conference was "proof if '1260 *days*' means days or years."[55] In light of Darby's 1830 defense of the historicist position on this topic, he most probably shifted his view due to the influence of the first two Powerscourt conferences. What appeared to be a more consistent reconciling of prophetic Scriptures could have led him to futurism. Since Darby critiqued and spurned works on futurism before 1830, to seek a direct influence on his thinking from the writings of Lacunza, Maitland, and Irving before Powerscourt seems inconclusive and unfruitful.[56]

The last day of the second Powerscourt conference was devoted to the relationship of Scripture to the present evil situation in the world and church. Darby's note suggests the failure of the church. "What is next to be looked for and expected?"[57] is followed by questions and Scriptures considered, which point out the degeneration of the age since apostolic times. No revival was anticipated. From consideration of these points, Darby's statement years later, "There is no event between me and *heaven*,"[58] could easily have been a logical conclusion at this early date.

Darby introduced the doctrine of the secret rapture of the

church, and clearly articulated the prophetic gap between the sixty-ninth and seventieth weeks of Daniel 9, at the third Powerscourt conference in 1833. Sandeen called these two concepts "basic tenets of the system of theology since referred to as dispensationalism."[59] His statement appears misleading, however, since the two concepts are really outgrowths of Darby's more basic tenet that distinguished the earthly and heavenly peoples of God. The rapture gathers the heavenly people to glory before God resumes dealings in an official way (the seventieth week) with His earthly people, the remnant of Israel.

Moreover, Sandeen seems to have mistakenly interpreted Darby's comments about how he came to believe in the secret rapture of the church.[60] Most probably by 1827, Darby came to believe in *the fact* of a rapture; but it was not until 1833 that he worked out *the timing* of the rapture. This explanation fits with Darby's own testimony about his conversion and enlightenment in 1827, concerning certain great ecclesiological and eschatological truths. "I was not able to put these things in their respective places or arrange them in order, as I can now [1855]; but the truths themselves were then revealed of God. . ."[61] The eschatological conclusions from the second conference certainly pointed in that direction, even if Darby had not voiced his opinions concerning them at that time. By 1843, B. W. Newton actively opposed Darby on the same two points.[62] Darby apparently was not contentious over the pretribulational rapture in his early years but became more convinced of that position from consistently applying his hermeneutical key, which distinguished the heavenly and earthly peoples of God.[63]

Antecedents to Darby's New Synthesis

Certainly Darby's thinking was influenced by those students of Scripture with whom he companied in his early years. The immediate occasion for fresh theological thinking for Darby was the ecclesiastical crisis he went through over Erastianism and church corruption. This was followed by a study of eschatology at Powerscourt, which helped crystallize his position on the earthly and heavenly peoples of God—his new synthesis of ecclesiology and eschatology.

It seems unwise to assert with any high degree of certitude that forces antecedent to those above had direct influence on Darby's new dispensational understanding. The synthesis represents the framing of a set of ideas in a unique manner. Nevertheless, the individual ideas comprising the set had historical precedents. Darby is an innovator of a system, but not a creator of the parts making up the system. That world of ideas which most likely could have formed the pool of possibilities in Darby's mind (his theological preunderstanding) will now be explored.

Difficulties in the Search for Sources

Acknowledgments given too infrequently. A premium placed on personal Bible study, a conscious effort to break with the assumptions of the past, and a failure to acknowledge sources from which help was derived, make searching for the extra-biblical sources of Darby's ideas difficult. Darby is clear as to the priority of the Word and the Spirit to attain to truth. He is equally clear in his disdain for the fathers of the church and past scholarship. He asserted, "None are more untrustworthy on every fundamental subject than the mass of primitive Fathers."[64] He confessed that he had profited from others on certain specific points, but that he rejected the system they had erected around those specifics. He rarely, if ever, acknowledged which specifics and what sources.[65]

Similarities perceived too superficially. Out of zeal to defend the historical nature of Darby's dispensational synthesis, and to downplay its novelty, some modern dispensationalists have sought to show dispensational schemes in selected writers since the apostolic period.[66] These well-meaning efforts fail on several accounts. Since Darby himself would not seek to demonstrate his synthesis from the fathers and later theologians, little is gained by trying to do so. Most attempts merely demonstrate that specific ideas used by Darby in his synthesis were around centuries earlier. But his synthesis was not, and has not been shown to exist, before the late 1820s. That Israel and the church are distinguished in the writings of early church fathers does not point to a source for Darby's synthesis.[67] How they are distinguished (earthly/heavenly) is the concept to be located in the family tree of ideas. Looking for sources long distance is inconclusive at best.

Cultural concerns related too hastily. Placing Darby in the context of the world of theological concerns debated in his youth and early ministry would appear to be a better starting point than would the church fathers. A few key concepts may serve to explain the time period during which Darby came to his ecclesiological-eschatological synthesis. Chadwick summarized "the leading questions before the nation, in the succession by which they troubled England" during the Victorian period as follows:

> First, whether representative government was compatible with an established church; that is, how religious inequality could be married to political equality. Second, whether Christian churches, established or dissenting, could adjust themselves to industrial revolution, speedy growth of population, and empire overseas. Third, whether the Christian church taught the truth.[68]

If these are accurate, Darby's concern over the nature and unity of the church is just a specific example of a general cultural concern.

Three religious forces infused the theological atmosphere of this period as well: the High Church tradition, the Oxford Movement, and the Dissenters. From Darby's personal testimony about his spiritual pilgrimage, it seems that Newman and the Oxford Movement had little influence on him. He claimed to have wrestled through the issues of their concern before the movement got started.[69] The third religious force—the Dissenters—may have emboldened Darby for his decision to break with the Establishment. He respected many dissenters "for their integrity of conscience, and often deep apprehensions of the mind of Christ."[70] He abhorred, however, their glorying in their distinctiveness, which to him contributed to the disunity of the church.

Some Dissenters were associated with Trinity College, Dublin, in the early nineteenth century and may have contributed to Darby's developing ecclesiology. John Walker, for example, was a fellow of the college until 1804. He taught the idea of a gathered church, held to weekly observance of the Lord's supper (which he called the breaking of bread), engaged in teaching and admonishing one another without distinction between clergy and laity, exercised discipline, sought to gather all true disciples together in separation from the world and the false church, denied that the gospel was intended to improve the condition of the world, and focused the believers' hope onto the second coming of Jesus Christ to earth.[71]

In spite of whatever influence they might have wielded on Darby's thinking, he distanced himself from the dissenting bodies. Darby believed that the Brethren provided a "third way," avoiding the problems of both the established church and the dissenting groups. To seek for sources for Darby's ideas among the Dissenters is potentially rewarding but difficult to establish with certainty.

In surveying the general concerns of the ecclesiastical world of Darby's developmental years, little of a conclusive nature appears. The closest possibility for an antecedent that might have contributed to his new ecclesiology is found in John Walker. That he was associated with Trinity College, Dublin, may provide a clue for more fruitful investigation.[72]

The Trinity College Connection

"To soil and clime no plant can be indifferent, the seed may fall on good or stony ground, and with good reason, therefore, do the Universities claim a share in the intellectual victories of their children."[73] If this sentiment be true, then Darby and Trinity College cannot be divorced. The intellectual climate of this institution most probably sustained an influence on young Darby's approach to study in general, and very possibly on the concepts that formed the reservoir of ideas out of which he later developed his unique formulations. From the college records and from the history written about the college, certain interesting facts emerge.

A proud heritage. Trinity College was known to be an innovative institution, first "to read the signs of the times, and show the way to her elder sisters,"[74] Oxford and Cambridge. Roman Catholics and Protestants alike contributed to the endowment of the college. A leader in open admission policy, Trinity never instituted religious tests for students. It was so open that it was the first university in the United Kingdom to grant degrees to Jews.[75]

Educational requirements. Open access to an educational opportunity at Trinity College did not lead it to lower its standards. Once admitted, the undergraduate studied philosophy, history, mathematics, composition, and rhetoric, besides his specialization. Emphasis was placed on debating, a feature which had continued since Edmund Burke founded the Historical Club in 1745 as a debating society at the college.[76]

In 1808, Dean Richard Graves (1763-1829) moved the college to include instruction in Bible for all students as a part of their academic education. Saturday lectures in Scripture "for the first time [were] set on a public and permanent footing."[77] Dixon explained: "The religious instruction of undergraduates was in the hands of the Catechist, while all resident Bachelors were obliged to attend lectures either with the Regius Professor of Divinity or Archbishop King's lecturer."[78] Graves was the Regius Professor of Divinity from 1815 to 1829, covering the period in which Darby was a resident student.

Prizes, as incentives to study, were first instituted in 1731, and from 1815 it was "customary to award a gold medal to the best answerer at the degree examination in mathematics and classics respectively."[79] Darby, as noted above, graduated Classical Gold Medalist in 1819. Interestingly, Richard Graves tutored classics and was popular among the students.[80] This man most likely had a direct influence on Darby, through lectures in both the classics and the Scriptures. Further investigation of those professors and tutors whose ideas could have informed Darby's thinking follows.

Darby's professors and tutors. Although Darby studied law, legal and theological training were not sharply divided during his days at Trinity College. Before 1850, the professorship of Civil Law was often held by a clergyman.[81] It was during Darby's early years that the requirements for taking Orders in the Church of England and Ireland were tightened. The deplorable state of the episcopacy from the 1790s into the early nineteenth century apparently motivated the administrative powers at Trinity College to promote the innovative and fervent-spirited Dean Richard Graves to Regius Professor of Divinity in 1815, to try to turn things around.[82]

In his first address in his new capacity, Graves outlined reforms and requirements. He desired to institute an annual examination of graduates who were preparing for ministry, requiring proof of attendance of a year's course of divinity lectures and attainment of a level of theological knowledge "suited to the importance of the sacred profession which they proposed to undertake."[83] Darby, who was ordained a priest in 1826, must have met these requirements. When he had a crisis of faith in 1822 and left the legal profession, "His father disinherited him, but thanks to the support of his uncle he was able to complete his theological studies."[84] Darby must have come under the instruction of Richard Graves, even though he rarely references him in his writings. Darby does indicate, however, a familiarity with Grave's work on the Pentateuch, in which his professor presented his clearest teachings on the future conversion and restoration of the Jews.[85]

The degree of influence a teacher wields over a student is hard to measure. The following observations about Graves' life and teaching are only meant to suggest possible sources for Darby's concepts concerning Israel and the church. Darby rejected some elements of Graves' teaching—notably his Arminianism.[86] Nevertheless, he adopted other elements of this man's lifestyle and teaching.

Richard Graves was a favorite with the students, for he cared for their spiritual and temporal welfare. He "put *heart* into his sermons...[and] gave *unction* to academic preaching."[87] He exemplified missionary zeal without political considerations for the conversion of Irish Catholics. Moreover, Graves wholeheartedly supported the London Society for Promoting Christianity Amongst the Jews. In 1811, he preached a remarkable sermon to sway people from contemporary anti-Jewish sentiments and to incite them to support Jewish evangelism.[88] In these respects, Darby was a model disciple of his teacher, whose example of devotion in evangelistic ministry he followed.

Of other professors and tutors who might have influenced Darby during his formative years of training, the records of Trinity College refer to two who seem to have had the greatest influence: Edward Hincks, who became sub-librarian of Trinity College in 1814, and Thomas Elrington, who served as Provost from 1811 to 1820.[89]

Edward Hincks was a brilliant man whose major interests were apologetics and ancient near eastern languages. The German Professor Tiele of Leyden, a contemporary of Hincks, acknowledged him as "that great pioneer in Oriental research and discovery."[90] He followed this with a list of nine published works by Hincks on Egyptian, Akkadian, Assyrian, and Babylonian languages, customs, and mythologies. Darby's translating skills, familiarity with the latest Old Testament scholarship of his day, and his penchant for apologetics might be traced back to Hincks. It was at this time also that the Grimms brothers were propounding their linguistics laws and espousing historical sensitivity and anthropological awareness for anyone studying ancient texts.[91] Darby's historical sensitivity as he read and interpreted the Old Testament led him to acknowledge the progressive stages in God's self-revelation. This biblical-theological slant is crucial to an understanding of Darby's view of Scripture. His sensitivity to the historical contexts of passages is marked throughout his *Synopsis*. Perhaps his tendency to distinguish among dispensations in order to preserve the historical integrity of passages (especially those dealing with unfulfilled prophecies) is dependent upon the linguistic influence of Edward Hincks.

Thomas Elrington had a special interest in Old Testament typology. Graves acknowledged the help he had received from Elrington on the typology of the Jewish feasts. Both Elrington and Graves stressed the typical character of the Old Testament for the gospel, yet they believed in a literal restoration of the Jews to Palestine in fulfillment of prophecy and the typology of the feast of tabernacles![92] Darby's teachings on typology are well known. Very possibly Elrington was the one who first fired Darby's imagination in this area of biblical interpretation.

Millenarian Expectations

The eschatological climate of 1827–33, previously surveyed, revealed that Darby arrived at his new synthesis in a time of heightened millennial expectations in the British empire. The French Revolution, and especially the Napoleonic wars, had stimulated speculation among premillennialists about the exact time of the coming of Christ. Darby shifted from a more historicist approach, to the interpretation of the 1260 days of Daniel and Revelation, to a futurist approach. In doing this he avoided date-setting pitfalls but preserved a doctrine of imminency.

The way in which Darby conceptualized the Christian's hope was only one of many different varieties of millenarian expectation to which he could have been exposed. As will be seen, both postmillennialists and premillennialists in Darby's student years expected an imminent change of dispensation. What is of special interest for this study is that the ordering of future events among postmillenarians at Trinity College, Dublin, was amazingly similar to the order of events among premillennial futurists. The millenarian ideas of the Anglican divines, and of the Puritans which influenced the intellectual history of Trinity College, are especially noteworthy.

In the first quarter of the nineteenth century, Darby's alma mater became the spawning ground of much prophetic writing, for reasons which remain unclear.[93] Trinity College graduates "were among the earliest and most able defenders of futurism."[94] Although it may be impossible to discover a direct link between Darby's concepts and those who most probably taught him at Trinity College, some very interesting eschatological notions are found in the works of Richard Graves, professor of divinity while Darby was a student.

That Graves was not the originator of most of the eschatological specifics that he taught is almost certain. Richard Watson (d. 1833) wrote of widely held opinions with which he disagreed: "It is *common with divines* to speak of the Jewish and Christian churches, as though they were *two distinct and totally different things*; but that is not a correct view of the matter."[95] In 1844 in America, Alexander reviewed a book on the conversion and restoration of Israel, commenting about those doctrines that "in the Church of England it has long been a favorite opinion, and among the Presbyterians of Great Britain a strong impulse has been given to it by the mission of the Scottish Deputation to the Jews...."[96]

The Puritan influence upon Trinity College was quite marked.[97] They had for a long time taught the future conversion of the Jews, as evidenced in the annotations on Romans 11 in the 1560 edition of the Geneva Bible.[98] Toon observed that in the seventeenth century, Moses Wall sought to persuade the English Parliament to readmit Jews to England. He provided eight reasons for doing this, one of which was that "God's covenant with the descendants of Abraham is not canceled; rather it is suspended and will begin to operate again in the last days."[99] One is almost startled by a sort of "postponement theory" at such an early date! Sandeen noted, "The most recent antecedents of the early nineteenth-century millenarians had been the Puritans, particularly that radical party known as the Fifth Monarchy Men."[100] Gisbertus Voetius (1589-1676), a Dutch theologian, stated that he differed from Calvin's interpretation of Romans 11:26 and favored the interpretation of the *majority* of the exegetes, especially "*the English theologians*—that the text points toward a general and future conversion of the Jews."[101] Van Den Berg added that "the idea of a general conversion of the main body of the Jewish people had become *communis opinio* in the circle of Reformed theologians in the Netherlands."[102] Therefore, the Anglican theological tradition in general, and the influences on Trinity

College specifically, indicate that Graves' eschatology was probably within the mainstream in his time.

Graves was a postmillennialist who rejected the historicism of earlier forms of postmillennialism. For example, Voetius believed in a millennium "in which Christ's reign became clearly visible in the conversion of the nations to the Christian faith—possibly the period between [a.d.] 73 and 1073."[103] Graves, on the other hand, was a futuristic postmillennialist; that is, he expected a future literal kingdom of Christ universally extended over the earth. "The kingdoms of this world shall become the kingdoms of the Lord and of his Christ" (Rev. 11:15) and would be accomplished "by the extension of the Gospel" and fulfilled "in the fullness of time."[104]

The elements of Graves' postmillennial scheme assume a literal approach to the interpretation of Scripture. Unfulfilled prophecies must yet be fulfilled. He used Isaiah 11:11 ("the second time to recover the remnant of his people") as a key support in his plea for Jewish evangelism.[105] Even the 1260 days, which for him were years, are still literally applied, for there will be 1260 real years which will come to a close before the Jews convert in mass and the millennial age dawns.[106]

As odd as it may seem to modern dispensational premillennial literalists, postmillennialists in Graves' day were known for their literalism with respect to prophecy. Alexander Keith (1791–1880), a contemporary of Graves, wrote a book in 1828 with "the Literal Fulfillment of Prophecy" as part of its title.[107] That this book ran through six editions in four years (1828–32) testifies to the interest and belief in the literal fulfillment of unfulfilled prophecies. "It is recognized," said Thomas Chalmers (1780–1847), another contemporary, "in our halls of theology as holding a high place in sacred literature, and it is found in almost every home and known as a household word throughout the land."[108]

Keith's was no obscure work. He not only held out a literal future for Israel, he also used a literal hermeneutic on prophecy as a genre. He filled his footnotes with Scripture, often emphasizing that "the prophecies . . . admit of a *literal* [Keith's emphasis] interpretation,"[109] and "in very truth the prophecy savours not in the least of hyperbole."[110] Certainly for Graves and Keith, unfulfilled prophecy was not to be explained away typologically, or interpreted figuratively, as if already being fulfilled in a different sense. Unfulfilled prophecy was yet to take place in space-time history.

Graves used the irrevocable promises of God to Abraham in conjunction with unfulfilled prophecy to defend the future conversion and restoration of Israel to Palestine. At present, explained Graves, the Jews may be experiencing chastisements, but these "were not to terminate in a final and irremediable destruction."[111] Graves' literal interpretation of Deuteronomy 28,30:1-6; and Leviticus 26:44 led him to expect a worldwide, protracted dispersion of the Jews, as well as certain reestablishment in Palestine, "secured to them in the original covenant with their great ancestor."[112] Keith also taught the unconditionality of the Abrahamic covenant: "The Scriptures also declare that the covenant with Abraham—that God would give the land of Canaan to his seed for an everlasting possession,—would never be broken...."[113]

For Graves, Israel's future national restoration would be her second and final return to Palestine (Isa. 11:10-16). It had been delayed so long in order that the fullness of the Gentiles might come in (Rom. 11:25).[114] This fullness would be brought in, and the time of Jewish conversion and restoration would occur after the 1260 years (he followed the day-for-a-year interpretation) of Daniel and Revelation were fulfilled.[115] Graves believed that the Christian could not know the dating of the 1260 years with precision, so that he "should pronounce his opinion with great caution and reserve."[116] But in 1811, he admitted that "the circumstances of the present time...[indicate] a rapidly approaching fulfillment of prophecy."[117]

Since the conversion of Israel (not the personal return of Christ) would mark the future change of dispensation to usher in a glorious period of earth history, Graves threw himself wholeheartedly behind the London Society for Promoting Christianity Amongst the Jews. Through the church, the gospel would be "re-echoed back again from us to them...repaying to her parent the means of existence."[118] Giving an exposition of Romans 11:15,30, and 31, Graves included a gathering of Gentiles into the church after the ascension of Christ and the fall of Israel. The Gentile church would then be instrumental in Israel's rising again as a nation. Thus the conversion and restoration of the Jews would be "a necessary preliminary to the final great and universal conversion of the Gentile world."[119] In other words, there would be two ingatherings of Gentiles. The second could be considered another "fullness of the Gentiles," in that glorious time on earth when the Jews, now converted, would be "a multitude of preachers, missionaries already dispersed through every region,"[120] culturally and linguistically suited for future gospel diffusion. This scenario of Jewish evangelists effectively finishing the job, which the church up to that point had been unable to do, is often recited by premillennialists. They usually relate the 144,000 of the Tribulation period to the picture.[121]

In his *Sermon*, Graves pointed out the "signs of the times which encourage us now to hope for success in attempting the conversion of the Jews rather than at any preceding period of the world."[122] Then would a new dispensation (a word Graves used quite frequently) be inaugurated on planet earth. Graves anticipated the rapid approach of this time, calling it a "grand era in the Divine dispensations."[123] The conversion of Israel was imminent, and it was in such a theological atmosphere of expectancy that Darby was schooled!

Graves called the evident reciprocity between Israel and the church, which will be fulfilled in the "grand era," "a wonderful harmony of the various parts of the divine economy."[124] Graves distinguished between "the Jewish scheme" (a phrase Darby would nearly wear out in years to come!), or dispensation, and the Gentile or Christian dispensation.[125] All the dispensations are:

> ...the scheme carried on under this Supreme Lord and King, according to the Scriptures, with an *uninterrupted progress* from the creation to this hour, and *still evidently progressive*; exhibiting *the Church of Christ, and the Jewish Nation* which rejects that Christ, as rendered equally subservient to this grand design of Providence; by which "the kingdoms of this world will finally become the kingdoms of the Lord and of his Christ:" and *the triumph of grace* here will prepare for the kingdom of glory hereafter.[126]

For Graves, one should contemplate "the Jewish and Christian dispensations united in one system,"[127] yet having distinction and progress within the historical outworking of that system. "The Church of Christ" and "the Jewish Nation" will be together in "the grand era."

Graves apparently followed many Anglican divines in distinguishing the Jewish and Gentile dispensations and the Jewish and Gentile (or Christian) churches. Secker,[128] writing before 1771, spoke of the church in its largest sense as comprehending "the whole Number of good Persons, in every Age...under whatever Dispensation of true Religion...."[129] He explained that the Scriptures usually apply the word "church" to the Christian assemblies after the ascension of Christ. He said, "But the Church, more especially meant here in the Creed, is the Christian: which, though in some Respects the same with the Jewish, in others differed from it."[130] Thus distinguishing Israel and the church in some respects was customary, while not a few drew the conclusion that "they were two distinct and totally different things."[131]

Conclusion

The theological grist for Darby's later synthesis was certainly present at Trinity College in his student days. Darby was trained in an atmosphere in which it was commonplace to refer to "the Church of Christ" and "the Jewish Nation" fulfilling different but related future roles. He was primed to anticipate a future dispensation in which Israel would play a distinctive part among the nations of the world, living in prosperity in their ancient land. Believing that the Gentile dispensation interposed between the Jewish dispensation and the future millennium, in which Israel would have her earthly portion, Darby called the Gentile dispensation "the Gentile parenthesis in their history."[132] It is a small step from the Gentile church and the Gentile parenthesis to the parenthesis church. The imprecise language for the church (the Jewish church, the Gentile church) of his Anglican forebears, and their distinguishing of the Jewish and Gentile dispensations possibly underlie Darby's earthly/heavenly insight.

Darby's Trinity College background cannot be discounted when analyzing his later doctrinal formulations. The atmosphere of millennial expectancy in which he was trained certainly affected his eschatology. The postmillennialism of Graves dealt very literally with unfulfilled prophecy and spawned an attitude of anticipation for an imminent change of dispensation. Israel would come into her rightful portion at that time. Within such a conceptual scheme, Darby made certain exegetical decisions. The literal return of Christ to earth, at which time Israel would be converted, was imminent for Darby, and not merely the conversion of the Jews. The change of dispensation would be accompanied by the rapture of the living saints and the resurrection of the dead saints. The change of body occasioned by these events for the saints carried the idea of a heavenly people in glorified bodies and an earthly people in natural bodies as being together in Christ's kingdom, the new dispensation.

How to get these two kinds of saints (heavenly and earthly) into the kingdom kept Darby open to further reflection on Daniel's seventieth week. Abandoning an earlier historicist interpretation for the 1260 days, he moved to a futurism with respect to Daniel's seventieth week. Here he had the clue as to how both kinds of saints could be in the kingdom at the same time. The rapture for glorification occurred prior to the 1260 days at least, allowing time for a remnant of Israel to develop and enter the kingdom in natural bodies

Thus exegetical decisions on certain specifics overlay the basic Anglican ecclesiology and eschatology of Darby's mentors. A new synthesis was born. Possible antecedents have pointed to pieces of the new synthesis he arrived at by 1833. These pieces were the raw material with which Darby worked. No one up to Darby, it appears, had espoused the exact finished product as he articulated it. Darby's ecclesiological decisions led him to emphasize the heavenly nature of the Christian church in the Gentile dispensation over against the earthly nature of the Jewish nation in the Jewish dispensation. The eschatological decisions which followed later moved him toward clearing the way for consistently holding to two kinds of saints— two peoples of God—in the coming dispensation of the kingdom.

Edward E. Hindson

The Rapture and the Return: Two Aspects of Christ's Coming

_____*OVERVIEW*

Is there a difference between the rapture and the second coming? Pretribulationists see clear biblical evidence for distinctions between the two events. Most opponents of pretribulationalism do not see these distinctions, even though the author finds overwhelming biblical evidence supporting a pretribulational rapture.

*A*nd so we can see there will be *no* rapture for the church!" The pastor thundered as he reached the end of his sermon. "All we can really look forward to is trouble, trouble, and more trouble!"

I sat bemused. It had been a classic defense of the amillennial position on the return of Christ. Like many amillennialists, the pastor, a dear friend, assumed that times of tribulation would continue throughout the church age and intensify toward the end times. Dismissing the idea of a pretribulational rapture (by which the church would escape the Tribulation), he then dismissed the idea of any rapture at all, conveniently throwing 1 Thessalonians 4:13-18 right out the stained-glass windows!

Many who do not believe in a pretribulational rapture falsely assume there will be no rapture at all. This is a complete misconception. If one takes seriously passages like 1 Thessalonians 4:17 ("We who are alive and remain shall be caught up together with them in the clouds, to meet the Lord in the air"—NASB), he or she is forced to conclude that there will be a rapture. The only real debate is over *when* it will occur.

Arguments raised against the rapture, on the basis that it is difficult to conceive of what it would be like for millions of people to suddenly disappear, are irrelevant. Joking remarks about bumping your head on the ceiling, or false teeth being left behind, or hundreds of car accidents suddenly occurring, are inconsequential in light of the fact that Scripture clearly states that we will be "caught up" (Greek, *harpazō*) into the air.

There will be a rapture! The only serious questions are: 1) When will it occur? and 2) What is its relationship to the return of Christ at the time of His second coming? If it can be proved that the body of believers (the church) will be "caught up" into heaven and that this "gathering together" (Greek, *episunagōgēs*, cf. 2 Thessalonians 2:1) is a separate event from the return of Christ in judgment, the pretribulationist has more than adequately made his case.

As John Feinberg has so convincingly demonstrated, one must first examine the basic passages about the rapture and the return and then look at secondary issues in light of the primary passages.[1] Pretribulationists merely need prove that the *dissimilarities* between the rapture passages and the return passages are significant enough to indicate that they are *separate* events.

The Nature of His Coming

The New Testament clearly teaches that Jesus Christ will "come again" (John 14:3 KJV) and "appear the second time" (Hebrews 9:28 KJV) for His own. He promised this to His disciples in the upper room. "I go to prepare a place for you," the Lord told His disciples, "and if I go and prepare a place for you, I will come again, and receive you unto myself; that where I am, there ye may be also" (John 14:2-3 KJV).

This is our Lord's first clear indication that He will return specifically and uniquely for His own. There is no reference in John 14 to a return in judgment upon the world. The promise of His return is specifically given to comfort the disciples during the time of His absence. Many believe this is the first clear reference in our Lord's teaching to the rapture of the believers.

In Hebrews 9:28, the writer also has believers in view when he states: "So Christ was once offered to bear the sins of many; and unto them that look for him shall he appear the second time without sin unto salvation." Again, the promise of our Lord's return for His own is sounded loud and clear.

At least nine biblical terms are used in the New Testament to describe the return of Christ:

1. *Ho erchomenos.* "The coming one," as in Hebrews 10:37: "For yet a little while, and he that shall come will come" (KJV).
2. *Erchomai.* The act of coming. Used often of Christ's return (Matt. 24:30; John 14:3; 2 Thess. 1:10; Jude 14; Rev. 1:7; 22:20).
3. *Katabainō.* To "come down" or descend, as in 1 Thessalonians 4:16: "For the Lord himself shall descend from heaven with a shout" (KJV).
4. *Hekō.* Result of one's coming, to have "arrived," as in Revelation 3:3: "I will come as a thief."

5. *Parousia.* Denotes arrival and presence (of a ruler), as in 1 Thessalonians 2:19: "For what is our hope, or joy, or crown of rejoicing? Are not you in the presence of our Lord Jesus Christ at his coming?" (KJV).

6. *Apokalupsis.* Meaning to "unveil" or "uncover." Rendered "appearing" (1 Peter 1:7 KJV) or "coming" (1 Corinthians 1:7 KJV), or "revelation" (Rev. 1:1 KJV). Involves the unveiling of His divine glory.

7. *Phaneroō.* To "appear" (John 21:1 KJV), or be "manifest" (1 John 3:5 KJV): As in 1 John 3:2: "It is not yet made manifest what we shall be. But we know that, if he shall be manifested, we shall be like him; for we shall see him even as he is" (KJV).

8. *Epiphainō.* To "appear" in full light or visibility. Denotes the "brightness" of His coming (2 Thessalonians 2:8 KJV) and the glory of "that day ... unto all them that love his appearing" (2 Tim. 4:8).

9. *Horaō.* To "see with the eyes," or to "appear" visibly, as in Hebrews 9:28: "and unto them that look for him shall he appear the second time" (KJV).

These terms are often used interchangeably to refer to the rapture or the return of Christ. One cannot build a convincing case for the distinction between the two events merely on the basis of the terms themselves.

The Time of His Coming

Most evangelicals agree as to the nature of Christ's coming, but there is substantial disagreement about the *time*. Millard Erickson observes: "The one eschatological doctrine on which orthodox theologians most agree is the second coming of Christ. It is indispensable to eschatology. It is the basis of the Christian's hope, the one event which will mark the beginning of the completion of God's plan."[2]

The New Testament picture of our Lord's return emphasizes at least six distinct aspects of the time of His coming. These may be summarized as follows:

1. *Future.* The entire emphasis of the New Testament points to a future return of Christ. He promised "I

will come again" (John 14:3 KJV). The angels promised He would return (Acts 1: 11). The apostles taught the certainty of His future return (Phil. 3:20; Titus 2:13; 2 Pet. 3:3-8; 1 John 3:2-3).

2. *Imminent.* The return of Jesus Christ is always described as potentially imminent or "at hand" (Rev. 1:3; 22:10 KJV). Every generation of believers is warned to be ready for His coming, as Luke 12:40 states: "Be...ready also: for the Son of Man comes at an hour you think not" (KJV). Believers are constantly urged to look for the coming of the Lord (Phil. 3:20; Heb. 9:28; Titus 2:13; 1 Thess. 5:6).

3. *Distant.* From God's perspective, Jesus is coming at any moment. But from the human perspective it has already been nearly 2000 years. Jesus hinted at this in the Olivet discourse in the illustration of the man who traveled into a "far country" (heaven) and was gone "a long time" (Matt. 25:19). Peter also implies this in his prediction that men will begin to scoff at the second coming, after a long period of time (2 Pet. 3:8-9).

4. *Undated.* While the rapture is the next major event on the prophetic calendar, it is undated, as is the glorious appearing of Christ. Jesus said: "But of that day and hour knoweth no man, not even the angels of heaven" (Matt. 24:36). Later he added: "It is not for you to know the times or the seasons" (Acts 1:7 KJV).

5. *Unexpected.* The mass of humanity will not be looking for Christ when He returns (Matt. 24:50; Luke 21:35). They will be saying "peace and safety," when suddenly caught unprepared by His return. So unexpected will His return be that, "as a snare shall it come upon them that dwell on the whole face of the earth" (Luke 21:35 KJV).

6. *Sudden.* The Bible warns that Jesus will come "as a thief in the night...(and) then sudden destruction" will come upon the unbelieving world (1 Thess. 5:2-3 KJV). His return for the bride will occur in a flash: "in a moment, in the twinkling of an eye...for the trumpet shall sound, and the dead (believers) shall be

raised incorruptible, and we (living believers) shall be changed" (1 Cor. 15:52 KJV).

Two Aspects of His Coming

There are certain similarities between the rapture passages and the second coming passages, since they both refer to future events relating to our Lord's return. But *similarity* does not mean they are referring to the *same* event. Pretribulationists believe that there are enough substantial differences between the two aspects of Christ's coming so as to render them as two separate and distinct events.

The distinction between these two phases of the second coming is substantiated by the contrast between those passages that refer to our Lord's coming for His church and those referring to His coming to judge the unbelieving world. Thomas Ice has provided the following list to identify those distinctions.[3]

Rapture Passages		Second Coming Passages	
John 14:1-3	2 Thessalonians 2:1	Daniel 2:44-45	Acts 1:9-11
Romans 8:19	1 Timothy 6:14	Daniel 7:9-14	Acts 3:19-21
1 Corinthians 1:7-8	2 Timothy 4:1	Daniel 12:1-3	1 Thessalonians 3:13
1 Corinthians 15:51-53	Titus 2:13	Zechariah 14:1-15	2 Thessalonians 1:6-10
1 Corinthians 16:22	Hebrews 9:28	Matthew 13:41	2 Thessalonians 2:8
Philippians 3:20-21	James 5:7-9	Matthew 24:15-31	2 Peter 3:1-14
Colossians 3:4	1 Peter 1:7,13	Matthew 26:64	Jude 14-15
1 Thessalonians 1:10	1 John 2:28-3:2	Mark 13:14-27	Revelation 1:7
1 Thessalonians 2:19	Jude 21	Mark 14:62	Revelation 19:11-20:6
1 Thessalonians 4:13-18	Revelation 2:25	Luke 21:25-28	Revelation 22:7,12,20
1 Thessalonians 5:9	Revelation 3:10		
1 Thessalonians 5:23			

Ice comments that the rapture is characterized in the New Testament as a "translation coming," in which Christ comes for His church, taking her to His Father's house (John 14:3; 1 Thess 4:15-17; 1 Cor. 15:51-52).[4] Here, He claims her as His bride and the marriage supper of the Lamb begins. Whatever view one holds in regard to our Lord's return, one thing is clear in prophetic Scripture The marriage occurs *in heaven* (Revelation 19:7-9) *before* the triumphal return of Christ with His redeemed church at His side (Rev 19:11-16)

Non-pretribulationists are at a virtual loss to explain how the church got to heaven prior to returning with Christ at the battle of Armageddon. At best, some suggest they are "caught up" after the Tribulation only to return immediately with the Lord.[5] This arrangement, however, leaves little or no time for the wedding!

The return of Christ is a series of events fulfilling all end-time prophecies. These include predictions of His coming *for* His church and His coming *with* His church. Pretribulationists divide the return of Christ in two main phases: the rapture of the church and the second coming of Christ. In the first aspect, our Lord comes to take His own (the living and the dead) to be with Him. In the second aspect, He returns with His resurrected and raptured saints to win the battle of Armageddon and to establish His kingdom on earth (Revelation 5:10, "and we shall reign on the earth").

The Bible is filled with detailed predictions about both aspects of Christ's return. Just as the Scripture predicted two aspects of our Lord's first coming (His suffering and His glory), so it predicts two aspects of His *second* coming. The different aspects of our Lord's return are clearly delineated in the Scripture. The only real issue in the eschatological debate is the time *interval* between them.

Pretribulationists place the seven-year Tribulation period between the rapture and the return. This allows for the proper fulfillment of Daniel's "seventieth week," and it clearly separates the rapture from the return. Others deal with this issue in the other chapters of this volume. It is my purpose merely to substantiate that there are adequate *dissimilarities* between the events of the rapture and the event associated with the return.

Contrast Between the Rapture and the Return

Rapture	Return
1. Christ comes *for* His own (John 14:3; 1 Thess. 14:17; 2 Thess. 2:1).	1. Christ comes *with* His own (1 Thess. 3:13; Jude 14; Rev. 19:14).
2. He comes in the *air* (1 Thess. 4:17).	2. He comes to the *earth* (Zech. 14:4; Acts 1:11).
3. He *claims* His bride (1 Thess. 4:16-17).	3. He comes *with* His bride (Rev. 19:6-14).
4. Removal of *believers* (1 Thess. 4:17).	4. Manifestation of *Christ* (Mal. 4:2).
5. *Only* His own see Him (1 Thess. 4:13-18).	5. *Every eye* shall see Him (Rev. 1:7).
6. *Tribulation* begins (2 Thess. 1:6-9).	6. Millennial *kingdom* begins (Rev. 20:1-7).
7. Saved are *delivered from wrath* (1 Thess. 1:10; 5-9).	7. Unsaved *experience the wrath* of God (Rev. 6:12-17).
8. *No signs* precede rapture (1 Thess. 5:1-3).	8. *Signs* precede second coming (Luke 21:11,15).

9. Focus: *Lord and church*
(1 Thess. 4:13-18).

9. Focus: *Israel and kingdom*
(Matthew 24:14).

10. *World* is deceived
(2 Thess. 2:3-12).

10. *Satan* is bound (Rev. 20:1-2).

Is the Rapture in the Bible?

The church's hope is the rapture. She awaits the Savior who is coming for His bride. The church may endure persecution, trouble, and difficulty in the meantime. But she is not the object of divine wrath. The church does not await destruction as the world does. Rather, she awaits the coming of her Lord and King. Peter explains that the present world is "reserved for fire, being kept for the day of judgment and destruction of *ungodly* men" (2 Pet. 3:7 KJV).

The church is pictured in Scripture as the wife of the Lamb (Rev. 19:7-9). She is not the object of the wrath of the Lamb. He does not beat her up and then marry her! Or marry her, then beat her up! He may discipline her in love. But His ultimate purpose is to present her to the Father as His perfect bride.

The rapture (or "translation") of the church is often paralleled to the "raptures" of Enoch (Genesis 5:24) and Elijah (2 Kings 2:12). In each case, the individual disappeared or was caught up into heaven. At His ascension, our Lord Himself was "taken up" into heaven (Acts 1:9 KJV). The biblical description of the rapture involves both the resurrection of deceased believers and the translation of living believers into the air to meet the Lord (1 Thess. 4:16-17; 1 Cor. 15:51-52).

The concept of the rapture is expressed in the biblical terms "caught up" (Greek, *harpazō*) and "gathered together" (Greek, *episunagōgēs*). Hogg and Vine observe that *harpazō* is the same verb used of Paul ("whether in the body, or apart from the body," 2 Corinthians 12:2-4 KJV); Philip ("spirit...caught away Philip," Acts 8:39 KJV); and the man child ("caught up to God," Revelation 12:5 KJV).[6] This explains that *harpazō* conveys the idea of force suddenly exercised and is best rendered "snatch" (John 10:28-29, where Jesus promises that no one can "snatch" (KJV) His own out of His hand). He alone does the "snatching" at the time of the rapture!

By contrast, *episunagōgēs* refers to that which results from the "catching up" (*harpazō*). Once caught up into the clouds, we shall be "gathered together" with the Lord. In commenting on 2 Thessalonians 2:1, Hogg and Vine observe: "Here it refers to the 'rapture' of the saints into the air to meet and to be forever with the

Lord."[7] The basic meaning is to "assemble together." The raptured church is pictured as the great "assembly" (synagogue) in the sky. Milligan observes: "The word goes back to the saying of the Lord in Mark 13:27 ("gather together His elect"), and is found elsewhere in the New Testament only in Hebrews 10:25, where it is applied to the ordinary religious assembling of believers as an anticipation of the great assembling at the Lord's coming."[8]

Of course there is a rapture! There can be no valid system of biblical eschatology without a rapture. The church will be "caught up" and "gathered together" with her Lord. The only real debate is over the question of when. Any eschatological system that dismisses the rapture as some hoax has forfeited the essential biblical teaching that Christ will come and snatch away His bride to the great assembly in heaven.

Amillennialists, postmillennialists, and posttribulationists alike must account for the rapture in their eschatological schemes. So away with all talk of debunking the very idea of the rapture. It is taught in these passages of Scripture as clearly as any other doctrine. And any legitimate eschatological system must account for it. There will be a rapture. The question is whether it is separate from the return of Christ or a part of the same event.

Are the Events of the Return Distinctly Different?

Those who reject a pretribulational rapture usually argue that the rapture happens simultaneous to the return of Christ.[9] The Lord descends from heaven, "catches up" the church, and then returns to set up His kingdom. In order to make the rapture occur simultaneous to the return, such systems emphasize the *similarities* between the two: In both Christ comes at the end of the age to bring in the consummation of all things.

However, a simple survey of the second coming passages reveals some significant differences. Unlike the rapture of the saints, several passages refer to our Lord's coming *with* His saints (1 Thessalonians 3:13, "at the coming of our Lord Jesus Christ with all his saints" [KJV]; Jude 14, "Behold, the Lord cometh with ten thousands of his saints" [KJV]; Revelation 19:14, "and the armies that were with him in heaven followed him upon white horses, clothed in fine linen, white and clean" [KJV]). Revelation 19:11-16 certainly refers to the church returning with Christ to judge the unbelieving world, overthrow the Antichrist and the false prophet, and to establish the millennial reign of Christ on earth.

Other second coming passages refer to a series of events that find no reference at all in the rapture passages: returning to the earth, splitting the Mount of Olives (Zech. 14:4); punishing the wicked in flaming fiery vengeance (2 Thess. 1:6-9); overthrowing political and ecclesiastical "Babylon" (Rev. 17-18); winning the battle of Armageddon (Rev. 16:16-21); defeating the Antichrist and the false prophet (Rev. 19:19-21); binding Satan in the bottomless pit (Rev. 20:1-3); establishing the reign of the saints upon the earth for a thousand years (Rev. 20:4-10).

All of these events associated with the return of Christ are completely distinct from the promise to rapture and assemble the church in heaven. These distinctions are surely sufficient to warrant viewing them as separate, though related, events. Having established this distinction, pretribulationists have adequate ground for viewing these events as being separated by the Tribulation period.

The church is promised that the coming of the Lord will result in her being "caught up" and "gathered together" unto Him. It is this promise of the rapture, not of the wrath, that is in view in Revelation 3:10, where the Scripture promises, "I will keep you *from* [Greek, *ek* 'out of'] the hour of trial that is going to come upon the whole world" (KJV). Only a pretribulational rapture makes this promise a reality.

Ten Reasons for a Pretribulational Rapture[10]

1. *Christ promised to keep the church from the Tribulation.* In Revelation 3:10, the risen Christ said the church would be *kept from* (literally, "preserved," or "protected *out* of") the hour of trial, or divine retribution, that is coming on the whole world.

2. *Tribulation judgments are the "wrath of the Lamb."* Revelation 6:16 depicts the cataclysmic judgments of the end times as the wrath of Christ. Revelation 19:7-9 depicts the church as the bride of the Lamb. She is not the object of His wrath, which is poured out on an unbelieving world.

3. *Jesus told His disciples to pray that they would escape the Tribulation.* In Luke 21:36, He said: "Be always on the watch, and pray that you may be able to escape all that is about to happen"

(KJV). Remember, even Lot was given a chance to escape Sodom before divine judgment fell.

4. *His coming in the clouds means the church's deliverance has come.* Jesus told His disciples: "Lift up your heads, because your redemption is drawing near" (Luke 21:28 KJV). The hope of the church is not in surviving the judgment of tribulation but in escaping it.

5. *God will call His ambassadors home before declaring war on the world.* In 2 Corinthians 5:20 (KJV), believers are called "Christ's ambassadors," who appeal to the world to be reconciled to God before it is too late. In biblical times, one's ambassadors were recalled when it was time to make war with the enemy.

6. *Moral restraint will disappear when the church is taken home.* Second Thessalonians 2:1-11 (KJV) warns that *after* the "coming of the Lord" and "our being gathered to Him," the "man of lawlessness" (Antichrist) will emerge on the world scene. The church's restraining ministry of "salt" and "light" will no longer hold back the tide of evil.

7. *The rapture will happen in the "twinkling of an eye."* First Corinthians 15:51-52 promises that "in a flash, in the twinkling of an eye...the dead shall be raised imperishable and we [living at the rapture] will be changed" (KJV). This instantaneous disappearance will terminate the church's earthly ministry.

8. *The rapture will take place in the air.* Unlike the glorious appearing, when Christ descends to earth, splits the Mount of Olives, overthrows Antichrist, and binds Satan, the rapture will occur when we are "caught up together...to meet the Lord in the air" (1 Thess. 4:17).

9. *The woman who suffers persecution during the Tribulation symbolizes Israel.* This is a very important point. The woman who delivers the male child (Christ) represents the nation of Israel. Israel, not the church brought forth Christ, and He in turn brought forth the church. He is the founder of the church, not its descendant. Therefore, the persecuted "saints" of the Tribulation are Jewish: the remnant of the woman's seed (Rev. 12:1-2,5-6,17).

10. *The Marriage of Christ (Lamb) and His bride (church) takes place before the battle of Armageddon.* The Bible describes the fall of "Babylon" (kingdom of Antichrist) in Revelation 17–18. But *before* it tells of Christ's return to conquer the Antichrist, it tells us "the wedding of the Lamb has come, and His bride has made

herself ready" (Rev. 19:7–8 KJV). This clearly indicates the bride has been taken to heaven earlier, and that she returns with Christ and the host of the "armies of heaven...dressed in fine linen, white and clean" (Rev. 19:8,14 KJV).

We have clearly seen from the New Testament that the rapture and the second coming are different in nature and therefore separate events. This observation, that there are two future comings, is an important element for determining the timing of the rapture. It is not surprising that non-pretribulationists often ignore these biblical distinctions. A literal interpretation of the passages involved in the two comings is best represented by a pretribulational perspective.

J. Dwight Pentecost

The Relationship of the Church to the Kingdom of God

_____*OVERVIEW*

What is the major theme or purpose that encompasses God's overall master plan? Dr. Pentecost believes that the drama of history revolves around the kingdom of God. This theme is traced from Genesis to Revelation, illustrating God's right to rule and the form that His kingdom takes through the various epochs of history. Anyone interested in the study of Bible prophecy has to deal with the vital issue of the role of the kingdom of God and how this important theme is developed throughout the Bible.

*G*od is sovereign, and as Sovereign He rules eternally in a kingdom in which He is the absolute authority. In order to understand the biblical concept of "kingdom," we must recognize that it includes several ideas: the *right* to rule, a *realm* in which ruling authority is exercised, and the *reality* of that authority actually being exercised.

The Kingdom in Eternity

Concerning God's kingdom, the Bible presents two aspects: the *eternal* aspect and the *temporal* aspect. The eternal kingdom is characterized by four essential truths: 1) It is timeless; 2) it is universal; 3) it is providential; 4) it is miraculous.

In eternity past, before the creation of the angels, the earth, and man, a kingdom existed in the sphere of "the heavenlies" because of the relationship among the members of the Trinity. God the Father was sovereign. God the Son, although equal in person, was subordinate to the Father. God the Holy Spirit was the active executor of the will of the Father (Gen. 1:2-3). Thus in eternity past there was a kingdom, involving the right to rule, as well as the sphere in which the right operated and the rule was exercised. Indeed, *all* the elements essential to a kingdom were present. This kingdom arises from the character of God and reaches from eternity to eternity.

God's kingdom was displayed in the angelic realm before it was developed on the earth. The created angelic hosts in that kingdom were subject to the Sovereign, and they worshiped Him and obeyed Him. This continued until the fall of Lucifer and the angels who followed him in rebellion.

The Kingdom on Earth (Pre-Abrahamic)

To demonstrate His right to rule, God ordered this earthly sphere as the place where He would rule. He populated it with creatures who were responsible to recognize that right, submit to it, and give the Ruler that which was due Him. Our sovereign God, in every period of theocratic administration, has ruled through those to whom He assigned His authority. It was the responsibility of administrators to subjugate all to God's authority, to reward those who do good, to punish evildoers, and to provide an atmosphere in which the subjects of the King might live in peace. In the garden, Adam was the theocratic administrator whose responsibility was to subject all creation to himself, so that through him creation might be subject to the authority of God. When this form of administration failed, God brought a judgment and expelled Adam and Eve from the garden.

God instituted a new form of theocratic administration in which He wrote His law in the hearts of men and subjected man to His law. That law was man's conscience (Rom. 2:15), and as men subjected themselves to the rule of conscience, they were in subjection to the authority of God. But that too failed. And when men rebelled against that form of theocratic administration, God wiped the human race off the face of the earth by a flood.

God then instituted a new form of theocratic administration in which authority was given to human government (Gen. 9:6). It was the responsibility of human government to curb lawlessness and to bring man in subjection to the authority of God. Again man failed miserably. And when men organized in open rebellion against God, "The Lord scattered them from there over all the earth, and they stopped building the city. That is why it was called Babel—because there the Lord confused the language of the whole world" (Gen. 11:8-9).

The Kingdom in Israel

With the call of Abraham, God introduced a new form of theocratic administration. He instituted the Abrahamic Covenant that promised Abraham a land, seed, and blessing. Throughout the Old Testament—through that expanding covenant program—God administered His theocracy here on earth.

The kingdom program was then developed with the nation Israel through the covenants God made with them: the Abrahamic (Gen. 15:18), the Davidic (2 Sam. 7:14), the New (Jer. 31:31-34), and the Palestinian (Deut. 28–30). These eternal, unconditional, irrevocable covenants determined the ultimate form of the kingdom of the God of heaven on earth.

While the covenants promised a kingdom here on earth, it was the prophets who described the glories of that kingdom. The prophets of the Old Testament had proclaimed a message of hope that caused Israel to eagerly anticipate the fulfillment of God's covenants and promises to them. David's son the Messiah would come to bring peace, righteousness, and prosperity to the nation. He would come as a Savior to redeem and as a Sovereign to reign. The nations which had persecuted Israel would be subjugated to Him, and Israel would know the promised peace which the Prince of Peace would bring. Her accumulated sins would be put away and she would experience forgiveness and life in righteousness. Such was the hope of Israel.

Years passed before an official proclamation was made by the prophesied forerunner, John the Baptist, who heralded his message to the nation: "Repent, for the kingdom of heaven is at hand" (Matt. 3:2 NASB). When Jesus began His ministry He made the same proclamation: "Repent, for the kingdom of heaven is at hand" (Matt. 4:17 NASB). The call to repentance shows that this was a contingent offer and that the blessings of the kingdom depended on the nation's response. This does not mean, however, it was not a genuine offer. The reference to the kingdom needed no explanation; it was the covenanted kingdom under David's son the Messiah, of which the prophets had so clearly spoken and for whom the nation was waiting. The nation was plunged into a great debate concerning His person. Who is this Jesus of Nazareth who claims to be the son of David and the Son of God? Is He what He claims to be? If so, He truly is the promised and covenanted Messiah. If not, He is a blasphemous impostor who is worthy of death. Jesus made His claims concerning His person very clear. He validated those claims convincingly by His miracles, and He challenged people to accept His claims and to put faith in Him, so as to receive a righteousness from Him that would enable them to enter His forthcoming kingdom.

From the inception of His ministry two responses to His presentation were evident. John says: "He came to His own [things], and His own did not receive Him. But as many as received Him, to them He gave the right to become children of God, even to those who believe in His name" (John 1:11-12). His rejection is clearly seen in the response of those in Nazareth, who heard Him claim to be the One who would fulfill the prophecy of Isaiah 61:1-2. These responses climax in the incident recorded in Matthew 12:22-24. There were those who, on the basis of the evidence He had presented about Himself as the son of David, the Messiah, expressed their willingness to accept Him as the Messiah. But there were also those who rejected the evidence and sought to explain it away, so that they would be guiltless for their rejection. There were two supernatural powers who could perform miracles: Satan and God. If the leaders acknowledged that Jesus performed miracles by God's power, they would be without excuse for their unbelief; but if He performed miracles by Satan's power, they could justify their rejection. Thus they sought to dissuade those who believed by saying: "This fellow does not cast out demons except by Beelzebub, the ruler of the demons" (Matt. 12:24).

Jesus' Judgment Upon Israel

Jesus viewed the explanation by the leaders as indicative of the course which that generation would follow. He viewed His rejection as if it were final, although it would not be finalized until His trial and crucifixion. The message that He began to proclaim was no longer "Come to Me, all who are weary and heavy-laden, and I will give you rest" (Matt. 11:28 NASB), but rather it was a message of judgment. Viewing the nation as being confirmed in their rejection and unbelief, Jesus from this time on speaks of the judgment to come.

In the parable of the wicked vinedressers (Matt. 21:33-44), after the leaders kill the heir, God, the owner, will destroy those wicked men miserably (Matt. 21:41). So, too, "the kingdom of God will be taken from you [that generation in Israel] and given to a nation [or generation] bearing the fruits of it. And whoever falls on this stone will be broken but on whomever it falls, it will grind him to powder" (Matt. 21:43-44, author's translation). This signifies the withdrawal of the offer of the covenanted kingdom to Israel and its postponement to the future.

This same judgment is depicted in Matthew 22:1-7, where the guests (the nation Israel), who had been invited to a wedding banquet (Messiah's kingdom) but refused to come, suffered the consequences of rejecting the king's invitation. The king "sent out his armies, destroyed those murderers, and burned up their city." This parable reveals the form of judgment: Roman armies, under Titus, would attack the city of Jerusalem, destroy it, and either kill or disperse its inhabitants.

Another specific prediction of the coming judgment is given in Matthew 23:37–24:2. Jesus declared He had sought to provide peace and security for Israel, but it was not experienced because "you were not willing." As a consequence, "Your house is left to you desolate" (Matt. 24:38). The house could refer to the temple, or to the city of Jerusalem, in which the temple stood, or to the Davidic house, whose throne would be left empty. The severity of the judgment is seen in the declaration: "Not one stone shall be left here upon another, that shall not be thrown down" (Matt. 24:2).

Luke is very specific in recording Jesus' message of judgment. In Luke 19:11-27 the nobleman declared, concerning the unfaithful, "Take the mina from him...but bring here those enemies of mine, who did not want me to reign over them, and slay them before me." In this parable it is significant that judgment fell on those who refused to submit themselves to the One who had the right to reign. This was the sin of that generation in Israel.

Once again, the judgment is predicted forcefully in Luke 21:20-24: "When you see Jerusalem surrounded by armies, then know that its desolation is near. Then let those in Judea flee to the mountains, let those who are in the midst of her depart, and let not those who are in the country enter her. For these are the days of vengeance that all things which are written may be fulfilled. But woe to those who are pregnant and to those who are nursing babies in those days! For there will be great distress in the land and wrath upon this people. And they will fall by the edge of the sword, and be led away captive into all nations. And Jerusalem will be trampled by Gentiles until the times of the Gentiles are fulfilled" (NKJV).

Thus we see that the message of Jesus was initially a message of hope, of blessing, and of salvation. But after the announcement by the leaders that Jesus received His power from Satan, and so was a blasphemous impostor, His message turned to one of judgment on that generation in Israel. While this announcement did not cancel the covenants and promises given to Israel concerning the earthly kingdom of David's greater Son, but only postponed the realization of those hopes, yet it did consign that generation to a physical and temporal judgment which was inescapable (Luke 19:27). Thus the kingdom program for Israel, which began with such high hopes at the beginning of Jesus' ministry, ends with the somber note of judgment and postponement.

The Kingdom in the Present Age

In light of all this, the following questions arise. What happens to God's kingdom, of which the Davidic millennial kingdom is only an earthly form, in this present age when the millennial kingdom has been postponed? What form does the kingdom take in this present age? What are the essential characteristics or features of God's kingdom in this present age?

In answer, Jesus referred to "the secrets of the kingdom" (Matt. 13:11). He was not referring to the covenanted Davidic, or millennial, kingdom. That there would be such a kingdom was no "secret" in the Old Testament! It clearly revealed the essential features or characteristics of the millennial kingdom. But what the Old Testament had not revealed was that *an entire age would intervene between the offer of the kingdom by the Messiah and Israel's reception of the King and enjoyment of full kingdom blessings.* With this background, we see that the time period covered by the parables in Matthew 13 extends from Israel's rejection until its future reception of the Messiah. Thus this new program began while Christ was still on the earth, and it will extend until His return to the earth in power and great glory.

Matthew 13

This period includes the time from Pentecost, in Acts 2, to the rapture; that is, the age of grace (which we also call the age of the Holy Spirit, or the church age). Although this period includes the church age, it extends beyond it, for the parables of Matthew 13 precede Pentecost and extend beyond the rapture. Thus these parables do not primarily concern the nature, function, and influence of the church. Rather, they show the previously unrevealed form in which God's theocratic rule would be exerted in a previously unrevealed age, made necessary by Israel's rejection of Jesus Christ. In Matthew 13 there are eight parables, each one providing an essential characteristic of the kingdom in this present age.

Seed, sowers, and soils. The first feature of this age is that it is characterized by a sowing of the seed by sowers and by varied responses to the sowing. In this parable, the seed (Matt. 13:3-8) represents the word, or "the message about the kingdom," and the field represents the "heart" of the individual hearer (v. 19). In Scripture, the "heart" often indicates intellectual capacity. A message, then, was being proclaimed and heard, but there were varying responses. Some seed showed no sign of life at all (that sown by the wayside). Some produced no fruit (that sown on rocky places). Some seed gave promise of bearing fruit but was eventually fruitless (that sown among the thorns). Finally there was seed that produced a crop, yielding a 100, 60, or 30 times what was sown (v. 23).

Mark recorded another parable by Jesus on the theme of sowing seed. This parable (Mark 4:26-29) was designed to teach that the *fruit depends not on the sower but on the life that is in the seed itself.* Regardless of what the sower did, the seed germinated, sprouted, grew, produced grain, and eventually yielded a bountiful harvest, which the man reaped. Jesus wanted to make it clear that any harvest they saw would be the result of sowing and then allowing the life in the seed to manifest itself by growth and yield.

Weeds among wheat. The second parable (13:24-29) was designed to supplement the first to teach that *there would be a false sowing alongside the sowing of the Word of God.* The field had been sown with good seed, and the sower could anticipate a harvest for his labors. Later, the sower was told that an enemy had sown the field with the seed of weeds.

This false sowing evidently took place immediately after the good seed had been sown. Then both kinds of seed germinated and sprouted. In the process of waiting for the harvest, it became evident that weeds had been sown in the wheat field. The presence of weeds would crowd out the growth of the fruit-bearing wheat. The servants, concerned as they were with the results of their labors, suggested that they try to remove the weeds from the field. However, the owner of the field recognized that it would be impossible to remove the weeds without destroying the wheat. So the servants were commanded to let both ripen, and at the time of wheat harvest they would then separate the good grain from the worthless weeds, without destroying the wheat. The weeds could be burned and destroyed, while the wheat would be gathered into storage. Through this parable Jesus prepared these men to be on guard for Satan's work of sowing false seed, or false doctrine, while they were sowing the good seed. Satan's false kingdom would continue to exist alongside the new form of God's kingdom.

The mustard seed. The third parable (13:31-32) reveals that *this new form of the kingdom will have an almost imperceptible beginning.* The emphasis in the parable is on the contrast between the size of the seed and the plants that are produced. "Small as a mustard seed" was a Jewish proverb to indicate a very minute particle. But out of that insignificant seed in one year would grow a plant which became large enough for birds to nest in. In Ezekiel 31:6 and Daniel 4:12, the figure of a spreading tree, in which birds lodge, indicates a great kingdom that can protect and provide benefits for many peoples. Christ would commission only 11 men to become His emissaries (John 17:18). This would seem to be an insignificant beginning, yet Jesus predicted that the world would hear His message from such a small beginning. Thus the parable teaches that the new form of the kingdom, while it did have an insignificant beginning, would eventually spread to the ends of the earth.

The hidden leaven. The fourth parable (13:33) was designed to show *how the kingdom program would develop and operate in the present age.* Some have referred to this as "The Parable of the Leaven," but that title puts emphasis on what leaven is or signifies. Actually, this is "The Parable of Leaven Hidden in Meal." In other words, the parable emphasizes what leaven does or how leaven works. When the leaven, or yeast, was introduced into the flour, a process began that was steady, continuous, and irreversible. That process continued until the whole mixture was leavened. Thus Jesus was teaching that the kingdom would not be established by outward means, since no external force could make the dough rise. Rather, this new form of the kingdom would operate according to an internal force that would be continuous and progressive until the whole mixture had been leavened. Here the emphasis was on the Holy Spirit and concerned His ministry to the world. Christ would again speak of this in John 15:26 and 16:7-11.

Hidden treasure and the expensive pearl. The fifth and sixth parables reveal *what accrues to God through the kingdom in this present age.* In the "Parable of the Treasure Hidden in the Field" (13:44), Jesus revealed that a multitude from Israel will become God's purchased possession through this present age. In the "Parable of the Merchant Looking for Fine Pearls" (13:45-46), Jesus revealed that God will obtain a treasure not only from the nation Israel but from the Gentiles as well. We understand this because a pearl comes out of the sea, and quite frequently in Scripture the sea represents Gentile nations. So again we see that a treasure from among the Gentiles becomes God's by purchase.

The dragnet. The seventh parable (vv. 47-50) reveals that *this new form of the kingdom will conclude in a judgment separating the righteous from the unrighteous.* The net drawn up from the sea brings all kinds of fish, some useful and some useless. Through this parable Christ taught that the age will end in a judgment to determine who enters the future millennial kingdom and who is excluded.

Righteousness is a prerequisite for entrance into the kingdom. The righteous are taken into it, but the unrighteous are excluded. The destiny of the wicked is not the blessing of the kingdom, but rather the judgment of eternal fire. This same truth, concerning the judgment prior to the institution of the millennial kingdom, is taught in Matthew 25:1-30, where Christ predicted judgment on the nation Israel, and in verses 31-46 where He described judgment on living Gentiles. The judgment predicted here is not a judgment on the dead but on the living, and it will take place at the time of Christ's second advent to the earth.

The householder. The eighth and final parable of Matthew 13 is that of the householder (v. 52), which teaches that *some features of the new form of the kingdom are identical to features previously revealed about the new and have no correspondence to what had been revealed about the millennial form of the kingdom.*

As we survey the Matthew 13 parables, we find that in light of Israel's rejection of Christ, He foresaw postponement of the millennial form of the kingdom. He announced the introduction of a new form of the kingdom, one that would span the period from Israel's rejection of Christ until Israel's future reception of Christ at His second advent.

This present age, with its new form of the kingdom, is characterized by the sowing of the Word, to which there will be varying responses depending on the soil's preparation (the soils). The harvest that results from the sowing is the result of the life that is in the sown seed (the seed growing of itself). Concurrent with the sowing of the Word is a false counter-sowing (the weeds). The new form of the kingdom had an insignificant beginning, but it will grow to great proportions (the mustard seed). The power in the kingdom is not external but internal (the leaven hidden in meal). God will gather a peculiar treasure to Himself through this present age (the hidden treasure and the pearl of great price). The present form of the kingdom will end in a judgment to determine who are righteous, and therefore eligible to enter the future millennial form of the kingdom, as well as who are unrighteous thus to be excluded from the millennial kingdom to come.

This revelation of the new form through which the theocracy would be administered in this present age was followed by a specific prophecy: "I will build My church" (Matt. 16:18). The nature and function of the church is not explained here, but it is revealed in its historical development in the book of Acts, with its doctrines explained in the epistles.

The Kingdom in Acts

Following His resurrection, Jesus spent time with those whom He had chosen (John 15:16), instructing them concerning the new form of the kingdom and preparing them for their ministry of introducing that new form to Jew and Gentile alike. He reiterated His promise of empowerment by the Holy Spirit for the work of their ministry. On Pentecost the promised Spirit was poured out and indwelt believers as His temple. In the book of Acts their ministry of proclaiming the new message of the new form of the kingdom is recorded, by which the gospel was proclaimed and spread throughout the world.

The kingdom of God in this present age, formed through the preaching of the gospel would be made up of Jews, Samaritans, and Gentiles. This was made clear to Peter in the vision given to him in Acts 10. When Peter, in obedience to the Levitical law, refused to eat that which was unclean, he was told, "Do not call anything impure that God has made clean" (v. 15). To make sure there was no misunderstanding, the command was repeated three times. It later became apparent that Peter understood that the distinctions inherent in the Levitical law had been removed, for when he was in the house of Cornelius he declared, "I now realize how true it is that God does not show favoritism but accepts men from every nation who fear Him and do what is right" (vv. 34-35).

Peter felt free to proclaim the gospel of the death and resurrection of Jesus Christ to the Gentiles assembled in Cornelius' house In response to their faith, "The Holy Spirit came on all who heard the message" (v. 44). The evidence that Gentiles had received the Holy Spirit was that they spoke with tongues (v. 46). Tongues were evidence to the apostles of the genuine conversion of the Gentiles and of their inclusion in the body of believers. In response, these

Gentiles showed their identification with Jesus Christ and the company of believers by being baptized.

Even so, Jerusalem had to be convinced of God's acceptance of Gentiles into the church and the kingdom. So Peter testified to the genuineness of their conversion by recounting in his dream what had happened next. And those in Jerusalem, "When they heard this, they had no further objections and praised God, saying, 'So then, God has granted even the Gentiles repentance unto life'" (11:18). This question was submitted to the apostles in Jerusalem, and Peter testified to the salvation of the Gentiles by faith in Jesus Christ apart from the law (15:7-11). His testimony is further corroborated by Barnabas and Paul (v. 12), and James, who presided at this council and rendered its decision. It was evident that God was dealing with Gentiles as Gentiles, "taking from the Gentiles a people for Himself" (v. 14)

James found this in keeping with the prophetic program. In Amos 9:11-12 it was prophesied that after the period in which Israel was disciplined because of disobedience (vv. 9-10), and the Davidic throne left empty for a time, the Davidic throne would be restored and the Davidic kingdom would be instituted. When it is reinstituted, the kingdom will include not only the physical descendants of Abraham but also a multitude of Gentiles. Therefore the restored Davidic kingdom under its rightful Davidic king would be composed of both Jews and Gentiles. In that kingdom Gentiles would not be made into Jews; instead, they would be in the kingdom as Gentiles. This allowed James to conclude that if God had a program for Gentiles, as Gentiles, in the future Davidic kingdom established here on the earth, there was no reason to deny that God could include Gentiles, as Gentiles, in this present form of the theocracy Through faith in Jesus Christ, Gentiles are equal participants with believing Jews in the present form of the kingdom of God.

Paul's life was dedicated to the preaching of the grace of God. He wrote, "Now I know that none of you among whom I have gone about preaching the kingdom will ever see me again" (Acts 20:25) Paul clearly equated preaching the gospel of the grace of God with the preaching of the kingdom of God. Once again we see that the two terms are used interchangeably, as in 28:23 when Paul arrived in Rome and "they arranged to meet Paul on a certain day and came in even larger numbers to the place where he was staying. From morning till evening he explained and declared to them the kingdom of God and tried to convince them about Jesus from the Law of Moses and from the Prophets." Again the preaching of the gospel was referred to as testimony concerning the kingdom of God. And in verses 30-31 this identification was again made, where "for two whole years Paul stayed there in his own rented house and welcomed all who came to see him. Boldly and without hindrance he preached the kingdom of God and taught about the Lord Jesus Christ."

Thus as we survey Paul's ministry from the book of Acts, we see him as an ambassador of the kingdom of God, but his message was salvation through the death and the resurrection of Jesus Christ. No reference is made to support the notion that the earthly Davidic kingdom had been established. Rather, the message concerns entrance into a present form of the kingdom of God by faith in Jesus Christ.

Uses of "the Kingdom"

While there are many references to the kingdom in the New Testament epistles, on closer examination we find the term "the kingdom" used in several different ways.

It is used of the *future earthly Davidic kingdom* to be established at the second advent of Jesus Christ. In 2 Timothy 4:1 Paul wrote, "In the presence of God and of Christ Jesus, who will judge the living and the dead, and in view of His appearing and His kingdom, I give you this charge." This must refer to the earthly Davidic kingdom that will be established on earth, since that is the kingdom which will follow the second advent of Jesus Christ and the judgments associated with that momentous event (Matt. 25:1-46).

Paul also wrote, "Christ, the firstfruits; then, when He comes, those who belong to Him. The end will come, when He hands over the kingdom to God the Father after He has destroyed all dominion, authority and power" (1 Cor. 15:23-24). Here Paul outlined a resurrection program that began with the resurrection of Christ and will continue with the resurrection of those that are Christ's at His second advent. The completion of the resurrection program does not come until after the reign of Christ here on earth, following His second coming. At the conclusion of that resurrection program, Christ will have delivered up the kingdom to God (v. 24). It is quite obvious, therefore, that the kingdom referred to here is the millennial kingdom over which Christ reigns on earth, following His second advent. Thus the idea of a future earthly Davidic kingdom is not at all foreign to the apostle's thinking.

Besides the *future earthly Davidic kingdom*, we also find that the *future eternal kingdom* is referred to in the epistles. In 2 Timothy 4:18 Paul declared, "The Lord will rescue me from every evil attack and will bring me safely to His heavenly kingdom." Paul obviously was anticipating the eternal reign of Christ in His eternal kingdom. Peter declared, "You will receive a rich welcome into the eternal kingdom of our Lord and Savior Jesus Christ" (2 Pet. 1:11). Peter likewise was anticipating his participation in that eternal reign of Christ.

Elsewhere Paul wrote, "Flesh and blood cannot inherit the kingdom of God, nor does the perishable inherit the imperishable" (1 Cor. 15:50). Here Paul seems to be using "kingdom of God" in reference to the eternal state of the believer. Thus "kingdom" or "kingdom of God" may refer to the eternal reign of Christ.

While the term "kingdom" is used in these two senses in the epistles, its third and most common use, by far, is in reference to the present form of the kingdom, that into which a believer enters by faith in Jesus Christ. Paul stated that God "has rescued us from the dominion of darkness and brought us into the kingdom of the Son He loves, in whom we have redemption, the forgiveness of sins" (Col. 1:13-14). Here the phrase "the kingdom of the Son He loves" is equated with the redemption and the forgiveness of sins received by faith in Jesus Christ.

In Galatians 5:19-21 Paul listed the works of the flesh and then declared "that those who live like this will not inherit the kingdom of God." He made a similar statement in Ephesians 5:3-5, where he listed grievous sins of the flesh and then stated that those who participate in such things do not have "any inheritance in the kingdom of Christ and of God" (Eph. 5:5). This concept is also found in 1 Corinthians 6:9,10. In these passages Paul is saying that men who are characterized by these sins are not saved, because it is evident they have never received by faith the salvation that comes through Jesus Christ. Therefore they are not participants in the kingdom of God. Thus we see again that the term "kingdom of God" is equated with salvation and must refer to participation in or exclusion from the present kingdom form.

Believers are exhorted to live lives worthy of God, who calls them into His kingdom and glory (1 Thess. 2:12). Here Paul seems to be referring to the participation of believers in the present form of the kingdom, who consequently are to walk worthy of that position. Paul commended the Thessalonians for their faithfulness and patience in the midst of persecutions and testings (2 Thess. 1:4), which validated their membership in the kingdom. By that conduct they were deemed "worthy of the kingdom of God," for which they were suffering (v. 5). Paul was not encouraging them to have patience and faithfulness in order to be able to participate in a future millennial kingdom; but, rather, to conduct themselves in a manner worthy of their participation in the kingdom's present form.

Paul told the Corinthians, "The kingdom of God is not a matter of talk but of power" (1 Cor. 4:20). In other words, if those in Corinth were actually saved and in the kingdom of God, they would demonstrate that by manifesting the power of the kingdom in their daily lives. Mere profession was not a sufficient demonstration of salvation or participation in the kingdom of God; that relationship must be established and demonstrated by the work of the Holy Spirit, who is the power in the present form of the kingdom of God.

James made reference to the kingdom in James 2:5, where he asserted that entrance into that kingdom is for those who are "rich in faith." A popular Jewish concept said that he whom the Lord loves He makes rich, and that those who had material wealth received it because God approved of their righteousness. Therefore, many sought riches as a basis for assurance of their acceptance by God. James, however, said that it is not those who are rich in this world's goods, but those who are rich in faith, who will "inherit the kingdom." Like Paul and Peter, James equated participation in the kingdom with salvation received by faith.

As a final note, according to Colossians 4:11 Paul considered himself a laborer on behalf of the kingdom of God, and he saw those faithful servants who worked with him as fellow workers in the kingdom.

From this survey, then, we see that the most frequent reference to the "kingdom" or the "kingdom of God" in the epistles is a reference to the present form of the kingdom, in which individuals by faith in Jesus Christ, and because of His death and resurrection, receive salvation and the gift of eternal life. All these are a part of the kingdom of God.

The Covenants in the Epistles

As we have already seen, biblical covenants dominated the thinking of the writers of Old Testament Scripture. And while those covenants play a prominent role in the Gospels, little reference is made to covenants in the New Testament epistles. This supports the idea that during this present age, in which a new form of the kingdom is being developed, God has temporarily set aside the nation of Israel, His covenant people, and is developing a new kingdom program.

Romans

We must also recognize, however, that the New Testament writers most certainly recognize the existence of the biblical covenants and refer to them when appropriate. For example, Paul, in his great epistle to the Romans, wrote to vindicate the righteousness of God. Paul, writing under the inspiration of the Holy Spirit, argued that God is righteous in judging sinners (1:18–3:20). He is righteous in justifying men by faith (3:21–5:21). He is righteous in providing for a believer's sanctification by identifying him with Christ in His death and resurrection (6:1–8:27). And He is righteous in providing for the believer's ultimate glorification (vv. 28-39).

Paul then showed that God is righteous in dealing with the nation Israel (Rom. 9–11). Paul proved this by pointing out that Israel's hope is based on the covenants and promises God gave to that people (9:4), but that those promises will only be realized by those who have Abraham's faith (vv. 6-13). God is sovereign in His display of mercy (vv. 14-24), and God's mercy may be extended even to the Gentiles (vv. 25-33). Therefore, Israel's covenanted promises are not realized, not because God is unfaithful, but because Israel refused to acknowledge their sin and to believe God (10:1-21).

Paul also said that though Israel has been set aside and is not now experiencing the fulfillment of the covenants, that does not mean God is unfaithful, for some in Israel are experiencing the blessings of salvation (11:1-6). In fact, the setting aside of Israel opens the door of opportunity to the Gentiles to find the salvation through Israel's Messiah (vv. 7-12). Israel, in keeping with the sovereign purposes of God, had been put in the place of blessing and became the channel through which God would accomplish His purposes in the world. Israel is viewed as a branch in a tree, drawing its life from the root. But because the nation was an unproductive branch it was cut off, and wild branches, that is the Gentiles, were grafted in. The Gentiles were put in the place of blessing and could by grace draw life from the root.

Warning was then given to the Gentiles that if they became unfruitful branches, they could be removed just as Israel had been removed. But the setting aside of Israel was not permanent, only temporary. Paul wrote, "If you were cut out of an olive tree that is wild by nature, and contrary to nature were grafted into a cultivated olive tree, how much more readily will these, the natural branches, be grafted into their own olive tree!" (v. 24). Paul assured his readers that, "The Deliverer will come from Zion; He will turn godlessness away from Jacob. And this is My covenant with them when I take away their sins" (vv. 26-27).

We can see clearly that in the analogy of the olive tree, Paul was viewing the root as the covenant that put Israel in a privileged position and guarantees restoration to that position when the Deliverer comes out of Zion and turns away ungodliness from Jacob. God's covenant program was prominent in the apostle's thinking as he vindicated the faithfulness of God in dealing with His people Israel.

Hebrews

Since the writer to the Hebrews was writing to Jewish believers, it's not surprising that we would find reference to the covenants in that epistle.

In Hebrews 5, in order to contrast the priesthood of Christ with the Aaronic priests, the writer referred to Psalm 110:4 where Christ was appointed high priest after the order of Melchizedek (Heb. 5:10). The Melchizedekian priesthood of Christ was then developed in chapters 7–8. The author went on to point out that the Aaronic priests derived their authority from the Mosaic covenant, but of the priesthood of Christ the author says, "The ministry Jesus has received is as superior to theirs as the covenant of which He is mediator is superior to the old one, and it is founded on better promises" (8:6).

Some feel that the "superior covenant" is a reference to the new covenant of Jeremiah 31:31-34, which was instituted for the house of Israel and the house of Judah by the death of Jesus Christ. This understanding may have some validity. However, the better covenant also may refer to the covenant God the Father made with God the Son at the time of His ascension into glory. There are two aspects to this covenant.

First, in Psalm 2:6-9 we read, " 'I have installed My King on Zion, My holy hill.' I will proclaim the decree of the Lord: He said to Me, 'You are My Son; today I have become Your Father. Ask of Me, and I will make the nations Your inheritance, the ends of the earth Your possession. You will rule them with an iron scepter; You will dash them to pieces like pottery.' " Here the psalmist recorded a decree, or covenant, that God the Father made with God the Son, which guarantees the Son the right to rule. The begetting of the Son referred to (v. 7) has to do with appointment to authority. This authority was conferred on Christ at the time of His enthronement at the right hand of the Father following His ascension.

The second aspect of the Father's covenant with the Son is recorded in Psalm 110, where the Father welcomed the Son into glory at the time of His ascension. There, He is seated at the Father's right hand until the time comes for Him to exercise the authority conferred on Him. There, He also is appointed "a Priest forever, in the order of Melchizedek" (v. 4). In other words, by the Father's covenants with the Son, the Son was given authority to rule as King-Priest

It may well be this covenant to which the writer of Hebrews refers in 8:6. The covenant that was the basis of the authority of the Aaronic priest was a conditional covenant, but the covenant that constituted Jesus Christ as King-Priest forever was unconditional, and therefore it is considered a better covenant, established on better promises

The writer to the Hebrews makes specific reference to the new covenant in verses 7–13, where he quoted Jeremiah 31:31-34. And while some say that the writer was quoting Jeremiah's new covenant in order to assert that the church supplants Israel as a covenant people, and that there is no future for the nation Israel, a careful study of the context reveals that this is not the author's intent.

Some to whom the author was writing still believed that the Mosaic covenant was a permanent covenant, and that men therefore were bound by the Mosaic law. It was the author's intent to show that even during the period in which the Mosaic law operated, it was viewed as a temporary, not a permanent, arrangement. He did this by quoting Jeremiah 31:31-34, to show that when God served notice that He would take away the Mosaic covenant and institute a new covenant with the house of Israel and of Judah, He was serving notice that the Mosaic covenant was a temporary and transitory covenant.

This is the point the writer was making when he said, "By calling this covenant 'new,' He has made the first one obsolete; and what is obsolete and aging will soon disappear" (Heb. 8:13). The writer made no attempt whatsoever to show that while the "old" covenant was made with Israel, the new covenant was made with the church so that believers today become God's people in place of Israel. However, he did effectively demonstrate that the Mosaic order was a temporary arrangement and consequently not binding on believers, who are participants in the new form of the kingdom.

In 10:16-17, the writer again made reference to the new covenant, quoting portions of Jeremiah 31:31-34. In that covenant God promised, "Their sins and lawless acts I will remember no more." The author was pointing out the limitations of the Old Testament sacrifices. At best, they provided only a temporary covering for sins, referring of course to that which was accomplished on the day of atonement. In contrast to that, the one sacrifice made by Jesus Christ put sins away permanently.

Therefore, instituting the new covenant with Israel by the death of Jesus Christ means there is no further need for the animal sacrifices required under the Mosaic law. This is the point: "Where these have been forgiven, there is no longer any sacrifice for sin" (Heb. 10:18). The answer, to those who felt that animal sacrifices continued to be efficacious, was to refer to the new covenant of Jeremiah 31:31-34, and to recognize that what was promised there had been instituted. Sins have been put away, so there is no further need for animal sacrifices. The writer further asserted in Hebrews 12:24 that Jesus is "the Mediator of a new covenant." Consequently, God is not dealing with sins on the basis of animal sacrifices but on the basis of the all-sufficient sacrifice of Jesus Christ.

Another reference to the covenant is made in Hebrews 13:20-21: "May the God of peace, who through the blood of the eternal covenant brought back from the dead our Lord Jesus, that great Shepherd of the sheep, equip you with everything good for doing His will, and may He work in us what is pleasing to Him, through Jesus Christ, to whom be glory forever and ever. Amen." The covenant here must of necessity refer to the new covenant of Jeremiah 31:31-34, since the blood of that covenant brings the believer to perfection or maturity. That covenant is referred to here as an "eternal covenant." This new covenant is in contrast to the Mosaic covenant which, as the writer of Hebrews has already shown, was viewed even during its time of operation as a temporary covenant.

This new covenant is an everlasting covenant. It is on the basis of the blood of this covenant that God will deal with sin. The work of Christ was to provide salvation and to bring all things into subjection to God's authority, so that this covenant will never need to be superseded by a better one.

It must be noted that, though reference is made to Israel's covenants in writing epistles to believers in the church, it does not mean that the church becomes Israel or deprives Israel of a future fulfillment of the covenants made with that nation.

Whenever "Israel" is used in the Scripture, whether in reference to an individual (Rom. 11:1) or a nation (9:4), without exception it refers to those who are physical descendants of Abraham. Paul makes this clear when he defines an Israelite as "a descendent of Abraham" in 11:1. Gentiles, by faith in Christ and by virtue of their relationship to Christ, who is a descendant of Abraham, are called the seed of Abraham (Gal. 3:29). The covenants were made with the physical descendants of Abraham. Those related to Abraham by faith may receive benefits from the covenants God gave that people, but they do not supplant the nation as recipients of the covenants.

The covenants did provide for universal blessings, which are applicable to Gentiles and to the church. Universal blessing was part of the Abrahamic promises (Gen. 12:3), which are fulfilled through Christ as Abraham's seed. Universal blessings are promised through the Davidic covenant, for Gentiles will be a part of the kingdom ruled over by David's son (Luke 2:10). These blessings come on the Gentiles who participate in Messiah's earthly rule. Universal blessings are promised through the new covenant (Joel 2:28-32). These blessings will be experienced by Gentiles when the Spirit is poured out on all flesh, so that "everyone who calls on the name of the Lord will be saved" (v. 32). However, the enjoyment of these blessings that flow from Israel's covenants does not mean that the nation will not eventually enjoy the fullness of those blessings into which we enter by faith today.

Four Realms of Authority

Following Israel's rejection of the Messiah, a new form of theocratic administration was instituted. Rather than investing authority in one individual, who would exercise authority in every realm of life, authority was assigned to administrators in four different realms in which we all live: the civil realm, the home, employment, and the religious realm. Those in authority in these four realms are effectively God's administrators, and to them is given the responsibility of curbing lawlessness in those realms and bringing man into subjection to God's authority in each of them.

Civil Government

The first realm is that of civil government. Paul in Romans 13:1-7, and Peter in 1 Peter 2:13-14, set forth a universal principle that all men are to be in subjection to governmental authorities. The reason obedience is commanded is because these authorities are God's ministers (Rom. 13:4).

Obviously a governmental authority is not a minister of the gospel; he is, however, an administrator of the theocracy in that portion of the kingdom to which he has been assigned. It is therefore the responsibility of the civil authority to curb lawlessness, to punish evildoers, to reward those who obey the law, and to provide an atmosphere in which righteousness may flourish and men may live in peace without fear. The authority of the civil ruler extends even to the removal of the lawless by death, the sword being the symbol of that power. As these civil administrators exercise their God-given authority and provide benefits for men as they exercise that authority, they are to be supported by taxes and respected because of the position they hold as God's administrators in His kingdom.

The Home

The second sphere of authority is the sphere of the home. It was developed by Paul in Ephesians 5:21-33 and by Peter in 1 Peter 3:1-7. These writers make it clear that the responsibility to curb lawlessness in the home is placed on the husband. Wives are to be in subjection to their husbands, because in subjecting themselves to their husbands they are showing subjection to the Lord. Similarly, responsibility is placed on children to recognize the authority of parents and to submit themselves to the rule of their parents. In so doing they are subjecting themselves to the rule of God. Sarah's submission to Abraham is given as an example of the submission that God requires (v. 6), and where these principles of submission are practiced the Lord will be ruling in that home. That home, in short, will constitute a miniature theocracy.

Relationships in this sphere were designed according to God's principles of marriage, which were laid down in the Garden of Eden to show the relationship existing between a believer and God. The husband or father portrays the authority that belongs to Christ, and he is to exercise his responsibilities in such a way that reflects the love and care Christ exercises over His own. Likewise, the wife represents the believer, and as the believer is rightly subject to the authority of Christ, so she portrays this relationship by subjection to her husband.

A home is not a Christian home because all in that home are Christians. A home cannot be considered a Christian home and a model of the theocracy unless those in the home are rightly related to each other according to God's established laws of marriage. Peter pointed out that one of the practical results of this relationship will be that an unbelieving husband may be brought to the Lord by the gracious submission of the wife to his authority.

It is crucial to recognize that the wife was *not* subjected to the authority of her husband as a punishment imposed on Eve for her rebellion against the revealed law of God. Rather, it was as a protection for her. She was relieved of the responsibility of making decisions. That responsibility is placed on her husband. Her responsibility is to submit to his protection and oversight. In this arrangement, the more difficult responsibility is given to the husband, who is commanded to love his wife as Christ also loved the church (Eph. 5:25).

Employer and Employee

The third realm in which lawlessness may abound, and in which God assigns administrative authority, is in the sphere of employment.

Paul dealt with this in Ephesians 6:5-9, while Peter addressed it in 1 Peter 2:18-20. The apostles commanded slaves and hired servants to recognize and to submit to the authority of their masters or employers because God has given administrative responsibility in the form of the theocracy to the employer in that realm. The submission that is given by the employee to the employer is the same submission he is expected to give to Christ. In submitting to Christ's administrator, he is submitting himself to Christ. Consequently any service that the employee renders his employer is viewed as a service for Christ.

Of course, an employer is responsible to treat employees as Christ would treat them, and in fact he is reminded that he is a servant of a Master who is in heaven. Thus they are Christ's representatives in that realm as theocratic administrators.

The Church

The fourth and final realm in which lawlessness may occur is within the religious realm, or the church itself. Peter in 1 Peter 5:1-7 deals with this sphere.

The elders with whom Peter identified himself were overseers of the flock. The flock refers to the body of believers, meaning that the elders are responsible to oversee the flock, so as to curb lawlessness and to bring those in the flock into subjection to the authority of Jesus Christ. It is their responsibility to feed the flock. The word "feed" includes the thought of taking care of every need the flock may have. They need to be fed, they need to be watered, they need to be led and guided, and they need to be corrected or disciplined. These are the responsibilities resting on those who are administrators in this part of the theocracy.

Peter commanded the younger ones (this would refer to the members of the flock) to submit themselves to the elders (v. 5). Logically, submission given by members of the flock to their shepherds is submission to Christ. When this proper relationship exists in the church we find a perfect miniature theocracy.

Thus we see that by dividing authority into the civil realm, the realm of the home, the realm of employment, and the realm of the church, administration is provided in all the spheres in which we live. The principle is the same in each sphere: *Submission to the administrator is submission to Christ.* Through this process Christ is effectively ruling through delegated representatives, to provide a kingdom in which peace prevails and righteousness persists, in which lawlessness is curbed, and in which those living in that kingdom can enjoy the blessings of Christ's rule.

Summary

God, in previous forms of theocratic administration, had centralized the authority in one individual or in one arrangement (as in human government). However, in the present age He has divided authority in four different realms, thus limiting the area committed to any administrator in the kingdom. The responsibility of those administrators is the same in any previous form: to bring those under their authority into submission to God, to maintain law and order, and to provide an atmosphere in which men may live in peace, because they are in subjection to appointed human authority and consequently to divine authority.

Thus we conclude that the church is a part of a kingdom of the God of heaven, falling in the inter-advent period. It was an unrevealed mystery in the Old Testament, but it was necessitated by Israel's rejection of the Messiah, which caused the postponement of the promised and covenant form of the kingdom, which will be inaugurated by the appearance of the King of kings and Lord of lords at His second advent.

The Eternal Kingdom

While the major emphasis in the epistles is on the present form of the kingdom, there is an anticipation of the merger of the present form of the kingdom into the Davidic kingdom to be established at the second advent of the Messiah, and the eventual merger of that Davidic kingdom into the eternal kingdom over which Messiah will rule by divine appointment. Paul sees this in 1 Corinthians 15:27-28, where at the end of His earthly rule, when all has been brought into subjection to the Father, either willingly or through judgment, the Father will assign rulership over the eternal kingdom to the Son. Thus, for the unending ages of eternity, God's fight to rule will be recognized. All in that kingdom will be in submission to Him and will join in worship of the Sovereign forever.

John S. Feinberg

Arguing About the Rapture: Who Must Prove What and How

_____*OVERVIEW*

What are the logical advantages and strengths of the pretribulational position? In this essay, Dr. Feinberg carefully evaluates the major strengths and weaknesses of the pre-, mid-, and posttribulational perspectives. If there is going to be meaningful discussion of the rapture positions there must be agreement on the proper methodology. Clear thinking enhances clear conclusions, which must prevail if the pretribulational rapture is going to be seriously proclaimed.

*S*ome years ago the symposium on the rapture of the church entitled *The Rapture—Pre-, Mid-, or Post-Tribulational?* by Gleason Archer, Paul Feinberg, and Douglas Moo, was published. The book is intriguing and helpful from a number of standpoints. It offers not only position papers but a chance for each author to interact with opposing views. It is generally well argued and makes a good contribution to the issue.

Many who read the book think that no one won this debate. I think there are various reasons for that, but one of the most important is that the three authors use different strategies in arguing their positions. As a result, one sees two or three different sets of arguments that do not necessarily address one another. As a result, readers may have difficulty evaluating who has made the best case, since the argument strategies are so different. Though some might think this unfortunate, I think it extremely important, for it vividly highlights different strategies and methodologies in arguing for one's views on the rapture. In so doing, it sheds light on what we all ought to be doing as we confront this issue.

In what follows I want first to make two methodological points as well as a theological and logical one. As to the former, I wish to: 1) lay bare the strategies that are typically used in arguing one's views on the rapture, and 2) suggest who is right and who is wrong. As to the latter, after clarifying methodology, I wish to apply the methodological points to the theological question of what one would have to prove in order to establish his position as correct. In so doing, I hope to set an agenda for discussing this issue, which I think will help us make greater headway than before. Finally, I want to give a general assessment of which position is best able to make its case.

Methodologies and Strategies

The difference in methodology is most strikingly illustrated by comparing Moo's piece with Feinberg's. Moo's discussion, as with many posttribulationists, proceeds by going to the passages that speak about the coming (*parousia*) of the Lord. Such passages typically deal with the second advent, which, of course, occurs at the end of the Tribulation. No clear, undisputed rapture passage (e.g., 1 Thess. 4:13-18, 1 Cor. 15:51ff) tells us whether the event under discussion is pre-, mid-, or posttribulational. Consequently, Moo offers a careful exegesis of parousia (coming) and rapture passages to show that the similarities between the two passages are so great that one must see the events of which they speak as occurring at the same time.[1] Typically, posttribulationists have relied heavily on exegesis of such passages to support their position. See, for example, J. Barton Payne's *The Imminent Appearing of Christ,* as well as the lengthy exegetical sections on Thessalonians, Revelation, and the Olivet discourse in Robert Gundry's *The Church and the Tribulation.*

On the other hand, Feinberg's procedure is different. Since true propositions accurately reflect the world, and since in the world there are no contradictory states of affairs, it is understood that if a view is correct it will not contradict other known truths. Thus, not only must a viewpoint fit the facts, but its implications must not contradict any other known truth. Feinberg takes this point seriously and structures a *reductio ad absurdum* argument. Granting the assumption that post- or midtribulationism is correct, let's see how they fit with others' theological and biblical principles that we know to be true. We'll see that those accepted truths do not fit with posttribulationism, and (in some cases) fit only slightly better with midtribulationism. Therefore, those views are wrong and pretribulationism, which does fit those other truths, must be correct. Such is a *reductio* type of argument.

Let me illustrate in regard to Feinberg. Feinberg's procedure is not to go to parousia passages and test them in the way Moo does. Instead, he appeals to such biblical teachings as the church's promised exemption from God's wrath, and the biblical teaching that there will be people who enter the millennial kingdom in nonglorified bodies. Granting these biblical and theological truths, Feinberg argues that the former point really doesn't square with either a mid- or posttrib position, and the latter really doesn't fit a posttrib view. But, since a truth cannot contradict some other known truth, post- and midtribulationism must be wrong. Pretribulationism, on the other hand, has no problem, Feinberg argues, with these theological truths. They actually provide support for pretribulationism.[2]

Feinberg's general strategy (a focus on theological and biblical truths to see how they square with the various views on the time of Christ's coming), is fairly typical of pretribulational handlings of the rapture question (cf. Walvoord's *The Rapture Question)*. There are, of course, some notable exceptions to these pretrib and posttrib strategies. For example, in Allan Beechick's *The Pretribulation Rapture,* the defense of a pretrib rapture includes an extended exegesis of parousia (coming) passages. On the other side of the question, Gundry, having started out as pretrib, and well aware of pretrib arguments, includes many chapters which address the theological ramifications of his views.

Archer's strategy is a bit different yet. He spends most of his time presenting arguments as to why pre- and posttrib views either cannot be correct or are at least very improbable. His arguments appeal both to theological and biblical truths other than to direct teachings about the rapture, and the second advent, and to some specific exegesis of parousia (coming) passages. His basic strategy is to show that opposing views are at best highly improbable, whereas his own view is the most satisfactory in regard to the issues he raises. Archer then raises several brief lines of positive support for his view.[3] As an interesting sidelight, the strategy of Norman B. Harrison (another midtribulationist) in *The End* is different again. When Harrison approaches the book of Revelation, he raises the rapture issue and attempts to show how passages like Revelation 4 do not support pretribulationism, whereas passages such as Revelation 11 do support midtribulationism.

The reason for noting different strategies is not to suggest that pretribulationists do not care about exegesis, or that posttribs do not care about theology, or that midtribs are, as we might suspect, in the middle on this methodological point. The reason is to point out the different methodologies used and to ask which is correct. That brings me to a second methodological point.

Granting what I have said about the methodologies generally used in this discussion, which is correct? In order to answer that, we must address a more fundamental question; namely, how should one formulate any doctrine? The answer is clear. Go first to those portions of Scripture that directly speak to the topic. For example, if one is formulating a doctrine of God, he should go to passages that directly speak of the nature of God, rather than about the nature of the church or of Scripture. In regard to the rapture, the principle is equally applicable. Go first to those passages that speak directly about the rapture and return of the Lord.

Proper methodology does not stop at this point, however. While one should begin with passages that speak directly about the doctrine under consideration, one must also pay attention to the implications of the doctrine. This is especially important if, as in the case of the rapture, the passages about the rapture and return of the Lord do not determine the question of the rapture's timing in relation to the time of the Tribulation. If one is working, for example, on the doctrine of divine sovereignty, he cannot merely look at passages that speak about God's control. He must also consider passages on human freedom. A doctrine of divine sovereignty that contradicts biblical teaching on human freedom is unwanted. Implications and relations of doctrines to one another are crucial. If one's position on a given theological issue is correct, it will fit with other known theological and biblical truths rather than contradict them.

As a reminder of this important methodological point, remember how many inerrantists respond to those who reject inerrancy on the grounds that the phenomena of Scripture contradict inerrancy. Methodologically, the appropriate response is that one must begin to formulate the doctrine of Scripture on the basis of passages that really address the nature of Scripture (e.g., 2 Tim. 3:16; 2 Pet. 1:21, John 17:17), rather than starting with passages about mustard seeds and cocks crowing. Inerrantists stress that the former, since they directly address the nature of Scripture, must be normative, while the latter must be interpreted in the light of the former. We need to follow the same methodology when handling other doctrines like the rapture.

The relation of the foregoing to the rapture issue should be obvious. Methodologically speaking, it is most appropriate to begin with the passages that directly speak about the event(s) in question—rapture, second advent, and Tribulation. Having formulated the clearest notion we can about the rapture and its relation to the second advent and Tribulation on the basis of careful exegesis of rapture and second advent passages, we must then look at the implications of our position on the rapture. If it does not square with other biblical teachings, then there is error somewhere. And, since the rapture is nowhere clearly and explicitly dated in Scripture, it is probably more likely than not that the mistake is in relation to our view of the rapture's timing.

The key point for all sides to remember is that proper theological methodology dare not allow us to ignore *either* the rapture and parousia passages or the doctrines that have implications for one's views on the rapture and second advent. Although study should begin with passages that speak directly to the topic at hand, both are equally important. It is surely no victory to uphold one's views on the timing of the rapture at the expense of denying what God's Word says, for example, about the relation of the church to God's judgmental wrath.

What lessons should we learn from this methodological point? For the pretrib (and probably midtribs as well), there is a need to get at the task of exegesis in regard to rapture and second advent passages. If posttribs are right that the similarity between the two types of passages is so great as to render them identical, then the battle is lost before the discussion ever can turn to the theological implications of the positions. What pretribs must do is squarely face those passages and see whether there is enough dissimilarity between rapture and second advent passages to warrant the possibility that the two events could occur at significantly separate times (like seven years apart). Midtribs need to do the same thing. And both pretribs and midtribs should *begin* at this point. They should not ignore it or address it at the end of the discussion. I doubt that pretribs and midtribs have much hope of convincing posttribs of very much so long as they shy away from that exegetical task.

For the posttrib, the lesson is a bit different but equally important. Posttribs must take more seriously questions about non-glorified bodies to populate the millennial kingdom and the question of God's wrath. Too often such issues have simply been ignored or relegated to a position of virtual insignificance. There is nothing wrong with beginning with the parousia passages as the posttrib wants; in fact, I am willing to grant that such is preferable in terms of proper theological method. But the posttrib needs to wrestle much more seriously than he has with the theological issues that pretribs and midtribs raise for him. And I doubt that posttribs have much hope of convincing pre- and midtribs of much, unless they start viewing these issues as more than minor problems for their view. To his credit, Feinberg does talk about dissimilarities between rapture and second advent passages, and Moo does somewhat address theological issues (especially in his responses), but in both cases the respective issues are treated as somewhat secondary.

All of this amounts to two important points. In regard to whose methodology is right, I am suggesting that in a way no one is entirely right or entirely wrong as we look at the way the positions are argued. Everyone needs to modify his methodology to some extent. The other point grows out of this. If the positions ever hope seriously to engage one another in dialogue, and even come to an agreement on this issue, they must take more seriously one another's strongest arguments (and the methodological points I have made about how to formulate doctrines, which points undergird the strongest arguments of the respective positions). It only stands to reason that if you tell me your strongest arguments for your view, and I basically shift the ground of the debate to my strongest arguments, we are not likely to convince one another of much.

What Must Be Proved?

One could grant my methodological points and still be puzzled about what he should attempt to prove with respect to his position. The pretrib might promise to look more closely at the exegesis of rapture and parousia passages, but he may wonder what he must prove about them. That brings me to the logical and theological aspects of this study. If one takes my methodological points seriously, what would it take, using the suggested methodology, to establish a particular position on the rapture as the most probable one (or even, perhaps, the correct one)? In what follows, I am not suggesting that nothing else could be offered as an argument for the three positions; I am only noting the issues that must be handled, regardless of whatever else is discussed.

What, then, must pretribs prove? Pretribulationists first should handle the parousia and rapture passages. Since second advent passages refer to the end of the Tribulation, and since clear rapture passages give no indication as to the time of the rapture, pretribulationists cannot expect to prove their position solely on the basis of these passages. Instead, all they can hope to show (and what they had better show) from an exegesis of these passages is that their view is not impossible. But what would make their view impossible? If it should be discovered that the similarity between clear second advent and clear rapture passages is so great as to warrant the conclusion that the events spoken of in both kinds of passages are identical, then pretribulationism would be impossible. As already noted, this is precisely what posttribs try to establish.

193

With this in mind, the pretribulationist must show that there is enough dissimilarity between clear rapture and clear second advent passages as to warrant the claim that the two kinds of passages *could* be speaking about two events, which *could* occur at different times. The pretribulationist does not have to prove at this point (and probably cannot) that the two events *must* occur at different times, but only that the exegetical data from rapture and second advent passages do not make it impossible for the events to occur at different times. If he can do that, the pretribulationist has shown that his view is not impossible. And he has answered the posttribulationist's strongest line of evidence.

After handling exegesis of rapture and second advent passages, the next move is to discuss various theological and biblical issues that have implications for the rapture issue. The pretrib must try not only to show that his position fits with those other biblical truths, but also that his opponents' views cannot be synthesized with those other issues, or at least not so well as his views can. In particular, the pretribulationist should raise the following four issues: 1) the wrath of God issue; 2) the non-glorified bodies to enter the millennial kingdom issue; 3) the timing of the marriage supper of the Lamb; 4) the timing of the bema seat judgment for the church. With regard to the first, the church is promised exemption from God's judgmental wrath (1 Thess. 1:10; 5:9). But God's judgmental wrath is poured out during the Tribulation. How, then, can God's tribulational wrath be avoided? Each rapture position has an answer. The pretribulationist needs to show that his is the most likely and that the others are either clearly false or very unlikely.

As to the non-glorified bodies, Scripture shows that some people will enter the millennial kingdom in natural bodies and then give birth to children (Isa. 65:20). Some of those children will rebel against the Lord (Rev. 20:7-10). But people in glorified bodies cannot give birth, nor do they sin. Thus, there must be some people who enter the kingdom in non-glorified bodies. But everyone who is raptured is glorified. So, if the rapture occurs posttribulationally, it seems that no one is left to enter the millennial kingdom in a non-glorified body. All rapture positions must confront this problem, and all have an answer. The pretrib must show his to be the best, if he can.

Third, given the context of the marriage supper of the Lamb as that of heaven (Rev. 19:1-10), followed by the second advent at the end of the Tribulation, and given semitic customs surrounding marriage,[4] which John most likely would have had in mind as he wrote Revelation 19, it appears that the church must be in heaven for this event somewhat prior to the end of the Tribulation. But how is one to explain the church's presence in heaven prior to the second advent? The rapture seems the most likely answer. But such an answer creates problems for posttribulationism, even if it does not for midtribulationism. The pretrib needs to discuss the timing and location of this event and to show, if he can, why his view can handle this issue better than other views.

Finally, Paul states that all believers must stand before the judgment seat of Christ. At that time our works will be evaluated by Christ and rewarded. When is that event most likely to occur? If during the kingdom, that needs to be proved. If during the Tribulation, while the church is in heaven, that needs to be proved. The former position surely fits better with posttribulationism than does the latter. The former view also fits either pre- or midtribulationism. The latter view fits equally well with pre- or midtribulationism, but it creates problems for posttribulationism. The pretrib needs to offer his answer and to show why it is the best of the possible answers.

If the pretrib can establish what I have suggested about the parousia and rapture passages, and if his answers to the theological issues can be shown to be the best of the three positions, then in essence he has won the debate. But what must the midtrib prove to establish his position as best? In regard to the parousia and rapture passages, he must by careful exegesis demonstrate the same thing the pretrib hopes to establish. That is, he must show that his position is not impossible, because the passages are not so similar as to rule out any possibility that the rapture could occur at a different time than the second advent.

Second, midtribulationists sometimes argue their case by associating the rapture trumpet with the seventh trumpet of Revelation, arguing that all occur at the midpoint of the Tribulation. Midtribs might even associate the last trump of the rapture with the trumpet of Matthew 24:31. All of this suggests several things the midtrib must do if he uses this line of argument. He must, for instance, demonstrate that the trumpet judgments of Revelation end at the middle of the Tribulation. Moreover, he must give exegetical reasons for associating the rapture trump with the seventh judgmental trump of Revelation. And if he associates all of these trumps with

Matthew 24:31, he must address the following problem: he must explain how he has avoided posttribulationism (since Matthew 24:31 is posttribulational). And if he maintains that the seventh trumpet and the rapture trumpet are the last trump, he must explain in what sense it is the last trump since there is still one more trumpet (Matthew 24:31) blown at the end of the Tribulation. This does not per se prove that the problems are unanswerable, but only that they must be confronted by a midtrib who wishes to argue his case by associating the various scriptural trumpets. As a sidelight, if the pretrib wants to correlate the trumpets of Scripture, he must also explain how the rapture trump can be the last trump when he believes it is blown seven years prior to the trump at the end of the Tribulation (Matthew 24:31). Since he doesn't associate the rapture trump with any of the trumpet judgments of Revelation, he need not show that the seventh trumpet judgment (regardless of when it occurs in the Tribulation) is the same as the rapture trumpet.

Finally, the midtrib must confront some theological issues. In addition to the four raised already, he must, if he is a dispensationalist, explain why the church was not present in the first 69 of Daniel's 70 weeks, but now is both in and taken out of Daniel's seventieth week. Nondispensational midtribs need not worry about this issue, but dispensational midtribs must address it. Midtribs must not only address these issues, they must show that their answers are better than their opponents' answers.

What about posttribulationists? What must they prove to establish their view? They should begin with an exegesis of parousia and rapture passages, but their task is not to prove that a rapture *could* be posttribulational, just as is the second advent. Since no passage explicitly dates the rapture, prima facie there is no impossibility about the rapture and second advent occurring at the same time. Instead, the posttrib needs to show that the rapture and second advent passages are so similar as to warrant the conclusion that they are actually speaking of the same time and the same event. The posttrib needs to do this for three reasons: 1) to eliminate the other views as incorrect; 2) this line of evidence clearly is the posttrib's best argument for his position, so he needs to make the most of it; 3) when he gets to the theological implications of his view, he faces the pretribs' strongest arguments against his position.

Having established whatever he can by means of this exegesis, the posttrib must still confront the theological issues. Even if he thinks he has established by exegesis that rapture and second advent passages speak about an identical time, proper theological method demands that he not ignore the implications of his view for other biblical and theological truths. If his view does not square with them, then despite what he thinks he has proved by his exegesis, there is still some problem with his views. Specifically, the posttrib must address the four theological and biblical issues raised earlier. In addition, if he is a dispensationalist (as Gundry claimed to be), he must explain why it is appropriate to see the church as absent from the first 69 of Daniel's 70 weeks but then present during the seventieth week. The posttrib must not only show that he can answer these theological issues, but as with pre- and midtribs, he must show that his answers are better than his opponents' responses.

By raising just the exegetical and theological issues I have mentioned, I do not mean to suggest that nothing else could be discussed in regard to the rapture. My point is merely that these seem to be the issues that are most at the core of the debate, regardless of what one holds on other matters. For example, some may think imminency is crucial to the debate and must be discussed, but I do not. On the one hand, even if one can prove that the Bible teaches imminency, I am not convinced that midtribs or posttribs cannot synthesize such a notion with their positions. As we all know, there are a number of different ways to define imminency. On the other hand, even if one could prove imminency wrong, that still would not preclude the rapture from occurring pretribulationally, whenever it does occur Consequently, though I believe in an imminent rapture, and think the matter of imminency is relevant to this debate, I do not see it as at the core of the debate.

Assessing the Positions

In regard to the central issues at stake in this debate, which side is best able to demonstrate what it needs to establish? A detailed answer is the subject of future study, but let me offer some initial words of assessment. As might be expected, I believe pretribulationism fares the best, and I need to explain why.

As to the exegesis of rapture and second advent passages, I do not think the posttribulationist can make his case that the two types of passages are so similar so as to conclude that the events of which they speak are identical. There are some differences between the passages that seem to make a difference. I mention three in particular. First, in the clear rapture passages (1 Thess. 4:13-18; 1 Cor. 15:51-55; John 14:1-3), the Lord's coming is presented as a coming in blessing for the saints. Nothing is said about His coming for judgment. On the other hand, passages about the second advent speak of the Lord's coming in judgment upon His enemies (Rev. 19:11ff; Joel 3:12-16; Zech. 14:3-5). Even Matthew 24:30-31, which occurs at the end of the Tribulation, invokes Zechariah 12:10, but the context of the event in Zechariah 12:10 is one in which the Lord goes forth to fight for his people Israel to destroy her enemies (see the whole context of Zechariah 12 and 14, which speak of the same events). Of course, even though the clear rapture passages do not mention any divine judgment when Christ comes for his people, it is surely possible that there might be judgment anyway. But it is just as possible that the reason no judgment is mentioned along with the coming at the rapture is that there is none. Not only is this possible, but it seems likely, in that when the posttribulational coming of the Lord is mentioned, invariably the biblical writer tells us that Christ is coming to judge the nations. Clearly, the second advent is a coming in judgment. But it seems that the rapture is not a coming in judgment, and that means it is possible that the two events are two separate events occurring at separate times.

A second difference is that second advent passages are invariably followed by talk of setting up the kingdom after the Lord's return (e.g., Matt. 24:31; 25:31ff; Zech. 14; Joel 3; Rev. 19–20). So, the second advent is preparatory to the establishment of the millennial kingdom. On the other hand, clear rapture passages give no hint that after the rapture the Lord establishes the kingdom. Granted, it is possible that the kingdom will follow the rapture, but it is also possible that the reason for the silence on the matter is that the kingdom does not immediately follow the rapture. At any rate, this is a significant difference between rapture and second advent passages, and it is a difference that makes it possible for the events to be at two separate times. And all the pretrib needs to show from exegesis of rapture and second advent passages is that it is *possible* that the events occur at different times

Third, it is very clear from 1 Thessalonians 4:13-18 and 1 Corinthians 15:51ff that at the rapture those gathered to the Lord will be glorified. On the other hand, second advent passages say nothing about anyone (living or dead) receiving a glorified body. The closest we come to it is Matthew 24:31, but all that verse says is that the elect will be gathered together. The imagery of the four winds and of one end of heaven to another is clearly poetic, suggesting that the Lord will gather the elect from wherever they are scattered at that time. It does not have to mean that any of the elect involved are literally in heaven at the time of the gathering (which would, I take it, necessitate being resurrected and glorified when they are gathered). So there is no indication that this verse necessitates giving the elect a glorified body. Again we see a difference. One event involves resurrection of dead saints and glorification of living and dead saints. The other event necessitates no resurrection of anyone. There is no hint in passages speaking about that event that anyone is glorified. Is it possible that someone gets a glorified body at the second advent, anyway? Perhaps, but where is the evidence for it? The lack of mention of any resurrection and any glorifying of bodies at the second advent surely makes it *possible* that this does not happen. This in turn makes it *possible* that the second advent and the rapture are two separate events occurring at separate times. As we have said, all that is necessary for pretribs and midtribs is that the exegesis of key rapture and second advent passages not make their positions impossible.

One further word is needed about Matthew 24:31. Some will say that it is clearly posttribulational, and that it clearly mentions gathering the elect. Doesn't this gathering of the elect with a trumpet call automatically equate this event with the gathering at the rapture? Not at all, for several reasons. As already mentioned, there is no indication that this gathering includes resurrecting and glorifying anyone, but the rapture includes those events. Second, just because a trumpet is mentioned in Matthew 24:31 and 1 Thessalonians 4:16 does not mean the events are the same. If we followed the logic that says the events are the same because there is a trumpet, then we would have to equate these passages with all seven trumpet judgments, which is, of course, absurd. Some will argue that it is not just that a trumpet is mentioned, but that a trumpet is used to gather the elect. This makes the Matthew 24 and 1 Thessalonians 4 passages different from the trumpet judgments. Indeed, it does, but I have already explained several respects in which the gatherings in 1 Thessalonians 4 and Matthew 24 still differ from one another. Gathering believers by a trumpet blast is not enough to guarantee that the events are the same.

A final point of difference between the Matthew 24: 31 gathering and the 1 Thessalonians 4 gathering is that in the former the gathering appears to be preparatory to the judgment of the sheep and goats (Matthew 25:31ff), and that judgment is preparatory to beginning the kingdom. Though there are many verses between Matthew 24:31 and 25:31, they are parables speaking primarily about the need for readiness at the Lord's return. Chronologically, there is no indication that the events of Matthew 25:31ff come long after 24:31. The Matthew 24:31 gathering seems to precede God's judgment of the nations. On the other hand, the gathering to the Lord mentioned in the clear rapture passages does not say that this event is preparatory to the judgment of the sheep and goats, or to the start of the kingdom. It could be the prelude to those events, but it need not be. Lack of mention of those events in conjunction with the rapture makes it at least *possible* that those events are not connected with the timing of the rapture. And if they are not connected, then it is possible that Matthew 24: 31 and 1 Thessalonians 4 speak of different times and different events. All the pretrib needs to show from his exegesis is that it *is possible* that these passages speak about two different events at two different times.

I conclude from this brief comparison of clear rapture passages with clear second advent passages that the similarities do not make either pretribulationism or midtribulationism impossible.[5] Among other things, that means that posttribulationism cannot make a conclusive case for its position solely on the basis of an exegesis of these passages. The posttribulationist's handling of those passages is, of course, a possible way to interpret them. But, as we have seen, it is not the only way. What the posttrib needed to show was that his handling of those passages was the *only* possible way to interpret them. Yet that is not so. The pre- and midtrib positions are still alive.

What happens when we turn to the theological issues? Which position handles these the best? Let us turn first to the need for nonglorified bodies to enter the millennial kingdom. According to pretribulationism, after the rapture the Tribulation begins. The gospel is preached throughout the Tribulation and there are some who believe. Though many who believe are killed (e.g., Revelation 13:7,15), not all believers are killed during the Tribulation. Those who live through the Tribulation go into the kingdom in natural bodies. In addition, some people accept the Lord when he returns at the end of the Tribulation (e.g., Zech. 12:10). Many of these people do not die at that point, and there is no evidence that they are given a glorified body when they receive Christ. These people are also available to go into the kingdom in natural bodies. For a pretrib position, there are seven years to get people saved prior to the kingdom, and some of those can go into the kingdom in natural bodies.

A midtrib position can also handle this problem. According to a midtrib, anyone saved in the first three-and-a-half years of the Tribulation is a member of the church and goes to be with the Lord at the midtribulational rapture. But there are still three-and-a-half more years of Tribulation left for other people to be saved. It is likely that some of those saved in the last three-and-a-half years make it to the end of the Tribulation without dying, especially since many are saved at the second advent. Midtribs have three-and-a-half years after the rapture to account for some believers who can go into the kingdom in natural bodies.

The position that is really in trouble with respect to this issue is the posttribulation rapture view. If everyone who goes at the rapture is glorified, and if the rapture occurs at the end of the Tribulation, who is left to enter the kingdom in a natural body? All believers will have been raptured and glorified by that time. Most posttribs don't seem to recognize the problem. To his credit Gundry does, and he offers four different answers. Let's see whether any work.

First, Gundry says that maybe the 144,000 who are protected throughout the Tribulation are those who go into the kingdom in natural bodies.[6] The main problem with this is that Scripture says they are all men, and they are all celibate (Rev. 14:4). So even if the 144,000 go into the kingdom in natural bodies, since they are all men, no children will be forthcoming from just them!

Gundry's second answer is that perhaps between the second advent and the start of the kingdom not all rebels will be destroyed. Maybe, then, some nonbelievers will enter the kingdom in natural bodies and give birth to children.[7] This may be the most amazing of all of Gundry's suggestions. When John the Baptist preached the coming of the kingdom, he announced the need to repent. When Jesus came and offered himself as King, he demanded a right spiritual relationship with God in order to enter the kingdom. No one can be a member of the church (and thereby a member of the kingdom, now or later) unless he meets the spiritual entrance requirements of the kingdom. Dispensational pretribulationists typically say that

Christ offered the full-blown kingdom at his first coming but postponed it because Israel refused to meet the spiritual entrance requirements of the kingdom. Despite all of this, Gundry wants us to believe that when the earthly kingdom actually arrives, God will change the rules for entrance. I find that hard to believe. If Christ begins His earthly reign with inhabitants of the kingdom who reject Him, then why not just begin the earthly reign 2000 years ago, despite his rejection by Israel as a whole? If some people can get into the kingdom at its outset without meeting its spiritual entrance requirements, then why not the Jews of Jesus' own day? This suggestion by Gundry doesn't make sense.

Gundry's third solution is that Jews saved during the Tribulation will be raptured with the church posttribulationally. However, at the second advent many Jews will turn to Christ when they look on him whom they have pierced (Zech. 12:10). It is these Jews who will enter the kingdom in natural bodies.[8] Though this may sound promising, it runs into significant problems in light of Gundry's understanding of Matthew 24. According to Gundry, the rapture occurs at Matthew 24:31,[9] and this is what we would expect him to say. However, one page later he explains that Matthew 24:30 is an allusion to Zechariah 12:10, the salvation of Israel at the end of the Tribulation. The problem should be obvious. If Matthew 24:30 refers to the salvation of Israel, then at the rapture (v. 31), those saved in Zechariah 12:10 and Matthew 24:30 will be raptured and glorified. So, the problem of unglorified bodies to enter the kingdom still remains.

There is another problem with this suggestion. Early in his book (p. 24) Gundry speaks of the salvation of Israel at the end of the Tribulation when Jesus returns at the second advent. He says these saved Israelites will not be raptured, because the rapture has already occurred before they turn to Christ. So the order of events is: rapture, salvation of Israel, and second advent. However, his later claim that Matthew 24:31 is the rapture, and that 24:30 is the salvation of Israel, means that Israel's salvation must precede the rapture. Again the problem should be obvious. Early in the book, Gundry says the salvation of Israel is after the rapture, whereas later he says it is before the rapture. You cannot have it both ways. And you surely cannot appeal to the salvation of these Jews as the answer to how to get unglorified people into the kingdom, if you aren't sure exactly whether their salvation comes before or after the rapture!

Gundry's final suggestion stems from Daniel 12:11-12. There is a time gap of some 75 days, according to Gundry, between the return of the Lord at the second advent and the start of the kingdom. Gundry wonders whether during this time gap some of the rebels will turn to Christ, and if they, therefore, will be the ones who go into the kingdom in natural bodies[10] (they are the sheep at the judgment of the sheep and goats). In some ways this is the most promising of Gundry's suggestions. There is little question that there is a time gap as indicated by Daniel 12:11-12. Moreover, the sheep and goats' judgment seems to occur prior to the setup of the kingdom, and there are both sheep and goats present at that judgment. Where would the sheep have come from? If they had been saved *during* the Tribulation, on a posttrib position they would have been raptured at the second advent, so there would be no Tribulation saints left in non-glorified bodies. But anyone saved *after* the second advent would not be raptured, and, hence, would not get a glorified body at that time. So all of this is possible. But we want to know which position has the most probable synthesis of this issue with the timing of the rapture. At this point, Gundry's view runs into trouble.

An initial problem is that Gundry says that the judgment of the sheep and goats comes at the end of the millennial kingdom (he associates it with the great white throne judgment of Revelation 20:11-15). But if that is so, then appeal to the judgment of the sheep and goats will prove nothing about how many people may or may not have gotten saved during the 75 days between the second advent and beginning of the kingdom. But perhaps the major difficulty with this suggestion is that there is no Scripture anywhere that says evangelism will occur during the 75-day interval. It is possible, but where is the biblical evidence? It is hard to make a case for any position from silence, since silence is consistent with everything and thus proves nothing.

So far, posttribulationists have not offered an adequate answer to how their view on the rapture allows time for people to be saved and enter the kingdom in natural bodies. But how do the various rapture positions fit with the marriage supper of the Lamb and the bema seat judgment? Here pretribs must admit that midtribs can handle these truths just as easily as can pretribulationism. Whether the gap between rapture and second advent is three-and-one-half or seven years, there is time for the church to be in heaven, appear at the bema seat judgment, and attend her wedding feast (Rev. 19:7-10). On the other hand, these two issues appear to be a problem for the posttrib position. Most likely, posttribs will claim that these events (at least the bema seat judgment) could occur after the return of the Lord at the second advent and the establishment of the kingdom. But since the Lord returns and sets up the kingdom on earth, it is hard to see how the marriage supper occurs at that time, since the scene of that event is clearly heaven (Rev. 19:1ff). Furthermore, after that event, the Lord rides out of heaven with His armies to destroy the wicked at the end of the Tribulation. So it is hard to see how the marriage supper can occur on earth after the second advent. And, if the marriage supper is in heaven before the second advent, then the church must have been raptured prior to the end of the Tribulation. Posttribulationism faces a significant problem with this issue.

Can the posttrib make a case for the bema seat judgment occurring after the second advent? Here again there are problems. If the posttrib says the judgment of the sheep, at the sheep and goats' judgment, is the bema seat, that is possible but not likely. Neither 1 Corinthians 3:12-15 or 2 Corinthians 5:10 even vaguely hint that there will be nonbelievers present at this event, but at the Matthew 25 judgment there clearly are nonbelievers (goats) present. Even if one wants to read nonbelievers into the 1 and 2 Corinthians passages, there is a further problem with seeing the bema seat judgment either at the second advent or early in the kingdom. In Revelation 19:7-10 we see the church at the marriage feast. She is adorned in her wedding gown, which represents the righteous deeds of the church. I take it that because the bride is wearing the gown she has already received her recognition and rewards for her righteous deeds.

Moreover, in Revelation 19:11ff, when the Lord rides out of heaven, He is accompanied with the armies of heaven. Revelation 19:14 says the armies were clothed in linen, white and clean. This is the same way the bride is described at the marriage supper (Rev. 19:8). Now, it is likely that the armies of heaven include angels, but it is just as likely that some of those clothed in linen, white and clean, are not angels but members of the church. If that is so, when the church rides out of heaven, at the *end of the tribulation* to do battle with the enemies of God, it has already received its reward and recognition for its faithful deeds of service. When would that have occurred? At the bema seat judgment. And this means that the bema seat judgment cannot occur after the return of the Lord at the second advent (either at the judgment of the sheep and goats, or early in the kingdom), but before the return.

I conclude, then, that posttribulationism is in serious trouble with respect to fitting both the marriage supper of the Lamb and the bema seat judgment into its framework. In regard to the three theological issues we have discussed, so far pre- and midtribulationism fare equally well. However, I think midtribulationism and posttribulationism are both in trouble with respect to the wrath of God issue.

Before turning to that matter, let me address other items that are problems for midtribulationism. First, how can a midtrib who is a dispensationalist justify keeping the church out of the first 69 of Daniel's 70 weeks, and then putting it in only to take it out in the middle of the seventieth week? Nondispensational midtribs need not worry about this problem, but there are other problems midtribs must face. A lot, of course, depends on how the midtrib argues his position, but many do so by associating the last trump of 1 Corinthians 15:52 and 1 Thessalonians 4:16 with the seventh trump of Revelation 11:15.[11] Archer does not agree (he thinks the rapture more likely occurs at Revelation 14[12]), but other midtribs do.

There are several concerns with this identification. The midtrib appeals to Revelation 11:18, which says of the events surrounding the seventh trump that the day of God's wrath has come. Now all of this fits with divine wrath as not beginning until the midpoint in the Tribulation, so long as the seventh trump actually occurs at the midpoint, rather than later on in the Tribulation (or even earlier). What makes it difficult to prove that the seventh trump falls at the midpoint is something else that midtribs are likely to hold. According to Scripture, the seal judgments precede the trumpet judgments. But note that, at the end of the sixth seal judgment, we read in Revelation 6:17 that the day of God's wrath has come. If the day of God's wrath does not begin until the midpoint of the Tribulation as midtribs say, then there is a major problem for midtribulationism. Put simply, Revelation 6:17 says the day of God's wrath arrives with the sixth seal judgment. This means that on a midtrib view, the sixth seal is at the middle of the Tribulation. If the trumpet judgments *follow* the seal judgment, it is hard to see how the seventh *trump* begins God's wrath at the midpoint of the Tribulation, since the sixth *seal* began God's wrath and midtribs say God's wrath begins at the middle of the Tribulation. In other words, God's wrath is said to begin one seal and seven trumpets too early for the midtrib to say the seventh trump is blown at the midpoint of the Tribulation. And if the seventh trumpet judgment is the last trump of the rapture, then the rapture trump is blown later than the midpoint. Posttribs may applaud this problem since, if they identify the last trump of the rapture with the seventh Tribulation trumpet judgment, that seems to fit better with posttribulationism; but, of course, this is a problem for midtribulationism. All in all, this is why I say that if the seventh trumpet of Revelation is the last trump of the rapture, the midtrib will have a hard time proving that it is blown at the midpoint of the Tribulation.[13]

All of these seem to be significant problems for midtribulationism to surmount. But there is a final problem that neither mid- nor posttribulationism seems able to handle adequately. It is the problem of the church's exemption from divine wrath. In 1 Thessalonians 1:10 and 5:9, Paul reminds believers that members of the body of Christ are exempt from divine wrath. Paul never guarantees exemption from afflictions and problems, but these passages guarantee that God's judgmental wrath will not fall on members of the church. Some people wonder if Scripture really teaches this, since at other times in history believers (Old Testament saints or Tribulation saints who are not members of the church) are present on earth when God pours out his judgmental wrath. But generally speaking, pre-, mid-, and posttribulationists agree that this is so, since all three positions explain how the church will escape God's judgmental wrath of the Tribulation. Pretribs argue that the church will be raptured before the Tribulation and in that way escape God's wrath (Rev. 3:10). Mid- and posttribs have other answers. We must look at those answers and see how well they square with biblical teaching.

Fundamentally, mid- and posttribs have dealt with the problem of the church's escape from divine wrath in one of two ways. The first way suggests that God will simply protect the church from His wrath while she is in the Tribulation. Even as God protected Israel in Egypt when He brought the plagues, so God will protect the church when He pours out His judgmental wrath upon the world. Let me suggest two problems with this. First, in the case of Israel and Egypt, it appears that when the ten plagues fell, they only fell upon the Egyptians, so the Jews did not get caught in the judgments.

However, the book of Revelation speaks about many people losing their lives during the Tribulation as God pours out His judgments on the world. Are we to assume that no believer will lose his life in these judgments? That's what is necessary if the church is present during the Tribulation when these divine judgments come, and if mid- and posttribs are right that God will protect the church from these judgments. But when you look at the nature of the seal, trumpet, and bowl judgments, many of them appear to fall upon the whole earth indiscriminately of whether the inhabitants are believers or nonbelievers. It is possible that God protects believers in the midst of these judgments, but where is the evidence that this is so?

The other problem with this suggestion is that it does not square with Matthew 24:21-22. Those verses speak of great tribulation, such as has never before been experienced. Jesus says that for the elect's sake God will shorten those days (how much, no one knows). Furthermore, He says that if it were not for that shortening, no one would survive. But the tribulation spoken of seems to refer to at least the last three-and-one-half years of the Tribulation, and surely divine wrath is poured out at that time. It should be clear that Matthew 24:22 is very odd if we accept the idea that God will protect His people from divine wrath during the Tribulation. If God protects His people, like He did with Israel in Egypt, why is there any need to shorten the days "for the elect's sake?" If they are protected, let it last 70 or 700 years. None of it will touch the elect if they are protected.

That God protects his people in the Tribulation from divine wrath is not a satisfactory explanation of how the church in the Tribulation avoids divine wrath. Incidentally, if any midtrib seriously proposes this resolution to the problem of divine wrath, then posttribs should respond by saying that if God can protect His church in the Tribulation for three-and-a-half years, He can do it for seven years. So one surely should not see any necessity to remove the church at the midpoint in order to escape the divine wrath of the second half of the Tribulation.

The second way that midtribs and posttribs have handled the issue of the church's escape from divine wrath is to distinguish divine wrath in the Tribulation from Satanic and human wrath. Gundry, for example, says that "the Tribulation of the seventieth week has to do, then, not with God's wrath against the sinners, but with the wrath of Satan, the Anti-christ, and the wicked against the saints."[14] On the other hand, divine wrath only is to be poured out on the unregenerate, and it is not until Armageddon when Jesus descends that God will do so.[15] So long as believers are raptured before the winds of divine wrath begin to blow, they can stay in the Tribulation and undergo Satanic and human wrath without contradicting the promise that the church will not experience divine wrath. Midtribs who handle the problem of escape from God's wrath in this way say the same sort of thing, except that they believe divine wrath begins at the midpoint of the Tribulation. Hence, the church is raptured prior to that.

What shall we say to this proposal? I find it deficient for several reasons. First, this proposal's underlying assumption is that in order for an act to be God's act, or even under His control, He must do it immediately, i.e., totally by Himself without any intermediary agents. Anyone who is a Calvinist should be very uncomfortable with that idea. Moreover, anyone (Calvinist or Arminian) who has read the book of Job, especially the first two chapters, where God's sovereign control over Satan's affliction of Job is obvious, should be uncomfortable with this suggestion. In addition, if we follow this logic, then acts like Assyria's attack on the northern kingdom of Israel must be human wrath, not divine wrath, in spite of the fact that Scripture clearly indicates that the attack was God's judgment upon Israel (Isa. 7:18ff).

This logic creates even further problems for prophecies about the end-times. Many posttribs would agree that Armageddon (and the events surrounding it) involves pouring out divine wrath. If so, then there is a real problem if God cannot do something unless He does it entirely Himself. Zechariah 12 and 14 speak of the attack of a worldwide confederacy against Israel. They also show that Israel is empowered to fight back, and that she participates in the destruction of her enemies. Zechariah 14 shows that the enemy will be so disoriented that its soldiers will start to attack one another. Since Zechariah 12 and 14 speak of Armageddon, there is a problem for the assumption that an act can only be God's if He does it entirely Himself. On the one hand, since human beings are involved in the attack and counterattack, Armageddon must be an expression only of human wrath (given the logic of the divine wrath versus the human and Satanic wrath distinction). But posttribs and midtribs agree that Armageddon sees the pouring out of God's judgmental wrath upon Israel's enemies. When you put this together, you come to the conclusion that Armageddon both is and is not divine wrath. I would suggest that the absurdity of this arises because of the assumption that an act can only be attributed to God or controlled by God if He does it entirely by Himself. Since this assumption underlies the divine wrath versus the human and Satanic wrath solution to the problem of the church's exemption from divine wrath, that solution is in deep trouble.

There is a final difficulty with trying to solve the problem of exemption from divine wrath by distinguishing divine from human and Satanic wrath. All sides agree that the seal, trumpet, and bowl judgments span the whole Tribulation. But notice how these judgments begin. As Revelation 5 begins, we see the book with seven seals. The opening of the first seal begins the sequence of judgments that last throughout the Tribulation. Scripture tells us that there was a search to find someone who was worthy to open the first seal. No one was found worthy except the Lamb, and he opened the first seal. But who is the Lamb? None other than Jesus Christ.

What does all of this mean? Some may reply that this is all symbolic, so we shouldn't make too much out of it. Granted, there is symbolism, but the symbolism cannot mean just anything. It must mean something. And the seal, trumpet, and bowl judgments are not just symbolic of something else; they are real judgments. What does the symbolism mean? It seems clear that it means that the sequence of judgments which spans the whole tribulation begins with an act of Jesus. That seems to suggest that all these judgments result from the instigation of God Himself. And that only suggests that attempting to distinguish Tribulation judgments that are human and Satanic wrath from those that are divine is doomed to failure. It's all divine wrath—not just Armageddon, and not just the last three-and-a-half years. If this is so, then it seems that the only way to be exempt from this time of divine wrath is either to be there but protected through it (and we have seen why that doesn't work), or not to be there at all, being raptured prior to it. Given all the evidence and argument I have offered, it seems that the best option for handling the church's exemption from divine Tribulational wrath is the option that says she escapes because she is not there at all.

Conclusion

The above explains part of why I believe that the pretribulation rapture position is the most successful of the three positions in making its case.[16] All sides must argue their case inferentially, since no passage sets the exact time of the rapture in relation to the Tribulation, and inferential reasoning is notoriously slippery. Nonetheless, it seems to me that of the three rapture positions, pretribulationism makes the best inferential case. There are other arguments one might adduce in favor of the position and against the other views, but that is another study. My primary intent here has been to clarify proper methodology for handling the rapture issue, and to point out what each side must do in order to establish its view as most probable. My hope is that we all will take seriously these matters of method and the logic of what needs to be established in this discussion. The net result would be a better grounding of each position in sound argument and exegesis, and a better addressing of one another's arguments. That would be a positive step forward in the discussion.

10
Elliott E. Johnson

Literal Interpretation: A Plea for Consensus

_____*OVERVIEW*

What is the starting point for properly understanding and interpreting prophecy? There is often confusion and disagreement among Christians as to the best method of approaching the interpretation of biblical texts. In this essay the author affirms both the inerrancy of Scripture as well as its ability to be understood when interpreted plainly and consistently. The Bible is authoritative, and the meanings expressed in the texts are true and have reference to what is real unless the context indicates otherwise.

Introduction

To promote "literal interpretation" in a post-modern environment would be futile unless people were sympathetic to some traditional values and open to consider the arguments. One value is the necessity to retain a view of truth and objective reality. A literal system is based on this view of objective reality, yet the literal principle cannot ensure objective practice in interpretation. In fact, rather than supposing an objectivity, I desire to promote "literal" as a believer in Christ and as one blessed with the presence and ministry of the Holy Spirit.

These two presuppositions will affect the objectivity of the thought process, but both faith and the illumination given by the Spirit are indispensable to reaching valid biblical interpretations.

Literal Interpretation

Literal interpretation formulates a system that takes what the Bible claims to be true of itself as a necessary framework for interpretation. Basic Reformation claims of *sola Scriptura, sola fide* and the perspicuity of Scripture frame a system of literal interpretation.

In addition to formulating this system, I acknowledge that there are other necessary influences on interpretation. An interpreter brings some preunderstandings that will influence the interpretation of individual texts. Irenaeus once described one as like placing together a grand mosaic, or like assembling Homeric verses into their correct and coherent plot structure. This influence involves a biblical theology of progressive revelation for the whole Bible. Further, it is necessary to reconstruct the historical references from a text to understand the world to which, and about which, the text speaks. While both a theology and a historical reconstruction may influence an interpretation of a text, they ought never override the commitments of a literal system.

While the task of gaining a consensus may seem futile and anachronistic to most, it may seem unnecessary for others. It is for these others that this essay is written, because, as Martin Marty has commented, "Literalists unite against their opponents, but they are far from unanimous on matters they regard as important."[1] The objective of this essay is to identify the necessary and sufficient concerns needed to formulate a system of literal interpretation. If "literal interpretation" is included in a doctrinal statement, it is important that there is agreement on what is believed.

The introduction of "literal" must consider the most comprehensive use of the term to refer to a system of interpretation. That system will then entail two related senses of literal.

Literal is a commitment to understanding that the Bible's authority is embedded in the meanings expressed in the words of the text

This first use of literal is a connotative sense, which reflects a shared belief about what the Bible claims to be true of itself; the Bible is God's Word written in human words.

Literal interpretation has traditionally been considered a staple in biblical studies, whether it was as the basic interpretation at Antioch or as a preliminary interpretation in an Alexandrian approach. These early and pre-critical approaches came under a fundamental challenge in the rise to prominence of historical criticism. Marty summarized the historical debate: "In England and America, at least, for over a century there have been intellectual defenses of biblical literalism. While Harper (Wm. Rainey Harper, 1892) and his kind were making Chicago, Yale, and Harvard advance stations for the 'scientific study of the Bible,' theologians at Princeton were turning that school into one of the bastions of a literalist approach to inerrant Scripture."[2] These Princetonians were concerned about the theological ramifications of critical interpretation, since they considered the Bible to be a special revelation of God. They concluded that the Bible in the original autographs was verbally and completely inspired, and thus authoritative. Those who considered this doctrine relevant, relied upon certain principles that explained interpretation. These principles are considered in the following summaries.

The Bible speaks with the authority of God. The Bible's authority resides in what God has to say about subjects, and what He has to say to various generations of His people.[3] This affirmation of the Bible's testimony about itself has been duly noted and developed by biblical scholars.[4]

The authoritative speaking of a written document resides in the type of meanings expressed by the words of the text. Scholars in legal fields, such as Robert H. Bork,[5] in literary fields, such as Leland Ryken,[6] and in philosophical fields, such as E. D. Hirsch,[7] have acknowledged the importance of the words of a text. Individual words must be taken seriously. Interpreters do not have the freedom to change wording without changing meaning. They do not have the right to disregard words, or even forms of letters, nor to manipulate the wording as critical scholars frequently do. Rather a text is read word by word, line upon line, as the reader gains a comprehension of the meaning expressed in a text.

The authoritative meanings are understood as messages expressed only if the words of a text are read in context. Words by themselves don't represent truths; messages expressed by words communicate truth or error.[8]

Thus words are read by themselves, and in relation to the immediate context, in an attempt to recognize the intended message. That message understood then summarizes, in the reader's mind, the type of meaning expressed in the text. And that message, validly understood by a reader, states the truth of the text.

The importance of reading the words of a text in context, to understand the intended sense, has been stated by David Cooper. In his "Golden Rule of Interpretation," he states, "When the plain sense of Scripture makes common sense, seek no other sense; therefore, take every word at its primary, ordinary, usual, literal meaning *unless the facts of the immediate context*... indicate clearly otherwise."[9] Although the influence of the immediate context is introduced by Cooper as a qualification, it is a determining qualification, overriding at times a plain sense. Thus I have chosen to introduce the determinative influence of *context* first as the controlling principle.

The determinative context is the immediate textual context because it directly influences word usage. Other contexts when relevant must be seen as providing a supporting influence. While the subject of "context" may seem easily defined, the grammatical, historical, literary, and theological factors are often difficult to recognize in their appropriate influence. Numerous contexts may come into consideration: parallel biblical passages; the human author's historical consciousness; Israel's cultural beliefs at the time of composition; antecedent canonical theology; social, cultural and communicative issues in the original communication; even contemporary problems and questions.[10] All of these may have a supporting influence in a final decision about the appropriate sense of a word, or words, but the determinative influence must go to *the immediate textual context.* That context fashions a textual usage which may be clarified and amplified by other supporting contexts.

In an attempt to clarify the abstract issues in the discussion of a literal system of interpretation, Isaiah 9:1-7 will be explored. One issue among contemporary interpreters is the person of the promised king of the line of David. Does the text say that he is a God-man or merely a historic king who is subsequently revealed to be, in fact, a God-man.[11] The literal system gives top priority to the wording of the text in the near-context of the oracle (9:1-7), and then it considers Isaiah's broader context (as 7:14, Immanuel, 11:1-16, and so on).

The oracle announces a word of joy to the dark land of Galilee because an unidentified leader shall appear. This person brings joy because he is involved in an enlarged nation that wins release as from an oppressive invader.

Then this person is introduced as one born to shoulder the government of David's kingdom. As unexpected as light in the midst of darkness, so are the names of this ruler—each name expresses a qualification of the ultimate hope of the Davidic line: Wonderful Counselor, Mighty God, Everlasting Father, Prince of Peace.

The question turns on the person of the one called "Mighty God." Does this name speak of the king as God? Contemporary scholars question whether seventh century Israel believed her Messiah would be a God-man. Delitszch questions whether that subject is even addressed in the Old Testament.[12] In order to answer the question, the force of the wording of the text will be examined more closely, under the related senses of literal.

So this connotative use of literal first of all refers to a *literal system of interpretation*, derived from the fact that the Bible is God's Word expressed in human's words. The two following senses of "literal" depend upon deciding what a word has *reference* to and what *sense* the word ought to have in context.

Literal is a commitment that the meanings expressed in a biblical text are true and have reference to what is real, unless the context indicates otherwise.

This commitment is based on the basic belief: the Bible is the Word of God and all that God says is true. This belief is about the type of statements found in the Bible, rather than the type of language, or language usage. "Any statement, literal or metaphorical, may be true or false, and its referent may be real or unreal."[13] The belief in inerrancy implies that biblical statements are true and have reference to reality. There may be an exception, like statements you find in parables, which imagine an experience, as in Luke 15:11 (NIV), "There was a man who had two sons..." The truth there does not have reference to the reality of a father and his sons existing in history, but to an attitude among the Pharisees, as imaged in the eldest son. Likewise, there may be statements like that of the devil, "All this I will give..." (Matthew 4:9 NIV), which may be a lie, and thus a reference to what is unreal. In each case, the near-context clarifies the type of statement expressed in the text.

While there are some exceptions (so clarified from the near-context), the Bible is the revelation of God, and so its statements are true in sense and real in reference. Thus historical narrative refers to past facts, prophetic discourses refer both to present and to future facts, and epistles refer to historical people and the factual workings of God in salvation.

The criticism raised is that "by deduction they argued that God, being God and thus inerrant, spoke through a necessarily inerrant Bible, which they turned into a kind of fact-book."[14] While the Bible is more than a fact-book, it is not less than that. A final answer to such a criticism would require an examination of the type of statement, text by text, and a demonstration of the probable historicity of each. A number of articles consider the issue of historicity.[15] But with our present stage of knowledge, attempts at demonstration have not proven persuasive to all. Yet such a deduction is clearly preferred to critical opinions, such as that the final myth of Exodus is clearly not meant to be a literal version of events.[16] In many such critical treatments, the myth is taken as true in some theological sense, but unreal historically. But what basis exists for any valid distinction, except for some personal preference?

When faith rests in the Bible's testimony that God speaks, and when God's authorship influences a biblical text, like Isaiah 9:6-7, then the reality of a text's reference must be carefully considered. Two questions must be asked: is Isaiah 9:6-7 a literal or a metaphorical statement, and, then, to what reality does the statement refer?

The statement in question is a list of names (v. 6). The sense of some names may be metaphorical (referring to a king as counselor or father), but in this essay, one name is at issue. If the text refers to the king as "Mighty God," to what reality is the text referring? If the name "Mighty God" refers to a man, then the ontological reality remains a man in history, or in prophecy, and the statement is metaphorical. There is nothing in the text to indicate that a god-like man becomes in fact God. Ontologically, a divine person is uncreated and infinite, while a human person is created and finite. The two references are distinct. It is textually incompatible for the same text to refer to a mere human, in a historical context, and to a God-man in the context of Jesus' advent. The statement would thus be taken as equivocal; in a historical context, metaphorical; and in a prophetic context, literal. Thus the true reality to which the statement refers is lost.

The question of Isaiah's comprehension of what he says, or the historic audience's understanding of these words, is not the determining issue. A prophet is not the ultimate source of his message (2 Pet. 1:20-21). Rather, at issue in the type of statement is the use of the language in the context. What is the textual evidence that the term "Mighty God" should be understood in a literal sense rather than a metaphorical sense? This is the issue to be considered now.

Literal is an expectation that the words are meant to be understood and used in their primary, matter-of-fact sense unless the context indicates otherwise.

The expectation of a literal sense reflects an important belief in the composition of the Bible. The biblical authors did not speak in an enigmatic fashion, so that a statement carries two textually unrelated or contradictory meanings. This is another way of talking about the perspicuity of Scripture, in which a text in context has only one sense: probably the plain sense. The historical-critical method has been faulted by believers because of the critical presuppositions that provide a foundation for the method.[17] In addition, the method raises further suspicion if it supports the valid understanding of the same text in two textually unrelated senses: what it meant and what it means.

This expectation of a single, plain, or literal, sense is also based on the belief that the Bible is composed in human words. But a literal sense, while easily illustrated, is difficult to define. So Ramm or Cooper use words like "plain, primary, ordinary, usual, or normal," but in spite of the multiplied descriptions, each simply represents a literary maxim. The maxim represents a first attempt at recognizing the word's meaning, in which a word probably is used in an unmarked or plain sense. Thomas Ice has appropriately concluded: "Cooper does not use the phrase 'common sense,' as critics suggest, by appealing to an abstract theory of common understanding latent in humanity. Instead he defines it within a literary context."[18] The reader of the text recognizes this plain sense as an initial expectation of the sense from a consideration of basic literacy. Yet each reader's basic literacy reflects the culture within which he has gained his literacy. This expectation opens the Bible to a layperson to read and study translations for himself. Such an expectation, with further education, can become a more sophisticated expectation of literal sense based on study of biblical vocabulary from lexical and semantic investigation. Still, the layperson, as any reader, must always test his expectation of a literal sense in view of the facts in the immediate context, and, as Cooper adds, "studied in light of related passages and axiomatic and fundamental truths."

The issue of a single, plain sense may be illustrated in the Isaiah 9:6 text. In the normal sense of language, our initial reading of the sense becomes the starting point in reading the oracle. In such a reading, "Mighty God" would name a divine person and "everlasting" would refer to a divine attribute. This initial reading is supported within the context of the text. The ultimate cause of this remarkable king is the "zeal of the Lord" (9:7), and the reign of this king will begin in history, "from that time on and forever" (9:7). The comprehensiveness of His government and peace knows no limits (9:7). This oracle could only be realized by a divine person if the language is taken at face value.

If, on the other hand, a historical king is what the text meant, then the name must be taken metaphorically. This has the support of a series of metaphors. In comparison to other sources of national direction, the king is a wonderful counselor. In comparing the nation to a family, the king is an everlasting father. In comparison to other human rulers with power, the king is like a mighty god. But was any king in Israel ever considered to be God, let alone the mighty God? Was any king ever worshiped in Jerusalem, as pagan kings had been worshiped? Does not the law prohibit such worship (Ex. 20:2-6)? So it is improbable that this name has the sense of a godlike king.

This exposes the untenable treatment that the historical-critical method often imposes on texts.[19] As a result, the text of Isaiah 9:6 would be treated as supporting two senses for which there is only supposed historical support. When such a method validates textually unrelated meanings between what it meant and what it means, the objective truth and reality of the text is lost. Either the text means a divine-human person or it means a merely human person. And this determination must be made based on the immediate textual context.

Conclusion

Martin Marty raises a final, important question: "What, if anything... does the literalist devotion to biblical inerrancy solve?"[20] The answer features two basic distinctives of the Reformation. The first frees the interpreter to operate consistently in faith toward God and what God says—*sola fide*. In distinction to a historical-critical method, in which everything to be interpreted is submitted to doubt or skepticism, a literal system begins in accepting the Bible's own claims. Such an approach represents the fairness that any author would desire, in which a sympathetic hearing would precede any critical judgments.

The second distinctive features the authority resident in *sola Scriptura*. The words of a text, understood in context, determine the type of meaning expressed in the Bible. As such, Scripture determines the meaning in distinction to some other person or context being treated as the determining authority.

The type of meaning involves the single *sense* of the message expressed in a text. This commitment prevents the words from being historically or culturally conditioned, so that, as in Isaiah 9:6, one truth is seen in a historical context and a different truth is seen in a prophetic context. At issue is the loss of truth expressed in a text and the corresponding *reference* to reality. And that loss is too great to sacrifice for a supposed historical or cultural necessity

Yet these definitions of literal interpretation, while necessary to preserve the interpretation of the truth taught in the Bible, are not sufficient to solve all the debates over interpretations. This insufficiency is because the definitions are neither innate to common sense nor complete in considering all the issues related to valid interpretation. On one side, it does not rest in Scottish Common Sense Philosophy, which is based "on the belief that reasonable people could intuit moral absolutes."[21] If such an intuition would provide a consensus about what determines the meaning, then the difficult choices of interpretation, as illustrated in Isaiah 9:6, would at least have an agreement on the basis for making these choices.

On the other side, the literal system is not a complete consideration of all the relevant issues related to interpretation; therefore, there should not be an unrealistic expectation that agreement in interpretations will be reached in literal interpretation of individual texts and particularly of problem texts. But the literal system does cast an appropriate framework within which validation can be considered in the examination of alternate interpretations of a text. Valid interpretations rely upon reason working with the wording of texts subject to the power of the Holy Spirit, and they rely on belief in an objective world of God's creation and the objective reality of God.

11
Gerald B. Stanton

The Doctrine of Imminency: Is It Biblical?

_____*OVERVIEW*

How important is the concept of imminency in prophecy? Pretribulationists believe that imminency accurately reflects the Scriptures, and that it makes prophecy relevant in the Christian's daily life. Imminency inspires hope for the any-moment return of our Lord. Imminency is a concept that has been held by Christians throughout the church's history and, yet, it has recently come under renewed attack by proponents of the pre-wrath rapture view. A denial of the doctrine of imminency erodes biblical truth and undermines holy living in the anticipation of Christ's return.

*T*he primary thought expressed by the word "imminency" is that something important is likely to happen, and could happen soon. While the event may not be immediate, or necessarily very soon, it is next on the program and may take place at any time. If the event is evil, or potentially dangerous, we call it "impending," for it is threatening to occur. But if it is an event full of hope and joyful expectation, we express it by the noun "imminence" or the adjective "imminent." Among believers, these words normally relate to the possible soon coming of our Lord Jesus Christ to catch up the church in that joyful and monumental event called the rapture.

The word "imminent" should not be confused with "immanent," which in theological language means that God is not only transcendent, or far above us, but that He is always with us and active on our behalf. Nor should it be confused with "eminent," which is a title of honor usually reserved for a king or other person of outstanding distinction. "Imminence" is used to describe the coming of Jesus Christ for the church, the rapture experience, and to declare that it is next on the prophetic program of God.

Actually, "imminency" normally implies the three following truths concerning our Lord's coming.

1) While no one knows the time of Christ's return, He may come at any moment and it is possible that He might come today. It is this hope that keeps the church singing:

> Jesus may come today, Glad day, Glad day!
> And I would see my Friend;
> Dangers and troubles would end
> If Jesus should come today.

Similarly, we sing with expectation: "Jesus is coming to earth again, What if it were today?" In the midst of trials and sorrows, the hope of Christ's imminent return never fails to encourage a troubled heart.

2) The rapture is signless, and it will be unannounced and largely unexpected. It is next on the revealed program of God, and is so presented in the Scripture that every generation may enjoy the hope, challenge, and other blessings of His appearing. We are all exhorted to *watch*, but no one can know the day nor the hour when the Bridegroom will come (Matt. 25:13).

3) No clearly prophesied event must transpire prior to the rapture, for this might date the time of His coming. If the return of Christ for the church is imminent, then obviously it will be before the coming period of Tribulation, with its clearly predicted signs and judgments. In theological language, the rapture must be *pretribulational*. We do not first look for an invasion of the Holy Land by Russia or some other northern confederation, or the revelation of Antichrist and his godless ambitions, or the predicted battle of Armageddon with its vast devastation. We look next for the coming of Christ from heaven to take His own to the Father's house (John 14:1-3). The Bible calls this our "blessed hope" (Titus 2:13).

This gives such great importance to our speaking of the "imminent return of Christ." We believe that the Bible teaches clearly that the rapture will take place before the great tribulation, the time of the outpoured wrath of God. This has become the cherished hope of a vast number of Christian people, especially those of conservative theology and premillennial expectation.

Why Believe in the Imminent Return of Christ?

There are a number of reasons why we believe Christ's return is imminent.

1) We see clearly that the rapture is not identical with the revelation, commonly called the second coming of Christ. These are two distinct events and there are some obvious differences. The rapture relates to the church, when the dead in Christ shall rise and the living will be translated to meet the Lord in the air (1 Cor. 15:52; 1 Thess. 4:16-17). It expresses *hope* and a warm *spirit of expectancy* (1 Thess. 1:10), all of which should result in a *victorious and purified life* (1 John 3:2-3).

On the other hand, the second coming of Jesus Christ does not deal primarily with the saint but with the sinner. When Christ returns to earth, Armageddon must be terminated (Rev. 19:17-18), the beast and the false prophet will be cast into the lake of fire (Rev. 19:19-20), Satan shall be bound in the abyss (Rev. 20:1-3), the nations of earth will be gathered and judged (Matt. 25:31-46), and Israel, which has gone through deep trial, will now behold and put their trust in Christ, their true Messiah (Zech. 12:10; Rom. 11:26-27).

2) There is a vast difference in the language used for these two events. While both relate to the end-time, and both describe actions on the part of Christ, early believers were taught to *look* for the Savior (Phil. 3:20; Titus 2:13). "Unto them that look for Him shall He appear the second time without sin unto salvation" (Heb. 9:28 KJV). Likewise, they were to *wait* for God's Son from heaven (1 Thess. 1:10). They were to *watch and be sober* (1 Thess. 5:6), and to *comfort one another* with the hope of Christ's coming (1 Thess. 4:18). These frequent exhortations caused them to believe that the return of Christ was *imminent.*

Paul seemed to include himself among those who looked for Christ's return (1 Thess. 4:15,17; 2 Thess. 2:1). Timothy was exhorted to "keep this commandment without spot, unrebukeable, until the appearing of our Lord Jesus Christ" (1 Tim. 6:14 KJV). Jewish converts were reminded that "yet a little while, and He that shall come will come, and will not tarry" (Heb. 10:37). Many have concluded that the expectation of some was so strong they had stopped work and had to be exhorted to return to their jobs (2 Thess. 3:10-12). All were exhorted to have patience (James 5:8). Finally, John concluded the book of Revelation, which closed the canon of Scripture, with the glad cry: "He which testifies these things says, Surely I come quickly. Amen. Even so, come, Lord Jesus" (Rev. 22:20 KJV). Such Scriptures form the very foundation for the widely acclaimed hope of Christ's imminent return.

How very different is the language of the second advent, when Christ returns to deal with the unbelief and rebellion of the wicked. In that day, He will "in flaming fire take vengeance on them that know not God, and that obey not the gospel of our Lord Jesus Christ" (2 Thess. 1:8 KJV). Failure to distinguish the rapture from the revelation has become a major source of confusion in the various schools of eschatology.

3) Imminency has been the consistent belief of evangelical Christians down through the centuries. While theological terms such as "trinity," "theophany," "imminency," "inerrancy," and "premillennial" developed gradually over the centuries," it is clear that, although they did not use the term, imminency was indeed the expectation of the apostolic church.

John F. Walvoord, an authority on eschatology, forcefully illustrates this: "The central feature of pretribulationism, the doctrine of imminency, is, however, a prominent feature of the doctrine of the early church...[which] lived in constant expectation of the coming of the Lord for His church."[1]

He then quotes *The Didache*, dated about A.D. 100–120, which contains the exhortation: "Watch for your life's sake. Let not your lamps be quenched, nor your loins unloosed; but be ye ready, for ye know not the hour in which our Lord cometh."[2]

Indeed, even Adolph Harnack, an early liberal theologian, out of sheer honesty as a historian, wrote:

> In the history of Christianity three main forces are found to have acted as auxiliaries to the gospel. They have elicited the ardent enthusiasm of men whom the bare preaching of the gospel would never have made decided converts. These [include] a belief in the speedy return of Christ and in His glorious reign on earth....First in point of time came the faith in the nearness of Christ's second advent and the establishing of His reign of glory on the earth. Indeed it appears so early that it might be questioned whether it ought not to be regarded as an essential part of the Christian religion.[3]

Jesse Forest Silver, in his excellent book *The Lord's Return*, has written of the apostolic fathers:

> They expected the return of the Lord in their day....
> They believed the time was imminent because their Lord had taught them to live in a watchful attitude. [And concerning the ante-Nicene fathers, he says:] By tradition they knew the faith of the apostles. They taught the doctrine of the imminent and premillennial return of the Lord.[4]

It is generally agreed that the church of the first three centuries was premillennial, although the common term used was "chiliasm," from the Greek word *chilas,* meaning "thousand." It is less clear when the concept of Christ's soon return was first explicitly stated as *imminent,* which is a theological word rather than a biblical one. Richard Reiter has traced it to the Niagara Bible Conference of 1878, and more specifically to the five resolutions of the first general American Bible and prophetic conference held in New York City the same year. Article 3 stated: "This second coming of the Lord is everywhere in the Scriptures represented as imminent, and may occur at any moment."[5] However, among the Niagara delegates arose three different definitions of "imminent": 1) Christ may appear at any moment, but this will be understood only by the final generation of the church (A. J. Gordon); 2) Christ could return within the lifetime of any individual generation of believers (Samuel H. Kellogg); 3) "Imminent" requires "the coming of Christ *for* his saints as possible any hour" (Arthur T. Pierson).

While this third "any moment" view was evidently dominant at Niagara, the years that followed brought some harsh disputes, especially by Canadian pastor Robert Cameron and Presbyterian theologian Nathaniel West, both of whom defended the posttribulational view. Their position was opposed by men like Lutheran minister George N. H. Peters, Congregational pastor C. I. Scofield, Presbyterian missionary spokesman Arthur T. Pierson, and Arno C. Gaebelein, editor of *Our Hope*; all of whom became strong champions of the pretribulational position. Ultimately, most posttribulationists gave up the concept of imminency, and "pretribulationism emerged as the dominant view of the rapture within American premillennialism."[6]

While most posttribulationists now vigorously repudiate imminency, it is significant that one of their number, J. Barton Payne, just as vigorously asserts that it was a major belief of the early Christian church. He even names his book on the subject *The Imminent Appearing of Christ.*[7]

When one studies the New Testament rapture passages and the exhortations to *look, watch,* and *wait* for Christ's coming, it is easy to see why so many of the Lord's people believe in and proclaim the doctrine of imminency. The expression has been incorporated into the doctrinal statement of many evangelical churches and missionary agencies. It forms part of the basic doctrine of many excellent Christian colleges and theological seminaries throughout the world. The great expectation of the church is to look for Christ and not Antichrist!

However, at this point there is still considerable disagreement among students of prophecy. Among those of premillennial persuasion, actually five different views have been proposed, frequently spoken of as pretrib, midtrib, posttrib, partial rapture, and pre-wrath rapture. While all of these may be evangelical, and some are held by prophetic scholars, the five views are mutually exclusive and all but one must be considered in error. Except possibly for some of the partial rapturists, only pretribulationists believe in the imminent return of Christ. *It is here proposed that this is the true and thoroughly defensible view of the Scriptures.*

The Attack Against Imminency

Since imminency is one way of stating that the church of Jesus Christ will be caught up in the rapture *before* the coming Tribulation, most of the opposition to this doctrine stems from the posttribulational camp. Probably the most extended (though not recent) attack against imminency came in 1922 from Robert Cameron. In his book *Scripture Truth About the Lord's Return,* he fills at least one-third of it with this argument.[8]

It is not our purpose here to review all of his arguments and give a considered rebuttal. This has already been accomplished in the book *Kept from the Hour*, in the chapter "The Imminency of the Coming of Christ for the Church."[9] In considerable detail, all of Cameron's arguments against imminency are answered, and the hope of the early church, as set forth in the New Testament, and the imminent return as an incentive to holiness are examined. To the present time, few have attacked imminency more vigorously than Cameron, and in *Kept from the Hour*, his objections have been answered fairly and convincingly.

However, in recent months the attack against imminency has come from a new and unexpected quarter. Marv Rosenthal, an evangelical and premillennialist ministering in Jewish evangelism, has rejected the pretribulational position, which he previously taught and defended during most of his ministry. He writes:

> I was a convinced, sincere, unbending, and, in retrospect, to my shame, intolerant pretribulation rapturist for thirty-five years. My pretribulation position was widely known. I had preached it with conviction and sincerity around the world.[10]

But under the prodding of a "persistent friend" (former publisher Robert Van Kampen), who phoned him almost daily for three months, and after much personal study, he renounced the pretrib position and wrote a new and surprisingly novel view, called the pre-wrath rapture of the church.[11] Typical of those who argue that the church must go through the Great Tribulation, he strongly renounced imminency and with frequent abrasiveness and much repetition, he argued for a rapture placed between the Great Tribulation and the Day of the Lord. This, to Rosenthal, will be three-fourths of the way through Daniel's seventieth week, and identified with the "innumerable multitude" of Revelation 7:9-17.

Concerning imminency, he declares that it is "invalid," an "insolvable problem" which "crumbles" and "is once again destroyed." This doctrine is a "false hope," which cannot "in the early Church be sustained." "The student of the Word will search in vain for exegetical evidence." "Pretribulation rapturism is once again mortally wounded."[12] It is a most annoying repetition.

He continues to defend his new prophetic views in a well-published bimonthly magazine called *Zion's Fire*. In the August-September 1990 issue, he asks the question, "Is the Return of Christ Imminent?" and then launches his major attack. He traces pre tribulationism back to J. N. Darby in the year 1830, and then ultimately to a charismatic and visionary woman named Margaret Macdonald. Such claims have been frequently answered. He discusses his view of the Day of the Lord, and repeatedly attacks the "unproven concept of imminence." In place of "imminency" he prefers the word "expectancy." And while he argues that "Christ can come during any generation of history," he believes that the church must first go through the Great Tribulation, which he waters down by calling it merely "a period of great difficulty."

Surprisingly, however, he can name only five objections to the doctrine of imminency, four of which are contained in one short paragraph.

Rosenthal's Five Objections to Imminency

1) He says: "There is no historical evidence to demonstrate that the early church believed in an any-moment rapture." But the evidence is right within the New Testament. They were instructed to look, watch, and wait for His coming, and to comfort one another with this happy expectation (1 Thess. 4:18). It would have been small comfort indeed to believe they must first go through a raging tribulation and probably die at the hands of the beast (Rev. 13:7). Such exhortations would have lost all significance if many years of unparalleled death and destruction must first intervene.

It is important to note that the writings of a great many early church leaders demonstrate that they did believe that Christ's return might be very soon. In addition to the hope so clearly expressed in *The Didache*, we read in the *First Epistle of Clement*, written about A.D. 96, "Of a truth, soon and suddenly shall His will be accomplished, as the Scripture also bears witness, saying, 'Speedily will He come, and will not tarry.'" Also, "The Lord shall suddenly come to His temple, even the Holy One for whom ye look."

In the *Second Epistle of Clement*, we read, "Let us every hour expect the kingdom of God in love and righteousness, because we know not the day of the Lord's appearing." And in the *Epistle of Barnabas*: "The Lord has cut short the times and the days that His Beloved may hasten"; also "The Lord is near, and His reward." Similarly, Ignatius, Bishop of Antioch, refers to "the last times" and exhorts in those times to "expect Him." Clement of Rome (ca. A.D. 40–100) preached the coming of Christ, and according to George N. H. Peters, Clement expressed the hope "that He shall come quickly and not tarry."[13] Crippen, in his *History of Doctrine*, declares: "The early Fathers lived in expectation of our Lord's speedy return."

The coming of Christ has long been the hope and expectation of great spiritual leaders such as John Wesley (1703–91), the father of Methodism, who fixed no dates but was always watchful for the Lord's return. He was hardly expecting to pass through seven years of raging tribulation when he wrote:

Perhaps He will appear as the dayspring from on high, before the morning light. Oh, do not set a time—expect Him every hour. Now He is nigh, even at the doors.[14]

In his day, Martin Luther declared:

I believe that all the signs which are to precede the last days have already appeared. Let us not think that the Coming of Christ is far off; let us look up with heads lifted up; let us expect our Redeemer's coming with longing and cheerful mind.

John Calvin wrote in his *Institutes of the Christian Religion:*

Scripture uniformly enjoins us to look with expectation for the advent of Christ.

To which hope Latimer (c.1485–1555) responded:

All those excellent and learned men, whom, without doubt, God has sent into the world in these latter days to give the world warning, do gather out of the Scriptures that the last days cannot be far off. Peradventure it may come in my day, old as I am, or in my children's days.[15]

Furthermore, in the *Shepherd of Hermas,* dated about A.D. 100–120, the author was told in a vision:

You have escaped from the great tribulation on account of your faith, and because you did not doubt in the presence of the beast.[16]

These quotations demonstrate clearly that the early church not only looked for Christ and His kingdom, but that they also expected His coming to be soon and even before the Tribulation. While we are not saying that the early church fathers, or even the Reformers, knew the details of eschatology, or were always consistent, it is a monumental error to declare that the concept of *imminency* was not found in the apostolic church but first appeared in the nineteenth century.

2) Rosenthal declares that the early church could not believe in imminence because "the gospel had to be preached throughout the world before Christ could return" (Acts 1:8). But we must remember the tremendous missionary impetus of the early church:

> When the vitality and zeal of Paul and other early converts, with their world-shaking testimony (Acts 17:6), is remembered, together with the size of the then-inhabited world (grown yet smaller by the unifying influence of Roman rule and Roman roads), it must be confessed that world evangelism was a greater possibility in Paul's day than in ours.[17]

3) "Peter was to live to be an old man (John 21:18-19). For the early church, that precluded an any-moment rapture." This argument, borrowed from Cameron, is readily answered. Peter himself encouraged believers to look for the coming of the Lord, calling those who did not do so "willingly ignorant" (2 Pet. 3:3-5). He knew that he might die suddenly (2 Peter 1:14), and Herod had just killed James and seized Peter with the same intention (Acts 12:1-3). Certainly believers expected Peter's early death, for when Rhoda bore the news of his release, they said "Thou art mad," and when he appeared to them "they were astonished" (Acts 12:15-16).

They had no concept that his would be a long life, and as they looked for the Savior they certainly did not run around asking, "I wonder if Peter is dead yet?" Actually, the passage in question, which recorded Christ's conversation with Peter, John 21:18, could not have been a factor in their thinking, for it was not written and sent to the churches until 20 or more years *after* Peter's death.

4) "The Temple was to be destroyed before Christ returned (Matt. 24:1-3). For the early church, that precluded an any-moment rapture." But in this passage, Christ was not discussing the rapture or the church age, for the Spirit had not yet come, nor had the church been established. He was teaching about the inter-advent age, that period between the first and the second coming of the king, and the affairs that concerned Israel. He predicted the destruction of the temple, a fact accomplished in A.D. 70 under the Roman, Titus. But there is nothing in this prophecy that relates the destruction of the temple to the timing of the rapture, nor vaguely suggests that it must happen first.

5) *"Antichrist will make a covenant with Israel to protect her for seven years" (Dan. 9:27). From A.D. 70 to May 14, 1948 "no Jewish nation or representative government existed....An any-moment rapture, therefore, was not possible before the modern state of Israel was resurrected out of the ashes of the second World War."* This may sound plausible until it is more fully considered. The prophecy does not say that the covenant will be made with the nation, Israel, but simply with "many." Nor can we assume that Daniel's prophecy, "shut up and sealed...to the time of the end" (12:4) was known and sufficiently understood by early Christians, to cause them to look for the reestablishment of Israel prior to the Lord's coming. It is obvious that they did not. In addition, Daniel was writing concerning the coming Antichrist and a covenant to be made during the last of the "seventy weeks." Since the catching up of the church occurs before the seventieth week, an event which takes place during the Tribulation has absolutely no bearing on the timing of the rapture.

It is not a question whether we now understand this ancient prophecy, especially in the light of the book of Revelation. The question is whether that prophecy was so clearly understood that it destroyed the hope and expectation of the church throughout the centuries. It is obvious that it did not, just as so many of us looked for the Lord from heaven many years before Israel became a nation in 1948. If Daniel's prophecy did not destroy our daily looking for Christ's coming during our own lifetime, why should it have destroyed hope and expectation in any lifetime? Can it be that Rosenthal's argument is simply a straw man set up in an attempt to protect an erroneous eschatology?

We must conclude that *imminency* and *pretribulationism* are intimately related, for the first is part of the evidence for the second. The difference is primarily a matter of focus. The word *pretribulational* focuses on the fact that the true church of Jesus Christ will be caught up to the Father's house before the "time of Jacob's trouble" (Jer. 30:7), before the "great day of God's wrath" (Rev. 6:16-17). The focus of the word *imminency* is upon Christ and His possible soon coming. We are not looking for signs or the fulfillment of other prophetic events. We are looking for Jesus Christ Himself!

His coming is next on the revealed program of God, and it may be near at hand. Hence, we look and watch and wait for our Lord from heaven. This is our bright and blessed hope, far higher and more in keeping with Scripture than looking for the Antichrist and the tragic years of the coming Tribulation. The next voice we shall hear from heaven will call us home!

Stanley D. Toussaint

Are the Church and the Rapture in Matthew 24?

_____*OVERVIEW*

Does Matthew 24 discuss the rapture and the church? Non-pretribulationists say "Yes" and pretribulationists say "No." More recently this issue has been a major battleground between the two positions. The recent rise of the "pre-wrath rapture" theory has reinvigorated the debate. Through clear biblical and theological analysis this study refutes those who would say "Yes." The clarity of this presentation will enrich anyone who desires a faithful understanding of this passage.

Introduction

A Statement of the Problem

All non-pretribulationists place both the church and the rapture in Matthew 24. This is essential to their position and for them no other interpretation is possible. However, pretribulationists exempt both the church and the rapture from Matthew 24. The question, contextually, exegetically, and theologically, is: are the church and/ or the rapture found in Matthew 24?

It should also be said that in the context of eschatology, the church and the rapture are so intimately bound together that if either is found in Matthew 24 the other is probably present also.

The Significance of the Problem

All premillennialists agree that the Tribulation and the Lord's return to reign are the primary themes of Matthew 24. To say, therefore, that the church and the rapture are discussed in this passage implies a non-pretribulational rapture. As stated above, it is essential to the non-pretribulational camps to have the church and the rapture in Matthew 24.

On the other hand, if the passage is best explained by seeing no reference to the church or the rapture, the pretribulational rapture position is strengthened. It should also be said that the pretribulational rapture doctrine is *not* based on Matthew 24. Consistent pretribulationists contend that the doctrine is found chronologically later in John 14 and is expanded by Paul in 1 Thessalonians 4 and 1 Corinthians 15. While a pretribulational rapture may be *implied* from Matthew 24, and pretribulationists would find it disconcerting to have either the church or the rapture in Matthew 24, the doctrine of the rapture occurring before the seven-year Tribulation rests on other biblical texts.

Organization of the Study

This study will briefly mention and discuss four primary views of Matthew 24: first, the critical interpretation; second, those that see Matthew 24 as basically fulfilled in the past (the preterist interpretation); third, the view that interprets Matthew 24 as being agelong in its outlook; and finally, premillennial posttribulationism.

The majority of this study, however, will discuss the question of the presence of the church and the rapture in Matthew 24 from Robert H. Gundry's posttribulational attack on pretribulationism. This emphasis is because Gundry is a dispensationalist and therefore his attempted refutation of the pretribulational viewpoint has been heard by many dispensationalists. The two questions of the church and the rapture will be discussed separately in this section. Also this study will discuss Matthew 24 as it bears on the recent view known as the pre-wrath rapture of the church.

Four Primary Views of Matthew 24

The Critical Interpretation

This view states that the majority of Jesus' Olivet discourse was created and produced by the early church. Beare, a proponent of this approach, wrote, "As will be seen, the whole discourse (at least to v. 31) is a chain of commonplaces of apocalyptic imagery and cannot be imagined to contain much that goes back to Jesus."[1] One critical scholar concedes, "Matthew believed that Jesus had taught that he would return in glory sometime within the years A.D. 30–110, although Jesus himself had not known the exact date of his coming and Matthew was probably right in thinking that Jesus had taught this."[2]

Critical scholars hold that the early church invented these sayings to meet some situation then current in the church. In such an approach it is obvious the church appears in Matthew 24. More conservative scholars, who take the Olivet discourse as containing the words and message of the Lord Jesus, reject the critical approach out of hand. Mounce gives one rebuttal to this critical approach:

> Critics who think that the bulk of Matthew comes
> from the early church rather than from Jesus himself
> are hard pressed to explain why there is no mention at

this point of the burning of the temple. A *vaticinium ex eventu* (prophecy after the event) would not have omitted such a specific item.[3]

Past Fulfillment

A second view of Matthew 24, sometimes held by amillennialists and widely found within postmillennialism, sees large sections of the chapter as fulfilled in the past, particularly in A.D. 70. Kik, who divides the chapter at 24:34 says:

> If the literal and well-defined meaning of this verse is accepted, it will be seen that this verse divides the chapter into two sections. Section One speaks of events which were to occur to the generation living at the time that Christ spoke these words. Section Two speaks of events to occur at the Second Coming of the Lord. Verse 34 is the division point of the two sections.[4]

In order to come to such an interpretation, Kik must wildly spiritualize some passages. For instance, he interprets Matthew 24:29 in the following manner:

> If the sun, moon, and stars refer to the Jewish nation and its prerogatives, then we have seen the fulfillment of this prophecy. The Jewish nation has been darkened and no longer shines for God. This has been true ever since the tribulation of those days.... The Sun of Judaism has been darkened; as the moon it no longer reflects the Light of God; bright stars, as were the prophets, no longer shine in the Israel of the flesh.[5]

Significantly, Hendriksen, a staunch amillennialist, presents another refutation of this view. He says that if this interpretation is taken, the Lord never answered the disciples' questions.[6] Furthermore, the Tribulation described in the passage immediately precedes the Lord's return (Matt. 24:29-31).

Age-Long Fulfillment

A third approach to Matthew 24 sees the chapter as essentially describing the entire inter-advent period with some emphasis on the close of the age. This is the most common view among amillennialists.[7] Clearly, those who hold this view see both the church and the rapture in Matthew 24. They believe in a return of the Lord Jesus Christ, a general resurrection, and final judgment.

An evaluation of this approach will be found in the next section because, although the opinions are very different, the reasons for rejecting the two views are essentially the same.

Premillennial Posttribulationism

Walvoord catalogs various kinds of posttribulationism in his work, *The Blessed Hope and the Tribulation,*[8] and these are also summarized in *The Rapture Question,*[9] where he notes certain premillennial posttribulationists as J. Barton Payne, Alexander Reese, and George E. Ladd. A more recent development of premillennial posttribulationism has been produced by Gundry, who is not only premillennial but also dispensational, in that he makes a distinction between Israel and the church.[10] The question being discussed in this chapter has particular relevance to Gundry arguments.

Gundry and the Church in Matthew 24

Bruce A. Ware skillfully discusses the arguments of Gundry, for seeing the church in Matthew 24, in an article titled, "Is the Church in View in Matthew 24–25?"[11] Ware summarizes Gundry's position under five points: the fallacy of hyper-dispensationalism; Matthew's relevance to the church; importance of the context; the time of Jerusalem's destruction; and the apostles' association with the church. Of these five, the most significant is Gundry's argument from the context of the Olivet discourse. Gundry contends that the bitter conflicts between the hierarchy of Israel and the Lord Jesus in Matthew 21–23 show that God was now rejecting Israel. He specifically mentions Matthew 21:43, "Therefore I say to you, the kingdom of God will be taken away from you and be given to a nation producing the fruit of it" (NASB).[12] Gundry describes the famous lament of Matthew 23:37-39 as the Lord's "sorrowful farewell to the Jewish nation."[13] Gundry concludes:

> We can hardly ask for more evidence that Jesus takes
> the standpoint of His rejection by the Jewish nation
> and His Father's rejection of the Jewish nation. It is

the chronology of the resultant present age which
Jesus now outlines. The context supports the relationship of the Olivet Discourse to the Church.[14]

He goes on to explain away the Jewish elements in Matthew 24
by saying they are addressed to Jewish and Judean Christians in the
church.[15]

Gundry's Omission

Gundry, however, is guilty of a serious omission. He fails to see
how the Lord's earlier pronouncements of judgment on Israel, as
recorded by Matthew, did not indicate Christ no longer had dealings
with Israel. It is not necessarily logical to argue that because Israel is
rejected by God in Matthew 21–23 that Matthew 24 concerns the
church. As far back as Matthew 11:20-24, Jesus pronounced a
scathing denunciation of Chorazin, Bethsaida, and Capernaum. In
12:39, Jesus also said, "An evil and adulterous generation craves for
a sign, and yet no sign shall be given to it but the sign of Jonah the
prophet" (NASB). He describes that generation as being under judgment in 12:41-45. Does this mean Israel is no longer in view in the
remainder of Matthew? Certainly the transfiguration recorded in
Matthew 17:1-13 was a confirmation of the kingdom for Israel (cf.
2 Pet. 1:16-18). Clearly Matthew 19:28, although it shows the
church's participation in the millennial kingdom, looks ahead to the
fulfillment of God's promises to Israel. Matthew 21, the Lord's so-
called "triumphal entry," was a presentation to Israel of Himself as
their Messiah and King. In spite of the pronouncements of woe and
judgment in chapters 11–12, the Lord was still dealing with Israel.
The Lord's rejection of Israel in Matthew 21–23 by no means indicates He cannot speak to or about Israel in Matthew 24.

The most glaring omission in Gundry's discussion of the context is his studied neglect of the questions asked by the disciples in
Matthew 24:3, "And as he was sitting on the Mount of Olives, the
disciples came to him privately, saying, 'Tell us, when will these
things be, and what will be the sign of Your coming, and of the end
of the age?'" (NASB). Gundry, in his entire chapter on the Olivet
discourse, makes only one passing reference to their questions when
he writes, "It is fitting that Jesus should give special instructions to
Jewish Christians who reside in Jerusalem and environs concerning

the future crisis of that city, especially since he is answering the apostles' question regarding the fate of the temple and the city."[16] It becomes obvious why Gundry says practically nothing about this critical aspect of the context of the Olivet discourse. *The question is totally Jewish!* Jesus had just predicted the complete destruction of the temple buildings (Matt. 24:1-2). If any institution was Jewish it was the temple! In addition, the end of the age mentioned by the disciples is marked by the coming of Israel's Messiah, to which they also refer in their questions.

It has been common for dispensational pretribulationists to say the first question is ignored by the Lord in Matthew 24, although He answers it in Luke's gospel. In Matthew He only answers the second two questions, concerning the sign of His coming and the end of the age.[17] It is contended that while the first question is overlooked in Matthew 24, Christ had already given his reply in Matthew 22:7, where God, portrayed as an angry king, destroys the city of those who spurned His call to a wedding feast.

A better approach to the questions of Matthew 24:3 might be to link all three together. In the disciples' minds a series of events seemed to follow in chronological order: 1) the destruction of Jerusalem; 2) the glorious presence of the Messiah to deliver His people; 3) the establishment of His kingdom. In other words, they believed the destruction of Jerusalem was closely associated with the coming of Christ and the end of the age.[18]

The disciples had good scriptural grounds for this thinking. Zechariah 14 has just such a sequence. In Zechariah 14:1-2 the prediction of Jerusalem's capture is followed by the Lord's mighty deliverance (14:3-5) and His subsequent reign on earth (14:6-21). It would be especially appropriate for the disciples to have Zechariah 14 in view because they are on the Mount of Olives, where Zechariah says the Lord will come in deliverance.[19]

The Parousia

A word should be said about *parousia*, the noun usually translated "coming" in Matthew 24:3. It has been commonly noted that in Greek literature the word looks at the coming of a king or dignitary to some locality. Of course, this usage is most appropriate for the second coming of Jesus Christ to earth. However, another more neglected meaning is found in Greek literature and may be in view in Matthew. It was used in a ritual or cultic sense to refer to the coming of a deity who somehow made his presence felt.[20]

The noun occurs only five times in the Septuagint, all in a non-religious sense, simply meaning "presence" (Neh. 2:6; Judith 10:18; 2 Macc. 8:12; 15:21; 3 Macc. 3:17). Significantly, in the intertestamental period *parousia* also was used in a religious sense, where it referred to the coming and aid of the Lord and also to the appearance of the Messiah. Colin Brown refers to Jewish apocalyptic texts where it is so used.[21] Josephus used it of the Shekinah glory (*Ant.* 3.80, 202), of the presence of God as seen in 2 Kings 6:17 (*Ant.* 9.55), and of God's presence in a very unusual if not miraculous rainstorm (*Ant.* 18.284). This religious sense may be in view in Matthew.

The term *parousia* occurs 24 times in the New Testament, but only four times in the Gospels, and *all in Matthew 24* (vv. 3,27,37,39). This means that the first time the term is used in the New Testament it probably included a Jewish religious sense of the appearance of the Messiah to deliver. If this is so, it gives the whole discourse in Matthew 24 an especially Jewish slant.

In a word, the questions of the disciples are completely Jewish and have nothing to do with the church! The disciples did not grasp the significance of the church at this point; they only gradually began to understand how God was building His church, as the book of Acts attests. The questions of the disciples are not only related to Israel, they form the basis for the entire discourse. Gundry is correct in saying the context deals with the Lord's rejection of Israel. But that is the point of the Olivet discourse. What is the future of Israel? How will God judge His chosen people and also establish the promised kingdom for them? The disciples wanted to know what God was going to do. Gundry's avoidance of the questions of the apostles in his discussion must be more than benign neglect.

Gundry not only passes by the disciples' questions, he also fails to see the Jewishness of the abomination of desolation in Matthew 24:15. He barely mentions it,[22] and yet it is as Jewish as anything in Matthew's Gospel. The abomination of desolation stands in the temple (cf. 2 Thess. 2:4), and it is the fulfillment of a prophecy dealing with Israel (Dan. 9:27; 11:31; 12:11). The mention of the Sabbath in 24:20 is also Jewish. Gundry explains this by saying, "He merely recognizes that reduction of services to travellers and extra-scriptural restrictions imposed and enforced in Jewish society might hamper the flight of Judean Christians."[23] But the fact remains that the passage is directed towards Jews! It is no wonder that David Hill, by no means a pretribulationist, let alone a premillennialist or a dispensationalist, says about Matthew 24:15-22, "These verses are among the most Jewish in the section."[24]

It is clear the disciples are representative of a group of believers living in the coming Tribulation period. Their representative nature is seen in Matthew 24:21-23:

> For then there will be a great tribulation, such as has not occurred since the beginning of the world until now, nor ever shall. And unless those days had been cut short, no life would have been saved; but for the sake of the elect those days shall be cut short. Then if anyone says to you, "Behold, here is the Christ," or "There he is," do not believe him (NASB).

The question is, do they represent believers in the church or Jewish believers who are on earth after the rapture? Gundry refers to a number of New Testament passages to say they portray the church (John 14:1-3; Acts 2:42; Eph. 2:20; 3:5-6; 4:11; 1 Cor. 12:28; Rev. 21:12-14). No one disputes these. Ware answers this argument graphically:

> But to show what the Apostles *became* is not to prove what they were in Matthew 24.... This is like arguing that Abraham Lincoln represented the United States of America while he was a young, rail-splitting youth because there is much evidence from later in his life that he in fact did represent the nation as its President.[25]

Certainly, the 12 apostles did not represent the church in Matthew 10:6, when Christ told them not to go to the Samaritans or Gentiles and minister to them! Later usage by itself does not indicate whom the disciples represent in the Gospels; *it must be the context.* In the case of Matthew 24, the Jewish nature of both its context and its contents argue for the disciples describing Jewish believers on earth after the rapture. It certainly must be concluded that the context does not argue for the presence of the church in Matthew 24, as Gundry contends.

Gundry and the Rapture in Matthew 24

First, Gundry says the rapture does not take place before the Tribulation because it is simply an assumption to say there is a pretribulational rapture. He says, "The burden of proof falls then on those who would put the rapture before the tribulation."[26] His second defense of posttribulationism is found in equating the gathering of the elect at the sound of a trumpet (Matt. 24:31) with the rapture (1 Thess. 4:16-17; 2 Thess. 2:1).[27] Third, Gundry makes the "taking" of Matthew 24:40-41 to be a reference to the rapture.[28]

These will be discussed considering the second and third points first, because once these are considered, the first becomes moot. In the second line of his defense, Gundry relates Matthew 24:31 to the rapture. Matthew 24:29-31 reads:

> But immediately after the tribulation of those days the sun will be darkened, and the moon will not give its light, and the stars will fall from the sky, and the powers of the heavens will be shaken, and then the sign of the Son of Man will appear in the sky, and then all the tribes of the earth will mourn, and they will see the Son of Man coming on the clouds of the sky with power and great glory. And He will send forth His angels with a great trumpet and they will gather together His elect from the four winds, from one end of the sky to the other (NASB).

Gundry goes on to show how in 1 Thessalonians 4:16-17 and 2 Thessalonians 2:1 there are similar elements—a trumpet, clouds, and a gathering of believers.[29] All agree that similar events are found in Matthew 24 and the Thessalonian epistles. It even must be conceded the same stem for "gather" is used in Matthew 24:31 (*episunagō*) and in 2 Thessalonians 2:1 (*episunagôgê*), also in Hebrews 10:25. Of course, this does not indicate equivalency. As Walvoord asserts, "The major objection to making this equivalent to the rapture is that there is no mention of either translation or resurrection, the two major features of the church."[30]

In addition, Gundry's association of the "gathering" of Matthew 24 with the rapture founders on the same problem that faces all who place the rapture at the conclusion of the Tribulation. Who will populate the millennium if all saved have glorified bodies? To counter this conundrum, Gundry believes there is only a partial destruction of the unsaved; the remaining saved will then populate the planet.[31] This is a strange view. If the Scriptures teach anything, they say all unbelievers will be judged and not permitted to enter the millennial kingdom. Israel will be purged of rebels (Ezek. 20:37-38), and Gentiles who are lost will be consigned to eternal punishment (Matt. 25:31-33,41-46). Certainly, the warning of John the Baptist leaves no room for "escapees" to enter Christ's kingdom on earth (Matt. 3:7-12). The subject of judgment preceding the earthly kingdom is common enough in Matthew (cf. 8:12; 13:40-42,49-50; 22:13; 25:31-46). The parable of the pounds puts it graphically in Luke 19:27, where it refers to slaughtering the ones who rejected Christ as king. To argue for a posttribulational rapture from the similar elements in Matthew 24, 1 Thessalonians 4:16-17, and 2 Thessalonians 2:1, as Gundry does, places a student into an inescapable maze.

The third line of Gundry's defense of his position is grounded in Matthew 24:40-41, "Then there shall be two men in the field; one will be taken, and one will be left. Two women will be grinding at the mill; one will be taken and one will be left" (NASB). Consistent pretribulationists interpret the "taking" in these verses as a removal for judgment. The context clearly supports this meaning. Just as sinners were taken away in the flood of Noah's day, so the lost will be removed from the earth so as not to enter the millennium (cf. Matt. 24:37-39). Gundry attempts to blunt the significance of the context by saying the parallel is in the element of surprise.[32] No one disagrees with this, but the unexpectedness of the Lord's coming does not rule out also His coming in judgment. The comparison is more complete than Gundry will admit. Just as unexpected judgment was seen in the flood, so it will occur when Christ returns at the end of the Tribulation.

He also advances a rather obtuse argument by saying that if this is a complete removal for judgment, "the pretribulational view of the judgment of the nations (Matt. 25:31-46) runs into trouble. For if all the wicked will be taken away in judgment at Christ's advent, who will remain to be the goats in the judgment of the nations?"[33]

The answer is simple. These are removed to stand before the Lord in judgment. Gundry argues, "God did not take away the wicked with the flood for the purpose of *subsequent* judgment. The flood *was* the judgment."[34] This is making the analogy too tight; every detail of the comparison need not match.

Gundry's strongest point rests on his distinction between the two verbs for "take" in verses 39-41. The verb *aírô* is used in verse 39 for the drowning of the lost in the flood and *paralambánô* is used for the taking when Christ comes. He says the latter verb is used in John 14:3. Gundry asserts, "In this light, the change from *αἴρω* [*aírô*] to *παραλαμβάνω* [*paralambánô*] indicates a change in topic and connotation: the former term refers to judgment similar in unexpectedness to the flood, the latter to reception of the saints at the rapture to be forever with their Lord (cf. 1 Thess. 4:17; John 14:3)."[35]

However, as Gundry parenthetically admits, *paralambánô* is used in an antagonistic sense in John 19:16, where Christ is taken to be crucified. The same verb is employed in Matthew 4:5, when the devil took the Lord Jesus to Jerusalem to tempt Him. In fact, this verb basically means "to take to oneself"[36] and may help explain Gundry's problem with reconciling this passage with the judgment of the nations (Matt. 25:31-46). The Lord takes these to Himself in preparation for judgment. Significantly, an alternative reading in the Greek text (manuscript D) in Acts 16:35 uses *paralambánô* to refer to the arrest and custody of Paul and Barnabas in Philippi. The context of Matthew 24:40-41 is strongly in favor of an antagonistic sense. Many pretribulationists have noted the taking away in Matthew 24:40-41 is a taking away to judgment.[37]

It becomes clear that neither Gundry's second argument for the rapture, the gathering of the elect in Matthew 24:31, is the same as the rapture, nor that his third contention, the "taking" of Matthew 24:40-41, is the rapture. Neither stands up under the light of theology, context, and exegesis. This makes Gundry's first assertion, that the placing of the rapture before the Tribulation is an assumption of pretribulationists, a moot point. It must be concluded that it is highly improbable that the church or the rapture are in Matthew 24, as Gundry would have pretribulationists believe.

The Pre-Wrath Rapture of the Church and Matthew 24

In 1990, Marvin Rosenthal published a rather novel and new view of the rapture, which he labeled the "pre-wrath rapture."[38] He believes Daniel's seventieth week has three major parts: 1) the first three-and-one-half years he calls "the beginning of sorrows" (Matt 24:8), which he says is not to be designated as "the tribulation", 2) the last three-and-one-half years contain the Great Tribulation and the Day of the Lord; 3) the church will not be raptured until just before the Day of the Lord, which is a time of God's wrath. In fact, God's wrath is not seen on earth until this third and final part of Daniel's seventieth week. Matthew 24 plays a large part in Rosenthal's scheme. He obviously sees both the church and the rapture in Matthew 24.

The core of Rosenthal's presentation begins with making the first six seals of Revelation 6:1-13 equivalent to Matthew 24:5-9 and 29.[39] Of course many pretribulationists have noted these, especially the correlation between the first four seals and Matthew 24:5-8. However, Rosenthal argues these first six seals are not a time of God's wrath, but are man-caused disasters on planet earth.[40] He contends that the church will fall victim to these humanly generated tragedies. Interestingly, Rosenthal never explains how the earthquakes in Matthew 24:7 are triggered by humans! He explains the famines as being the result of war, but he never interprets Revelation 6:6, where the third horse rider is told, "Do not harm the oil and the wine" (NASB). This appears to be a divinely caused famine and certainly contradicts Rosenthal's assertion that "it is not the seals which hurt the earth, sea, and trees, but the trumpet judgments which follow (Rev. 8:7-11)."[41] Rosenthal agrees that the first horseman (the first seal) represents the coming of the first beast, but then he goes on to say, "To attribute the emergence of the Antichrist to God is obviously preposterous."[42] But is it? This is exactly what Paul says God does in judgment in 2 Thessalonians 2:11-12: "And for this reason God will send upon them a deluding influence so that they might believe what is false, in order that they all may be judged who did not believe the truth, but took pleasure in wickedness" (NASB). Certainly the revelation of God's wrath in Romans 1:18 is seen in His giving people over to greater sin (Rom. 1:24,26,28). If this is true today, how much more can God in wrath give permission for the Man of Sin to become a world ruler and object of worship during the Tribulation? The passive verb *edothê* in Revelation 13:5b and 17 (two times) looks at God's sovereignty in giving the Antichrist his authority

Rosenthal argues that the aorist tense of *edothê*, which is *ēlthen* in Revelation 6:17, is anticipating the event (i.e., proleptic) and looks ahead to the opening of the seventh seal. This is possible, but it more normally has a past tense in the indicative mood. If this is so, it certainly looks back to divine wrath as seen in the seal judgments.

Rosenthal uses another chapter to defend his view of the pre-wrath rapture of the church, based on the words "coming" and "end" in Matthew 24:3. He insists that the noun "coming" must be associated with the rapture of the church.[43] However, he makes a distinction between "the end" and the rapture. He says, "The church will be raptured, and then the end—God's wrath—will fall upon an unrepentant world."[44] To buttress this interpretation he uses 1 Corinthians 15:24, a passage most premillennialists apply to the end of the millennium. It is strange to make a distinction between the two in the Olivet discourse. His coming in Matthew 24 is obviously at the end of the Tribulation in Matthew 24.

In connection with discussing the coming of the Lord, Rosenthal insists it means an arrival and continuing presence.[45] Then he says, "That would be contradicted by the concept of a coming at the beginning of the seventieth week and another at its end, as pretribulationism has often taught."[46] But Rosenthal has the same problem as pretribulationists. If the rapture occurs before the Lord's wrath, as seen in the trumpet and bowl judgments, how can Christ be viewed as having a continuing presence? Rosenthal simply declares, "Christ's coming (*parousia*) includes both His coming and consequent presence to accomplish His purposes."[47] Pretribulationists could say exactly the same thing and hold to their own view! Christ's activity in Daniel's seventieth week will be a demonstration of His presence. To be honest with his view, Rosenthal must admit a coming of Christ occurs in Revelation 19, *after* the trumpet and seal judgments.

Rosenthal also argues for a pretribulational rapture from the warnings and exhortations that are found in Matthew 24:42–25:30. He declares, "The pretribulation rapture, by its insistence that the church will be gone before the seventieth week begins, negates those warnings."[48] Pretribulationists recognize these warnings are addressed to people living during the Tribulation after the church has been raptured, but they also see present-day applications relating to the church. Second Peter 3:10,11 clearly indicates that believers in this age can have lessons for life taught to them by events which are future and in which they will not participate.

Some other interesting views are given as well by Rosenthal to shore up his presentation. For instance, he believes the verb "shortened" in Matthew 24:22 means that the time for the Great Tribulation between the beginning of sorrows and the Day of the Lord will be abbreviated.[49] This will be done for the sake of Israel.[50] He contends this supports the pre-wrath view because it makes the day and hour of the Lord's return unknowable. The duration of the last half of Daniel's seventieth week is three-and-a-half years, or forty-two months, or 1260 days, or time, times and a half time. Within this period of time the Great Tribulation occurs. Because the Great Tribulation is shortened, the time of the rapture is unknown; but it occurs before the Day of the Lord with its wrath.

Here one must think theologically. If according to Acts 17:26, God has marked out the times for the nations, His sovereignty would include the length of time of the Great Tribulation. Another passage says the very day of entering God's rest has been determined (Heb. 4:7). Certainly, the shortening of the days is fixed. Who is to deny that the three-and-a-half years have already been amputated from what they may have been? Certainly the world and Israel deserve more than seven years of tribulation! This shortening to seven years is an evidence of God's grace.

The book carries a number of other points, but the basic thesis is found in saying that the seals which parallel Matthew 24 are not a time of God's wrath but are humanely generated cataclysms. This has been seen to be fallacious, and consequently the view is seriously damaged.

Conclusion

The Olivet discourse, according to this study, is the Lord's response to three questions of the disciples, all revolving around the conclusion of the Tribulation: the destruction of Jerusalem, the coming of the Lord, and the end of the age.

It appears that the Lord's answer is seen in the three time markers of verses 6, 8, and 14. In verse 6 the Lord says, "That is not yet the end" (NASB). That answer is introduced in verse 4, with a warning not to be misled. The presence of false messiahs, wars, and rumors of wars is so characteristic of all depraved humanity and of human history that they do not necessarily characterize the end. This may be why the Lord here uses the verb "must" (*dei*) in verse 6. The disciples could be misled by the turmoil of society, and even the overthrow of Jerusalem, but the world is fallen and it is therefore necessary for these things to occur. Such conduct on the part of humanity has marked history.

The second time indicator, in verse 8, may look at the first half of the Tribulation period. The advance in the conditions described in verse 7 seems to parallel, at least in part, the first four seals of Revelation 6. These are the beginning of birth-pangs (Matt. 24:8).

The third time marker, found in verse 14, looks back to verses 9-13. The conditions here may be a general survey of the last half of the Tribulation. From verses 15-28, the coming of the Man of Sin is contrasted with the Lord's coming. Verses 29-31 describe the glory of His return, as verse 27 anticipates. The application for Israel is given in Matthew 24:32-51. The passage, as was said earlier, is Jewish and relates to a very Jewish context. Because of its Jewishness, neither the church nor the rapture are in view in Matthew 24.

John F. Walvoord

1 Thessalonians 4:
A Central Rapture Passage

_____*OVERVIEW*

How difficult is prophecy to understand? In this essay the author makes a case for literal interpretation of prophecy. This is demonstrated through his interpretation of 1 Thessalonians 4, which he believes is a key to understanding the New Testament teaching of the rapture. Many errors in prophetic teaching arise from attempts to exchange the normal literal approach with an allegorical interpretation.

*A*n amazing feature surrounding much of the current discussion about prophecy is the almost universal assumption that prophecy cannot be interpreted literally. This, undoubtedly, is the major cause of the current confusion and the diversity of views. If statements of prophecy that are clear are accepted for what they say, it usually yields only one interpretation. But if it is claimed that the normal, or literal, interpretation is not what is intended, then it is anyone's guess as to what the passage means. This accounts for the great proliferation of prophetical theories, practically all of which are based on the idea that prophecy has to be interpreted non-literally.

What About the Year 2000?

Another major cause of confusion is inattention to what the Bible says about limiting our understanding of future events to what the Bible actually reveals. In current literature a lot of attention is paid to the twenty-first century, and it is seldom pointed out that the Bible does not teach anything about the twenty-first century. The ancient theory that the world will go on for 7000 years—2000 years before Abraham, 2000 years after Abraham, 2000 years after Christ, and then a millennial kingdom as the seventh thousand—has no scriptural support at all. In the Bible the period before Abraham is simply not dated, as the genealogies are not complete, and Usher's dates do not permit the universal flood in that period. Without giving in to the wild guesses of evolutionists who postulate millions of years, it is obvious that the Bible does not give us specific information about the time of Adam's creation.

The Allegory of Alexandria

In current discussions, this whole matter of the proper interpretation of prophecy is bypassed and not even considered, even though in the history of the doctrine it is rather plain that the major cause for confusion of prophecy is the adoption of the point of view which basically originated in the Alexandrian school of theology about A.D. 200. The Alexandrian school was the forerunner of modern liberalism. They were enamored with Platonic philosophy's pure idealism and wanted to harmonize it with Scripture. The only way this could be done was by denying what the Scriptures plainly said, and they came out with a theory that all Scripture is a huge allegory that does not mean what it appears to mean but has a hidden meaning which must be discovered. This, naturally, undermined all existing theology and was strenuously opposed by the church. It triumphed, however, in northern Africa and devastated the African church which previously had been premillennial. The result was that North Africa was a desert for biblical Christianity until our twentieth century.

The prevailing opinion of the church, however, opposed their view and successfully supported the idea that the Bible should be interpreted in its literal, or normal sense. In the field of prophecy this was harder to support, as prophecies had not yet been fulfilled. The result was continued confusion in eschatology and the rapid decline in chiliasm, the belief in a future millennial kingdom, which characterized the first and second century church. The matter was finally brought to solution by Augustine (354–430), the famous bishop and theologian of North Africa, who concluded upon his investigation that Scripture as a whole should be interpreted in its plain, grammatical, and historical sense, but that prophecy was a special case. He especially disagreed with the concept of a future millennial kingdom, though he interpreted literally the second coming, heaven, and hell. He came to this conclusion because certain premillennial sects had advocated the idea that the millennium was a time of carnal physical feasts, and he considered this too materialistic to be accepted.

What Augustine would do with a carefully presented premillennial point of view in the twentieth century would be very interesting. Augustine, however, succeeded in normalizing the whole matter, and his point of view was accepted by the Roman Catholic church, and the Protestant Reformers—Martin Luther, Calvin, and others—resorted to his solution of the problem of interpretation. The result was that the Reformed church was largely amillennial, as it is to this day. Any consideration of prophecy requires a clear understanding that the problem is whether or not prophecy is literal.

Literal Interpretation:
The Only Way to Go

This writer in 1991 published a book entitled *Prophecy Knowledge Handbook,* which attempts to explain every prophecy in the Bible from Genesis to Revelation. At the outset, it seemed to be an impossible task in light of the many views on almost every biblical prophecy. However, an approach was taken that prophecies should be examined for what they state; and if what they state is understandable, it should be accepted at face value, in other words, literally, or in its natural sense. The ancient motto, "If the natural sense makes sense don't seek any other sense," was found to be the key to prophetic interpretation. Using this, it was relatively simple to approach each clear passage and interpret it in that sense. Passages which were not clear had to be interpreted by those that were clear. The resulting 800-page volume presents a system of prophetic interpretation that is not contradictory and is based upon plain biblical statements.

When the task was completed, the discussion had dealt with 1000 passages of prophecy, some single verses, some chapters, and 50 percent of them were found to have already been literally fulfilled. This justifies the prospect of literal fulfillment in expectation of prophecies yet to be fulfilled.

Admittedly, the subject of prophecy is complex because it deals with many details that must be harmonized if one accepts the inerrancy of the Bible. In addition to the problem of literal, or natural, interpretation is the fact that Scripture, like all literature, has figures of speech, which must be understood as such. These are not complex, hidden mysteries, but rather obvious in their intended meaning. It is easily understood that when Christ declared He was the Good Shepherd (John 10:14), He never literally had cared for sheep but that His followers were ministered to much as a shepherd ministers to his sheep. When referring to Himself as the door (John 10:9), it is clearly understood that He is the Savior by which one must enter into the fold of salvation. When Christ declared that He was the light of the world (John 8:12), He did not mean He was a light beam but that He was the vehicle of revelation of divine truth. Figures of speech are designed to illustrate, not to hide the truth.

Prophecy does have the peculiarity of sometimes being presented in symbolic form. This is especially true in Daniel, Ezekiel,

Zechariah, and the book of Revelation. In most cases, however, the symbols are interpreted in the larger context of Scripture. An illustration of this is Daniel 7:7, where the fourth beast is said to have seven horns. Later in the same chapter, in verse 24, the statement is made that "ten horns are ten kings." It is not true that the introduction of symbols makes a book of the Bible incomprehensible, but it does require comparing Scripture with Scripture.

Interspersed between symbolic revelations are the plain statements of Scripture, which can be taken in their ordinary meaning. As in the book of Revelation, for instance, even a casual reading by one uninformed would yield the result that the book is describing a time of judgment from God connected with the second coming of Christ. It is unfortunate that some interpreters, in the effort to make their point of view scriptural, build upon what seems to them to be obscurity of Scripture.

Interpreting the Unclear
in Light of the Clear

The central passage on the rapture of the church is found in 1 Thessalonians 4:13-18. So often, this passage is neglected in the discussion of prophecy as a whole, and another look at it will yield some helpful insights into God's prophetic program. At the outset it should be observed that this prophecy is not given in obscure or symbolic language; it is a plain statement about what will occur at the rapture of the church. As in all prophecy interpretation, it is important to observe what is said and not add to what is said.

The passage begins with a statement by Paul that he does not want the Thessalonians to be ignorant or uninformed concerning future things. It is significant that the apostle Paul, once he received the revelation of the rapture of the church, included it in his missionary messages as part of the gospel. Though he was in the Thessalonian church only a short time before being driven out, he left behind his teaching about the first coming of Jesus Christ and His death and resurrection, as well as his teaching that Christ could be coming back at any time to take His own out of the world. The emphasis on this subject of the Lord's coming is sadly neglected by much of the church today. It is evident from this passage and many others that God intends us to study prophecy even though all the details are not revealed. The purpose of prophecy as a whole is to provide hope and comfort in the time of bereavement, as Paul states in verse 13.

What follows is a plain statement of what the rapture is all about. Just as the Bible teaches that Christ in His first coming died and rose again, so also at the rapture God will bring with Jesus those who have fallen asleep. This statement plainly indicates that when Christ returns in the event being described, He will bring the souls of Christians who have died with Him. In the nature of physical death a soul departs from the body and goes to heaven. The body is buried. At the time of Christ's coming the Scriptures here make plain that the body will be resurrected and the soul will reenter the body.

The grand event is described as coming by divine revelation from Jesus Christ Himself. The rapture is not a subject of prophecy in the Old Testament, though the second coming of Christ is. For this reason, Paul does not quote any Old Testament Scriptures but presents the truth of the rapture as a new doctrine given by direct revelation to him. The facts he outlines are not difficult to understand.

Apparently, the Thessalonians had some questions as to whether the dead would be raised at the time of their own transformation when being caught up to glory. The order of events is plainly indicated here. Christians who are living at the time of this event will not precede those who have died, the order of events being that the resurrection of the righteous comes first and is followed immediately by the translation and transformation of living Christians. This is described in verse 16, "For the Lord himself will come down from heaven, with a loud command, with the voice of the archangel and the trumpet call of God, and the dead in Christ will rise first" (NIV).

There is nothing symbolic or obscure in this passage. Christians who have died will be resurrected at the time Christ comes for His own. Immediately following, however, those who are living at the time will be caught up with them in the clouds to meet the Lord in the air. Further light is cast on this in 1 Corinthians 15, where it is made clear that Christians who have not died will be instantly changed like those resurrected from the grave. Together, Christians will meet the Lord in the air.

It is obvious that this is a beginning of a journey from earth to heaven. In John 14:3, on the night before His crucifixion, Christ said, "If I go and prepare a place for you, I will come back and take you to be with me that you also may be where I am" (NIV).The rapture is a movement from earth to heaven.

Important Contrasts

A comparison of the rapture doctrine as presented here, with the second coming of Christ, described in Revelation 19, should make it abundantly clear that the two events are quite different and do not occur at the same time, though this has been the common doctrine of the church, which does not necessarily pay attention to the details of prophecy. The rapture of the church has one purpose: the removal of the church from the world. The second coming does not have this purpose and is entirely different. In Revelation, at the second coming, Christ is accompanied by the armies of angels and saints in heaven, and it is a major movement of the whole group from heaven to the millennial earth. His purpose is to "strike the nations" (Rev. 19:15 NIV). His coming is the time of expression of the "fierceness and wrath of Almighty God" (v. 15). Events that follow justify this, as the armies mounted against Christ are destroyed, and the world ruler, and the false prophet associated with him, are cast into the lake of fire. There is no removal of the saints from the earth, as they are going to be in the millennial kingdom with Christ throughout the thousand years. It would be difficult to describe two occasions that are more different than the rapture and the second coming of Christ, though in both cases they are properly described as the coming of Christ. In the rapture, however, He does not touch the earth; whereas, in the second coming His feet touch the Mount of Olives (Zech. 14:4).

The events that follow the second coming are also totally different than the events that follow the rapture. From other Scriptures we gather that the rapture takes the church to heaven, where it is judged and joins Christ at the marriage feast of the Lamb. In Revelation, the aftermath of the second coming is the binding of Satan for 1000 years (Rev. 20:1-3), the resurrection of the martyred dead who join with Christ in His 1000-year kingdom (Rev. 20:4-6), and the 1000-year reign of Christ on earth. No such events follow the rapture of the church immediately.

The error of combining the rapture and the second coming, though very common and especially held by the amillenarians and postmillenarians, can only be justified on the basic principle that you cannot interpret prophecy literally, which is a false assumption.

It is perhaps unnecessary to point out that there is no obscurity about this in 1 Thessalonians 4:13-18. The entire prophecy is couched in plain, ordinary language that is understandable in its natural, or literal, meaning. As such, it should guide the student of prophecy through all other Scriptures that deal with the end times. Most important is the contrast between the rapture, the catching up of the church, which is mentioned here, and the second coming of Christ which is a totally different event.

In brief, the second coming of Christ, as portrayed in Revelation 19, is a movement from heaven to earth in which Christ will be accompanied by all the hosts of heaven, in which He is coming to judge a wicked world and to establish His kingdom on earth. If the church is caught up to heaven earlier than this event, as many believe, it will accompany Christ in His return to the earth and will be with Him throughout the millennial kingdom.

Conclusion

In current discussion of prophecy, a frequent claim is made that any attempt to understand specific events of the future is an extreme literal interpretation of the Bible. It is overlooked that literal, or natural, interpretation is the norm, not the extreme, and it is the only method of interpretation which will yield any kind of harmony in the prophetic Word. One does not have to be an accomplished scholar or capable of very abstract reasoning to understand the rapture in 1 Thessalonians 4. Properly understood, it serves as a rudder to guide us through all other prophecies of the end times.

Much of the confusion in modern prophecy would be removed if proper attention were paid to 1 Thessalonians 4 Almost every wrong interpretation ignores this passage, even though it is plainly written and easily understood. Scholars are often too busy justifying their position on other matters, and they consider this a minor issue; whereas, instead, it is one of the central issues of prophecy in its interpretation in the New Testament.

Understanding the rapture doctrine is not only a theological issue but also a very practical one. The early church, obviously, was looking for the coming of Christ at any time. This is what the Thessalonians were taught, and this is what they believed. Early

Christians were characterized as loving His appearing (2 Tim. 4:8), meaning that they not only loved the Savior but also the prospect of seeing Him face-to-face in all His glory and being joined to Him forever. A neglect of the rapture doctrine leads to a neglect of this marvelous hope which is intended to be a guiding star to Christian life and testimony and its future expectation and hope.

14
H. Wayne House

Apostasia in 2 Thessalonians 2:3: Apostasy or Rapture?

_____ *OVERVIEW*

What is the best understanding of the Greek term apostasia *in 2 Thessalonians 2:3? Should it refer to religious apostasy or rebellion as is most commonly understood, even by pretribulationists? Or should it be understood to refer to a physical departure or disappearance? Either view is possible within the range of the word's meaning. In this essay, Dr. House makes a case for* apostasia *as a reference to the rapture. If this is true, then the case for the pretribulational rapture would not only be greatly strengthened, it would be virtually established.*

*T*he Thessalonian epistles furnish much of the exegetical ore from which those concerned with the nature and timing of Christ's return have mined their eschatology. This is appropriate since the apostle Paul introduces many statements regarding the coming of our Lord. Unfortunately, even in passages that have sufficient context and development to determine the most significant issues of the Day of Christ and subsequent happenings on this earth, there is considerable difference of opinion among biblical eschatologists. In order to come to a proper understanding of this blessed hope, the disagreements are not confined to those who hold diverse millennial perspectives, or even different tribulational views, but they are found among pretribulational, premillennial scholars. Those who accept this nomenclature proudly nonetheless differ about the details. Arduous exegetical spadework is still necessary to get the finer granules of theological gold.

One of the more technical points that needs to be addressed in 2 Thessalonians 2 is the identification of the meaning of *apostasia* in verse 3, the subject to which I will restrict my presentation, fully recognizing that this is but one piece of the grand puzzle of this fascinating portion of Scripture.

How Biblical Scholars Have Understood *Apostasia* in 2 Thessalonians 2:3

There are four primary interpretations of the meaning of this Greek term historically, and the proper understanding of the word can shed much light on whether a pretributional understanding of events surrounding our Lord's return is the correct one or not. Let us briefly look at each option.

As an Appositive

The perspective that the term *apostasia* in 2 Thessalonians 2:2 refers to the "man of sin" in the same verse is known as the appositional view. Generally this has not been held in recent times. In the first centuries of the church, however, Alford writes that several fathers believed this to be the case, including Chrysostom, Theophylact, and Augustine.[1] For example, Chrysostom says, "What is the *apostasia*; he calls the antichrist himself the *apostasia*."[2] Theophylact says, "The *apostasia* is the antichrist."[3] Augustine comments, "And the day of judgment will not come, unless that should come first, which he calls the fugitive."[4] Modern commentators are divided on the matter. John Eadie pointedly disagrees that *apostasia* is equivalent of the "man of sin" ("Nor can ἀποστάσια [*apostasia*] be taken as the abstract for the concrete, meaning Antichrist himself, as Chrysostom, and the Greek fathers, with Augustine"). But James Moffatt seems to identify the two (a small minority view):

> [T]he apostasy and the appearance (so of Beliar, *Asc. Isa.*, iv. 18) of the personal anti-Christ or pseudo-Christ form a single phenomenon. From the use of ἡ ἀποστασία [*hē apostasia* = *the departure/revolt*] as a Greek equivalent for Belial (LXX of 1 Kings xxi. 13, A, and Aquila), this eschatological application of the term would naturally flow, especially as איש בליעל [*ish belial* = *man of wickedness*] might well be represented by ὁ ἄνθρωπος τῆς ἀνομίας [*ho anthropos tēs anomias* = *the man of lawlessness*] the analogy of 2 Sam. xxii. 5 (LXX) = Ps. xvii. (xviii).[5]

As "Falling Away" from the Faith

A second view is that *apostasia* refers to a religious defection or falling away in the last days, after which the "man of sin" or Antichrist will be revealed. As Edmond Hiebert explains, "The first sign which Paul insists must precede the Day of the Lord is 'the falling away' (*hē apostasia*), the term from which our English word "apostasy" is derived. It denotes a deliberate abandonment of a formerly professed position or view, a defection, a rejection of a former allegiance."[6] Bloesch also holds that the "falling away" is a sign that precedes the *parousia* of Christ:

> Though the *parousia* will be sudden and unexpected, the Bible nonetheless speaks of signs for those who

have the eyes to see and the ears to hear. They are not empirical evidences or proofs but reminders to the faithful that his coming is on the horizon. Among these signs are...a falling away from faith accompanied by false prophets with signs and wonders (Matt. 24:10-11,24; 1 Tim. 4:1; 2 Tim. 4:3,4; 2 Thess. 2:3,9).[7]

As will be explained in more detail below, this view seems to originate with the King James Version in 1611. Many scholars today hold to this viewpoint, but they differ as to who actually falls away. Some believe this refers to apostasy within the church (Erdman, Ockenga, Hendriksen, Mason, Calvin).[8] Others think this speaks of a falling away of Jewish people during the Tribulation (Rosenthal),[9] while others believe the falling away is of non-Christians as a whole (Marshall, Bruce).[10]

Professing church

Charles Ryrie, for example, sees the apostasy of 2 Thessalonians 2:3 as being the future great apostasy in which people turn away from a truth formerly accepted. He relates it to apostasy in the professing church. Ryrie thinks that the future great apostasy mentioned in 2 Thessalonians 2:3 is possibly discussed in Revelation 17 and 2 Timothy 3:1.[11]

This also seems to be the perspective of Louis Berkhof, when he says that immediately before the end the Bible indicates a time of great apostasy, "when the faith of many will wax cold, and when they who are loyal to Christ will be subjected to bitter sufferings, and will in some cases even seal their confession with their blood...."[12]

Jews

Others view the *apostasia* as the rejection of God by the Jewish people during the time of the Tribulation. Marvin Rosenthal says that the first two uses of *apostasia* in the New Testament are in the context of Paul being accused of asking Jews to abandon or forsake the teachings of Moses. Rosenthal then says that this is the same sense in 2 Thessalonians 2:3, in which Paul "was speaking of Jews who, during the seventieth week of Daniel, will totally abandon the

God of their fathers and their messianic hope in favor of a false religion (humanism) and a false messiah (the Antichrist, 2 Thess. 2:2-12)."[13] Rosenthal believes, then, that the *apostasia* is the Jewish abandonment of their covenantal relationship with the Lord during the first half of the Tribulation, and so it cannot be an event preceding, or at the beginning of, the seventieth week.[14]

Non-Christians

Other scholars consider that the apostasy or rebellion is of "nonChristians as a whole, of the sons of disobedience in whom the prince of the power of the air, the evil spirit, is now operating (cf. Eph. 2.2)."[15]

C. F Hogg and W. E. Vine argue that the apostasy is a revolt by man against the claim of a superior being, namely, God: "All apostasy is essentially religious, i.e. it is revolt against God. This apostasy is not merely a revolt against God, it is a denial of any being, or order of beings, superior to man. It is the claim of man to absolute supremacy not only in the world but in the universe."[16]

Lewis Sperry Chafer identifies the apostasy in 2 Thessalonians 2:3 with the final apostasy before the man of sin appears, and he sees it as a final deception upon those who receive not the love of the truth so that they might be saved.[17] In another statement, Chafer clearly indicates that he sees the apostasy as being only non-Christians:

> The elect company of true believers is ever beset with tendencies to formality, unbelief, and worldliness. This condition, as predicted, has continued throughout the age. In 2 Thessalonians 2:3 it is stated, "Let no man deceive you by any means: for that day [the day of the Lord] shall not come, except there come a [the] falling away first." Here the definite article (cf. R.V.) isolates this apostasy from every other. It precedes the Day of Jehovah, and is evidently that final form of religious union and profession which will obtain in the tribulation after the true Church has been removed from the earth [brackets his].[18]

A.T. Robertson leaves the question in the air, when he says, "It is not clear whether Paul means revolt of the Jews from God, of

Gentiles from God, of Christians from God, or of the apostasy that includes all classes within and without the body of Christians."[19]

As a Revolt or Rebellion

For some writers there may not be a clear distinction between *apostasia* as being a "falling away" or a "revolt," but a revolt or rebellion appears to imply a forceful active rejection of God, while defection appears to be more passive. This is especially true when one draws imagery of a political, armed revolt against a governmental authority.

A. L. Moore states that the apostasy is the final revolt against God and has as its heart religious rebellion:

> **[T]he rebellion comes first**: here Paul uses imagery drawn probably from Daniel 11:36 (and cf. Isa. 14:13ff; Ezek. 28:2). Rebellion, *apostasia*, could refer to political apostasy or military revolt in classical Greek, but in the LXX it denotes religious rebellion against God (cf. Jos. 22:22; Jer. 2:19). With the article (as here) it signifies a definite event of which the converts have knowledge (cf. verse 5). The thought is, we suggest, that when the moment comes for Christ to appear in glory and for all that rebels against God to be unmasked and cast out, the forces of evil will arise as never before in a last desperate effort against God. It is not the same thought as we find in Mark 13:6ff; 1 Timothy 4:1ff; 2 Timothy 3:1-9, where rebellion and lawlessness are "signs of the End" (as here, too, in verse 4-7) for the final upsurge of evil here described is thought of as actually belonging to the complex of events which constitute the End.[20]

I. Howard Marshall says, "The thought is of a general increase in ungodliness with the world at large rather than a large-scale apostasy within the church, although the probability of the attitude in the world at large affecting some within the church should not be overlooked."[21]

Similarly, Leon Morris states:

> While the coming of "the Day of the Lord" will be
> unexpected (1 Thess. 5:2-3), certain things will pre-
> cede it. One is *the rebellion*. The definite article
> shows that the rebellion was well known to the
> readers; evidently it had formed part of Paul's pre-
> vious teaching. Our difficulty is that we do not know
> what he had told them. In classical Greek *apostasia*
> meant a political or military rebellion, but in LXX it is
> used of rebellion against God (e.g. Jos. 22:22), and
> this became the accepted biblical usage. Paul is say-
> ing that in the last times there will be a great uprising
> of the powers of evil against God (Mt. 24:10ff; 1 Tim.
> 4:1-3; 2 Tim. 3:1-9; 4:3-4). It is as though Satan were
> throwing all his forces into one last despairing effort.[22]

David Williams states that there is no real difference between
rebellion and apostasy, and that the apostasy may have been political in nature in view of Romans 13:1:

> At all events, in common with other New Testament
> writers and like Jesus himself (Matt. 24:10-13), Paul
> envisages a final upsurge of evil before the end of the
> age, heralding the onset of the end. Some have under-
> stood the *apostasia* as a falling away within the
> church, but the word expresses not so much apathy as
> deliberate opposition, and it is better to see this as a
> reference to events outside the church which, how-
> ever, will profoundly affect the church. The rebellion
> will be the church's "great tribulation" (Rev. 7:14).[23]

F. F. Bruce argues, like Williams, that the rebellion is a "large-
scale revolt against public order," and that rebellion against "gov-
erning authorities" is rebellion against God since He instituted
them.[24]

As the Rapture

The fourth view is that *apostasia* refers to the rapture; that is,
the departure of the church prior to the coming of the man of sin

(2 Thess. 2:2ff) and the Tribulation period of seven years (though this view of *apostasia* could equally be used by a midtribulation person). Among the scholars who have adopted the rapture understanding of *apostasia* are MacRae, Ellisen, Lewis, English, Pentecost, and Wuest. As seen from the preceding list, proponents of this view essentially represent scholars of pretribulation persuasion, though certainly the majority of pretribulationists have not adopted this understanding of *apostasia*. Richard Reiter indicates:

> In his series "Re-thinking the Rapture" in *Our Hope*, editor E. Schuyler English concluded that *apostasia* in 2 Thessalonians 2:3 meant "departure" or "withdrawal" rather than the more common translations of "falling away" or "rebellion." English based his case on lexical possibilities and contexual considerations to solve a theological problem. He also published replies by conservative scholars—some agreed but many disagreed. Allan A. MacRae, president of Faith Theological Seminary in Philadelphia at that time, felt that the interpretation solved a serious problem for pretribulational interpretation. Kenneth S. Wuest of Moody Bible Institute approved it, yet most pretribulationists rejected it. Probably none recalled that J. S. Mabie, connected with the earlier Bible conference movement, suggested "a most original answer" to the interpretation of *apostasia* at the Annual Conference on the Lord's Coming, Los Angeles, in November, 1895. It was the rapture of the church set forth in 1 Thessalonians 4:14-18.[25]

A recent proponent is Stanley Ellisen, who acknowledges that the term *apostasia* has come to be identified almost universally as defection, usually associated with the retraction from godliness and the gospel as found in passages such as 1 Timothy 4:1, and 2 Timothy 3:1ff, and 1 John 2:18ff. Due to this, says Ellisen, a doctrine of a major defection from the faith in the last days has been constructed, so that dictionaries uniformly define "apostasy" as desertion of one's faith. Ellisen then comments:

> At the risk of being out of step with most commentaries on the subject, may we suggest the greater

acceptability of an alternate view: the evidence for a
great singular defection from the faith, occurring just
prior to the rapture or to the Day of the Lord, is really
based on questionable ground. In the first reference
generally appealed to (1 Tim. 4), Paul does speak of
an apostasy from the faith, but not as a unique end-
time event. Rather, he described it as a trend or movement that was already present. This he characterized
as erroneous doctrine, hypocritical living, and improper
legalism. In using the term here, he qualified it with
the phrase "from the faith." By itself it meant simply
"departure."

In the second reference to defection, 2 Timothy 3:1ff.,
Paul does not use the term apostasy, but merely
speaks of evil men in general in the latter times. His
point here is that evil men will become more and
more depraved as the age wears on (2 Timothy 3:13).
Thus this passage has no real relation to apostasy
from the faith and certainly does not warn of some
specific final defection that will precede the rapture or
introduce the Day of the Lord.[26]

Similarly Gordon Lewis argues that *apostasia* may rightly be
translated other than "defection" or "revolt" and refer to a spatial
departure:

The verb [for *apostasia*] may mean to remove spatially. There is little reason then to deny that the noun
can mean such a spatial removal or departure. Since
the noun is used only one other time in the New Testament of apostasy from Moses (Acts 21:21), we can
hardly conclude that its Biblical meaning is necessarily determined. The verb is used fifteen times in
the New Testament. Of these fifteen, only three have
anything to do with a departure from the faith (Luke
8:13; 1 Tim. 4:1; Heb. 3:12). The word is used for
departing from iniquity (2 Tim. 2:19), from ungodly
men (1 Tim. 6:5), from the temple (Luke 2:27), from
the body (2 Cor. 12:8), and from persons (Acts 12:10;
Luke 4:13).[27]

How *Apostasia* Has Been Translated

Now that we have briefly looked at how commentators and theologians view the translation of *apostasia*, let us look at how the various versions of the Bible have translated the term. The translation of *apostasia* varies little for the first 15 centuries of translation. The Vulgate uses the Latin word *discessio*, meaning "departure" (*Ne quis vos seducat ullo modo: quoniam nisi venerit discessio primum....*"). This fourth-century Latin translation by Jerome presented the standard understanding until Beza, a member of the Geneva Bible Translation Committee, departed from the traditional translation of "departure" and instead transliterated the Greek term as *apostasia*.

In view of this history, prior to Beza, the earliest English versions used the neutral term of "departure" in translating *apostasia*, either translating the term with a verb or a noun and not indicating what was intended by the term, whether departure from the faith or departure in a spatial sense. Note the seven translations and their dates:

Apostasia
as departure or departing

1384	Wycliffe Bible	Departynge first
1526	Tyndale Bible	Departynge first
1535	Coverdale Bible	Departynge first
1539	Cranmer Bible	Departynge first
1576	Breeches Bible	Departing first
1583	Beza Bible	Departing first
1608	Geneva Bible	Departing first

It is uncertain why Beza decided to depart from Jerome's translation and transliterate the Greek term rather than translating it. Possibly this was due to the fact that Jerome was a Roman Catholic, and Beza, Calvin's disciple, was Protestant. But this would hardly explain why he would transliterate *apostasia* unless so doing would bring theological benefit in the controversy with Romanism. In fact, the sense of *apostasy* may have seemed very appropriate to describe the perspective of the coming of Christ in view of the popish apostasy, i.e., him being the man of sin. Whatever the reason may be, the word "departure" as the translation of *apostasia* ceases after Beza and the new translation, the 1611 King James Version. To my knowledge the KJV is the first English translation to introduce an alternative translation, rather than Beza's transliteration, that of "falling away:" "Let no man deceive you by any means: for *that day shall not come*, except there come *a falling away* first, and that man of sin be revealed, the son of perdition...." (KJV).

Modern translations since the King James Version have followed its practice in not using "departure." These translations of *apostasia* in 2 Thessalonians 2:3 generally have settled on the translations of "rebellion" or "falling away." Other meanings similar to these are "apostasy," "great revolt," and "rejection." The following are some modern presentations from standard New Testament translations:

Apostasia as "Rebellion" or a Synonymous Concept

"Don't let anyone deceive you in any way, for that day will not come until the *rebellion* occurs and the man of lawlessness is revealed, the man doomed to destruction." NIV)

"Let no one deceive you in any way; for that day will not come unless the *rebellion* comes first and the lawless one is revealed, the one destined for destruction." (NRSV)

"You must let anyone deceive you at all. For that is not until the *rebellion* takes place and the embodiment of disobedience makes his appearance—he who is doomed to destruction.. . " (Goodspeed)

"Let no one deceive you in any way; for that day will not come, unless the *rebellion* comes first, and the man of lawlessness is revealed, the son of perdition...." (RSV)

"Let nobody delude you into this belief, whatever he may say. It will not come till *the Rebellion* takes place first of all, with the revealing of the Lawless One, the doomed One.. " (Moffatt)

"Don't let anyone deceive you by any means whatsoever. That day will not come before there arises *a definite rejection of God* and the appearance of the lawless man. He is the product of all that leads to death...." (Phillips)

"Never let anyone deceive you in this way. It cannot happen until *the Great Revolt* has taken place and the Rebel, the Lost One, has appeared." (Jerusalem Bible)

"Do not let anybody at all deceive you about this, because that cannot take place until *the great revolt* occurs and the representative of lawlessness is uncovered, the one who is doomed to destruction...." (Williams)

Apostasia as "Falling Away" or Synonymous Concept

"Let no one in any way deceive you; for the *apostasy* is to come first, and the man of sin is to be revealed, the one doomed to hell.. ." (Berkeley)

"Let no man beguile you in any wise: for it will not be, except *the falling away* comes first, and the man of sin be revealed, the son of perdition...." (ASV)

"Let no one deceive you by any means; for that Day will not come unless *the falling away* comes first, and the man of sin is revealed, the son of perdition...." (NKJV)

Arguments that Tend to Favor the Rapture View

Lexicographical Considerations That Favor the Rapture View

The Indeterminacy of the Meaning of *Apostasia*

There can be little question that the noun *apostasia* has been translated generally as carrying a nonspatial meaning, usually "defection," "rebellion," "falling away," or "revolt" in extra-biblical literature. Also in the LXX, the noun regularly refers either to a revolt against a government or defection from faith in Yahweh.[28] The lexica provide additional proof for these meanings.[29] If one merely counted the times *apostasia* is used with these meanings, or wholly relied on the lexica, then the case would be closed on the rapture view. However, such an approach would not yield a fully developed understanding of the word. There can be no question that the verb form allows the idea of spatial departure and is used that way many times in the LXX, in fact more times than the ideas of defection or revolt combined (see interaction below with Gundry). The response to this is that even if this is true, the noun form does not carry the idea of a spatial departure. But this is not accurate.

The noun form allows for *apostasia* as a simple departure in the classical period, proved by examples from Liddell and Scott. Their lexicon gives "departure" and "disappearance" as secondary meanings.[30] If one says that this is not important because this meaning is only classical or ancient and thus lost its meaning by the time of the New Testament period, then I may turn to this same root meaning for *apostasia* in the patristic era immediately following the New Testament period, as indicated in definitions for the noun form in Lampe's Patristic Greek Lexicon.[31] Although the noun used in the sense of a spatial departure is not the normal meaning (though it is true for the verb) during New Testament times, the word is found with this meaning in time periods before and after the New Testament era, and it is likely to have been understood this way at least sometimes. It was also understood to have this meaning in 2 Thessalonians 2:3 by the fourth-century translator Jerome, where in his text he translates *hē apostasia* as the Latin *discessio*, meaning "departure."

The real question is why the noun *apostasia*, which can mean "departure," is so often used for "defection" or "revolt," but is used so few times for "departure," unlike the verb? Certainly I have no final answer, but the idea of departure from the faith of Israel, or rebellion against a foreign power, became a natural use of the word, and we find it repeatedly in such contexts. But the key is that it does not inherently carry the meaning of defection or revolt. It does so only because of the contexts in which it is found.

Comparison of 2 Thessalonians with 1 Maccabees 2:15

Some believe that the example of the articular *apostasia* in 1 Maccabees 2:15, translated "defection," provides proof that *apostasia* in 2 Thessalonians 2:3 should be translated "religious defection."[32] Three examples of an articular *apostasia* occur in the Old Testament,[33] one in the Apocrypha, and one in the New Testament. Unlike the passages in 2 Chronicles and Jeremiah, the articular *apostasia* in 1 Maccabees 2:15 and 2 Thessalonians 2:3 has *no* qualifier. This is so because the former passage is the only example of an absolute *apostasia* (with an article and no qualifiers present), just as one finds in 2 Thessalonians 2:3.[34]

When a word occurs like this without any qualifier of meaning, the understanding is that what the word refers to is so definite in the reader's mind that no qualifier is needed. One can simply read the narrative of 1 Maccabees until 2:15, and the translation of religious defection is clear. Chapters 1 and 2 describe the Greek takeover of Palestine by Alexander to the time of Antiochus Epiphanes. The introduction concerns the infamous invasion and desecration of the temple by Antiochus, in which he was joined by many Jewish traitors. The writer of 1 Maccabees describes the whole movement of Jewish traitors as "the apostasy" (2:15). In the preceding 46 verses the author described that departure as "from God," "from the covenant," "from the Law," and so on. The term with the article needs no further qualification, although the word is translated many ways in the LXX.[35]

When one studies the context of 2 Thessalonians 2:3 in the same manner as the contextual markings provided in 1 Maccabees 2:15, the idea of *apostasia* being a reference to the rapture seems totally plausible (see below).

Contextual Considerations That Favor the Rapture View

There are two major contexual factors that favor the understanding of *apostasia* as the rapture. The first is that the rapture of the church is the primary doctrinal view which Paul develops in 1 Thessalonians, and also in 2 Thessalonians, where he tries to correct some false teaching and provide the Thessalonians with some hope. The second consideration supporting this view is the antithetical parallel between the *apostasia* and the man of sin in 2:3 to the restrainer and the man of sin in verses 6 and 7.

The Rapture in the Thessalonian Epistles

The prior context of 1 Maccabees 2:15 provided invaluable assistance in determing the sense of the absolute *apostasia* as being "religious defection." The article with *apostasia*, and the fact that no qualifiers are present, indicates that the readers were expected to understand the idea of departure as present in the noun. The meaning was clear based on their prior knowledge; namely, defection from the Jewish faith. Similarly, the prior context of 2 Thessalonians 2:3, found in the letters to the Thessalonians, indicate that the absolute *apostasia* in 2:3 very reasonably may be understood to

mean the "departure of the church," a subject repeatedly encountered by the Thessalonians, both in the oral teaching of Paul and the
letters he wrote to them.

Almost every chapter of 1 Thessalonians has a direct reference
to the departure of the church. In 1 Thessalonians 1:9-10a, the
apostle indicates that they had turned from the idols and waited on
God's Son from heaven to *rescue* (*rhuomenon*) them from the coming wrath. In 2:19, Paul indicates that the Thessalonians provide him
with his hope and joy at the coming of Christ. Chapter 4 provides
the most complete statement of Christ's *coming* (*parousia*) for
believers. In verses 13-17, Paul speaks of the dead rising first and
believers being *caught up together* (*harpagēsometha*) to meet
Christ in the air. In 5:1-11, the apostle says that believers obtain
salvation (*sōterias*), referring back to the same ideas developed in
the preceding chapter. Last of all, the verses immediately preceding
2:3 speak of the coming of Christ and our gathering together with
Him, ideas that summarize the entire emphasis on Christ's coming
given in 1 Thessalonians.

In the instances just given, the apostle uses a variety of Greek
words to express the same event of our departure from the earth to
be with Jesus Christ. Should it be so surprising that the apostle now
uses still another term to express this departure that must precede
the revelation of the man of lawlessless during the Tribulation
period? Remember, the Thessalonians had been led astray by the
false teaching (2:2-3) that the Day of the Lord had already come.
This was confusing because Paul offered great hope, in the first
letter, of a departure to be with Christ and a rescue from God's
wrath. Now a letter purporting to be from Paul seems to say that
they would first have to go through the Day of the Lord. Paul then
clarified his prior teaching by emphasizing that they had no need to
worry. They could again be comforted because the departure he had
discussed in his first letter, and in his teaching while with them, was
still the truth. The departure of Christians to be with Christ, and the
subsequent revelation of the lawless one, Paul argues, is proof that
the Day of the Lord had not begun as they had thought. This understanding of *apostasia* makes much more sense than the view that
they are to be comforted (v. 2) because a defection from the faith
must precede the Day of the Lord. The entire second chapter (as
well as 1 Thessalonians 4:18; 5:11) serves to comfort (see vv. 2,3,17),

supplied by a reassurance of Christ's coming as taught in his first letter.

The Restrainer

The antithetical parallel of *apostasia* and the man of lawlessness in verse 3 to the same type of parallelism in verses 6 and 7 supports *apostasia* as being the rapture. [36]

Characteristically, the restrainer in verses 6 and 7 has been taken as a reference to the Holy Spirit or to the church (a few have seen this as a reference to government, but this is unlikely). Lewis Sperry Chafer presents the Holy Spirit as being the restrainer:

> The mystery of lawlessness which he consummates was begun in the Apostle's day and would have been completed at an earlier time had not that lawlessness, promoted by Satan, been restrained. The Restrainer will go on restraining until He, the Restrainer, is taken out of the way. Then shall "that Wicked" one be revealed, and not before. But who is the Restrainer? The notion it is the church herself is corrected at once by the disclosure that the Restrainer is a Person, for the identification is of one who may be designated with the masculine gender. Likewise, the claim that this Person is Satan is as untenable, since Satan cannot be said to restrain himself. That the Restrainer is accomplishing a stupendous, supernatural task classes Him at once as one of the Godhead Three; and since the Holy Spirit is the active agency of the Trinity in the world throughout this age, it is a well-established conclusion that the Restrainer is the Holy Spirit of God. Some portion of this restraint is, no doubt, wrought through the church, which is the temple of the Spirit (cf. 1 Cor. 6:19; Eph. 2:19-22).
>
> Nothing needs to be imposed upon fallen humanity to set up the great tribulation in the earth: that tribulation will automatically result when the Spirit's restraint is removed. The removal of the Holy Spirit is the reversing of Pentecost. On the Day of Pentecost He who had been omnipresent in relation to the world became resident in the world, and when He is removed He who is

now resident will be again omnipresent in His relation to the world. This explains the seeming paradox that He who was already here on earth because infinite came on the Day of Pentecost, and He who is removed will still be present. So far as its being a mere inference that the church—the Spirit's present abode in the world—will remain here after the Spirit is removed, her departure with the Holy Spirit, though that departure is not expressly mentioned in this context, is a necessity.[37]

I think that the Holy Spirit is surely in view in these verses, but also that the church still on earth may also be a restrainer. Interestingly, Paul uses both a masculine and a neuter in his development of what keeps the man of sin from being revealed. The person of the Holy Spirit restrains, or prevents, his revelation. I believe this to be indicated in verse 7, where Paul says the *one* who restrains the man of lawlessness will do so until this restraining one is taken out of the way. On the other hand, the contrast of another restrainer holding down the man of lawlessness in verse 6 indicates a thing that hinders the lawless one's revelation. Paul challenges the Thessalonians to remember what he had taught them (v. 5), which he expects they should now understand. If they realize that the Day of the Lord will not occur until the church is removed, and that the departure of the church must precede the revelation of the man of lawlessness, then it is reasonable for them to now know that the presence of the church (what is restraining him) in the world prevents the revelation of the man of lawlessness. This would provide comfort, for until the church's departure or *apostasia* the man of lawlessness, and subsequently the Day of the Lord, could not begin.

Interaction With Those Who Reject the Rapture View

The rapture view has not been well received by a large number of scholars from various eschatological positions, and some scholars have made specific attempts to discredit the view that *apostasia* could mean "departure" or "rapture."

When Schuyler English came upon the idea that *apostasia* in 2 Thessalonians 2:3 might be translated "departure," speaking of the rapture, he sent his idea to a number of well-known biblical scholars, asking for their evaluation. One to whom he wrote was well-known theologian J. Oliver Buswell. His response was pointedly negative.[38] In a later writing about this matter he says:

> In recent years a group of premillennial Bible teachers have advanced the idea that *apostasia* in 2 Thessalonians 2:3 means the "departure" of the church in the rapture. Against this view is the fact that *apostasia* quite uniformly stands for the departure or standing away, or removal of that which is hostile to the point of view of the writer. I cannot find any instance in which this word, either as verb or as a noun, refers to a departure in which the speaker or writer or his friends depart. It always designates a departure in a hostile sense.[39]

Buswell's analysis of the uses of *apostasia*, as we shall see below, is incomplete and not in full accord with the perimeters that he has given to the word. In fact, there are a number of examples of *apostasia* and its verbal counterpart that occur in just the sense that Buswell disclaims as the word's meaning.

This skepticism is not limited to those who are not pretribulationists. Well-known pretribulationist John Walvoord has also concluded, reluctantly and with resignation, that *apostasia* cannot refer to a rapture. Walvoord says that *apostasia* and the revelation of the man of sin are sequential events that must precede the Day of the Lord.[40] He then mentions that "E. Schuyler English and others have suggested that the word means literally 'departure' and refers to the rapture itself,"[41] but then he comments that Gundry argues convincingly against the interpretation of "rapture" in *apostasia*. He says that Wuest joins English but that this view "has not met with general acceptance by either pretribulationists or posttribulationists."[42] Walvoord then concludes: "In that case [against "rapture" in *apostasia*] Gundry, seconded by Ladd, is probably right: the word refers to doctrinal defection of the special character that will be revealed in the Day of the Lord."[43]

Possibly the most thorough analysis of the arguments for *apostasia* as referring to the rapture has been from posttribulationist Robert Gundry. He notes that English finds some evidence for

"departure" in the classical period, but that this is the least important evidence for the New Testament meaning in 2 Thess. 2:3. He
continues:

> The meaning and connotation of a New Testament
> word are determined from four sources: 1) other
> appearances in the New Testament; 2) the LXX; 3) the
> *koine* (of which New Testament Greek is a species);
> and 4) classical Greek. The last makes the least
> important of all sources and, significantly, it is from
> this least important source that English draws his
> argument. But even in classical Greek simple depar-
> ture by no means predominates.[44]

I find it extremely interesting that Gundry limits the determination of word meanings to four and omits (possibly by accident) the
most important factor in determining the specific meaning of any
given word; namely, context. Certainly, even in context a word
cannot mean just anything one chooses, but within the range (i.e.,
semantic distance of a word) of meaning any given word may have,
context is the most important consideration, and this is especially
pertinent in the present discussion.

When considering the four sources for *apostasia*, Gundry
argues:

> [T]he first three sources indicates that at the time the
> New Testament was written, ἀποστασία had acquired
> the limited meaning of departure in the spheres of
> religion and politics, i.e. political revolt and religious
> apostasy. The only other occurrence of the word in the
> New Testament (Acts 21:21) bears the sense of reli-
> gious apostasy. Ἀποστασία and its cognate and earlier
> forms appear over forty times in the LXX (including
> several appearances in the versions of Aquila, The-
> odotion, and Symmachus)—every time with the mean-
> ing of religious or political defection. In matters of
> vocabulary and style the LXX strongly influenced the
> New Testament writers, whose Bible for the most part
> was the LXX. The high number of occurrences of
> ἀποστασία in the LXX and their broad distribution
> evince a well-established usage.[45]

Gundry's statement that *apostasia* and its cognates occur over 40 times in the Septuagint (LXX) is perplexing to me because it is a gross understatement. In reality *apostasia* and its cognates occur over 220 times in the LXX. Moreover, contrary to Gundry's dogmatic comment that *apostasia* and its cognates occur "every time with the meaning of religious or political defection," *apostasia* and its cognates carry different senses in the LXX. At least 66 times they express spatial separation from someone or something. The terms mean religious defection approximately 53 times and political defection only about eight times. Gundry's "well-established" usage (read "political revolt" or "religious apostasy"), at least in the LXX, is simply inaccurate.

After coming to the previous overly broad and unfounded conclusions, Gundry then attempts to bolster his conclusions by appealing to the standard lexica and commentators:

> Our remaining primary source, the *koine*, as given by MM [Moulton and Milligan], offers several examples of political rebellion and religious apostasy, but not one example of simple spatial departure. No wonder, then, that New Testament lexicons uniformly give ἀποστασία the special senses of religious apostasy and political rebellion—BAG [Bauer, Arndt, and Gingrich], Kittel, Cremer, Abbott-Smith, Thayer, and others. No wonder also that scholarly commentators on 2 Thessalonians interpret ἀποστασία as bearing this meaning—Alford, Ellicott, Moffatt, F. F. Bruce, Frame, Milligan, Morris, and others.[46]

Certainly this reference to notable authorities is both prima facie persuasive and formidable. This argument is the most compelling to me, since I wonder how the major lexica and scholars studying this passage could be in such harmony on this meaning of the word *apostasia* and yet be in error regarding 2 Thessalonians 2:3.

Before attempting to interact with why I am not fully convinced by this appeal to authority, I should point out that Gundry has misstated the evidence provided by Moulton and Milligan and by Kittel, unless he is excluding the cognate verb of *apostasia* in his statement.[47] For example, MM provides three examples of the verb *aphistēmi* (a cognate of *apostasia*) as carrying the sense of spatial departure;[48] you unfeelingly *went off* without taking your brother's body (P. Grenf. II. 77:9, A.D. 3–4); Ears *standing out* from the head (P. Lond. 1209.12, 89 B.C.); only *left me* after he had forced me to sign (P. Rein 7:18, 141? B.C.).

Moreover, Kittel recognizes that *apostasia* and its cognates can carry the spatial sense:

> ἀφίστημι, Trans. "'to remove,' either spatially or from the context of a state or relationship (τινά τινος or τινά; ἀπό τινος), or from fellowship with a person = 'to seduce,' 'to win away' from someone, ether [sic] privately or politically. Hence also the intrans. sense 'to remove oneself,' 'to resign,' 'to desist,' 'to fall away.' "[49]

Other than the exceptions listed above, I grant that Gundry has important support to bolster his claims, and because of my respect for these sources I desire to tread lightly. I also recognize, however, that it is not unusual for these same lexical sources and biblical scholars to quote one another without doing a fresh or independent study of the evidence. A simple example of this is the understanding of the Hebrew word *tesuqah*, translated "desire" in Genesis 3:16. New insight given to it by Susan Foh reveals the proper understanding, an insight overlooked by lexicographers, Hebrew scholars, and commentators alike.[50] I believe this may also be the case in the proper understanding of *apostasia* in 2 Thessalonians 2:3.

Gundry counters the appeal by English to translators during the Reformation who used "departure" for *apostasia*, such as Tyndale (c. 1526), Coverdale (1535), Cranmer (1539), Geneva Bible (1557), and Beza (1565). He retorts: "But the appeal to early English translations unwittingly reveals weakness, because in the era of those versions lexical studies in New Testament Greek were almost non-existent and continued to be so for many years. The papyri had not yet been discovered, and the study of the LXX had hardly begun. That subsequent versions uniformly departed from the earlier rendering points to a correction based on sound and scholarly reasons."[51]

I fail to follow Gundry's logic here. He argues that these early translations err in translating *apostasia* (see section below on translations) as "departure" because they did not have the advantage of lexical studies in the New Testament and the LXX. He then indicates that subsequent versions deviated from this translation because they are based on sounder and more scholarly sources. How can this be? The 1611 King James Version, without any better access to more New Testament or Septuagintal studies than its predecessors, not to mention papyriological and other extra-biblical sources, changed from "departure" to "fall away." With the King James Version winning the day as the translation of the English-speaking world, translators characteristically, if not slavishly, followed its lead on *apostasia*.

Gundry then criticizes English and Wuest for bypassing lexical evidence for the noun *apostasia* in favor of the verb *aphistēmi*. Gundry is correct that oftentimes nouns acquire special meanings. He then argues that during Paul's time the noun had acquired the special sense of religious apostasy or political defection:

> Whereas ἀφίστημι very many times carries the simple meaning of spatial departure, ἀποστασία appears elsewhere in the New Testament and many times throughout the LXX *solely* with the special meaning. Such usage counts far more than etymology. We should take the meaning which a word had during the time and in the culture in which it was written instead of making recourse to a literal definition of the root. Thus, the terms "apostasy," "falling away," and "rebellion" do not overlay the Greek word with a questionable interpretation. They rather represent a valid and necessary recognition of the *usus loquendi*– i.e., they are true translations.[52]

Though he is essentially correct that nouns often develop special meanings different from their verbs, this is by no means the rule. Generally nouns and verbs stay within the same field of usage, nouns still participating in the meaning of the root verb from which the noun evolved. Consequently, though nouns may vary considerably in meaning from the verb, it is not necessarily so. The development of both nouns and verbs from the root meaning of a given word may be illustrated from the following two graphs, in which "to deliver" and "to depart" often developed specialized, and often richer, meanings, but they generally are still within the perimeter of the root meaning. One must then use context to determine exactly which nuance should be expressed in translation.

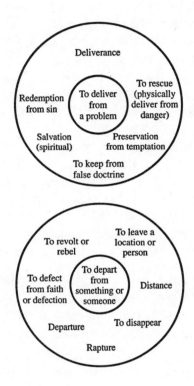

After dealing with the meaning of "rapture" given by English for *apostasia*, Gundry turns his attention to the contexual arguments of English and Wuest.

They argue that the meaning of "religious defection" for *apostasia* always comes from the context and qualifying phrases, not from the word itself [53] Gundry admits that the idea of defection must come from the context. However, he believes that "when the word appears exclusively or predominantly in such contexts—in the NT, the LXX, the *koine*, and classical Greek—defection becomes inherent to the meaning. Where a question arises, there fore, we are bound to recognize the prevailing connotation of the word."[54]

Here Gundry begs the question, for the connotation of the word in the context of 2 Thessalonians 2:3 is the very point to be established. Whereas a plethora of examples of *apostasia* as meaning "defection" or "revolt" can be adduced with little effort, in each of these the context *naturally* provides for such a translation. This is not the case in 2 Thessalonians. In fact, as argument will later show, when one follows a careful contextual study of *apostasia* in 2 Thessalonians 2:3, due consideration given to the Thessalonian epistles, there is an interesting comparison with the same type of contexual factors that produce the translation of "revolt" for *hē apostasia* in 2 Maccabees 2:15.

Wuest argues that the definite article with *apostasia*, with no qualifying phrase, in 2 Thessalonians 2:3 points to something well known to the Thessalonians and is explained in the previous context. Rather than Wuest's explanation that the definite article explains an identity in the preceding context, Gundry believes it may instead "anticipate a following explanation. Or he may provide no explanation at all: the article then bears the sense, 'the well known..' or the 'the special....' "[55] Based on this, Gundry offers three explanations:

> First, the article points to a previous explanation (v. 1; 1 Thess. 4:16ff). But it is unthinkable that Paul would use for the rapture a word the connotation of which overwhelmingly has to do with civil and religious defection.

> Second, the article points to a well known apostasy about which Paul had already informed the Thessalonians through his oral teaching. English calls this possibility "pure conjecture," *but the apostle himself writes,* [italics his] "Do you not remember that while I was still with you, I was telling you these things?" (v. 5). The very fact that Paul inserts thrs rhetorical question suggests that we are not to look for an ἀποστασία which he delineated in 1 Thessalonians, but for an item in Paul's initital ministry by word of mouth.

> Third, the definite article points to a special apostasy which gets further explanation in the ensuing discussion. One must read the passage blindfolded not to see

that the immediately following context bristles with references to and explanations of "the apostasy." The man of lawlessness will lead a rebellion against God by opposing and exalting himself "above every so-called god or object of worship, so that he takes his seat in the temple of God, displaying himself as being God" (v. 4). The subsequent verses abound with yet further descriptive expressions: "the mystery of law-lessness," "the lawless one," "the activity of Satan, with all power and signs and false wonders, and with all the deception of wickedness," "a deluding influ-ence so that they might believe what is false." *The* [italics his] apostasy will be a rebellion against God led by the Antichrist during the tribulation.[56]

Gundry's first argument is circular. He believes that *apostasia* cannot mean "rapture" here because the word normally means "defection." But what it connotes in 2 Thessalonians 2:3 is the very point of the discussion. The argument that *apostasia* cannot mean "rapture" here because it generally means "defection" elsewhere proves nothing but that it assumes what he seeks to prove. Context determines meaning, not how the word is used in other contexts dealing with matters relating to revolt or defection.

Gundry's second argument could be correct; that is, that the content explained by *hē apostasia* may only have been given by Paul to the Thessalonians in oral form. It is just as likely that the oral teaching Paul refers to in 2 Thessalonians 2:5 has been confirmed to them in writing, so that they *now* clearly understand what has been restraining the revelation of the man of sin (2:6). It is illogical to believe that a defection from the faith or a revolt against God is what restrains the revelation of the man of lawlessness, for this would actually bring in his reign, not hold it back. More likely is the view that the presence of God's people in the world, and the work of the Spirit through them, restrains this final expression of evil. After the church is removed, then sin holds sway.

His last argument (according to Gundry, lost on those of us who are blindfolded), also poses major difficulties. It is possible that *hē apostasia* refers to what follows, but I think it more likely refers to what precedes.[57] Paul says the *apostasia* occurs *first prōton*, and then the man of sin is revealed. Gundry sees the man of sin as leading a rebellion, but how can *apostasia* refer to the rebellion as a prerequisite to the Day of the Lord if it is an event within the Day of the Lord? If this is not what Gundry means, but, instead, that the man of sin comes out of the rebellion, other problems arise. J. Dwight Pentecost offers one problem with Gundry's view:

> If we take 2 Thess. 2:3 in its generally accepted use and make it read "That day shall not come, except there come the apostasy first, and that man of sin be revealed," it seems to me the inference would be that the man of sin, or the apostate one, would come out of the apostasy, or the apostate church, while the picture in Revelation 13 is that the man of sin, or the first Beast, comes from the nations as the head of the Revived Empire. The man of sin is not dependent on an apostate church but a "removed" church.[58]

Conclusion

I have sought to demonstrate that the departure of the church may be the proper understanding found in the Greek word *apostasia* in 2 Thessalonians 2:3. Certainly the case is not conclusive, but it should not be dismissed out of hand as many have done. If *apostasia* means departure, in the context of the departure of Christians before the Day of the Lord, then the word corresponds with Paul's other terms to describe the deliverance of Christians from this world and their gathering to Jesus Christ. The meaning of *apostasia* in Greek literature, the grammar of the passage, and contextual considerations found in the Thessalonian epistles, fit well with this interpretation and may provide hope and comfort to Christians today, even as it did to the Thessalonian Christians of the first century.

Appendix A

Lexica

Liddell, Scott, Jones, McKenzie

ἀποστασία, late form of ἀπόστασιας, *defection, revolt*; esp. ın religious sense, *rebellion against God, apostasy*; 2. *departure, disappearance*; 3. *distinguishing*, c. gen; 4. *distance*.

ἀφίστημι, Causal in pres. and impf. *put away, remove, keep out of the way*; 2. *cause to revolt*; Intr. in Pass. stand away or aloof from.

Kittel's *Theological Dictionary of the New Testament*

ἀφίστημι, Trans. " 'to remove,' either spatially or from the context of a state or relationship (τινά τινος or τινά ἀπό τινος), or from fellowship with a person = 'to seduce,' 'to win away' from someone, ether [sic] privately or politically. Hence also the intrans. sense 'to remove oneself,' 'to resign,' 'to desist.' "

ἀποστασία, "The word presupposes the concept ἀποστάτης 'to be an apostate,' and thus signifies the state of apostasy, whereas ajpovstasi denotes the act."

"In 2 Th. 2:3 ἀποστασία is used in the absol. sense as an event of the last days alongside or prior to (?) the appearance of the ἄνθρωπος τῆς ἀνομίας. Here a Jewish tradition is adopted which speaks of complete apostasy from God and His Torah shortly before the appearance of the Messiah."

Bauer-Ardnt-Gingrich-Danker

ἀποστασία, from classical ἀπόστασις, meaning *rebellion, abandonment* in religious sense, *apostasy* from something τινος.

ἀφίστημι, in transitive meaning cause to *revolt, mislead*; intrans. *go away, withdraw* from something or someone; *fall away*.

New International Dictionary of New Testament Theology, Colin Brown, ed. (p. 606).

ἀφίστημι—The word means (trans.) "to put away, remove: (a) in a spatial sense; (b) from a condition or relationship; (c) from association with a person. It also means to turn someone (either privately or politically) against a person, to cause to revolt." Intrans. it means "to remove oneself, go away; to stand aloof, withdraw from, cease, give up; recoil, separate oneself; to fall away. From it are derived the nouns *apostasis*, revolt (first found in cl. Gk., from the time of Thc., 1, 122); *apostates*, deserter, political rebel (e.g. 'against the king', 'against the country'; a later term found in Polybius); *apostasia*, a late form of the classical *apostasis*, meaning, state of rebellion or apostasy (e.g. 'from Nero'; 'from the Romans'); and *apostasion*, a legal term for handing over at purchase, conveyance, and used of a bill of divorce (Deut. 24:1, 3; Matt. 5:31; 19:7; Mk. 10:4)."

Louw and Nida, *Greek-English Lexicon*

ἀποστασία, "to rise up in open defiance of authority, with the presumed intention to overthrow it or to act in complete opposition to its demands—'to rebel against, to revolt, to engage in insurrection, rebellion.' "

ἀφίστημι, "to cause people to rebel against or to reject authority—'to incite to revolt, to cause to rebel.' "

Moulton and Milligan, *Vocabulary of the Greek New Testament*, illustrated from the Papyri and other non-literary sources

ἀποστασία, the term is used in the literature to express rebels, and rebellion.

ἀφίστημι, used in contracts for repelling individuals making claims, or of renouncing a claim; or to leave someone or something.

Lampe, *A Patristic Greek Lexicon*

ἀφίστημι, withdraw from communion (ἀφιστάμενος τῇ τῶν ἀδελφῶν συνοδίας Iren. *haer. 3.4.2.*), apostatize (ἔνιαι εἶ τὸ παντελὲς ἀπέστησαν Iren. *haer.* I.13.7), give up, cease.

ἀποστασία, 1. revolt, defection; 2. apostasy; from paganism, from Judaism, from Christianity, from orthodoxy; 3. divorce; 4. departure; 5. standing aloof.

ἀπόστασις, 1. departure; 2. defection, revolt; apostasy; 3. giving up, renunication; 4. absence; 5. separation; 6. divorce.

The LXX and the Hebrew Text

Canonical books

2 Chronicles 28:19: ὅτι ἐταπείνωσεν κύριο τὸν ιουδαν δι αχαζ βασιλέα Ιουδα, οτι ἀπέστη *ἀποστάσει* ἀπὸ κυρίου.

For the Lord humbles Juda because of Achaz king of Juda, because he grievously *departed* from the Lord.

כִּי־הִכְנִיעַ יְהוָה֙ אֶת־יְהוּדָ֔ה בַּעֲב֖וּר אָחָ֣ז מֶֽלֶךְ־יִשְׂרָאֵ֑ל כִּ֤י הִפְרִ֙יעַ֙ בִּיהוּדָ֔ה
וּמָע֥וֹל מַ֖עַל [unfaithfulness: v. מַעַל] בַּֽיהוָֽה׃

For Yahweh had humbled Judah because of Ahaz the king of Israel because he loosed [immorality] in Judah and *dealt treachously* against Yahweh.

2 Chronicles 29:19: *Καὶ πάντα τὰ σκεύη, α ἐμίανεν Αχαζ ὁ βασιλεὺς ἐν τῇ βασιλείᾳ αὐτοῦ ἐν τῇ ἀποστασίᾳ αὐτοῦ, ἡτοιμάκαμεν καὶ ἡγνίκαμεν, ἰδού ἐστιν ἐναντίον τοῦ θυσιαστηρίου κυρίου.*

And all the vessels, which king Achaz polluted in his reign in his *apostasy*, we have prepared and purified, behold, they are before the altar of the Lord.

וְאֵת כָּל־הַכֵּלִים אֲשֶׁר הִזְנִיחַ הַמֶּלֶךְ אָחָז בְּמַלְכוּתוֹ בְּמַעֲלוֹ

[in his unfaithfulness: v. מַעַל] הֵכַנּוּ וְהִקְדָּשְׁנוּ וְהִנָּם לִפְנֵי מִזְבַּח יְהוָה:

And all the utensils that king Ahaz cast aside in his reign, in his *treachery*, we have prepared and sanctified; and behold, they are before the altar of Yahweh.

2 Chronicles 33:19: *Προσευχῆς αὐτοῦ, καὶ ὡς ἐπήκουσεν αὐτοῦ, καὶ πᾶσαι αἱ ἁμαρτίαι αὐτοῦ καὶ αἱ ἀποστάσεις αὐτοῦ καὶ οἱ τόποι, ἐφ οις ᾠκοδόμησεν τὰ ὑψηλὰ καὶ ἔστησεν ἐκεῖ ἄλση καὶ γλυπτὰ πρὸ τοῦ ἐπιστρέψαι, ἰδοὺ γέγραπται ἐπὶ τῶν λόγων τῶν ὁρώντων.*

[and his unfaithfulness: v. מַעַל] וּתְפִלָּתוֹ וְהֵעָתֶר־לוֹ וְכָל־חַטָּאתוֹ וּמַעְלוֹ
וְהַמְּקֹמוֹת אֲשֶׁר בָּנָה בָהֶם בָּמוֹת וְהֶעֱמִיד הָאֲשֵׁרִים וְהַפְּסִלִים לִפְנֵי הִכָּנְעוֹ הִנָּם
כְּתוּבִים עַל דִּבְרֵי חוֹזָי:

And his prayer, and his entreaty, and all his sin, and his *trespass*, and the places in which he had built high places and made stand the Asherim and the graven images before he was humbled, behold, they are written in the Matters of the Seers.

Joshua 22:22: *Ὁ θεὸ θεὸ ἐστιν κύριὸ, καὶ ὁ θεὸ θεὸ κύριὸ αὐτὸ οιϳεν, καὶ Ισραηλ αὐτὸ γνώσεται· εἰ ἐν ἀποστασίᾳ ἐπλημμελήσαμεν ἔναντι τοῦ κυρίου, μὴ ρύσαιτο ἡμᾶ ἐν ταύτῃ·*

אֵל׀ אֱלֹהִים׀ יְהוָֹה׀ אֵל׀ אֱלֹהִים׀ יְהוָֹה הוּא יֹדֵעַ וְיִשְׂרָאֵל הוּא יֵדָע
אִם־בְּמֶרֶד [in rebellion: v. מָרַד] וְאִם־בְּמַעַל בַּיהוָה אַל־תּוֹשִׁיעֵנוּ הַיּוֹם הַזֶּה:

Yahweh is the God of gods; Yahweh is the God of gods! He knows, and Israel shall know if it is in *rebellion*, and if it is in treachery against Yahweh, you shall not save us alive today.

Jeremiah 2:19: παιδεύσει σε ἡ *ἀποστασία* σου, καὶ ἡ κακία σου ἐλέγξει σε καὶ γνῶθι καὶ ἰδὲ οτι πικρόν σοι τὸ καταλιπεῖν σε ἐμέ, λέγει κύριὸ ὁ θεὸ σου· καὶ οὐκ εὐδόκησα ἐπὶ σοί, λέγει κύριὸ ὁ θεὸ σου.

תִּיסְרֵךְ רָעָתֵךְ וּמְשֻׁבוֹתַיִךְ [and your backslidings: v. שׁוּב] תּוֹכִחֻךְ וּדְעִי וּרְאִי כִּי־רַע וָמָר עָזְבֵךְ אֶת־יְהוָה אֱלֹהָיִךְ וְלֹא פַחְדָּתִי אֵלַיִךְ נְאֻם־אֲדֹנָי יְהוָה צְבָאוֹת׃

Your own evil shall teach you, and your *apostasies* shall reprove you. Know, then, and see that is evil and bitter your forsaking Yahweh your God; and My fear is not ın you declares the Lord Yahweh of Hosts.

Isaiah 30:1: Οὐαὶ τέκνα *ἀποστάται*, τάδε λέγει κύριὸ, εποιήσατε βουλὴν οὐ δῑ ἐμοῦ καὶ συνθῆκᾶ οὐ διὰ τοῦ πνεύματὸ μου προσθεῖναι ἀμαρτίᾶ ἐϕ ἀμαρτίαῖ,

הוֹי בָּנִים סוֹרְרִים [ones being obstinate: v. סוּר] נְאֻם־יְהוָה לַעֲשׂוֹת עֵצָה וְלֹא מִנִּי וְלִנְסֹךְ מַסֵּכָה וְלֹא רוּחִי לְמַעַן סְפוֹת חַטָּאת עַל־חַטָּאת׃

Woe to **rebellious** sons, declares Yahweh, to make counsel, but not from Me; and to weave a covering web, but not of My Spirit, in order to add sın on sın.

Apocrypha

1 Esdras 2:27: ἐπέταξα ουν ἐπισκέψασθαι, καὶ εὑρέθη οτι ἐστὶν ἡ πόλῑ ἐκείνη ἐξ αἰῶνὸ βασιλεῦσιν ἀντιπαρατάσσουσα καὶ οι ἄνθρωποι *ἀποστάσεῑ* καὶ πολέμου ἐν αὐτῇ συντελοῦντὲ

Therefore I commanded to make diligent search, and it has been found that that city was from the beginning practising against kings; and the men therein were given to **rebellion** and war

1 Maccabees 2:15: Καὶ ηλθον οι παρὰ τοῦ βασιλέὼ οι καταναγκάζοντὲ *τὴν ἀποστασίαν* εῑ Μωδειν τὴν πόλιν, ινα θυσιάσωσιν.

In the mean while, the kings officers, such as compelled the people to *revolt,* came into the city Modin, to make them sacrifice

2 Maccabees 5:8: πέρᾶ ουν κακῇ καταστροφῇ ἔτυχεν. ἐγκλη-θεῖ πρὸ͂Αρέταν τὸν τῶν͂Αράβων τύραννον πόλιν ἐκ πόλεὼ *φεύγων διωκόμενο ὑπὸ πάντων στυγούμενο ὦ τῶν νόμων **ἀποστάτῇ** καὶ βδελυσσόμενο ὦ πατρίδο καὶ πολιτῶν δήμιο εἶ Αἴγυπτον ἐξεβράσθη,*

In the end therefore he had an unhappy return, being accused before Aretas the king of the Arabians, fleeing from city to city, pursued of all men, hated as a **forsaker** of the laws and being had in abomination as an open enemy of his country and countrymen, he was cast out into Egypt.

New Testament

As a Verbal

Luke 2:37: *καὶ αὐτὴ χήρα ἕως ἐτῶν ὀγδοήκοντα τεσσάρων, ἥ οὐκ **ἀφίστατο** τοῦ ἱεροῦ νηστείαῖ καὶ δεήσεσιν λατρεύουσα νύκτα καὶ ἡμέραν.*

and then as a widow to the age of eighty-four. And she never **left** the temple, serving night and day with fastings and prayers.

Luke 4:13 *Καὶ συντελέσᾶ πάντα πειρασμὸν ὁ διάβολο̂ **ἀπέστη** ἀπ᾽ αὐτοῦ ἄχρι καιροῦ.*

And when the devil had finished every temptation, he departed from Him until an opportune time.

Luke 8:13: *οἱ δὲ ἐπὶ τῆς πέτρᾶ οἵ ὅταν ἀκούσωσιν μετὰ χαρᾶ δέχονται τὸν λόγον, καὶ οὗτοι ῥίζαν οὐκ ἔχουσιν, οἵ πρὸς καιρὸν πιστεύουσιν καὶ ἐν καιρῷ πειρασμοῦ **ἀφίστανται***

"And those on the rocky soil are those who, when they hear, receive the word with joy; and these have no firm root; they believe for a while, and in time of temptation **fall away.**

Luke 13:27: *καὶ ἐρεῖ λέγων ὑμῖν, Οὐκ οἶδα [ὑμᾶς] πόθεν ἐστέ· **ἀπόστητε** ἀπ᾽ ἐμοῦ, πάντᾶ ἐργάται ἀδικίᾶ.*

and He will say, "I tell you, I do not know where you are from; **depart** from Me, all you evildoers."

Acts 5:37: *μετὰ τοῦτον ἀνέστη Ἰούδας ὁ Γαλιλαῖος ἐν ταῖς ἡμέραῖ τῆ ἀπογραφῆ καὶ **ἀπέστησεν** λαὸν ὀπίσω αὐτοῦ· κἀκεῖνος ἀπώλετο καὶ πάντες ὅσοι ἐπείθοντο αὐτῷ διεσκορπίσθησαν.*

After this man Judas of Galilee rose up in the days of the census, and drew away some people after him, he too perished, and all those who followed him were scattered.

Acts 5:38: καὶ τὰ νῦν λέγω ὑμῖν, **ἀπόστητε** ἀπὸ τῶν ἀνθρώπων τούτων καὶ ἄφετε αὐτοῦ ὅτι ἐὰν ᾖ ἐξ ἀνθρώπων ἡ βουλὴ αὕτη ἢ τὸ ἔργον τοῦτο, καταλυθήσεται,

And so in the present case, I say to you, stay away from these men and let them alone, for if this plan or action should be of men, it will be overthrown;

Acts 12:10: διελθόντες δὲ πρώτην φυλακὴν καὶ δευτέραν ηλθαν ἐπὶ τὴν πύλην τὴν σιδηρᾶν τὴν φέρουσαν εἰς τὴν πόλιν, ἥτις αὐτομάτη ἡνοίγη αὐτοῖ καὶ ἐξελθόντε προῆλθον ῥύμην μίαν, καὶ εὐθέῶ ἀπέστη ὁ ἄγγελὀ ἀπ᾽ αὐτοῦ.

And when they had passed the first and second guard, they came to the iron gate that leads into the city, which opened for them by itself; and they went out and went along one street, and immediately the angel departed from him.

Acts 15:38: Παῦλος δὲ ἠξίου, τὸν **ἀποστάντα** ἀπ᾽ αὐτῶν ἀπὸ Παμφυλίᾶ καὶ μὴ συνελθόντα αὐτοῖ εἰς τὸ ἔργον μὴ συμπαραλαμβάνειν τοῦτον.

But Paul kept insisting that they should not take him along who had deserted them in Pamphylia and had not gone with them to the work.

Acts 19:9: ὡς δέ τινες ἐσκληρύνοντο καὶ ἠπείθουν κακολογοῦντὲ τὴν ὁδὸν ἐνώπιον τοῦ πλήθοῦ, **ἀποστὰς** ἀπ᾽ αὐτῶν ἀφώρισεν τοῦ μαθητᾶ καθ᾽ ἡμέραν διαλεγόμενὀ ἐν τῇ σχολῇ τυράννου.

But when some were becoming hardened and disobedient, speaking evil of the Way before the multitude, he withdrew from them and took away the disciples, reasoning daily in the school of Tyrannus.

Acts 22:29: εὐθέως οὖν **ἀπέστησαν** ἀπ᾽ αὐτοῦ οἱ μέλλοντες αὐτὸν ἀνετάζειν, καὶ ὁ χιλίαρχος δὲ ἐφοβήθη ἐπιγνοὺς ὅτι Ῥωμαῖός ἐστιν καὶ ὅτι αὐτὸν ἦν δεδεκώς.

Therefore those who were about to examine him immediately let go of him; and the commander also was afraid when he found out that he was a Roman, and because he had put him in chains.

2 Cor. 12:8: ὑπὲρ τούτου τρὶς τὸν κύριον παρεκάλεσα ἵνα **ἀποστῇ** ἀπ᾽ ἐμοῦ.

Concerning this I entreated the Lord three times that it might depart from me.

1 Tim. 4:1: *Τὸ δὲ πνεῦμα ῥητῶ λέγει οτι ἐν ὑστέροῖ καιροῖ* **ἀποστήσονταί** *τινê τῇ πίστεῶ προσέχοντê πνεύμασιν πλάνοῖ καὶ διδασκαλίαῖ δαιμονίων.*

But the Spirit explicitly says that in later times some will fall away from the faith, paying attention to deceitful spirits and doctrines of demons.

1 Tim. 6:5: *διαπαρατριβαὶ διεφθαρμένων ἀνθρώπων τὸν νοῦν καὶ ἀπεστερημένων τῆς ἀληθείας νομιζόντων πορισμὸν εἶναι τὴν εὐσέβειαν.*

and constant friction between men of depraved mind and deprived of the truth, who suppose that godliness is a means of gain.

2 Tim. 2:19: *ὁ μέντοι στερεὸς θεμέλιος τοῦ θεοῦ εστηκεν, ἔχων τὴν σφραγῖδα ταύτην· Ἔγνω κύριος τοὺς ὄντας αὐτοῦ, καί,* *Ἀποστήτω ἀπὸ ἀδικίας πᾶς ὁ ὀνομάζων τὸ ὄνομα κυρίου.*

Nevertheless, the firm foundation of God stands, having this seal, "The Lord knows those who are His," and, "Let everyone who names the name of the Lord abstain from wickedness."

Heb. 3:12: *Βλέπετε, ἀδελφοί, μήποτε ἔσται ἔν τινι ὑμῶν καρδία πονηρὰ ἀπιστίας ἐν τῷ* **ἀποστῆναι** *ἀπὸ θεοῦ ζῶντος.*

Take care, brethren, lest there should be in any one of you an evil, unbelieving heart, in falling away from the living God.

As a Noun (Feminine)

Acts 21:21: *κατηχήθησαν δὲ περὶ σοῦ ὅτι* **ἀποστασίαν** *διδάσκεις ἀπὸ Μωυσέως κατὰ τὰ ἔθνη πάντας Ἰουδαίους λέγων μὴ περιτέμνειν αὐτοῦ τὰ τέκνα μηδὲ τοῖς ἔθεσιν περιπατεῖν.*

and they have been told about you, that you are teaching all the Jews who are among the Gentiles to forsake Moses, telling them not to circumcise their children nor to walk according to the customs.

2 Thess. 2:3: *μή τις ὑμᾶς ἐξαπατήσῃ κατὰ μηδένα τρόπον. ὅτι ἐὰν μὴ ἔλθῃ ἡ* **ἀποστασία** *πρῶτον καὶ ἀποκαλυφθῇ ὁ ἄνθρωπος τῆς ἀνομίας, ὁ υἱὸς τῆς ἀπωλείας.*

Let no one in any way deceive you, for it will not come unless the apostasy comes first, and the man of lawlessness is revealed, the son of destruction.

As a Noun (Masculine)

Matt. 5:31: Ἐρρέθη δέ, Ὃς ἂν ἀπολύσῃ τὴν γυναῖκα αὐτοῦ, δότω αὐτῇ **ἀποστάσιον.**

And it was said, "Whoever sends his wife away, let him give her a certificate of divorce."

Matt. 19:7: λέγουσιν αὐτῷ, Τί ουν Μωϋσῆ ἐνετείλατο δοῦναι βιβλίον **ἀποστασίου** καὶ ἀπολῦσαι [αὐτήν];

They said to Him, "Why then did Moses command to give her a certificate of divorce and send her away?"

Mark 10:4: οἱ δὲ εἶπαν, Ἐπέτρεψεν Μωϋσῆς βιβλίον **ἀποστασίου** γράψαι καὶ ἀπολῦσαι.

And they said, "Moses permitted a man to write a certificate of divorce and send her away."

The Papyri

ἀφίστημι
ἀλόῃῶ ἀπέστητε μὴ ἄραντες τὸ σῶμα τοῦ ἀδελφοῦ ὑμῶν.
You unfeelingly went off without taking your brother's body. P Grenf. II. 77:9 (A.D. 3/4).

ὦτα ἀφεστηκότα
Ears standing out from the head. P. Lond. 1209.12 (89 b.c.)

ἐμπλεκείς τέ μοι οὐκ ἀπέστηι εἰ μὴ ἠνάηκασε κτλ.
Only left me after he had force me to sign. P. Rein 7:18 (B.C. 141?)

ἀποστασία
ἠνγκάσθην ὑπὸ τῶν Αἰγυπτίων ἀποστατῶν ἐνέγκαι τὰς συνγραφὰς καὶ ταύτας κατακαῦσαι.
The title deeds were taken by force by the Egyptian rebels and these they burned. P. Amh. II. 30:33ff (2 B.C.)

βουλόομενοι ἐξσπάσαι με καὶ ἀγαγῆσαι, καθάπερ καὶ ἐν τοῖς πρότερον χρόνοις ἐπεχείρησαν, οὔσης ἀποσταάσεως.

Desiring to draw me out and to lead me just as also in the former time they attacked being rebels. P. Par. 36:13 (2 B.C.)

Josephus

παρὰ Οὐάρου δ' ἐκομίσθησαν ἐκ Συρίας ἐπισταλοι περί τῆς Ἰουδαίαν ἀποστάσεως.

And dispatches arrived from Varus in Syria concerning the revolt of the Jews. Josephus, *Jewish Wars*, 2.39.

πολλὰ ποιήσειν αὐτοις κακά, τῆς ἀποστάσεως ἀμυνόμενον

He would make them suffer severely in taking revenge for their revolt. Josephus, *Antiquities*, 13.219.

την ἀποστασίαν τὴν ἀπὸ Ῥωμαίων

The revolt against the Romans Josephus, *Vita*, 43.

Appendix B

2 Thess. 2:1: Ερωτῶμεν δὲ ὑμᾶς, ἀδελφοί, ὑπὲρ τῆς παρουσίας τοῦ κυρίου ἡμῶν Ἰησοῦ Χριστοῦ καὶ ἡμῶν ἐπισυναγωγῆς ἐπ' αὐτόν.	
Now we request you, brethren, with regard to the coming of our Lord Jesus Christ, and our gathering together to Him,	
2 Thess. 2:2: εἰς τὸ μὴ ταχέως σαλευθῆναι ὑμᾶς ἀπὸ τοῦ νοὸς μηδὲ θροεῖσθαι, μήτε διὰ πνεύματος μήτε διὰ λόγου μήτε δια' ἐπιστολῆς ὡς δι' ἡμῶν, ὡς ὅτι ἐνέστηκεν ἡ ἡμέρα τοῦ κυρίου.	
that you may not be quickly shaken from your composure or be disturbed either by a spirit or a message or a letter as if from us, to the effect that the day of the Lord has come.	
2 Thess. 2:3: μή τις ὑμᾶς ἐξαπατήσῃ κατὰ μηδένα τρόπον. Let no one ın any way deceive you, for ıt will not come	
ὅτι ἐὰν μὴ ἔλθῃ ἡ ἀποστασία πρῶτον unless the apostasy comes first,	καὶ ἀποκαλυφθῇ ὁ ἄνθρωπος τῆς ἀνομίας, ὁ υἱὸς τῆς ἀπωλείας, and the man of lawlessness is revealed, the son of destruction,

	2 Thess. 2:4: *ὁ ἀντικείμενος καὶ ὑπεραιρόμενος ἐπὶ πάντα λεγόμενον θεὸν ἢ σέβασμα, ὥστε αὐτὸν εἰς τὸν ναὸν τοῦ θεοῦ καθίσαι ἀποδεικνύντα ἑαυτὸν ὅτι ἔστιν θεός.* who opposes and exalts himself above every so-called god or object of worship, so that he takes his seat in the temple of God, displaying himself as being God.
2 Thess. 2:5: *Οὐ μνημονεύετε ὅτι ἔτι ὢν πρὸς ὑμᾶς ταῦτα ἔλεγον ὑμῖν* Do you not remember that while I was still with you, I was telling you these things?	
2 Thess. 2:6: *καὶ νῦν τὸ κατέχον οἴδατε* And you know what restrains him now,	*εἰς τὸ ἀποκαλυφθῆναι αὐτὸν ἐν τῷ ἑαυτοῦ καιρῷ.* so that in his time he may be revealed.
2 Thess. 2:7: *τὸ γὰρ μυστήριον ἤδη ἐνεργεῖται τῆς ἀνομίας·* For the mystery of lawlessness is already at work;	*μόνον ὁ κατέχων ἄρτι ἕως ἐκ μέσου γένηται.* only he who now restrains will do so until he is taken out of the way.

2 Thess. 2:8: *καὶ τότε ἀποκαλυφθήσεται ὁ ἄνομος, ὅν ὁ κύριος Ἰησοῦς ἀνελεῖ τῷ πνεύματι τοῦ στόματος αὐτοῦ καὶ καταργήσει τῇ ἐπιφανείᾳ τῆς παρουσίας αὐτοῦ.*

And then that lawless one will be revealed whom the Lord will slay with the breath of His mouth and bring to an end by the appearance of His coming;

15
Paul D. Feinberg

2 Thessalonians 2 and the Rapture

_____ *OVERVIEW*

What is one of the most significant passages in the New Testament relating to the timing of the rapture? Second Thessalonians 2 is one of the most-debated New Testament passages that relates to the timing of the rapture. In this essay, Dr. Paul Feinberg deals with three of the most important issues relating to the timing of the rapture in 2 Thessalonians 2. He demonstrates from the Scripture why the pretribulational position best explains the problems and issues in this important passage.

*T*he Thessalonian epistles are Paul's eschatological epistles. We would expect therefore that Paul would have things to say about the rapture, and we are not disappointed. The Thessalonian church was not only an exemplary church (1 Thess. 1:8); it was an expectant church. Paul writes that the Thessalonians "turned to God from idols to serve the living and true God, and to wait for his Son from heaven" (1 Thess. 1:9-10). In his first Thessalonian letter Paul writes to urge Christians not to neglect daily work even though they were to look for the Lord's return (4:11-12), and he writes to comfort those who had lost loved ones, assuring them that those who had died would meet the Lord in the air (4:13,15).

Paul's second Thessalonian letter is written about six months later. In chapter 2 he writes to correct some false teaching that was troubling believers in Thessalonica. Paul is trying to save the doctrine of the second coming of Christ from some misconceptions that were held by the Thessalonians. This chapter and its relationship to the rapture question is our subject here. I shall focus primarily on the first seven verses. There are three issues that I wish to address: 1) the relationship between 2 Thessalonians 2:1 and Matthew 24:29-31 and the time of the rapture; 2) the silence of Paul about a pretribulational rapture in correcting false teaching in 2 Thessalonians 2:2-4; 3) the identity of the restrainer in 2 Thessalonians 2:5-7.

The Relationship Between
2 Thessalonians 2:1 and Matthew 24:29-31

There is a twofold argument that relates 2 Thessalonians 2:1 with Matthew 24:29-31 and sets the time of the rapture as posttribulational. One finds these arguments in Robert H. Gundry's *The Church and the Tribulation*.[1] The arguments are as follows. First, Gundry argues that "the coming of our Lord Jesus Christ and our being gathered to him" is a reference to the return of Christ and the rapture at the end of the Tribulation period. He bases this argument on the idea that 1 Thessalonians 4:16–5:9 is a reference to a rapture that will take place just before the Day of the Lord which begins at the end of the Tribulation.[2] Moreover, Paul makes no distinction between his description of the second coming given in 2 Thessalonians 1:7-10 and the coming in 1 Thessalonians 4:16ff. Further, he introduces the phrase "our gathering together to him" in 2 Thessalonians 2:1 without any observable shift in reference from 1:7-10, which is a posttribulational coming in judgment to destroy the wicked. Finally, Paul writes about an event that will take place in the Tribulation, the Antichrist and his demise. Gundry concludes, "Hence, outstandingly posttribulational references surround the highly debated section 2:1-7. The very setting of the section should make us wary of unnecessarily interpolating the idea of a pretribulational rapture."[3] And again, "If then the context of 2:1 leads us to regard the parousia there as posttribulational, it is singularly strange that 'our gathering together to Him' should be connected with it and mentioned second in order—unless the rapture, too, is posttribulational."[4]

To summarize what Gundry has done to this point, he has related Paul's discussions of the coming of Christ in the Thessalonian epistles to one another: 1 Thessalonians 4 and 5 to 2 Thessalonians 1:7-10 to 2 Thessalonians 2:1. He has also argued that, in their context in the Thessalonian epistles, these are references to a posttribulational return and rapture.

To this argument is added a second one which relates 2 Thessalonians 2:1 to Matthew 24:29-31. In Gundry's discussion of the Olivet discourse, he tries to establish the place of the rapture. He says that no reference to it would place it before the Tribulation. He rejects what he sees as common pretrib reasoning for this omission, namely that the Olivet discourse is about the Jewish age and is a Jewish discourse. Therefore we should not expect it to teach about a pretribulational rapture of the church. Gundry thinks this is simply false. He argues against an exclusively Jewish understanding of the Olivet discourse on the grounds that: 1) the disciples are a transitional group (one time representing the believing remnant in Israel, another time standing for the church); 2) that Jesus is teaching about the church just two days later in the Upper Room discourse (John 14); 3) that Matthew, the Gospel written to the Jews, teaches about the church (Matt. 16:13-18; 18:15-18).[5]

Posttribulationalists, therefore, identify the rapture with the gathering of the elect by the angels at the sound of the trumpet in Matthew 24:31. This clearly sets the rapture as posttribulational because Matthew 24:29 introduces the events that follow as occurring "immediately after the distress of those days." The correctness of this identification is further supported by a number of parallels with 1 Thessalonians 4:16,17, where we read of a trumpet and clouds and 2 Thessalonians 2:1, where Paul discusses a gathering of believers just as in the Olivet discourse.[6]

In summary, Gundry has argued that the gathering together at the coming of the Lord (2 Thessalonians 2:1) is a reference to the rapture of the church, and that that gathering is the same as the gathering of the elect in Matthew 24:31, decisively establishing the time of the rapture as posttribulational. If this argument is correct, then a pretribulational rapture of the church *cannot* be correct.

However, if this argument is a good one, it is equally as decisive against a midtribulational rapture as it is against a pretribulational one. Second, this argument is good only if two conditions are met. The "gathering together" of 2 Thessalonians 2:1 must be a reference to the rapture of the church, and the gathering of the elect in Matthew 24:31 must be identical with it. I shall argue that first condition is met and is true but that second is false, because arguments aimed at identification fail. Therefore, this argument fails as an objection to a pretribulational rapture.

Here is a more thorough discussion of the aforementioned conditions. First, to what does the "gathering together to Him" of 2 Thessalonians 2:1 refer? There are only two answers: to a rapture, the time of which would be determined later, or to the coming and revelation of Christ on His return to this earth after the Tribulation. Clearly, the majority view is that it refers to the coming of Christ at the end of the Tribulation. It is fair to say that many commentators on this verse do not relate it to the rapture issue at all. Their argument is that Paul discusses the return of Christ in these two epistles, and there is no reason to make any distinctions related to this eschatological event. For instance, 2 Thessalonians 1:7-10 teaches about a judgment that is to take place at the end of time, and there is no reason to think that 2:1 is a reference to anything else. This whole argument, in my judgment, is not an inconsequential one; but in the end I think that this is not a reference to the second coming of Christ to this earth.

The second option is the minority view. It identifies the gathering together with the rapture of the church. Interestingly enough, that is the view both of Gundry[7] and Thomas,[8] though the former thinks that the rapture is posttribulational and the latter pretribulational. I have already mentioned Gundry's reasons for taking it as the rapture. Thomas holds that "the being gathered" specifies what *part* of the "coming" is under discussion. It is the great event described more fully in 1 Thessalonians 4:14-17. The gathering is of those who go to meet the Lord in the air, en route to meeting the Father in heaven. Both of these texts speak of a gathering, though 1 Thessalonians 4 says we "will be caught up together," while 2 Thessalonians describes it as "being gathered to Him." The ideas are clearly parallel. This too is a substantial argument, but the decisive matter in favor of identifying this phrase with the rapture is that Paul calls it *our* gathering to him. He is definitely speaking to Thessalonian Christians who were members of the church. He uses the first person pronoun in 1 Thessalonians 4. Therefore, I cannot escape identifying the gathering with the catching up.

What remains to be examined is when this rapture will take place. It must be a posttribulational rapture for Gundry's argument to be established. This could be done on one or all of the three grounds suggested by Gundry. The first is that Paul only discusses the coming of Christ as a single complex event coming at the end of a time of Tribulation, since 1 Thessalonians 4:16ff, 2 Thessalonians 1:7-10, and 2 Thessalonians 2:1 are discussed without any appeal to a distinction between a pretribulational rapture and posttribulational second coming of Christ. The important link in this argument is the relationship of 1 Thessalonians 4:14-17 to the rest of the references to the coming of the Lord, especially 1 Thessalonians 5:1-9. The point is that if you can tie 4:14-17 to posttribulational rapture, and identify 2 Thessalonians 2:1 with 4:14-17, and support the posttribulational timing of the rapture by its relationship to 2 Thessalonians 1:7-10, which everyone takes to be after the Tribulation, then you have the rapture in the Thessalonian epistles consistently a posttribulational.

Again, the key to making this argument is to show that 1 Thessalonians 4:14-17, is so related to 5:1-9 that a posttribulational rapture is required. It is just at this crucial point in the argument that a pretribulationist disagrees, and rightly so in my judgment. While Gundry thinks that 1 Thessalonians 4:14-17, on its own, best fits a posttribulational rapture, another important reason is its relationship to 5:1-9. The connection between the two sections is through the Greek particle *de*. According to Gundry, this particle has "a mixture of a continuative sense and a slightly adversative sense. In other words, the particle implies a shift in thought, but not without close connection with the foregoing thought. Sometimes the adversative sense drops out altogether."[9] Gundry's argument is based on a misreading of the text, as the connection between 4:14-17 and 5:1-9 is not through the particle *de*, but *peri de*. This is Paul's usual way of introducing a new subject (e.g., 1 Thess. 4:9,13). While it may be true that the two subjects discussed are not so different that they are completely unrelated to one another, or in contrast to one another, it is also true that they are not simply the continuation of the same subject. "The proper interpretation recognizes a shift in thought, but not without some connection with the foregoing."[10] I suggest that the topic remains the coming of the Lord, but that there is a discussion of two distinct phases of it. This is further supported by the change from the use of "we" to "they" and "you" in 1 Thessalonians 5. Gundry does not think that this is significant, but to a pretribulationist's mind it certainly is. Once 1 Thessalonians 4:14-17 is no longer connected in the simple way that Gundry suggests, his argument is going to fail.[11]

A second reason for identifying the Thessalonian references as a posttribulational coming of Christ is the linguistic parallel between the "gathering to him" of 2 Thessalonian 2:1, and the "gathering of his elect," in Matthew 24:31. 2 Thessalonians 2:1 uses the noun *episunagogēs*, while Jesus uses the verb *episunachēi* in Matthew 24:31. On the basis of the use of related words, it might be argued that the two gatherings are the same and that they are clearly posttribulational, since Matthew says that this is "immediately after the distress of those days."

Such an argument fails. Methodologically, one cannot simply identify two events merely because they are described by the same word. Further, to do so in the context where the debate is whether the events are the same or different is to beg the question. There is one way out of this dilemma. One might argue that the word in question has become a technical term, such that wherever it occurs it has a constant meaning. In this case the argument would be that the verb *episunagein* and its cognate noun have the status of a technical term relating to a posttribulational gathering of God's children to

Himself. However, an examination of the evidence shows this argument is simply false. There are nine occurrences of the noun and verb in the New Testament. Of those nine only three have an eschatological significance. They are the two under discussion here and a third instance in the synoptic parallel in Mark 13:27. Six occurrences are very general: the citizens of a city coming to see a dignitary. Therefore, to claim that a term has become a technical term based upon three occurrences, two of which are parallels in the synoptic Gospels, is to claim too much.[12]

In fairness to those who make this identification, they do not all do it simply on the linguistic parallel mentioned. They would offer a third reason, which, in combination with the second reason, they believe constitutes the case for identifying the gatherings. It is the similarity of *detail* along with the linguistic parallel that justifies the claim that the two gatherings are the same event and therefore posttribulational. There is the use of a trumpet, there are clouds, and there is a gathering of saints to the Lord. This argument, if true, is more substantial.

Close consideration, however, shows this argument is unconvincing to a pretribulationist.[13] The parallel between trumpets, clouds, and saints being caught up to meet the Lord in Thessalonians and Matthew, depends on establishing 1 Thessalonians 4:14-17 as posttribulational. At the center of this argument is its relationship to 5:1-9, which we have previously rejected. Moreover, any argument of this sort must not only be based on similarities; it must also be sensitive to differences. Similarities between events may be because they are *similar,* not the *same.* Gundry himself recognizes that there are differences, but he tries to show that they are compatible with one another and/or insignificant. The gathering may be related to that of dispersed Jews at the coming of their Messiah as taught in Deuteronomy 30:4 and Isaiah 27:12,13. Those who are gathered in Matthew are called *the elect*, a term Gundry himself says may refer to Israel, the church, or both. The one who gathers the saints is different. It is angels in Matthew and the Lord Himself in 1 Thessalonians 4. Gundry calls the Olivet discourse the most complete description of what will take place at the rapture, but there is the curious omission of any statement about the resurrection of the dead.[14]

In summary, the similarities that are cited between the Thessalonian epistles and Matthew are all based on making 1 Thessalonians 4:14-17 posttribulational and treating the differences as explainable. Both of these approaches will be unconvincing to a pretribulationist.

The Silence About a Rapture
in Correcting False Teaching

A second issue is the Paul's silence about a rapture in his correction of the false teaching that was troubling the Thessalonian believers, in 2 Thessalonians 2:2-4. An important reason for Paul's writing this second epistle so shortly after the first is found in these verses. The false teaching that was troubling the Thessalonians came to them either by a variety of means (a prophecy, a report, a letter) or by one of these means. The content of this false teaching is clear: "The Day of the Lord has come" (2:2). The teaching was that these believers were in the day of the Lord. This teaching was unsettling and alarming them. Paul writes to correct this false teaching, which was also incorrectly attributed to him.

Gundry thinks that there are two ways in which pretribulationists can interpret this passage. First, they can argue that the Thessalonians were unaware of a pretribulational rapture, and because of this ignorance they believed that they were in the Day of the Lord. This move, however, comes at a price. It requires that the entire case for a pretribulational rapture in the Thessalonian epistles be invalidated. If they did not know of such a rapture both from the first epistle and Paul's oral teaching, it is unlikely that we, who lack the latter, would be able to discern such a teaching. Furthermore, Paul merely reminds them of what he has taught them in order to correct their error. Thus, if they were unaware of such teaching, the case for a pretribulational rapture fails in 2 Thessalonians as well.[15]

Second, pretribulationists can hold that Paul taught a pretribulational rapture in 1 Thessalonians and orally, but that the believers forgot about it. Their forgetfulness caused them to believe the false teaching, and this was the source of their agitation. This is more likely the approach that a pretribulationist will take, but it too has a price. The problem here is that Paul had a very simple and decisive response to the Thessalonian error. He could have, and on Gundry's view ought to have, said that the Thessalonians should not worry because he had taught them that a pretribulational rapture had to occur before the Day of the Lord was going to begin. Paul is silent on this issue. He makes no mention of the rapture, and this counts severely against a pretrib rapture. Paul's answer is that the Thessalonians cannot be in the Day of the Lord because the apostasy had not occurred and the man of lawlessness had not been revealed.

There are a number of points that one can make in response to this claim. First, I can agree with Gundry that it would have been nice to have had an unequivocal statement about the time of the rapture here. However, the Spirit of God did not see fit to do that, and as I will argue that is not necessary here.

Second, there are some pretribulationists who do think that there is a reference to the rapture in Paul's response. For them, the reference comes in the statement that the apostasy must come before the Day of the Lord. They take the word "apostasy" not only to have the meaning of a religious defection but also to mean a physical departure. Were this the case, and I do not think it is,[16] then Paul corrected the Thessalonian believers by reminding them that the rapture had to occur before the Day of the Lord began.

Third, let us grant that there is no reference to the rapture in Paul's answer to the false teaching. Does that invalidate a pretribulational rapture? I think not! I can put my reason both negatively and positively. Negatively, what *would* invalidate a pretrib rapture would be teaching by Paul that was inconsistent with or contradictory to such a rapture. Positively, as long as Paul's teaching is compatible with a pretrib rapture there is no problem, as long as there is sufficient basis for such a belief elsewhere. In sum, all that is required is that Paul's teaching does not contradict a pretrib rapture and that such a rapture is based on biblical teaching elsewhere. I think that both of these conditions are met, although an unequivocal statement by Paul would have been nice.

Fourth, the problem of Paul's silence about a rapture in correcting the false teaching about the Day of the Lord is every bit as unresolved on a posttribulational understanding of the rapture. Put slightly differently, posttribulationists have either the same or a similar problem on the assumption of the correctness of their view. There are, I suggest, three interpretive options open to the posttribulationist. First, Paul taught no view of the rapture in 1 Thessalonians, or else the believers were unaware of it. If this is so, then the problem for the posttrib is the same as the problem for the pretrib in

Gundry's first option. Second, it can be argued that Paul taught a posttrib, pre-Day of the Lord rapture. This is the view that I would attribute to Gundry. If this is so, Gundry has the same problem that the pretrib does on the second interpretative option set out above. The Thessalonians thought that the Day of the Lord had come. The decisive answer here, as well, would have been, "You are wrong in your belief; don't you remember I taught you a posttrib, pre-Day of the Lord rapture?" The text is silent about such a rapture too. Third, posttribulationists may hold that Paul taught a posttrib, Day of the Lord rapture. That is, the rapture will be both posttribulational and *in* the Day of the Lord. In this case, the problem is not the same but similar. It is not why Paul is silent about the rapture but why the Thessalonians are unsettled and alarmed, two strong words. On this interpretation, the Day of the Lord would have to come before the rapture could take place. If the Thessalonians thought they were in the Day of the Lord, even though erroneously, they should not have been unsettled and alarmed, for the coming of the Lord to rapture them was imminent; it was about to occur. Joy and expectancy should have been their attitudes. Those who were not working because they thought the Lord was about to return, were in fact vindicated. The rapture was about to occur.

In sum, it would have been nice to have had some unequivocal statement about the time of the rapture in answer to the false teaching. But that was not the Holy Spirit's intention, and it may be profitless to speculate why. However, if this is a problem, it constitutes the *same* problem for certain posttribulational views of the rapture, and a *similar* one for other interpretations.

The Identity of the Restrainer

A final theological and exegetical question in 2 Thessalonians 2 is the identity of the restrainer and its importance for the question of the time of the rapture. This issue is a bit different than the previous two. The first two matters dealt with arguments that posttribulationists offer against pretribulationism. This issue deals more with an argument that pretribulationists bring in support of their position and against mid- or posttribulationism. The argument is that the restrainer in 2 Thessalonians 2:6,7 is the Holy Spirit, and that the removal of His restraint comes at the rapture. This removal supports a pretribulational rapture.

The first step in dealing with this argument is to identify the restrainer.[17] As we might expect, we have a variety of interpretations. Let me just give an overview of the most common approaches. First, the predominant view in the early church was that the restrainer was the Roman Empire. The restraining power was embodied in the person of the emperor. As time passed, conflict arose between the civil and ecclesiastical power, and this text was interpreted as meaning that the civil power was restraining the papacy until the coming of the Lord, at which time the latter would be destroyed. This view was defended on the grounds of Paul's vagueness about the restrainer, since if this letter fell into the hands of the civil authority they might view Paul's claim about the restraint being removed as an act of sedition. The vagueness of the reference, however, seems to be related to the fact that the Thessalonians already know of this matter. Moreover, the Roman Empire no longer exists, and the man of lawlessness has not appeared.

Second, growing out of the first view is the interpretation that the restrainer is human government, particularly as it is expressed in the rule of law. Restraint through the rule of law is the opposite of the man of sin and the mystery of lawlessness. This view has gained popularity among interpreters of all views on the rapture. One cannot rule out the possibility that this is the correct identification. Though human governments are often given to excesses, Paul teaches that their rightful duty is the restraint of evil (Rom. 13:1-7). At the same time we should not dismiss the possibility that the restraint of evil requires something stronger, more supernatural, than mere human government, which praises welldoers and punishes evildoers.

Third, many identify the restrainer with the Holy Spirit. This interpretation seems best to me. It too was widely held in the early church, being found in the writings of Theodoret, Theodore of Mopsuestia, and Chrysostom. The view may reflect apostolic teaching. Moreover, it would seem that a person is required to restrain a person, and a supernatural one to restrain this man of lawlessness who is motivated by Satan himself. Finally, this view best accounts for the change in gender between verses 6 and 7. Verse 6 uses a neuter to identify the restrainer, most likely a reference to the Greek noun for spirit, *pneuma*. The change in verse 7 to the masculine is a reference to the personality of the Holy Spirit. Thus, I conclude that the most likely reference is to the Holy Spirit, for even if the restraining of evil is through human government, ultimately that is only possible through the power given it by the Holy Spirit.

Having identified the restrainer as the Holy Spirit does not settle the issue of the relationship of this to the rapture. For this to be used as an argument for pretribulationism, it must be shown that the Holy Spirit *only* restrains the revelation of the man of lawlessness through the church. It is only in this way that the removal of the church is identical with the removal of the restraint. As long as the Holy Spirit is active during the Tribulation period, it is possible that He will act to restrain the final manifestation of evil independently of the church and its restraining activity. There seems to be abundant evidence that the Holy Spirit will be active in the earth during the Tribulation period. He will empower His witnesses (Mark 13:11). Evangelism will be more effective than it has ever been (Matt. 24:14; Rev. 7:9-14). It is reasonable to assume that as Satanic activity increases, so will the activity of the Holy Spirit. As a matter of fact, this passage does not say, nor does any other, that the restraint of the appearance of the man of lawlessness is an activity that the church has been called to do. We are to be salt and light, but it is unlikely that Jesus meant that this was the restraining of the final form of iniquity. If this is so, then any view of the rapture can meet the requirements of this passage. The Holy Spirit will be active during the Tribulation, and the church at best is one, not the only one, who restrains the revelation of the man of lawlessness. We may think that because of the special relationship between the Holy Spirit and the church, a pretribulational rapture best serves the meaning of the text, but, at least in my judgment, it is not the only possible interpretation. Thus, those of us who are pretribulationists need to be careful in the use of this argument, that we do not claim for it more than is justified.[18]

Conclusion

In conclusion I have tried to deal with one of the most difficult eschatological texts in the New Testament. I have tried to show that on the three issues raised in 2 Thessalonians 2:1-7, there is no exegetical or theological matter that makes a pretribulational rapture impossible, or even improbable.

Appendix

While the majority of commentators on 2 Thessalonians 2:3 take *apostasía* to refer to apostasy or religious defection, some argue that it is reference to the rapture.[19] If this claim is defensible, then Paul *does* use his teaching about a pretribulational rapture to instruct the Thessalonian believers about the Day of the Lord. The accuracy and defensibility of this claim rests on the *etymology* and *usage* of the Greek verb *aphistēmi* and its cognate nouns.

Aphistēmi and its cognates are found widely in Greek literature. The verb is first thought to have been found in the writings of Thucydides (Thuc., 1, 122). In the period from second century B.C. to first century A.D. there are at least 355 occurrences of this word group,[20] making these rather common words in the Greek language. *Aphistēmi* is a compound verb from *apo* (from) and *histēmi* (to stand). It is both a transitive verb, meaning "to cause to revolt, mislead," and an intransitive verb, meaning "to go away, withdraw, depart, fall away." From this verb are derived two nouns, *apostasion* and *apostasía*. *Apostasion* comes to have a fixed meaning, "a bill of divorce," while *apostasía* means "rebellion, abandonment, state of apostasy" or "defection." It is the latter noun that is found in our text.

The question that we are now ready to answer is whether the noun *apostasía* ever refers to a *physical* departure, allowing Paul to make a reference to the rapture of the church by using this word. Let us take how the words are used in the biblical Greek (the LXX and the New Testament) as the context for establishing how these words are used. These would be the primary contexts for setting the usage of any biblical term, although at least in this case what is true in biblical Greek is true more generally. The first thing that we can say is that the verb *aphistēmi* is clearly used of physical departure in both testaments. In the Old Testament (the LXX) the verb is used in Genesis 12:8 of Abram's departure from Shechem toward the hills east of Bethel. It is used of the physical separation of persons as in 1 Samuel 18:13, where it is used of David's departure from Saul, and in Psalm 6:8, of the physical separation of the wicked from God's presence. In New Testament Greek there are clear examples of the use of the verb to express physical departure or separation. Forms of this verb appear 15 times. Luke uses this word 10 times (Luke 2:37; 4:13; 8:13; 13:27; Acts 5:37-38; 12:10; 15:38; 19:9; 22:29). It is found four times in Paul (2 Cor. 12:8; 1 Tim. 4:1; 6:5; 2 Tim. 2:19). It is used once by the writer of Hebrews (Heb. 3:12). All but Acts 5:37 are intransitive uses. The idea of physical departure is prominent in many of the occurrences. In Luke 2:37 Anna is said to have never left the temple. In Acts 19:9 Paul was teaching in the synagogue in Ephesus for three months, but he left or departed when some obstinate hearers refused to believe. Thus, there are clear examples where the verb means to physically depart or leave in both the Greek Old Testament and New Testament.

There are fewer uses of the two related nouns in biblical literature, but again both are found in the Greek Old Testament and New Testament. *Apostasion* is found with a fixed meaning in both testaments. It is related to the breaking of the marriage covenant (Mal. 2:14). And it means "a certificate of divorce" (Deut. 24:1,3; Isa. 50:1; Jer. 3:8; Matt. 5:31; 19:7; Mark 10:4).

This leads us to the noun in 2 Thessalonians 2:3, *apostasía*. It is found in the Greek Old Testament and has the idea of rebellion (Joshua 22:22), wickedness (Jeremiah 2:19), and unfaithfulness (2 Chr. 28:19; 29:19; 33:19). *Apostasía* is found twice in the New Testament, in our text and in Acts 21:21. In Acts, the noun is used in Paul's teaching that the Jews who lived among the Gentiles that *forsake* the teaching of Moses about circumcision. *None* of the uses of the noun in either testament indicate a physical departure of any sort. The point can be made even more strongly. If one searches for the uses of the noun "apostasy" in the 355 occurrences over the 300-year period between the second century B.C. and the first century A.D., one will not find a single instance where this word refers to a physical departure. The uses outside biblical Greek are exactly parallel to those in it.

Let me summarize my findings: 1) *aphistēmi* and its cognates are found widely in Greek literature; 2) the verb *aphistēmi* has many and clear uses where a physical departure can only be meant; 3) the noun *apostasion* has a clear and fixed meaning that relates it to the marriage covenant, and it is the common way of expressing the giving of a certificate of divorce; 4) the other noun, *apostasía,* has a variety of meanings, but none of them relate to a physical departure. It seems that any fair assessment of the data leads to the conclusion that Paul does not refer to the rapture in 2 Thessalonians 2:3.

Before I conclude this appendix, let me state and respond to two possible objections to the conclusions that I have argued for above.

It might be argued that though the derivative noun may never be used of a physical departure, the idea is nonetheless justified because of the underlying verb which has that etymology and usage. In other words, one rests the rapture interpretation of this text not on *apostasía* but on the verb *aphistēmi*. This simply cannot be done. In most cases the meaning of the underlying verb carries over to its derivative noun. But there are instances where this is not the case, and to do so leads to false conclusions. This is even true where the word is a compound. *Anaginōskō* is a word in the New Testament. It is a compound from the preposition *ana* which means "up, upwards" and *ginōskō* which means "to know." To base the meaning of the compound on the meaning of its parts leaves one with a meaning for *anaginōskō* of "to know up" or "to know upwards," when in fact the word means "to know certainly, recognize" or "to read."[21] There is at least another clear example of the difference between a verb and its cognate noun. There is a verb *eperōtaō* which is found a number of times in the New Testament, 53 times in the Gospels, and five times in the epistles (e.g., Matt. 12:10; Luke 3:10; Rom. 10:20). The meaning of the verb, invariably, is "to ask" or "consult." A derivative noun occurs once in the New Testament, in 1 Pet. 3:21. The noun is *eperōtēma*. The idea here is of a pledge, quite different from its cognate verb meaning.[22] That is, water baptism is "a pledge of a good conscience toward God." Thus, the meaning of derivative nouns must be established through *their usage*.

A second objection to what has been argued is that, in the history of the interpretation of this text, there are some interpreters, important ones too, who have suggested that a physical departure is at least a part of the meaning of this word. That may be, but that does not settle the matter. If they came to their conclusions on the basis of the etymology and usage of *aphistēmi*, they were wrong, at least in my judgment. If, on the other hand, they reached their conclusions for some other reason, then we would have to know what those reasons were, so that they could be evaluated. However, it does seem that given what we presently know, there is no reason to understand Paul's use of *apostasía* as a reference to the rapture.

16
John McLean

Chronology and Sequential Structure of John's Revelation

_____*OVERVIEW*

How important is the structure of the book of Revelation? Many interpreters seek to rearrange the events of John's Revelation in the same way that one would shuffle a deck of cards. Is this necessary or consistent with literal interpretation? In this essay, the author argues for a straightforward and sequential approach to understanding the book. While all acknowledge the complexity and uniqueness of Revelation, this essay demonstrates that a chronological and sequential approach best explains John's vision.

*P*eople always like to know when something is going to happen. Whether it is a weekend of activities, a church service, or a day at work, a schedule of events is always appreciated.

What Is the Schedule of Events?

The book of Revelation gives us a schedule of events for the period that is called the end times. Revelation provides both a chronological and sequential presentation of God's final eschatological judgment which is known as the Tribulation. Scripture does not give us enough information to set dates for future events. In fact, we are told that only the Father knows the time of the second coming of Jesus Christ (Matt 24:36; Mark 13:32). This is an exhortation to avoid date-setting or guessing. It is even difficult to look at world events and say with certainty that these things are a fulfillment of prophetic Scripture. It is probably better to understand the things that appear to be fulfilling prophetic Scripture as possibilities or stages in the final development of future fulfillment.

The person who does understand the structure of Revelation (the Apocalypse) will know the chronological and sequential timetable of the events contained in the book. This structure does not tell us when the Tribulation begins, but it does give us a schedule of events to understand what happens after it begins.

The comfort for the believer is that these events will not take place until after the rapture of the church. God has promised that He has not destined us to wrath but to obtaining salvation (deliverance) through Jesus Christ (1 Thess. 1:10; 5:9). This deliverance, designated as the rapture, is provided through the gathering together of the saints in the air to meet Jesus Christ. Paul wrote in 1 Thessalonians 4:16-17: "For the Lord himself will come down from heaven, with a loud command, with the voice of the archangel and with the trumpet call of God, and the dead in Christ will rise first. After that, we who are still alive and are left will be caught up together with them in the clouds to meet the Lord in the air. And so we will be with the Lord forever."

There are four major principles that define the structure of Revelation and show that it is both chronological and sequential. The book unfolds according to a prophetic timetable as well as a literary sequence of events that reveals more precise definition and detail about the closing events of a period which is called "The Tribulation and Great Tribulation."

Epistolary Structure

The first principle is the recognition of the epistolary nature of the book. Revelation begins with a prologue (1:1-8) and closes with an epilogue (22:6-21). The book contains seven exhortations to seven churches in Asia Minor. Although other common elements of epistolary literature are absent from Revelation, these missing elements should not dissuade a person from acknowledging this aspect of the structure.

Revelation 1:19

The second principle is stated in Revelation 1:19: "Write therefore the things which you have seen, and the things which are, and the things which shall take place after these things" (NASB). Revelation is structured in part by the three time periods that are mentioned in this verse: 1) the things which you have seen; 2) the things which are; 3) the things that shall take place after these things.

This threefold division does not control the major content of the book, as evidenced by the disproportional character of the three sections (1:1-20; 2:1–3:22; 4:1–22:5). Greg K. Beale suggests this threefold division is based on Daniel 2.[1] He maintains: "It would appear not to be from mere accidental placement that John introduces the book and three subsequent major sections in Revelation with an allusion to Daniel 2:28-29,45."[2] Jan Lambrecht contends the division should stand even if Revelation 1:19 is not accepted as a proof text.[3]

The "things which you have seen" are recorded in chapter 1. John recorded the initial vision of the glorified Jesus Christ, in which he was commissioned to write the entire book of Revelation. Chapters 2 and 3 contain the "things which are." This is evidenced by the command to John: "Write in a book what you see" (Rev.

1:11 NASB), indicating the existence of these churches in John's day and the present aspect of the "things which are." This section closes with the opening of the third section, "the things which shall take place after these things." Revelation 4–21 comprises this third section, as indicated by 4:1: "*After these things* I looked, and behold, a door standing open in heaven, and the first voice which I had heard, like the sound of a trumpet speaking with me, said, Come up here, and I will show you *what must take place after these things*." John clearly provided a chronological division to the book with this three-fold segmentation.[4]

Sequential Nature of the Septet Judgments

The third principle concerns the sequential nature of the three septet judgments (seals, trumpets, bowls) of Revelation. There are two basic views of the sequence of the septet judgments. John M. Court notes, "The three plague sequences, the seven seals, the seven trumpets, and the seven bowls have an important role to play in any interpretation of the structure of the book of Revelation."[5] The structure of Revelation is determined, in part, by one's understanding of whether the three septet judgments are sequential or simultaneous. The sequential view understands the seals, trumpets, and bowls as successive judgments that proceed out of each other. The simultaneous view sees a recapitulation of the septets, in which the judgments are parallel to each other. Each recapitulation reviews previous events and adds further details. Court summarizes the conundrum: "The problem for the Recapitulation theory was to show how events which appeared to be different were different only in the way they were described. For the chronological theory the converse is a problem: how can the interpreter make a clear distinction between sequences which have superficial similarities?"[6]

This chapter argues for the sequential view of the septet judgments, i.e., the trumpets follow the seals and the bowls follow the trumpets. The sequential structure does not negate a recapitulation, or review, of other visions in John that portray visionary scenes which preview eschatological events to come (Rev. 7:9-17; 14:8-13). G. Bornkamm cites as examples the five visions of chapter 14 (the Lamb on Mt. Zion; the angel proclaiming the gospel; the proclamation of judgment on Babylon; the torment of the beast worshipers; and the son of man with a sickle), which events parallel the coming of the Lamb in Revelation 19:1-21.[7] Robert Mounce notes: "At times he [John] moves ahead quickly to the eternal state in order to encourage the redeemed with a vision of the bliss that awaits them. At other times he returns to the past to interpret the source of the hostility being experienced by the church in the present time."[8]

That there is continuity between the septets is evidenced by similar patterns of devastation. Each set of judgments is more intense and destructive than the previous ones.[9] The second trumpet destroys one-third of seas while the second bowl turns all of the seas into blood (Rev. 8:8-9; 16:3). The third trumpet pollutes one-third of the rivers and springs, while the third bowl transforms all of the rivers and springs into blood (Rev. 8:10-11; 16:4-7). The fourth trumpet smites one-third of the sun, moon, and stars, while the fourth bowl causes the sun to intensify and scorch the people of the earth (Rev. 8:12-13; 16:10-11).

Although there are many similarities between the septets, the differences are more crucial and determinative. The seals generally differ in content from the trumpet and bowl plagues. There is no alignment between the first, fifth, and seventh parallel judgments of the septets. Dale Davis notes: "The sequence within each series is diverse from the sequence within other series, and even where they are apparently similar the content of the judgment reveals a disparity."[10] These differences argue against the simultaneous view and suggest the sequential, or successive, view as the probable option. The following reasons are offered as strong evidence for the successive structure of the seal, trumpet, and bowl judgments.

A "plain face" reading of the book suggests that the septets (seals, trumpets, bowls) are sequential. The two Greek phrases *kai eiden* (*and I saw*) and *meta tauta* (*after these things*) indicate a sequential movement of the visions beyond just the reception of these visions by John. It should also be admitted that these phrases indicate a chronological movement as seen in the contexts of Revelation 1:19; 9:12; 15:15; 19:1; 20:3 (*meta tauta*), and 5:1,2,6,11; 6:1,2,5,12; 7:2; 8:2; 9:1; 15:1,2; 17:3,6; 19:11,17,19; 20:1,4,11,12; 22:1 (*kai; eidon*).

The seven seals are followed by the seven trumpets, and the seven bowls follow the seven trumpets (Rev. 6:1-17; 8:1-9,21; 16:1-21). The bowls evidence a sequential pattern, as they are called "the last, because in them the wrath of God is finished" (Rev. 15:1). Sequential character is manifested within each septet. The ordinal numbers indicate succession: [*deuteran, tritēn, tetartēn, pemptēn, ektēn, ebtomēn*] (second, third, etc.). There is also a successive building within each septet to a climactic conclusion.[11] Sequential progression is also noted by the parallels between the three woes and the fifth, sixth, and seventh trumpets (Rev. 8:13; 9:12; 11:14).[12]

Ugo Vanni contends the seventh part of each septet encompasses the judgments that follow.[13] The successive nature of the judgments is evidenced in the breaking of the seventh seal: "And when He broke the seventh seal, there was silence in heaven for about half an hour. And I saw the seven angels who stand before God; and seven trumpets were given to them" (Rev. 8:1-2 NASB). The seven angels then execute the seven trumpet judgments, bringing an intensification of destruction on the earth (Rev. 8:7–9:21).

The seventh trumpet is linked to the seven bowls. John states that when the seventh angel sounds the trumpet, "then the mystery of God is finished" (Rev. 10:7). At both the introduction and conclusion of the bowl judgments, the writer emphasizes that in them the wrath of God is finished (Rev. 15:1,8; 16:17). The seventh trumpet brings forth the execution of the seven bowls and the completion of God's wrath.

Davis points out two contextual clues that indicate a sequential pattern. One hundred and forty-four thousand people are protectively sealed on their foreheads after the sixth seal and before the release of the plague by the four angels (Rev. 7:1-8). The fifth trumpet brings a demonic plague on mankind and torments "only the men who do not have the seal of God on their foreheads" (Rev. 9:4). Therefore Davis concludes: "John depicts an event under the trumpets as clearly following after other events under the seals."[14]

In summary, the crucial differences between the judgments include: the "plain face" reading of the text; the sequential character within each septet; the use of ordinal numbers; the sequential aspect of the seventh part of each septet; the contextual clues of progression that argue for the successive approach.

The following structural outline represents a descriptive view of the development of Revelation. The climax of Revelation is the coming of the Son of Man. The major motif that leads up to the second coming is the intensification of the septet judgments (4:1–19:21). The septets unfold out of each other until the final climax of worldwide destruction. John intermittently suspends the progressive movement and disclosure of the septets in order to introduce pertinent information. The information is inserted by means of narrative previews or narrative synopses. Narrative previews prophetically amplify major characters or events that are enunciated later in Revelation. Narrative synopses provide apocalyptic scenes that review past events and lead the reader to future episodes.

Outline designations (1A-6A) mark major divisions in the book. The major section of the book is 3A which has four primary subsections (1B-4B) that develop it. The progression of letters in the alphabet and numbers represents further sublevels of structuration and supportive development.

Structural Outline of Revelation

1A Prologue: *"Things Which You Have Seen,"* 1:1-20

2A Letters to the seven churches: *"Things Which Are,"* 2:1–3:22

3A God's Wrath, Great Tribulation: *"Things Which Shall Take Place After These Things,"* 4:1–19:21

    1B Introduction to the seven seal judgments, 4:1–5:14

        1C Throne of God in heaven, 4:1-11

        2C The scroll of the Lamb, 5:1-14

    2B The six seal judgments, 6:1–7:17

        1C First seal: white horse, 6:1-2

        2C Second seal: red horse, 6:3-4

        3C Third seal: black horse, 6:5-6

        4C Fourth seal: ashen horse, 6:7-8

        5C Fifth seal: martyrs under the altar, 6:9-11

        6C Sixth seal: great day of God's wrath, 6:12-17

        7C Narrative preview: redeemed of God, 7:1-17

           1D Sealing of the 144,000, 7:1-8

           2D Martyrs from the Great Tribulation, 7:9-17

    3B The seventh seal judgment: the seven trumpets, 8:1–18:24

        1C Breaking of the seventh seal: introduction to the seven trumpets, 8:1-6

        2C First trumpet: one-third of the earth destroyed, 8:7

3C Second trumpet: one-third of the sea destroyed, 8:8-9

4C Third trumpet: one-third of the water destroyed, 8:10-11

5C Fourth trumpet: one-third of the celestial destroyed, 8:12

6C Introduction of the three woes, 8:13

7C Fifth trumpet, first woe: men tormented, 9:1-12

8C Sixth trumpet, second woe: one-third of mankind destroyed, 9:13–11:14

    1D Sixth trumpet, one-third of mankind destroyed, 9:13-21

    2D Narrative preview: little scroll final judgment, 10:1-11

    3D Narrative synopsis: witnesses' persecution, 11:1-14

9C The seventh trumpet: the seven bowls, third woe, 11:15–18:24

    1D The seventh trumpet and proclamation of God's kingdom, 11:15-19

    2D Narrative synopsis, 12:1–14:13

        1E A woman, male child, Satan in conflict, 12:1-6

        2E Angelic war in heaven, 12:7-12

        3E War on earth, 12:13-17

        4E Beast out of the sea, 13:1-10

        5E Beast out of the earth, 13:11-18

        6E Narrative preview, 14:1-13

    3D Introduction of the seven bowls, 14:14–15:8

        1E Son of Man with a sickle, 14:14-16

        2E Winepress of God's wrath, 14:17-20

        3E Seven angels of the seven plagues, 15:1

        4E Worship of God and the Lamb, 15:2-4

        5E Seven angels receive the bowls, 15:5-8

4D The seven bowl judgments: the end,
16:1–18:24

   1E First bowl: malignant sores, 16:1-2

   2E Second bowl: sea destroyed, 16:3

   3E Third bowl: rivers destroyed, 16:4-7

   4E Fourth bowl: scorching heat, 16:8-9

   5E Fifth bowl: darkness, 16:10-11

   6E Sixth bowl: preparation for war,
   16:12-16

   7E Seventh bowl: worldwide
   destruction, 16:17-21

   8E Narrative synopsis, 17:1–18:24

      1F Description and destruction of
      the harlot, 17:1-18

      2F Condemnation and destruction of
      Babylon, 18:1-24

4B The advent of Jesus Christ, 19:1-21

   1C Introduction and praise of the advent,
   19:1-10

   2C *Parousia* of Jesus Christ, 19:11-16

   3C The judgment of the beast, false prophet, and
   people, 19:17-21

4A Millennial kingdom of God: *"Things Which Shall
Take Place After These Things,"* 20:1-15

   1B Satan is bound in the abyss, 20:1-3

   2B Saints are resurrected, 20:4-6

   3B Final judgment of Satan, 20:7-10

   4B Final judgment of mankind, 20:11-15

5A The new Jerusalem, 21:1–22:5

6A Epilogue: 22:6-21

Seventh Week
of Daniel and Revelation 4–19

The fourth principle for understanding the structure of Revelation is the correlation of the seventieth week of Daniel 9:27 with the synoptic eschatological discourses of Matthew 24, Mark 13, Luke 21, and Revelation 4–19. The first step is to analyze thematic parallels between the "birth pangs" of the synoptics (Matt. 24:4-14; Mark 13:5-13; Luke 21:8-19) and the first six seals of Revelation

(6:1-11). These affinities evidence chronological and structural parallels between the synoptic eschatological discourses and Revelation.

The second step is to analyze some eschatological sections in Luke (Luke 21:22-23; 23:28-31) that provide a literary key for establishing a structural bench mark for the midpoint of Daniel's seventieth week in Revelation 6. The entire judgment section of Revelation (4–19) is then compared in order to discover further correlations between the synoptics and Revelation.

The third section suggests thematic and linguistic correlations between the synoptics and the Apocalypse. These signature themes evidence the imprint of the synoptics on the content and structure of Revelation.

The First Half of Daniel's Seventieth Week

The relationship between the synoptics and seals has been recognized in part by several expositors.[15] The opening of the first seal calls forth a rider on a white horse (Rev. 6:1). Zane Hodges maintains: "Although the book of Revelation has always provided a fertile field for differing interpretations, few—if any—of its prophetic visions have received more widely divergent explanations than that of the first of the famous four horsemen of the Apocalypse."[16] Hodges argues that the first horseman is Jesus Christ beginning the judgment of the book of Revelation. He proposes three arguments in support of his view.[17] He notes that Zechariah's prophecy presents divine agents of judgment under the symbols of horsemen. This symbolic parallel should lead to the identification of these horsemen as divine agents. He also points to similarities between the messianic deliverer of Psalm 45 and the rider of Revelation 6:1-2. These correspondences point to a divine rider on the first horse who is executing the judgment of God. Third, he notes the parallels between Revelation 6:1-2 and Revelation 19, where the rider is clearly identified as Jesus Christ (Rev. 19:1-16).

Against this interpretation is the ambiguity of the identification of this rider with Jesus Christ. It is Jesus Christ, the Lamb, whom John identifies as opening the seals (Rev. 6:1). J. P. M. Sweet concurs: "This interpretation is rejected by most modern scholars: the rider cannot be Christ since he opens the seal, and the context gives no hint of the gospel."[18]

John clearly reveals the identity of Jesus when He is presented in the book (Rev. 1:1-8; 5:6-14; 6:16; 19:11-16). The Lamb is included as part of the sixth seal, and therefore it seems awkward to insert him as the rider of the first horse (Rev. 6:16).

There are significant differences between the riders of Revelation 6 and 19. The two riders wear different crowns. The first rider wears a *stephanos* (*wreath crown*), while the second rider wears a *diadēmata* (diadem crown). The first rider carries a *bow* (*toxon*), while the second rider has a sharp *sword* (*rhomphaia*) that proceeds from his mouth. The description of the second rider is so detailed that John leaves little doubt he is referring to Jesus Christ.

Mathias Rissi argues that the rider of the first horse is the Antichrist.[19] He notes the parallels that exist between the eschatological synoptic discourses and the four horsemen. The first sign of the beginning of birth pangs is the presence of pseudo-messiahs. The disciples are warned not to be deceived by men who come in the name of Jesus (Matt. 24:5; Mark 13:6; Luke 21:8). He maintains the four horsemen are part of a group of demonic agents.[20]

The acceptance of this view, in part, is dependent on how much weight is given to the parallels between the synoptics and Revelation. The synoptics do not state that the Antichrist is the first sign of birth pangs but that the pseudo-messiahs are. It may be better to view the first rider as a general symbolic reference to pseudo-messiahs who stir up the people to war and insurrection. The rider is said to go out "conquering and to conquer," but open warfare is not present until the second seal.

The rider of the red horse is given a large sword and power to take peace from the earth. The red color of the horse indicates bloodshed, as men slay each other in war. The *large sword* (*machaire megalē*) is used in the Old Testament in other eschatological judgment passages (Isa. 27:1; 34:5; Ezek. 21:3).

The second seal clearly parallels Matthew 24:6-7 and the synoptics: "And you will be hearing of wars and rumors of wars; see that you are not frightened, for those things must take place, but that is not yet the end. For nation will rise against nation, and kingdom against kingdom" (NASB).

The third rider on a black horse brings famine. The rider holds a pair of scales in his hand. The scales were used to weigh out the approximate weight of grain for sale. The rider proclaims: "A quart of wheat for a denarius, and three quarts of barley for a denarius; and do not harm the oil and the wine" (Rev. 6:6 NASB). A denarius was a small silver coin with the approximate value of 18 to 20

Roman cents. It was devalued in the days of Nero to about 8 cents.[21] The denarius was the standard wage for one man's workday. Adela Y. Collins suggests a denarius under good circumstances could purchase 8 to 16 times more wheat and 8 times more barley than proclaimed by the rider.[22] Two things indicate a scarcity of food: 1) the high price of grains is due to inflated cost from short supply and high demand; 2) the text indicates the third rider has damaged the grain and wheat harvest. The oil and wine harvests are not harmed by this plague.

Famine is also a common result of war. Foreign enemies would scorch the land with fire, cut down fruit-bearing trees, and salt agricultural fields in order to weaken the people in the coming years. All three synoptic writers list famine as one of the plagues following the turbulence of wars and rumors of wars (Matt. 24:7; Mark 13:8; Luke 21:11).

The rider of the pale horse is named "Death" (*thanatos*). *Thanatos* can refer to physical death by various causes or a fatal pestilence that results in death. Court notes, "In the realities of the ancient world one sense of thanatos (pestilence) most frequently led to the other sense (death)."[23] The name of this plague is symbolic as one-fourth of the earth's population is killed. *Hades* [*hadēs*] follows closely behind the fourth rider. Hades in the New Testament lies at the heart of the earth and is a place of abode for the dead. In Revelation, Hades is controlled by Jesus Christ (Rev. 1:18), and it is a place of judgment for the wicked who will ultimately be thrown into the lake of fire (Rev. 20:13). The implication may be that the people killed by this plague are God's enemies, who are judged to death and a place of torment. The people of the earth are killed by *sword* (*romphaia*), famine (*limō*), *pestilence* (*thanatos*), and *wild beasts* (*thērion*). The third destroyer is *thanatos* (*Death*). The greatest number of casualties from war and famine are often the result of pestilences. Dead bodies are breeding grounds for devastating diseases. Unsanitary military camps can breed rabid rodents and bring plagues that are able to wipe out entire units. Malnutrition results in weakened bodies that are susceptible to all forms of disease.

The final instrument of death is *wild beasts* (*thērion*). There is some question as to whether *thērion* should be understood literally or figuratively. *Thērion* is used of *wild animals* that fought in arenas, and also of animal-like beings of a supernatural kind.[24] The writer emphasizes these are wild beasts of the earth, and therefore it is better to understand this as a reference to wild beasts which roam the wilderness.

The fourth seal aligns well with the synoptic discourses. Famines, pestilences, and death are part of the beginning of birth pangs (Matt. 24:7; Mark 13:8; Luke 21:11). Luke employs the word *loimoi*, which specifically refers to *pestilences* where John chooses *thanato*, a more general term that includes pestilences and death.[25]

John envisions martyrs under an altar after the fifth seal is broken. Their place under the altar signifies the location where the blood of their sacrifice collects. These people are slain because of their testimony to the Word of God. The synoptics warn the disciples that persecution and martyrdom are expected during a time of tribulation (Matt. 24:9-12; Mark 13:9-13; Luke 21:12-19). The disciples would be hated, betrayed by family members, beaten in the synagogues and civil courts, thrown into prison, and put to death.

The martyrs cry out: "How long, Sovereign Lord, holy and true, until you judge the inhabitants of the earth and avenge our blood?" (Rev. 6:10). This prayer is in keeping with their concept of the just demands of the law and character of God. The retribution is avenged on "the inhabitants of the earth" (Rev. 6:10).[26]

Each of the souls is given a white robe (*stolē leukē*) to wear. Charles points out that Jewish and early Christian literature taught that martyrs were to be given white robes as spiritual bodies, while the rest of the faithful had to wait for their robes until the final judgment.[27] The martyrs are informed they must wait a little longer, until the slaughter is completed and their fellow servants and brothers are also killed (Rev. 6:11).

The synoptic writers seek to comfort the disciples by saying that the Holy Spirit will be with them and give them words to speak in their hour of trial (Mark 13:11; Luke 21:15). The disciples are said to proclaim the gospel before kings and governors and ultimately to the whole world. Luke warns that some of them will be put to death, while others will not have a hair of their head perish (Luke 21:16-18).

A great earthquake occurs at the breaking of the sixth seal. The motif of earthquakes is used by John throughout Revelation to herald the coming judgment of God (Rev. 6:12; 8:5; 11:13,19; 16:18).[28] Each earthquake brings an intensification of judgments. The sun's light is darkened and the moon appears red as blood.

Cosmic phenomena are common in other Old Testament prophetic works. Joel 2:28–3:3 (cf. Acts 2:19-20) records similar corresponding events of the sun and moon. The context of Joel portends the coming judgment on the nations that have been enemies of Jerusalem. The Day of Yahweh in Joel brings judgment on the nations and deliverance and restoration to the people of Jerusalem. Stars are said to fall from the sky like ripe figs dropping from a tree. John describes the sky rolling back like a scroll, and every mountain and island is moved by the catastrophic events.

The people cry for the mountains to cover them from the wrath of God: "For the great day of their [God and the Lamb] wrath has come, and who can stand?" (Rev. 6:17 NASB). The sixth seal incorporates aspects of the synoptics from the midtribulational events and signs of the coming of the Son of Man. It will be argued later in this chapter that the flight and hiding of the people relate to the time period of the abomination of desolation. The celestial and terrestrial phenomena of the sixth seal are also signs of the coming of the Son of Man in the synoptics (Matt. 24:29; Mark 13:24-25; Luke 21:25-26 NASB). The sixth seal reflects the Lucan account more closely as Luke includes, with the coming of the Son of Man, the aspect of men "fainting from fear and the expectation of the things which are coming upon the world" (Luke 21:26). It appears that John uses the sixth seal to introduce the beginning of the end, the "Great Tribulation" (Matt. 24:21; Mark 13:19; Luke 21:23; Rev. 6:17; 7:14), and to give the reader a glimpse of God's eschatological final judgment that has begun to fall on the whole world.

The following chart visualizes the parallels between the synoptics and seal judgments.

Textual Parallels Between the Synoptics and Seal Judgments

	Revelation 6	Matthew 24	Mark 13	Luke 21
False Messiahs, Prophets	2	5,11	6	8
Wars	2-4	6-7	7	9
International Discord	3-4	7	8	10
Famines	5-8	7	8	11
Pestilences	8			11
Persecution/Martyrdom	9-11	9	9-13	12-17
Earthquakes	12	7	8	11
Cosmic Phenomena	12-14			11

The Seventieth Week Midpoint in Relationship to the Apocalypse

Luke intersperses eschatological statements throughout his closing chapters (Luke 17:20-37; 19:41-44; 21:5-38; 23:26-31). The last disclosure of eschatological teaching (Luke 23:26-31) is set in the context of Jesus' crucifixion. Luke states: "And there were following Him [Jesus] a great multitude of people, and of women who were mourning and lamenting Him. But Jesus turning to them said, 'Daughters of Jerusalem, stop weeping for Me, but weep for yourselves and for your children. For behold, the days are coming when they will say, Blessed are the barren, and the wombs that never bore, and the breasts that never nursed'" (Luke 23:27-29 NASB).

The phrase "For behold, *the days are coming,*" [*oti idou erchontai ēmerai*] (Luke 23:29) clearly denotes the eschatological nature of the statements that follow. This phraseology is used elsewhere by Luke and the synoptic writers to introduce prophetic announcements (Luke 17:22,26-31; 19:43; 21:22-23,37; cf. Matt. 24:19,22,29; Mark 13:17,19,20,24). This prophetic announcement is paradoxical in that barrenness is often viewed in biblical writings as a curse from God rather than a blessing (Gen. 16:2; 20:17,18; 29:32; 30:22,23; 1 Sam. 1:6,7; 2:1-11; Isa. 4:1; Luke 1:25). It appears the blessedness of this situation is the freedom from pregnancy and small children during a time of trouble. Luke ironically states as a blessing (Luke 23:29) what he previously stated as a warning (Luke 21:23 NASB). Each of the synoptic writers identically records the negative version of this teaching: "Woe to those who are with child and to those who nurse babes in those days" (Matt. 24:19; Mark 13:17; Luke 21:23)

This admonition is in view of the persecution that results from the abomination of desolation and the destruction of Jerusalem (Matt. 24:15-24; Mark 13:14-23; Luke 21:20-24). The people of Jerusalem are warned to flee to the mountains of Judea in order to protect themselves from the impending persecution. A woe is pronounced over pregnant women and women with small children because their flight will be impeded due to their responsibilities and concerns for others. Blessed are the women who are free from these burdens, because their flight will be quicker and easier. It appears that Luke has the time frame of Jerusalem's destruction in mind when he records this declaration (Luke 23:29; cf. 21:23).

A second event in this discourse describes the reaction of some people to the resulting tribulation: "*Then* (*tote*) they will begin to say to the mountains, 'Fall on us,' and to the hills, 'Cover us'" (Luke 23:30 NASB). *Tote*, which can be translated, "at that time," indicates the sequential proximity of these two events.[29] People who flee to the mountains will cry out for the mountains and hills to hide them. Luke 23:30 may be an allusion to Isaiah 2:19 and Hosea 10:8. Isaiah 2:19 relates to a scene of men who are fleeing from the judgment and terror of Yahweh: "And men will go into caves of the rocks, and into holes of the ground before the terror of the LORD, and before the splendor of His majesty, when He arises to make the earth tremble." The judgment, according to Isaiah, is the result of Israel's idolatry (Isa. 2:12-18 NASB).

The language of Hosea 10:8 is particularly similar to Revelation: "They will say to the mountains, 'Cover us!' And to the hills, 'Fall on us!'" This prophetic oracle also concerns Yahweh's judgment of Israel's idolatry (Hos. 10:1-8).

Luke adapts this prophetic motif and applies it to the tribulation surrounding Jerusalem's destruction. The resulting sequence has a close time proximity: 1) the abomination of desolation and siege of Jerusalem, the midpoint of Daniel's seventieth week and the synoptic eschatological discourses; 2) then, people flee from Jerusalem to the mountains, and pregnant women have a particularly difficult time; 3) then, some people cry out for the mountains and hills to cover them.

A comparison of Luke 23:30 with the sixth seal of Revelation 6:12-17 demonstrates a further correlation. Revelation 6:15-17 states: "And the kings of the earth and the great men and the commanders and the rich and the strong and every slave and free man, hid themselves in the caves and among the rocks of the mountains; and they said to the mountains and to the rocks, 'Fall on us and hide us from the presence of Him who sits on the throne, and from the wrath of the Lamb; for the great day of their wrath has come; and who is able to stand?'" (NASB). The Apocalypse expands on this prophetic announcement by elaborating on the type of people who will cry out. Isaiah and Hosea focus upon idolaters in Israel; Revelation amplifies the prophecy to include Gentiles from every level of society. Charles notes there are seven classes of people enumerated, from the emperor to the slave, the rich to the poor, a motif that is repeated again by the writer (Rev. 6:15; 13:16; 19:18).[30]

Luke 23:30 does not explicitly state who is causing the judgment, but Revelation attributes the catastrophic judgment to the eschatological wrath of "Him who sits on the throne, and from the wrath of the Lamb" (Rev. 6:16). The synoptic gospels describe the flight of Jerusalem residents, probably consisting primarily of believing and nonbelieving Jews. These believing Jews, at least in part, will be protected by God as they flee into the wilderness (Rev. 11:6-17). Luke does not identify who cries out for the mountains and hills to cover them. The context suggests that they are Jewish people fleeing the judgment of God. Both of these passages relate back to the same Old Testament prophets of Hosea and Isaiah, and they provide similar but slightly different perspectives.

A further correlation with other parallel eschatological discourses of Luke shows he also conceives of this period as a time "of great distress upon the land, and wrath to the people" (Luke 21:23). An integration of these correspondences with the synoptics suggests the sixth seal is an expansion of the synoptic eschatological discourses, and in particular, the Gospel of Luke. The proposal is that John has sequentially placed the sixth seal in conjunction with the abomination of desolation without making specific reference to it in the context of Revelation 6. The prophetic sequence would be: 1) the abomination of desolation and the destruction of Jerusalem at the midpoint of Daniel's seventieth week (Matt. 24:15; Mark 13:14; Luke 21:20); 2) people flee to the mountains (Matt. 24:16-18; Mark 13:15-16; Luke 21:21); 3) people cry for the mountains and rocks to fall on them and hide them from the wrath of God and the Lamb (Luke 23:30; Rev. 6:15-17).

A mathematical formula may help to illustrate this analogy. If A=B, and B=C, and C=D, then A=D. Applying this logic to the texts, if the time sequence of A (the abomination of desolation is the midpoint of the seventieth week of Daniel and the Tribulation of the synoptics), equals B (at this time the people flee to the mountains and women are warned about impending dangers); and the time frame of B equals C (the people cry out for the mountains to fall on them); and reference C equals D (the sixth seal of Revelation when the wrath of God and the Lamb initiate the great day of their wrath and people cry for the mountains to fall on them), then A (the abomination of desolation at the midpoint of Daniel's seventieth week), equals or occurs at the time as D (the time of the sixth seal of Revelation). Textual correlations that develop the expansion and chronological framework of the seventieth week of Daniel are: 1) the abomination of desolation: Daniel 9:27 equals Matthew 24:15-19, Mark 13:14-17, and Luke 21:20-21; 2) people flee from persecution: Matthew 24:15-19, Mark 13:14-17, and Luke 21:20-21 equals Luke 23:29-31; 3) people cry for the rocks to hide them: Luke 23:29-31 equals Revelation 6:12-17; therefore, 4) Daniel 9:27 equals Revelation 6:12-17.

If this correlation is correct, then a structural bench mark is established. The bench mark is that the sixth seal is the midpoint of Daniel's seventieth week. The Apocalypse has amplified this framework, as expanded on by the synoptic writers in Matthew 24, Mark 13, and Luke 21. The first five seals have been demonstrated to be remarkably parallel and sequential to the "birth pangs" of the synoptics, therefore it is suggest that the sixth seal can be accepted as the dividing point of Daniel's seventieth week. The cumulative parallels argue strongly for the chronological and sequential structure of Revelation. This would also suggest that further affinities between Daniel's seventieth week and the synoptics should be observed in the latter portion of the judgment section of Revelation.

A Correlation of the Synoptics to the Apocalypse (Rev. 7–19) Within the Second Half of the Seventieth Week

The third part of this section compares Revelation 7–19 with the eschatological synoptic discourses to discover further structural and literary parallels.[31] Revelation 7:1-8 describes the sealing of 144,000 people, 12,000 from each of the 12 tribes, with the "seal of the living God" (Rev. 7:2). The seal is for their protection from the plague that is about to be released by the four angels who are standing at the four corners of the world. Revelation 9:4 indicates the judgments are on the people of the world rather than those who follow the Lamb and are sealed by God.

This section may correspond to the synoptic writers' descriptions of events which follow the flight of the people from the persecution that follows the abomination of desolation. Matthew and Mark suggest there is divine protection for some of the elect during this period: "And unless those days had been cut short, no life would have been saved; but for the sake of the elect those days shall be cut short" (Matt. 24:22; Mark 13:20 NASB). An angel ascends "from the rising of the sun," and stops the plague of the four angels until the elect of God are sealed for protection (Rev. 7:2-3).

The second part of this chapter includes a vision of a great multitude from every nation and all peoples of the earth (Rev

7:9-17). This Gentile multitude, clothed with white robes, is standing before the throne of God and the Lamb. The white robes suggest that these people are martyrs similar to those who were seen under the altar of the fifth seal (Rev. 7:9; cf. 6:9-11). They are described as those "who come out of the *great tribulation*," and they have washed their robes and made them white in the blood of the Lamb (Rev. 7:14). They serve in the temple of God and are protected by the Lamb (Rev. 7:14-17).

John may be seeking by this vision to comfort the believers who are under persecution during the Great Tribulation. The synoptics indicate that immediately following the abomination of desolation, great persecution and death fall on the people of Jerusalem, in particular, and on the rest of the world (Matt. 24:16-22; Mark 13:14-20; Luke 21:20-21). John portrays the final state of the persecuted by placing them in heaven with the Lamb. The synoptics pronounce a woe of judgment on the people of the world, while John suggests final deliverance for those who follow the Lamb: "They shall hunger no more, neither thirst anymore; neither shall the sun beat down on them, nor any heat; for the Lamb in the center of the throne shall be their shepherd, and shall guide them to springs of the water of life; and God shall wipe every tear from their eyes" (Rev. 7:16-17). This time of unprecedented persecution on earth results in deliverance in heaven, as the cries of agony on earth become the cries of worship in heaven (Rev. 7:1-17).

John envisions a temple of God with an altar and with worship taking place (11:1). He is commanded to measure the temple precinct but to "leave out the court which is outside the temple, and...not measure it, for it has been given to the nations (*ethnesin*), and they will tread under foot (*patēsousin*) the holy city for forty-two months" (Rev. 11:2). The Apocalypse appears to be paralleling a statement in Luke 21:24: "Jerusalem [the holy city] will be trampled under foot (*patoumenē*) by the Gentiles (*ethnōn*) until the times of the Gentiles be fulfilled."

This numerical sequence of three-and-a-half years certainly fits the theory that Revelation is structured by the seventieth week of Daniel, as elaborated by the synoptics, and divided into two periods of three-and-a-half years each. John envisions the temple being desecrated for a period of three-and-a-half years. This time frame is restated in Revelation 11:3: "And I will grant authority to my two witnesses, and they will prophesy for twelve hundred and sixty days (forty-two months or three-and-a-half years), clothed in sackcloth."

The two witnesses are described as two olives trees and two lampstands, which is similar to symbolism found in Zechariah 4:3-14. The witnesses are given supernatural powers to defend themselves, which is reminiscent of the narratives about Elijah and Moses (Ex. 7:20; 8:1-12:29; 1 Kings 17:1; 18:41-45; 2 Kings 1:10-12). The beast that arises from the abyss wars against them and kills them. This beast arises out of the abyss in the latter part of the Great Tribulation (Rev. 17:8), confirming that the two witnesses minister during the second half of the Tribulation. Their bodies lie dead in the streets for three-and-a-half days. After this time, they are resurrected and ascend to heaven. Judgment descends on Jerusalem and the second woe is completed.

John introduces another series of narrative contemplations in order to establish a setting for the eschatological end (Rev. 12:1–14:20). Revelation 12:1–13:8 portrays the warriors of Satan who oppose the kingdom of God. The first vision depicts war on earth between the dragon (Satan) and the woman (Israel). The woman represents the people of Israel. Arguments in support of this view are: 1) the symbolism reflects the dream of Joseph in Genesis 37, which depicts the foundation of the nation; 2) there is a symbolic reference to the birth of a manchild from the woman, and the man-child is a veiled reference to Jesus; 3) the woman flees to the wilderness for protection, which corresponds to the flight of the people of Jerusalem to the mountains (Matt. 24:16-20; Mark 13:14-19; Luke 21:20-24). The correlation of protection for the woman by God for 1260 days is clearly a reference to the three-and-a-half-year period of the second half of the Tribulation, the second half of the seventieth week of Daniel (Rev. 12:6).

The second part of the vision depicts war in heaven (Rev 12:7-12). The Apocalypse describes the cosmic conflict between Michael with his angels, and Satan with his angels. The mention of Michael is reminiscent of Daniel 12:1: "Now at that time Michael, the great prince who stands guard over the sons of your people [Israel], will arise. And there will be a time of distress such as never occurred since there was a nation until that time; and at that time your people, everyone who is found written in the book, will be rescued" (NASB). John signifies by this vision that Satan's end is near and deliverance for the saints will arrive.

The third aspect of this vision is Satan's attack on the woman, Israel. The woman flees to the wilderness with the aid of divine help. She is protected for "time and times and half a time" (Rev. 12:14). These events, and particularly this phrase, are reminiscent of Daniel 7:25 and 12:7. A similar beast who persecutes Israel is described by Daniel and John (Dan. 7:23-24; Rev. 12:3). Daniel 7:25 and 12:7 relate to a period of persecution that lasts for three-and-a-half years. John envisions the persecution of Israel lasting for three-and-a-half years, the time period from the committing of the abomination of desolation until the coming of the Son of Man.

In chapter 13, Revelation focuses on a beast that rises up out of the sea (Rev. 13:1-10). The description of this beast is similar to the great red dragon who persecutes the nation of Israel (Rev. 12:3; 13:1). The beast also represents a combination of beasts from Daniel 7:4-8, a leopard, bear, and lion (Rev. 13:2).[32] The beast is fatally wounded and supernaturally healed. As a result of this miracle, the "whole earth is amazed and follows after the beast and they worship the dragon" (Rev. 13:3-4). The synoptics state that "false christs and false prophets will arise and will show great signs and wonders, so as to mislead, if possible, even the elect" (Matt. 24:24; Mark 4:22 NASB).

The beast is given authority for 42 months during which he blasphemes God and makes war against the saints (Rev. 13:5-7). This is the fifth reference in Revelation to a period of three-and-a-half years. John portrays the abomination of desolation under the symbolism of the beast that rises up out of the sea. John's language parallels the Lucan account, as seen in the following: 1) *captivity* (*aichmalōsian*, Rev. 13:10; cf. Luke 21:24); 2) death by the *sword* (*machairē*, Rev. 13:10; cf. Luke 21:24); and 3) *perseverance* of faith (*upomonē*, Rev. 13:10, cf. Luke 21:19).

Another beast arises, "coming up out of the earth; and he had two horns like a lamb and he spoke as a dragon" (Rev. 13:11-18 NASB). The beast out of the earth causes people to worship the beast out of the sea. He performs great signs and miracles with the result that he deceives "those who dwell on the earth" (Rev. 13·13-14). The Apocalypse envisions him giving life to a statue of the first beast. He imposes the mark of the first beast, "666," on "the people of the earth." Those who do not accept the mark of the beast are either killed or ostracized from society (Rev. 13:15-18)

The second beast represents a pseudo-prophet or pseudo-messiah. John describes him as a lamb (Rev. 13:11), an obvious parallel to Jesus, the true Lamb, in Revelation (Rev. 5:6-13; 7:9-17; 12:11; 13:8; 14:1-10; 17:14; 19:7-9). This beast corresponds to the pseudo-prophets and pseudo-messiahs, which the synoptics indicate precede the coming of the Son of Man (Matt. 24:24-26; Mark 13:21-22). The miracle of giving animation to the statue of the first beast seems to correlate with the synoptics' view of the resurrection of Jesus, the Messiah.

Another angel proclaims the eternal gospel to all the people of the earth and exhorts them to fear and worship God because the hour of His final judgment is coming (Rev. 14:6-7). The language intensifies as the "hour of His [God's] judgment has come" (Rev. 14:7). This phrase is thematically repeated with greater intensity as the eschatological end draws near (14:15; 17:12; 18:10,17,19; one day, 18:8). This vision may be a parallel to Matthew 24:24: "And this gospel of the kingdom shall be preached in the whole world for a witness to all the nations, and then the end shall come" (NASB; cf. Mark 13:10).

The last vision of chapter 14 pictures "one like a Son of Man" preparing to thrust a sickle of judgment into the earth (Rev. 14:14-20 NASB). This is a prelude to the *parousia* of Jesus and the judgment of Babylon. The symbolism represents the final stroke of God's wrath on the world. Other angels come out of the temple—one with a sharp sickle, another with fire—and they execute God's wrath on the earth. John takes traditional apocalyptic imagery and unfolds prophetic judgments that are similar to the synoptic gospels (Matt. 24:29-31; Mark 13:24-27; Luke 21:25-28).

Chapter 15 describes a sign in heaven, which introduces the last septet of judgments. John states that these seven angels with seven plagues "are the last, because in them the wrath of God is finished" (Rev. 15:1 NASB). This phrase echoes Revelation 10:7, where the angel of the seventh trumpet "is about to sound, the mystery of God is finished, as He preached to His servants the prophets" (NASB). These final eschatological judgments and signs correlate further with the fulfillment of the disciples' questions concerning signs of the end of the age (Matt. 24:3; Mark 13:4; Luke 21:7).

The seven bowls of God's wrath are the most devastating of the three septets (Rev. 16). The first bowl judgment gives loathsome and malignant sores to those who have the mark of the beast (16:2).

The second and third bowls transform the water systems of the earth into blood (Rev. 16:3-7). An interpretation of these judgments is offered by John: "O Holy One, because Thou didst judge these things; for they poured out the blood of the saints and prophets, and Thou hast given them blood to drink" (Rev. 16:5-6 NASB). The next two bowls affect the impact of the sun on the earth. The fourth bowl intensifies the rays of the sun, so that men are scorched by its fierce heat. The fifth bowl blocks out the light of the sun, so that the kingdom of the beast is darkened. The people of the beast gnaw their tongues in pain and blaspheme God because of the tormenting sores that have been inflicted on them.

The sixth bowl dries up the Euphrates River and prepares a way for the kings from the east to invade Palestine (Rev. 16:12-16). The dragon, the beast, and the false prophet, send forth three demonic spirits to deceptively persuade the kings of the whole world to gather at Har-Mageddon and fight against God. The sixth seal may be reflective of some parables that follow the synoptic eschatological discourses. Matthew suggests that the coming of the Son of Man will be a time of devastation for the people of the earth (Matt. 24:36-39; cf. Luke 17:21-37). The Apocalypse exhorts the reader to watchfulness (Rev. 16:15), which may parallel the parabolic exhortations of: 1) the fig tree (Matt. 24:32-36; Mark 13:28-32; Luke 21:29-33); 2) the days of Noah (Matt. 24:36-39; Luke 17:26-27); 3) the watchful householder (Matt. 24:42-44; Mark 13:33-37; Luke 21:34-36); 4) the wise servant (Matt. 24:45-51; Luke 12:42-46).

The seventh bowl announces the consummation of God's judgment (Rev. 16:17-21). A scene of unprecedented lightning, earthquakes, and hailstones announces the final catastrophic judgment (Rev. 16:18). The earthquakes cause worldwide destruction, particularly in the city of Babylon: "And the great city was split into three parts, and the cities of the nations fell. And Babylon the great was remembered before God, to give her the cup of the wine of His fierce wrath" (Rev. 16:19 NASB).

Chapters 17 and 18 record God's judgment on Babylon the great. Babylon is depicted in chapter 17 as a harlot who leads the nations into immorality and abominations (Rev. 17:1-7). John amplifies the abomination of desolation under the symbolism of the great harlot (Matt. 24:15; Mark 13:14). The harlot is identified as a "great city, which reigns over the kings of the earth" (Rev. 17:18). She is sitting on a beast that is representative of world powers and leaders. This beast is the beast out of the sea in chapter 13, since both creatures are identified as having seven heads and ten horns (Rev. 13:1; 17:3). The harlot is depicted as a persecutor who has murdered the saints and witnesses of Jesus. This is a common motif of Revelation, as each of the beasts murders the saints (11:7; 12:13; 13:7,17).

Another angel announces: "Fallen, fallen is Babylon the great! And she has become a dwelling place of demons and a prison of every unclean spirit, and a prison of every unclean and hateful bird" (Rev. 18:2 NASB). Chapter 18 focuses on the reaction of the people to the destruction of Babylon. God's vengeance is executed on Babylon because of her sensual and immoral character (Rev. 16:6-8) and murderous persecution of the saints (Rev. 16:24). In a similar thought, the synoptics maintain that God's enemies will be thoroughly destroyed at the *parousia* of the Son of Man (Matt. 24:36-41; Luke 17:26-30).

The kings, merchants, and people of the world lament the fiery destruction of the city because she is a great source of commerce and pleasure to them. The Apocalypse presents the destruction as a swift and catastrophic event that totally annihilates the city (Rev. 18:8,10,17,19). The writer contrasts the reaction of the people of the world and the saints in heaven; the former group mourn the destruction, while the latter rejoice because at last their blood is avenged (Rev. 18:20). Matthew emphasizes that the people of the earth will mourn the events of the *parousia* of the Son of Man (Matt. 24:30).

Chapters 17 and 18 are an apocalyptic portrayal of the final judgment recorded in the synoptic Gospels, and they are the conclusion of the seventieth week of Daniel. Correlations to the synoptics include: 1) the world is filled with abominations; 2) the saints and witnesses of God are persecuted and murdered; 3) the Son of Man returns and overcomes His enemies and delivers His elect people.

The climax of the seventieth week of Daniel and the eschatological synoptic discourses are amplified in chapter 19. The coming of the Son of Man brings vengeance on His enemies and deliverance to the elect. A great multitude in heaven proclaims "Hallelujah" to God in view of His judgments. The saints are pictured as the bride of the Lamb in contrast to the harlot of Babylon (19:7-9). John portrays the Son of Man coming out of heaven on a white horse. He is accompanied by the armies of heaven and executes judgment and war on His enemies. The beast, false prophet, and people who worship the beast are all destroyed by the power of the Lamb (19:17-21). God's elect are delivered and His kingdom is established.

There are numerous thematic and linguistic parallels between the synoptic eschatological discourses and the judgment section of Revelation.[33] These thematic affinities demonstrate a further correlation between Revelation and the synoptics. The following chart illustrates the textual correlations identified in this study.

Textual Parallels
Between the Synoptics and Revelation

The Setting in the Temple

Rev. 4:1–5:14; Matt. 24:1-3; Mark 13:1-4; Luke 21:1-7

The Beginning of Birth Pangs

Rev. 6:1-17; Matt. 24:4-14; Mark 13:5-13; Luke 21:8-17; 23:27-31

Unprecedented Great Tribulation

Rev. 7:1–9:21; Matt. 24:21-22; Mark 13:19-20; Luke 21:18-19

The Abomination of Desolation and Persecution

Rev. 10:1–14:13; Matt. 24:15-28; Mark 13:14-23; Luke 21:20

Final Judgment and *Parousia* of the Son of Man

Rev. 14:14–19:21; Matt. 24:29-31; Mark 13:24-27; Luke 21:25-28; Matt. 24:36-39; Luke 17:22-30

Summary

The Apocalypse clearly evidences the influence of the synoptic eschatological discourses on its content and structure. The first five seals patently parallel the "birth pangs" of the synoptics. These judgments follow the sequential order of all three synoptic Gospels. Furthermore, the sixth seal has been shown to correlate with the eschatological passages in Luke to evidence the establishment of the midpoint of Daniel's seventieth week. The cumulative testimony of thematic and linguistic affinities strongly suggests that John contains synoptic motifs in the development of the latter chapters of Revelation. Revelation amplifies on the synoptic eschatological discourses by means of apocalyptic imagery about end-time events.

The following chart shows the structural relationships between the seventieth week of Daniel 9 and the judgment section of Revelation. The Apocalypse is divided according to the correlations established between the seventieth week of Daniel 9, the synoptic eschatological discourses, and the content of Revelation 4–19.

This chart is a compilation of several charts by Marvin Rosenthal and Robert Van Kampen in their book *The Prewrath Rapture*.[34] A close examination of the chart reveals a number of problems with their chronological and sequential structure of the Revelation. Their presentation of the pre-wrath rapture is little more than a new twist on a modified midtribulational or posttribulational rapture theory.

A critical evaluation of Rosenthal's pre-wrath rapture theory, and suggested exegetical insights and corrections, will demonstrate that a pre-wrath rapture is pretribulational.[35]

The Tribulation Midpoint:
The Sixth Seal

An examination of Rosenthal's structure of Revelation clearly shows that he places the midpoint of the seventieth week of Daniel between the fourth and fifth seals. It was demonstrated earlier in this chapter that the midpoint of the seventieth week is the sixth seal of Revelation. Rosenthal has to arbitrarily move the sixth seal deep into the second half of the Tribulation so that he can have more time to remove the church before the wrath of God falls on the earth. A correction of Rosenthal's structure at this point forces him into a midtribulational viewpoint at best.

This arbitrary structure also forces Rosenthal to ignore some basic grammatical and contextual clues that concern the timing of the wrath of God. Rosenthal seeks to exploit the indefiniteness of the Greek aorist tense of Revelation 6:17 (*ēlthen*) to obviate or confuse the plain understanding of the text. The pagan world under the catastrophic judgments of the sixth seal understand that "the great day of their wrath (*orgēs*) has come, and who can stand?"[36] These people are making this statement on the basis of events that have taken place, not on the basis of events that will take place. The Day of the Lord may not be proven to include the entire period of the Tribulation by this text, but it certainly includes events beginning with the sixth seal. Furthermore, even if the Day of the Lord

REVELATION IN CORRELATION TO THE
SEVENTIETH WEEK OF DANIEL

DANIEL 9:27A

F
I
R
S
T

Revelation
Introduction of Seven Seals 4:1-5:14
First Seal: White horse 6:1-2
Second Seal: Red horse 6:3-4
Third Seal: Black horse 6:5-6
Fourth Seal: Ashen horse 6:7-8

H
A
L
F

Fifth Seal: Martyrs under the altar 6:9-11
Sixth Seal: Great day of God's wrath 6:12-17

Matt. 24:4–14; Mark 13:4–13; Luke 21:8–19

DANIEL 9:27B

M
I
D

&

S
E
C
O
N
D

H
A
L
F

Revelation
Redeemed of God 7:1-17
Breaking of Seventh Seal, Seven Trumpets 8:1-6
First Trumpet: 1/3 earth destroyed 8:7
Second Trumpet: 1/3 sea destroyed 8:8-9
Third Trumpet: 1/3 water destroyed 8:10-11
Fourth Trumpet: 1/3 celestial destroyed 8:12
Introduction of the three Woes
Fifth Trumpet, First Woe: men tormented 9:1-12
Sixth Trumpet, Second Woe: 1/3 mankind 9:13-21
Little Scroll Final Judgment 10:1-11
Two Witnesses Persecuted 11:1-14
The Seventh Trumpet 11:15-19
A Woman, Male child, Satan in conflict 12:1-17
Beast out of the sea 13:1-10
Beast out of the earth 13:11-18

Matt. 24:15-28; Mark 14:14-23; Luke 21:20-24

DANIEL 9:27B

Revelation
Visions and Proclamations of the End 14:1-20

F
I
N
A
L

Introduction: Seven Bowls 15:1-8
First Bowl: malignant sores 16:1-2
Second Bowl: sea destroyed 16:3
Third Bowl: rivers destroyed 16:4-7
Fourth Bowl: scorching heat 16:8-9
Fifth Bowl: darkness 16:10-11

D
A
Y
S

Sixth Bowl: preparation for war 16:17-21
Seventh Bowl: worldwide destruction 16:17-21
Destruction of Babylon 17:1-18:24
Parousia of Jesus Christ 19:1-16
Judgment: beast, false prophet 19:17-21

Matt. 24:29-31; Mark 13:24-27; Luke 21:25-28

AN EXAMINATION OF THE PRE-WRATH RAPTURE

Seals—Man's wrath through Antichrist
Trumpets—God's wrath on mankind
Bowls—God's wrath on the nations

		Pre-Wrath Rapture	Christ's Coming
	Abomination of Desolation	**God's Wrath**	
Beginning of Sorrows	Great Tribulation	Day of Lord	Dan. 12:11
Seals		7 Trumpets	Bowls
1　　　　　4	5　　　　　6	7　　Years	1　　　　7
◄　3½ Years　►	◄　3½	►	

does not begin until the sixth seal, it does not demand that the rapture take place immediately before the sixth seal in order to be pre-wrath. Pretribulationalism is also pre-wrath. The context suggests that the aorist tense be understood with a past action nuance, indicating that the *wrath of God has come.*

Can the Entire Seventieth Week Be Called "The Tribulation"?

Rosenthal's major thesis is that the church must be removed before the wrath (*orgē*) of God comes on the world. The major passages that Rosenthal argues from are 1 Thessalonians 1:10 and 5:9. Most pretribulationalists would fully agree with this thesis. The difficulty is in the determination of when the wrath of God begins in relationship to the seventieth week of Daniel 9:27. Rosenthal argues that:

> The designation *the tribulation period* should properly be omitted from an honest consideration of the time of the Rapture of the Church. The term *tribulation period* is normally used by pretribulation rapturists as a synonym for the seventieth week of the book of Daniel (Dan. 9:27); that is, to describe the seven years that immediately precede Christ's physical return to the earth to establish His millennial kingdom. Although popular and used by competent preachers, teachers, and theologians, *such a designation has no biblical justification....* A clear fact emerges from an examination of the word *tribulation* as used in the Bible. In a prophetic context, it is used to describe only the period of time that begins in the middle of Daniel's

seventieth week—*never of the first half of it. Based
on that indisputable fact, to call the entire seven-year
time frame the tribulation period is to coin a technical
phrase and superimpose it upon the Scriptures, reading into the biblical text that which does not itself
declare.*[37]

Rosenthal has not only overstated his case but has stated as true
fact that which is clearly false. A cursory reading of a Greek concordance reveals that the word "tribulation" (*thlipsis*) is used in
prophetic contexts to refer to both the first and second halves of the
seventieth week of Daniel. Matthew 24:9, which chronologically
relates to the first half of the seventieth week as evidenced by its
preceding the midpoint of the abomination of desolation (Matt.
24:15-21) states: "Then they will deliver you to *tribulation* (*thlipsis*),
and will kill you, and you will be hated by all nations on account of
My name" (NASB). Clearly the biblical text describes the first half of
the seventieth week as a time of *tribulation*.

The second half of the seventieth week is also described as a
time of tribulation. Second Thessalonians 1:6 uses the Greek word
thlipsin while referring to the second coming of Christ which occurs
during the second half of the seventieth week of Daniel: "For after
all it is only just for God to repay with *affliction* (*thlipsin*) those who
afflicted you" (NASB). Therefore, it is proper and even biblical to
refer to, and even describe, the seventieth week of Daniel as "The
Tribulation," or "A Time of Tribulation".

Is the Great Tribulation Shorter Than
Three-and-One-Half Years?

I agree with Rosenthal that the designation "The Great Tribulation" should be reserved for the second half of Daniel's seventieth
week, but he denies that the term "Great Tribulation" can refer to
the entire portion of the second half period (Matt. 24:21; Rev. 7:14).
Rosenthal argues:

This, then is clear. The entire seventieth week is not
shortened. The last three-and-one-half years of that
seventieth week are not shortened. What the Lord
Himself teaches is shortened in the Great Tribulation.

It is less than three and one-half years in duration. It begins in the middle of the seventieth week, but it does not run until the end of the seventieth week.... The following facts cannot be set aside: 1) The Great Tribulation begins in the middle of the seventieth week, but it does not run to the end of that week. It is cut short.[38]

Once again a reading of the biblical text demonstrates the error of Rosenthal's statement. Daniel 12:1 states: "Now at that time Michael, the great prince who stands guard over the sons of your people, will arise. And there will be a *time of distress* (LXX, *kairos*; *thlipses*), such (*thlipsis*) *as never occurred since there was a nation until that time*; and at that time your people, everyone who is found written in the book, will be rescued" (NASB). Matthew 24:21 echoes the language of Daniel 12:1 while referring to events that include and follow the midpoint of the abomination of desolation: "For then there will be a *great tribulation (thlipsis megalē), such as has not occurred since the beginning of the world until now, nor ever shall.*"

It is quite obvious that Daniel 12:1 and Matthew 24:21 are both referring to a time which is further defined as the "Great Tribulation." Daniel 12:6-7 defines the length of this period of time: "And one said to the man dressed in linen, who was above the waters of the river, 'How long will it be until the end of these wonders?' And I heard the man dressed in linen, who was above the waters of the river, as he raised his right hand and his left toward heaven, and swore by Him who lives forever that it would be for a *time, times, and half a time*; and as soon as they finish shattering the power of the holy people, all these events will be completed" (NASB).

Revelation 12:14 further corroborates this correlation as Michael and his angels wage war with the dragon and his angels with the result that the dragon persecutes the woman (Israel), who is then protected by God for *time and times and half a time*. The term *"time and times and half a time,"* is defined by parallel statements in this context as "one thousand two hundred and sixty days (12:6)," and "forty-two months" (13:5). Therefore, the Great Tribulation is a period of *time, times, and half a time* or 1260 days which is three-and-one-half years. The Great Tribulation spans the entire second half of Daniel's seventieth week.

Is the Day of the Lord Completely Separate
from the Great Tribulation?

A further difficulty for the pre-wrath rapture theory is the separation of the Day of the Lord and the Great Tribulation into two
distinct and separate time periods. This distinction is foundational
for Rosenthal's pre-wrath theory since the Day of the Lord is the
time of *God's wrath and tribulation,* and therefore the church must
be removed from this time frame. Rosenthal writes:

> The error of such logic (that the Day of the Lord
> begins the tribulation) is that it assumes that the Day
> of the Lord commences when the seventieth week of
> Daniel begins. But a careful examination of the bibli-
> cal data will clearly indicate that *it does not!* The false
> assumption [according to Rosenthal, this assumption
> is made by pretribulationalists] just mentioned is per-
> haps the single greatest error in the debate concerning
> the timing of the Rapture.[39]

I believe that the majority but not all of the passages that
address the Day of the Lord focus primarily on events, such as the
battle of Armageddon, that surround the second coming of Christ.
Isaiah 2, 13 and Zechariah 14 are three important chapters that
suggest the Day of the Lord also covers the same period as the Great
Tribulation.

An example is seen in Isaiah 2 where the language of Isaiah
echoes the events of the sixth seal of Revelation 6:12-17: "In the
last days (Isaiah 2:2)...the common man has been humbled, and the
man of importance has been abased, but do not forgive them. Enter
the rock and hide in the dust from the terror of the Lord and from the
splendor of His majesty (Isaiah 2:9-10)....For the Lord of hosts
will have a day of reckoning (Isaiah 2:12)" (NASB).

A further example is seen in a comparison of catastrophic cosmic phenomena in Isaiah 13:6-13 and the sixth seal of Revelation
(see particularly Isaiah 13:10,13 and Rev. 6:12,13,17). The events of
these chapters clearly parallel each other. In addition, Zechariah 14
parallels events from the persecution of the Jews, which arises out of
the abomination of desolation at the midpoint, to the second coming
of Christ at the end of the Tribulation. Therefore, the parallel language and content of these passages renders the conclusion that the

Day of the Lord is not separate from the Great Tribulation. It is probably better to accept these two designations as describing the same time frame which is the second half of the seventieth week of Daniel.

Therefore, this conclusion moves the pre-wrath rapture timetable back to at least a period before the sixth seal, which is in contradiction to Rosenthal's position that the rapture occurs after the sixth seal.[40] The Day of the Lord and the Great Tribulation are two designations that, at least in part, share the same events within the same time frame.

Does Revelation 4:1–6:11
Contain God's Judgment?

A further question to be asked in relationship to the pre-wrath rapture theory is whether or not Revelation 4–6:11 should also be included as part of God's tribulation judgment of wrath on the world. It was demonstrated previously in this study that the first half of Daniel's seventieth week should be described or titled "The Tribulation." The fact that there is tribulation during this time suggests an examination of the presence of the church in this time frame. Rosenthal understands the tension of the presence of the church in the midst of tribulation that is initiated by God because this contradicts his placement of his pre-wrath rapture in Revelation 8. He writes:

> Pretribulationism suggests that in the book of Revelation it is the Lamb of God who takes the scroll out of the right hand of Him who sits upon the throne (Rev. 5:6-7). The scroll, as it is opened, brings to fruition the seventieth week of Daniel. Since it is the Lamb alone who had the right to open the scroll and loose the seals thereof (Rev. 5:9), the entire tribulation period is the outpouring of His wrath. This argument totally ignores the distinction between God's active will and permissive will, both of which are equally under His sovereign control.[41]

Rosenthal goes on to suggest that since the first five seals are committed by the agency of man that the seals are not a part of God's judgment. This logic sets up an artificial principle of interpretation that ignores the plain teaching of God's control and execution of events throughout the revelation. One example is found in the destruction of the harlot of Babylon (Rev. 17–18). This judgment is the will of God but it is carried out by the forces of the beast: "And the ten horns which you saw, and the beast, these will hate the harlot and will make her desolate and naked, and will eat her flesh and will burn her up with fire. For *God* has put it in their hearts to execute His purpose by having a *common purpose*, and by giving their kingdom to the beast, until the *words of God should be fulfilled*" (Rev. 17:17-18 NASB).

A second line of evidence is that Jesus Christ is the One who breaks the seals and initiates the judgment (Rev. 6). Christ is beginning the completion of the process of establishing His rule on earth in which mankind will honor Him (Rev. 5). John 5:22-23,27 states: "For not even the Father judges anyone, but He has given *all judgment* to the Son, in order that all may *honor* the Son, even as they honor the Father.... And He gave Him authority to *execute judgment*, because He is the Son of Man" (NASB); see also Daniel 7:13-14). The implication is clear: the church must be removed before the seal judgments because the seals contain God's judgment as executed by Jesus Christ during the Tribulation.

A third line of evidence that Revelation 4–5 contain the judgment of God is the cosmic phenomena that issue forth from the throne of God. Each of the septet judgments: seals, trumpets, bowls, as well as other plagues, are preceded by the execution of cosmic phenomena such as lightning, thunder, and earthquakes, which come forth from the throne of God (Rev. 4:5; 6:12-14; 8:5; 11:19; 15:8; 16:18). These cosmic phenomena signal the outpouring of God's judgment on the world. These judgments are filled with His wrath and bring devastating destruction. The presence of these signals of judgment prior to the breaking of the seals certainly indicates that the seals are part of *God's judgment* during the Tribulation.[42] If the rapture of the church is defined as *pre-wrath*, which is biblically and theologically correct, then the church must be removed prior to the beginning of God's judgment in Revelation 4.

The final line of evidence that Revelation 4:1–6:11 contains the judgment of God is the corroboration that the seal judgments are characteristic of God's wrath. Ezekiel 14:21 is an example of judgments from God that are similar to the first five seals: "For thus says the Lord God, 'How much more when I send *My four severe judgments* against Jerusalem: *sword, famine, wild beasts, and plague* to cut off man and beast from it" (NASB). See also passages like Leviticus 26:22-25; Deuteronomy 28:21-25; Jeremiah 15:2-4; 16:4; Ezekiel 5:12-17 for further examples of cosmic catastrophes which parallel the five seals and are characteristic of God's wrath.

Do the Bowl Judgments Follow the Second Coming?

The final critical evaluation of Rosenthal's view is his placing of the bowl judgments after the second coming of Christ. He states: "Christ will literally return to assume His kingdom at the seventh trumpet (Rev. 11:15-17)."[43] He defines the last trump of 1 Corinthians 15:52 as the seven trumpets of Revelation.[44] He takes the seven trumpets which are plural, and squeezes them into one trump which is singular, and then states: "That interpretation is unstrained and biblically accurate."[45] The difficulty with this view is that it wrenches the septet bowl judgments (Rev. 15–16) out of John's literary, sequential, and chronological order by placing them after the second coming of Christ (Rev. 19).[46] After the execution of the bowl judgments, one of the seven angels of the bowl judgments shows John the coming destruction of Babylon (Rev. 17:1). After the destruction of Babylon, it states in Revelation 19:1,11: "*After these things* I heard, as it were, a loud voice of a great multitude in heaven saying, 'Hallelujah! Salvation and glory and power belong to our God.... And I saw heaven opened; and behold, a white horse, and He who sat upon it is called Faithful and True; and in righteousness He judges and wages war" (NASB). Therefore, since the bowl judgments precede the destruction of Babylon; and since the destruction of Babylon precedes the second coming of Christ, it is impossible to place the bowl judgments after the coming of Christ without disregarding the plain sequential statements of the text.

A Pre-Wrath Rapture Is Pretribulational

Let's go back to Rosenthal's basic thesis: The rapture must precede the wrath of God. But how are we to define the wrath (*orgē*) of God. A comparison of Ephesians 5:6; 1 Thessalonians 1:10; 5:9; with 2 Thessalonians 1:5-10 provides a parallel definition. Ephesians 5:6 states: "Let no one deceive you with empty words, for because of these things the *wrath* (*orgē*) of God comes upon the sons of *disobedience*" (NASB). Second Thessalonians 1:5-8 states as a result of the persecution of the Thessalonians that: "This is a plain indication of God's righteous judgment. . . . For after all it is only just for God to repay with *affliction* (*thlipsin*) those who afflict you, and to give relief to you who are afflicted and to us as well when the Lord Jesus shall be revealed from heaven with His mighty angels in flaming fire, dealing out retribution to those who do not know God and to those who *do not obey* the gospel of our Lord Jesus" (NASB). *Orgē* should not be restricted to a definition that cannot also incorporate tribulation (*thlipsis*). *Orgē* is seen as a parallel term to *thlipsis* in these two passages.

Luke 21:23 and the parallel synoptic accounts, in the context of a midtribulational time frame, provide another parallel: "Woe to those who are with child and to those who nurse babes in those days; for there will be great *distress* (Luke, *anagkē*; Matt. 24:21 and Mark 13:19, *thlipsis*), upon the land, and *wrath* (*orgē*) to this people" (NASB). These parallels indicate that the *wrath of God* does involve *tribulation*. Tribulation can be seen as a part of God's wrath. First Thessalonians 5:9 and 1:10 clearly state that God has not appointed believers to wrath (*orgē*) and will deliver them from it.

It has been previously shown in this chapter that the first half and even the entire seven years of Daniel's seventieth week should be designated as "The Tribulation," or "A Time of Tribulation." The second half is certainly "The Great Tribulation." Revelation 4–19, which spans the seventieth week of Daniel, contains the judgment of God, i.e., His tribulation and wrath.

A PRETRIBULATIONAL RAPTURE WHICH IS PRE-WRATH
A TIME OF GOD'S WRATH AND TRIBULATION
THE DAY OF THE LORD

Pre-Wrath Rapture

Signing of Covenant God's judgment begins						God's judgment intensifies	
Tribulation						Great Tribulation	
Beginning of Birth Pangs Seals					Abomination Desolation	Trumpets	Christ's Coming Bowls
1	2	3	4	5	6	7 1 2 3 4 5 6 7	1----7
◄		3½ Years			►	◄ 3½ Years	►

Therefore, the church must be removed before the beginning of the seventieth week of Daniel which is elaborated on in Revelation 4–19. The preceding chart reflects the necessary exegetical corrections for the pre-wrath rapture view and represents a biblical viewpoint on the timing of the rapture.

Midtribulational Rapture Theory

A major advocate of the midtribulational or mid-seventieth-week rapture theory has been Gleason L. Archer. He argues from a midtribulational rapture that takes place in Revelation 14:14-16.[47] Archer confuses the spiritual nature of people in Revelation 14:6 by referring to this group as "true believers in every kindred, nation, and tribe."[48] The group is described as "those who live on the earth." This phrase is better understood as referring to unbelievers. The phrase is used in Revelation 3:10 and 11:10 to refer to unbelievers. The angel is said to preach an eternal gospel to these people, hardly a message that is needed for "true believers." His misunderstanding continues through Revelation 14, resulting in an illogical conclusion. He writes: "This (a declaration of the coming of the Armageddon judgment) should alert us to the fact that John does not follow a neatly segmented chronological sequence in the series of visions revealed to him, but rather, there is occasional overlap or preliminary anticipation from time to time, which is taken up again and brought to its conclusion later in the book."[49]

The fact that Revelation offers the reader narrative synopses and previews to highlight and focus on important events and people does not dictate that the book is without chronological and sequential structure. Archer's placement of the rapture in chapter 14 forces the expositor to reshuffle the chapters like a deck of cards so that the desired chronology is established. It seems better to this author to recognize the previously argued structure and accept the sixth seal as the midpoint and chapters 7 through 18 as referring to the second half of the Tribulation. A rapture in Revelation 14 would force an author to a late tribulational viewpoint rather than midtribulational position.

J. Oliver Buswell Jr. argues that the seventh trumpet (Rev. 11:15-19) is the midtribulational point of the revelation.[50] He equates this with the last trump of 1 Corinthians 15:52. This loose cross-reference association should be abandoned in light of a clearer understanding of the structure of Revelation. The seventh trumpet is executed sometime later in the second half of the Tribulation. This means that Buswell's cross-reference correlation would result in a rapture that was later during the Great Tribulation. There is no exegetical evidence to relate 1 Corinthians 15:52 to the seventh trumpet judgment. The seventh trumpet, which results in the seven bowl judgments, probably takes place during the last few weeks of the Great Tribulation since the results of these judgments leave the earth in an uninhabitable state. A midtribulational seventh trumpet is not sequentially possible according to the previously argued structure.

Posttribulational Rapture Position

Douglas Moo is a proponent of a posttribulational rapture position. He places the rapture of the church in Revelation 11. He argues:

> Of more significance is the depiction of events in chapter 11. Although there are many details that are obscure in this chapter it seems reasonably clear that 11:11-12 describes the resurrection of the two witnesses. Does this resurrection have anything to do with the Rapture? The fact that the two are said to go up "in a cloud" may suggest this, for clouds are consistently mentioned in descriptions of the Rapture (cf. Matt. 24:30; Acts 1:9; 1 Thess. 4:17; Rev. 14:14). And, as elsewhere when the Rapture is mentioned, a trumpet is found in this text (11:15).[51]

The problem that faces Moo is explaining the details of the rest of the chapter as well as the chronological indicators.[52] These two witnesses are said to prophesy for 1260 days (Rev. 11:3). Their bodies are said to lie in the streets for three-and-one-half days (Rev. 11:9). This would force the posttribulational rapture to the very end of the seventieth week and well after the wrath of God is released under the seal judgments. The judgment that results from their death is the conclusion of the second woe (Rev. 11:14). The second woe is chronologically part of a three-woe sequence that parallels with the fifth through seventh trumpets. The placement of the rapture in Revelation 11 would force the displacement of the sequential nature of the septet judgments as demonstrated earlier in this paper. Moo must rearrange the chronological and sequential nature of Revelation in order to fit this posttribulational viewpoint into the book. He offers the following structure for Revelation.[53]

Notice that Moo places the sixth element of each septet in parallel with the others. This is done so that he can arrange other passages that he suggests refer to Christ's *parousia* in a parallel chronological order. Moo forces the structure of Revelation into an unnatural order in order to support his posttribulation view. This structure disregards the many textual clues that were offered earlier in this chapter that demonstrated the chronological and sequential order of the entire book of Revelation. Moo needs to explain the coordination of the sequential and structural order of the other chapters of Revelation since he has moved them out of their literary sequence. He also must explain why the seventh seal does not constitute the seven trumpets, and why the seventh trumpet does not constitute the seven bowls. Finally, Moo must explain how his structure contains so many judgments that execute the wrath of God when the church is promised that "God has not destined you to wrath" (1 Thess. 1:10; 5:9). These problems are easily solved by accepting the chronological and sequential structure of Revelation in the context of a pre-seventieth-week rapture.

Robert Gundry senses this predicament of removing the church prior to the wrath of God. In his posttribulational understanding of the Revelation, he piles up the wrath judgments at the end of the seventieth week. He argues:

> The universally acknowledged Semitic style of Revelation favors the second view (concurrent judgments piled up at the end), according to which the seals, trumpets, and bowls will find somewhat concurrent fulfillment. .. Chronologically, the apocalyptic visions dart back and forth with swiftness that sometimes bewilders our Western minds.[54]

Gundry's bewilderment is not necessary if a person understands the chronological and sequential nature of the Revelation. The acceptance of Semitic style doesn't necessitate bewilderment on the part of the reader or lack of sequential structure within the literary product. Gundry's view at best is a late tribulational view since he must allow at least six months for the execution of the trumpets with the fifth trumpet being five months in duration. Gundry faces the difficulty of every posttribulational writer in that the seventieth week of Daniel, as fulfilled in Revelation 4–19, contains the wrath and tribulation of God throughout its contents.

Conclusion

A pre-wrath rapture must be pre-seventieth week, or what has been historically understood as pretribulational. The wrath of God begins in Revelation 4–5 with the preparatory vision of the judgment throne of God. Jesus Christ executes the wrath of God by breaking the seal judgments. The first five seals are part of the first half of the seven-year Tribulation (Rev. 6). The sixth seal is the transitional midpoint with the execution of the abomination of desolation. The seventh seal, which is the seven trumpets and seven bowl judgments (Rev. 7–18), continues the intensity of God's wrath through the second half of the Tribulation until the coming of Jesus Christ in Revelation 19. Only a pre-seventieth-week or pretribulational rapture can consistently fulfill the promises of 1 Thessalonians 1:10 and 5:9

17

Robert Gromacki

Where is "the Church" in Revelation 4–19?

_____*OVERVIEW*

Where is the church during the seven-year Tribulation, as outlined in Revelation 4–19? If posttribulationism were correct, you would expect to see the church mentioned as being on earth during this time. However, that is not the picture one sees in Revelation 4–19. This writer demonstrates through investigating many of the details of Revelation 4–19 that the church is pictured in heaven with Christ, having been raptured before the Tribulation began. You can become informed of the overwhelming support for the pretribulational understanding of this issue through this essary.

*T*he Roman emperor Domitian banished the apostle John to the island of Patmos in the Aegean Sea (Rev. 1:9). It was there that John heard the command of Jesus Christ: "What you see, write in a book, and send it to the seven churches which are in Asia" (Rev. 1:11 NKJV). John recorded what he saw and heard, and then he sent the volume to seven local churches located in key cities within the Roman province of Asia; namely Ephesus, Smyrna, Pergamos, Thyatira, Sardis, Philadelphia, and Laodicea (Rev. 1:11).

The content of the book of Revelation can be divided into three sections, based upon Christ's command: "Write the things which you have seen, and the things which are, and the things which will take place after this" (Rev. 1:19 NKJV). These three sections reveal a time sequence: past, present, and future.

What had John just seen? He had just seen a symbolic vision of Jesus Christ standing in the midst of seven lampstands that represented the seven local churches (Rev. 1:12-18,20). This content forms the *past* section of the book ("the things which you have seen"). The *present* section ("the things which are") can be seen in the seven individual letters to the churches (Rev. 2–3). The *future* section thus forms the major part of the book (Rev. 4–22). The prepositional phrase "after this" (*meta tauta*) literally means "after these things." It is found three times (1:19; 4:1 [twice]). The third section begins with these words: "After these things I looked, and behold, a door standing open in heaven. And the first voice which I heard was like a trumpet speaking with me, saying, Come up here, and I will show you things which must take place after this" (4:1 NKJV).

The *future* section (Rev. 4–22) contains an introduction, revealing the throne of God the Father in heaven and the taking of the seven-sealed scroll by Jesus Christ (4–5). The seal, trumpet, and bowl judgments are then described (5–16). The judgment of Babylon is then set forth (17–18). The second coming of Jesus Christ to the earth is finally presented (19:11-21). The millennial kingdom, the great white throne judgment, and the eternal state close out the prophetic revelation (20–22).

The typical futurist interpretation of the book contends that chapters 4–19 describe what will take place in the seven years preceding the second coming of Christ to the earth (19:11-21). Consistent advocates of premillennialism hold this position regardless of their particular view on the rapture of the church.

However, only those who embrace the pretribulational rapture (or the pre-seventieth-week-of-Daniel rapture) will argue for the absence of the genuine church on the earth during these entire seven years. What evidence can be found within Revelation 4–19 to show that the true church is in heaven when the events of these chapters are taking place? The following looks at nine indications.

The Mention of the Church

The words "church" or "churches," so prominent in chapters 1–3, do not appear again in the book until the last chapter (22:16). The singular "church" and the plural "churches" together occur 19 times in the first three chapters (1:4,11,20 [twice]; 2:1,7,8,11, 12,17,18,12,19; 3:1,6,7,13,14,22).

The term "church" (*ekklesia*) literally means "a called out group." It has two main usages in the New Testament. It can be used of the body of Christ, which He is building in this age (Matt. 16:18; 1 Cor. 12:13; Eph. 1:22-23; 4:1-6). It is composed of believing Jews and believing Gentiles made one in Christ (Eph. 2:15-16). The term can also be used of a local congregation of believers (Acts 14:27; Gal. 1:2). It is so used in this second sense in the book of Revelation.

However, there is a strange silence of the term in chapters 4–19. That fact is especially noteworthy when you contrast that absence with its frequent presence in the first three chapters. One good reason for this phenomenon is the absence of the true church and true evangelical churches in the seven years preceding the second coming. The true believers of the church have gone into the presence of Jesus Christ in heaven before the onset of the events of the seven-year period. The church is not mentioned during the seal, trumpet, and bowl judgments because the church is not here during the outpouring of these judgments.

The Admonition

The recurring phrase "unto the churches" (2:7,11,17,29; 3:6,13,22) is conspicuously absent in a similar admonition (13:9). All seven letters to the churches end with this admonition by Christ: "He who has an ear, let him hear what the Spirit says to the churches" (NKJV). Each individual person in each individual local church was to hear and to apply the truth that Christ gave to all of the local churches. For example, a believer in the church at Ephesus could profit spiritually from what the Savior said to the churches at Pergamos or at Philadelphia.

Satan, the beast, and the false prophet are the three main enemies of God and His people during the seven-year period (13:1-18; 19:20–20:3). The beast, symbolic of the military-political dictator of the end times, will rule for 42 months, the second half of the seven-year period. John recorded this truth about him: "All who dwell on the earth will worship him, whose names have not been written in the Book of Life of the Lamb slain from the foundation of the world" (13:8).

At this point, John records the warning: "If anyone has an ear, let him hear" (13:9). Period! There is no mention of "saying to the churches," a phrase which is repeated seven times in the seven letters. If the previously mentioned churches (Rev. 1–3) could possibly be in the seven-year period to face the wrath of the beast, then why wasn't the admonition addressed to them? The obvious answer is that they won't be on earth at that time.

There is the mention of "saints" in the context (13:7,10). These saints, however, are those who get saved during the seven years after the true church has been taken into heaven.

The Wife of the Lamb

The church, as a body-unit, is not seen after chapters 1–3 until the marriage of the Lamb is discussed (19:7-9). Here is the description:

> Let us be glad and rejoice and give Him glory, for the marriage of the Lamb has come, and His wife has made herself ready. And to her it was granted to be arrayed in fine linen, clean and bright, for the fine linen is the righteous acts of the saints (19:7-8).

The church is called Christ's "wife" (*gunē*). Paul used the metaphor of husband and wife to describe the relationship of Jesus Christ to the church (Eph. 5:22-33). The wife is seen as a complete, definite unit in heaven even before the actual second coming of Christ to the earth (19:7; cf. 19:11-16). There is no sense that part of the wife is in heaven and another part is on earth.

The wife has also been rewarded prior to the second coming of Christ to the earth. Her accountability can be seen in the fact that she "has made herself ready" (19:7). However, no believer deserves any reward for what he has done for the Lord. The divine conferral of reward is still an expression of His redemptive grace, thus the text reads: "And to her it was granted to be arrayed in fine linen" (19:8). The linen is defined as "the righteous acts of the saints" (19:8 NKJV). The phrase "righteous acts" is the translation of a plural noun (*ta dikaiōmata*). It seems to refer to the righteous deeds done by genuine believers rather than to the imputed positional righteousness of Christ (Rom. 3:22; 4:22–5:1).

Thus, the judgment seat of Christ has already taken place in heaven before He returns to the earth. All believers in this church age know that they will have to give an account for what they have done since they have been saved (1 Cor. 3:11-15; 2 Cor. 5:10).

Since the wife has been rewarded prior to the return of Christ to the earth, then the wife had to be raptured into heaven before that event.

Christ's Activity

The focus of Christ's activity changes from chapters 1–3 to chapters 4–19. In the first three chapters, His ministry was in the midst of the seven churches on earth. He is commending, criticizing, and correcting them. In chapters 4–19, however, His activity occurs in heaven. He is occupied with the seven-sealed scroll and the judgments that proceed from it.

As the living Head of the church, His body, He is presently building His church (Matt. 16:18). He is in us and we are in Him His attention is on the church. However, that emphasis disappears in chapters 4–19. In the seven years prior to His return to the earth, He is preparing the world and Israel for His coming. The church is now completely with Him in heaven by way of resurrection, translation, and rapture. That phase of His creative and redemptive purpose has been finalized.

24 Elders

If the 24 elders represent the church, then the church is already in heaven before the opening of the seal judgments. The elders have a prominent part in chapters 4–19. They are mentioned 12 times (4:4,10; 5:5,6,8,11,14; 7:11,13; 11:16; 14:3; 19:4). They are first mentioned as present in heaven around the throne of God the Father: "Around the throne were twenty-four thrones, and on the thrones I saw twenty-four elders sitting, clothed in white robes; and they had crowns of gold on their heads" (4:4 NKJV).

Who are these elders? Do they represent angels or men? If human, do they symbolize Old Testament believers, New Testament believers, or both?

The numerical adjective "twenty-four" is significant. King David divided the Levitical priesthood into 24 orders (1 Chron. 24). Each order performed priestly functions at the tabernacle and at the temple for eight days, from Sabbath to Sabbath. In the distribution of the work load, each order would function two weeks per year. In so doing, each order represented the entire priestly tribe and the nation of Israel before God. Thus, the number "twenty-four" came to be representative of a larger, complete group. Thus, the "twenty-four elders" is a phrase which denotes more than two dozen specific persons; rather, the elders stand in for an entire group of personal beings, either angels or humans.

Three features about their description are striking. First, they are "sitting" on thrones. They are not standing, flying, or hovering. Have angels ever sat in the presence of God? No Scripture verse says that they have ever done so. However, Jesus promised every believer in the church age: "To him who overcomes I will grant to sit with Me on My throne, as I also over came and sat down with My Father on His throne" (Rev. 3:21 NKJV). God positionally has made every believer to "sit together in the heavenly places in Christ Jesus" (Eph. 2:6). The "sitting" feature of the elders better suits men than angels.

Second, the elders were "clothed in white robes" (*himatiois leukois*). These words were previously used of believers within the churches (3:5,18).

Third, the elders had "crowns" (*stephanous*) on their heads. These are crowns gained by achievement and victory. Again, believers in the churches were promised crowns (2:10; 3:11; same word). In the epistles, believers in this church age are promised crowns for specific accomplishments: the incorruptible crown for living a spiritually disciplined life (1 Cor. 9:25); the crown of rejoicing for impacting lives to receive Jesus Christ as Savior (1 Thess. 2:19); the crown of righteousness for loving the appearing of Christ (2 Tim. 4:8); the crown of life for loving Christ in the endurance of trials (James 1:12; cf. Rev. 2:10: the crown of life given to the believer-overcomer at Smyrna for being faithful unto death); and the crown of glory for faithful pastors (1 Peter 5:4). Holy angels do not wear crowns, but believers can and will wear them.

The triple description of the 24 elders as sitting, clothed, and crowned speaks for an identity of redeemed people, notably the believers of this church age.

A text-translation problem within the context of the praise of the elders must be addressed (5:8-10). The elders sang a new song, saying:

> You are worthy to take the scroll, and to open its seals; for you were slain, and have redeemed us to God by your blood out of every tribe and tongue and people and nation, and have made us kings and priests to our God; and we shall reign on the earth (5:9-10 NKJV).

In this song of redemption, notice the first person plural personal pronouns ("us" and "we"). Both the King James version and the New King James version, based upon the received Greek text (*Textus Receptus*), indicate that the elders are praising God for their own salvation.

On the other hand, the New International version, based upon the critical Greek text, has this translation:

> You purchased men for God from every tribe and language and people and nation. You have made them to be a kingdom and priests to serve our God and they will reign on the earth.

Notice the usage of the third person plural personal pronouns ("them" and "they"). The *New American Standard Bible* also has the third person pronoun. The *Majority Greek Text* has the third-person pronouns, and that fact is noted in the margin of the New King James version. With the usage of the third-person pronouns, the elders seem to be praising God for the salvation of another group. Those who believe that the elders are angels are quick to point out that interpretation.

However, can people speak about themselves in the third-person rather than in the first person? The song of Moses and of the children of Israel, expressed after their deliverance from Egyptian bondage and their passage through the Red Sea, contains these words: "You in Your mercy have led forth the people whom You have redeemed; You have guided them in Your strength to Your holy habitation" (Exod. 15:13 NKJV). The Israelites are definitely singing about themselves, and yet they sing in the third person. Thus, if the third-person text translation (in Rev. 5:8-10) is accepted as the preferred, original text translation, that fact alone does not preclude the possibility that the elders are singing about their own salvation.

Again, if the third-person text translation is viewed as the original, then the fact that other Greek texts before 1611 (the year that the King James version was published) contained the first person is very significant. It shows that people before 1611 held to the view that the elders were redeemed people. Critics of the pretribulational rapture position, consequently, cannot argue that the proponents of the pretribulational rapture have superimposed their dispensational bias upon the passage.

Angels are set in contrast to the elders: "Then I looked, and I heard the voice of many angels around the throne, the living creatures, and the elders" (Rev. 5:11 NKJV). They sang praise to Christ without any reference to their redemption or to the salvation of others: "Worthy is the Lamb who was slain to receive power and riches and wisdom, and strength and honor and glory and blessing" (5:12 NKJV). If the elders are angels, then the song would appear to be redundant. The second song and the contrast between the elders and the angels suggest that the elders are humans.

The term "elder" (*presbuteros*) is never used of angels in the Bible. The word itself denotes maturity and growth. It is contrasted with "younger" (1 Tim. 5:1-2). How could angels be designated as elders when all of the holy angels were created at the same time. In other words, they are of the same age. In contrast, the elders of a local church were to be men of spiritual experience (1 Tim. 3:1-7;

Titus 1:5-9). When Paul called "for the elders of the church" at Ephesus to meet him at Miletus, they came as the official leaders and as the representatives of all the believers in Ephesus.

The more plausible explanation of the 24 elders is that they represent a group of redeemed people. Who are these people? Since the believers within the Old Testament period will not be resurrected until the return of Jesus Christ to the earth (Dan. 12:1-3; Rev. 20:4-6), the elders more likely represent the redeemed of the church.

The Heaven-Dwellers

The beast, that great military-political leader of the end time, will open his mouth "in blasphemy against God, to blaspheme His name, His tabernacle, and those who dwell in heaven" (Rev. 13:6 NKJV). Who are these heaven-dwellers? They are contrasted with earth-dwellers (12:12; 13:8,14). The earth-dwellers are both human and unsaved. Thus, the heaven-dwellers seem to be human and saved. The verb "dwell" (*skēnountas*) is the same word used for Jesus Christ's incarnation: "And the Word became flesh and dwelt among us" (John 1:14 NKJV). A similar word (*skenos*) is used to describe the believer's present body as a "tent" (2 Cor. 5:1,4). The verb ("to dwell") or the noun ("tent") is never used of angelic activities or bodies.

In the critical Greek text, the phrase "those who dwell in heaven" is in apposition to "His tabernacle" (the connective "and" is omitted). This equation suggests that the heaven-dwellers, as God's tabernacle, is a specific group with none to be added. If that is so, then their description better fits the raptured church, since more people will be saved in the second half of the seven-year period.

John's Experience

John's experience should not be equated with the rapture of the church. John wrote: "After these things I looked, and behold, a door standing open in heaven. And the first voice which I heard was like a trumpet speaking with me saying, Come up here, and I will show you things which must take place after this" (4:11 NKJV). Some claim that this event clearly indicates the fulfillment of the main rapture prediction (1 Thess. 4:13-18; *Old Scofield Bible,* p. 1334). Others see the experience of the apostle as a symbolic representation of the translation of the church (*New Scofield Bible,* p. 1356).

There are some similarities: the voice and the trumpet (4:1; cf. 1 Thess. 4:16). However, the differences in the two accounts are much greater. At the rapture, the believers will hear the voice of an archangel, whereas John directly heard the voice of Christ (4:1; cf. 1:10). There is no mention of Christ's descent from heaven when John went into heaven. There is no mention of a meeting in the air at a point between heaven and earth. There was no permanent change in the body of John. The experience of John parallels those of Paul (2 Cor. 12:1-7) and of Philip (Acts 8:39).

The Lampstands and the Lamps

The individual lampstands, which represented the seven churches (Rev. 1:12,20), should not be equated with "the seven lamps of fire burning before the throne" (Rev. 4:5). Hal Lindsey claimed that the movement of the lamps from earth to heaven was evidence for the removal of the church from earth into heaven before the outpouring of divine judgment (*There's a New World Coming*, p. 86).

However, there is a difference in the Greek words translated as "lampstands" (*luchnias*; 1:12,20) and "lamps" (*lampades*; 4:5). Thus, they cannot be seen as equal symbols for the church. If they could, then why did John use a different word? In addition, the "lamps" are defined as "the seven spirits of God" (4:5).

The so-called equation of the lampstands with the lamps should not be used as a proof for a pretribulational rapture.

Israel's Prominence

Israel and God's covenant program with Israel are the central focus of the seven years prior to the return of Jesus Christ. That emphasis accounts for the silence of any reference to the church on earth at the same time.

When John went into heaven, he first saw the throne of God the Father (4:2). He then gave this symbolic description of God: "And He who sat there was like a jasper and a sardius stone in appearance; and there was a rainbow around the throne, in appearance like an emerald" (4:3 KJV).

Why did God reveal Himself in this way? There is a clue in the two precious stones. The jasper (*iaspidi*) and the sardius (*sardiō*) are the same two words used in the *Septuagint*, the Greek translation of the Hebrew Old Testament, in the description of the breastplate of the high priest of Israel (Exod. 28:17-21). The breastplate contained 12 stones, one for each of the 12 tribes of Israel. They were set in four rows with three stones in each row. The sardius was the first stone in the first row; thus it represented Reuben, the oldest of Jacob's sons. The jasper was the last stone in the last row; thus it represented Benjamin, the youngest of the 12 sons.

These two stones, in the description of God, may represent the relationship of God to His chosen people, the nation of Israel. The appearance of the rainbow further substantiates His covenant relationship and the integrity of His pledged word. Thus, these key chapters (4–19) open with God and His relationship to the people of Israel on earth.

The intercalation of the church age is over. God will now complete His program with Israel through the fulfillment of the seventieth week of Daniel (Dan. 9:24-27). The focus has shifted from the church (Rev. 1–3) to Israel (Rev. 4–19).

When Jesus Christ took the seven-sealed scroll, He was described as "the Lion of the tribe of Judah, the Root of David" (5:5). This description is based upon two Old Testament passages that relate the promised Messiah to Israel.

In the first passage, Jacob informed his 12 sons about what would happen to them "in the last days" (Gen. 49:1). Concerning Judah, he said:

> Judah, you are he whom your brothers shall praise; Your hand shall be on the neck of your enemies; Your father's children shall bow down before you. Judah is a lion's whelp; from the prey, my son, you have gone up. He bows down, he lies down as a lion; and as a lion, who shall rouse him? The scepter shall not depart from Judah, nor a lawgiver from between his feet, until Shiloh comes; and to him shall be the obedience of the people (Gen. 49:8-10 NKJV).

In the second passage, God gave this promise concerning Israel, the future kingdom, and the Messiah:

> There shall come forth a Rod from the stem of Jesse, and a Branch shall grow out of his roots. The Spirit of the Lord shall rest upon Him. The spirit of wisdom

and understanding, the spirit of counsel and might, the Spirit of knowledge and of the fear of the Lord. And in that day there shall be a Root of Jesse, who shall stand as a banner to the people; for the Gentiles shall seek Him, and His resting place shall be glorious (Isa. 22:1-2,10 NKJV).

The seven-sealed scroll symbolizes the right to rule as earth's king. The contents of those seven seals will then occur during the seven-year period prior to Jesus' return to the earth (described in Rev. 4–19). Jesus Christ's right to that scroll is viewed from His relationship to Israel rather than from His relationship to the church. He is the head of His body, the church (Eph. 1:22-23), but that description is not given here.

A prominent group in the seventieth week of Daniel is the 144,000, the sealed servants of God (7:3-4; 14:1-5). They are "of all the tribes of the children of Israel" (7:4), namely: Judah, Reuben, Gad, Asher, Naphtali, Manasseh, Simeon, Levi, Issachar, Zebulun, Joseph [Ephraim], and Benjamin (7:5-8). This passage shows the presence of Israel as a national, ethnic entity on the earth and its tribal divisions in that day.

Mounce, who holds to a posttribulational rapture, claims that ten of the tribes disappeared at the Assyrian conquest of the northern kingdom of Israel (722 B.C.) and that the other two lost their identity when Rome destroyed Jerusalem (A.D. 70). He denies the literalness of the number and the names (*The Book of Revelation*, p. 168). However, Anna is identified as a member of the tribe of Asher during the infancy of Jesus (Luke 2:36). Also, if Judah is not literal in 7:5, is it literal in 5:5? A better explanation is that God is using Israel, rather than the church, to serve Him on earth during the seven years prior to Christ's return to the earth.

The second half of the seven-year period will begin with the forced exit of Satan from heaven to earth and his subsequent persecution of a "woman" (Rev. 23:1-17). Who is this woman? She has been seen as Mary, the mother of Jesus, the New Testament church, and as Israel.

John saw this description of her: "Now a great sign appeared in heaven: a woman clothed with the sun, with the moon under her feet, and on her head a garland of twelve stars" (12:1 NKJV). The mention of the sun, moon, and 12 stars should take us back to the dream of Joseph: "Then he dreamed still another dream and told it to his brothers, and said, 'Look, I have dreamed another dream. And this time, the sun, the moon, and the eleven stars bowed down to me'" (Gen. 37:9 NKJV). Jacob understood the meaning and said: "Shall your mother and I and your brothers indeed come to bow down to the earth before you?" (Gen. 37:10 NKJV). In the interpretation, Jacob is the sun, Leah (or perhaps Rachel) is the moon, and the 12 sons of Jacob are the 12 stars.

The woman was present at the birth of Christ (12:5) and will also be present on earth during the 1260 days prior to Christ's return to the earth (12:6,13-17). In using the "law of previous reference" as a principle of interpretation, only the nation of Israel would qualify as the meaning of the woman. This position finds support in the Old Testament passage (Gen. 37:9-10), in the actual historical situation at the time of Christ's birth, and in the promise of a restored, regenerated nation of Israel.

Where is the church in Revelation 4–19? An investigation into those chapters will show that the church will be in heaven with Jesus Christ. When will she go there? She will be raptured there before the events of Revelation 4–19 occur.

18
Jeffrey L. Townsend

The Rapture in Revelation 3:10

_____*OVERVIEW*

Why is Revelation 3:10 such a hotly contested passage between pretribulationists and non-pretribulationists? It is important since it is a text claimed by pretribulationists to teach that the church will be kept out of the Tribulation. Jeffrey Townsend has written perhaps the best study ever done in defense of the pretribulational understanding of this key passage. He demonstrates from the Greek New Testament that the church will be removed before the seventieth week of Daniel begins.

*E*qually sincere and devout students of the prophetic Scripture hold differing views on the time of the church's rapture in relation to the Tribulation. This is due in large measure to the fact that no biblical verse specifically states that relationship. But Revelation 3:10 comes close: "Because you have kept the word of My perseverance, I also will keep you from the hour of testing, that hour which is about to come upon the whole world, to test those who dwell upon the earth" (NASB). Consequently, as Gundry has stated, "Probably the most debated verse in the whole discussion about the time of the church's rapture is Revelation 3:10."[1]

In Revelation 3:10, the church at Philadelphia is promised protection from the hour of testing. The great pretribulational/posttribulational debate over this verse concerns the nature of the promised protection. Pretribulationists maintain that the church is here promised preservation *outside* the hour of testing by means of the Rapture (external preservation). Posttribulationists argue that the Church is preserved *in* the hour of testing (internal preservation). The solution to the problem of promised protection is bound up in the phrase: *se tēreso ek tēs hōras tou peirasmou* (I will keep you from the hour of testing).

The Meaning of "Keep From"

Although *tēreo* is often translated "keep," a better rendering in Revelation 3:10 would be "preserve" or "protect," since great trials are in view in the "hour of testing."[2] Whatever the promise involves, its great fruit will be the genuine preservation and protection of the church during the hour of testing.

This presents an immediate problem for posttribulationism, which holds that the church will be preserved on earth in the hour of testing. Yet verses such as Revelation 6:9-10; 7:9,13,14; 13:15; 14:13; 16:6; 18:24; and 20:4 present a time of unprecedented persecution and martyrdom for the saints of the Tribulation period.

Gundry identifies these saints as members of the church.[3] One wonders, with Sproule, "If multitudes of Christians are going to die under the fierce persecution of Antichrist, Satan, and the wicked, then *in what way* has God preserved them through the Tribula— tion?"[4] Moreover, it must be questioned whether this kind of "preservation" would be of any comfort and encouragement to the persecuted Philadelphians. In effect the posttribulational scheme denies the meaning of "preservation" in *tēreō* (keep).[5]

The preposition *ek* is the focal point of the debate over whether Revelation 3:10 promises internal or external preservation. The standard lexicons and grammars are in agreement on the basic meaning of this preposition. According to Robertson, "The word means 'out of,' 'from within,' not like *apo* or *para*."[6]

Applying this meaning to Revelation 3:10, posttribulationists interpret the verse two ways. Reese states both views: "The use of *ek* in Revelation 3:10 distinctly implies that the Overseer would be in the hour of tribulation; the promise refers, either to removal from out of the midst of it, or preservation through it."[7] Posttribulation- ists who hold the latter view tend not to see any reference to the rapture in Revelation 3:10. They only see the preservation of the church in the hour of testing.[8] This is an untenable position because the idea of preservation in and through the hour of testing would normally have been expressed by *en* or *para*.[9]

This leaves Reese's first view, which, in modified form, is Gun- dry's view. In a rather lengthy study of *ek*, Gundry asserts the following:

> Essentially, ἐκ, a preposition of motion concerning thought or physical direction, means out from within. ʹΕκ does not denote a stationary position outside its object, as some have mistakenly supposed in thinking that the ἐκ of Revelation 3:10 refers to a position *already* taken outside the earthly sphere of tribula- tion....If ἐκ ever occurs without the thought of emergence, it does so very exceptionally.[10]

These statements pose a very real problem for pretribulation- ism, for it appears that *tēreō ek* must look at "protection issuing in emission," a concept in line with posttribulationism.[11]

However, sufficient evidence exists throughout the history of the meaning and usage of *ek* to indicate that this preposition may also denote *a position outside its object with no thought of prior existence within the object or of emergence from the object.*

Eκ in Classical Literature

Liddell and Scott list several examples of *ek*, chiefly in the early writers, with the heading, "of Position, *outside of, beyond.*"[12] For example, in the following quotation from Murray's translation of *The Iliad*, the italicized portion is the translator's rendering of *ek beleōn*: "Thereafter will we hold ourselves aloof from the fight, *beyond the range of missiles,* lest haply any take wound on wound...."[13] In this and other references listed by Liddell and Scott, the meaning of *ek* is clearly *not* motion "out from within."[14] Gundry notes this evidence, but relegates it to early classical writers and certain lingering, frozen forms of expression.[15] However, these writers have the effect of establishing that from the earliest times *ek* can denote outside position (as well as motion "out from within").

Eκ in the Septuagint

Proverbs 21:23 exemplifies the fact that the idiom of "outside position" expressed by *ek* continued into the era of the Septuagint: "The one who guards his mouth and tongue *keeps* (*diatērei*) his soul *from* (*ek*) trouble."[16] This verse is significant not only because it provides an example of *ek* as meaning "outside position," but also because it does so by using *diatēreō* with the preposition. Although there are no examples of *tēreō* with *ek* in the Septuagint, *diatēreō* with *ek* has a very similar meaning. The preposition διά in composition with *tēreō* simply intensifies the idea of "keeping" (hence: to keep continually or carefully).[17] Thus the Septuagint contains a very comparable idiom to that found in Revelation 3:10, and the meaning in the Septuagint is not "keep by bringing out from within," but rather "keep outside of." The ideas of prior existence in the object and emission from it are missing.[18]

Proverbs 21:23 is not an isolated case. *Ek* with the idea of outside position is also found in expressions employing synonyms of *tēreō* (cf. *exaireō* with *ek* in Josh. 2:13; *rhuomai* with *ek* in Ps. 33:19 [Septuagint, 32:19]; 56:13 [Septuagint, 55:13]; Prov. 23:14).[19] Abbott notes that in Psalm 59 "*sōson ek, exelou ek, rhusai ek,* may mean, not 'Bring me safe out after I have fallen in,' but 'Save me [by *keeping* me] out (of the hands of my enemies who surround me).'"[20] In summary, the Septuagint offers examples of expressions which are not frozen forms and where *ek* has the idea of outside position.

EK in Josephus

The works of Josephus also provide examples of *ek* used to express "outside position" rather than "motion out from within." In perhaps the clearest example, the italicized portion is Thackeray's translation of *rhuomai* with *ek*: "He *delivered* them from those dire consequences which would have ensued from their sedition but for Moses' watchful care."[21] The idea here is preservation rather than removal, since the judgment of God was prevented by Moses' intercession.

EK in the New Testament

Examples of *ek* carrying the idea of "outside position" have been found in each period of the development of the Greek language. Acts 15:29 establishes the fact that this meaning of *ek* is also found in the New Testament. In Acts 15:28-29, the brethren in Jerusalem concluded their letter to the Gentiles in Antioch with instructions to abstain from certain practices that would be especially offensive to Jewish brethren. Their concluding remark is found at the end of verse 29: "*Keeping yourselves free from (ex...diatērountes)* such things, you will do well." The expression employs *diatēreō* in the form of a circumstantial participle with *ek*. Like the expression with *Diatēreō* and *ek* in Proverbs 21:23, the idea is outside position, not motion out from within.[22] The thrust of verses 28 and 29 is a request for future abstention (cf. *apekesthai*, v. 29a) from certain practices (outside position), not an accusation of current vices from which the brethren in Antioch must desist (motion out from within). As noted previously, *diatēreō* differs from *tēreō* only in the strength of the idea of keeping (hence "keeping...free" rather than simply "keeping"). Consequently, Acts 15:29 provides another construction which is very similar to *tēreō ek* in Revelation 3:10, and again the meaning is not keeping out from within, but keeping outside the object of the preposition.

In addition to Acts 15:29, at least four other verses in the New Testament contain verbal constructions with *ek* in which *ek* seems to indicate a position outside its object.[23] Each of these verses needs to be examined in some detail.

John 12:27. The use of *ek* in John 12:27 is important because this verse can shed light on John's usage of the same preposition in the book of Revelation.[24] Whether or not Jesus' words, "Father, save Me from this hour," express a question or a petition is relatively unimportant to the present discussion. The question at hand is whether Jesus was speaking about preservation from the coming hour of His death (*ek* meaning outside position) or deliverance out of an hour that had already come to pass (*ek* meaning motion out from within). The verb *sōzō* is capable of either idea.[25] Robertson is certain that Jesus had already entered the hour.[26] However, John 7:30 and 8:20, along with the immediate context of 12:23-24, seem to use "the hour" in reference to Jesus' betrayal and death, which would be followed by His glorious resurrection. Evidently the request of the Greeks in 12:21 vividly brought to mind the hour of the Lord's impending death, but the actual occurrence of the hour was yet future. This is the conclusion of Smith, who writes a helpful appendix on the significance of John 12:27 in relation to the rapture question in Revelation 3:10:

> That Jesus' suffering at this time was proleptic and anticipatory and that the "hour" spoken of was in reality still in the future is evident in that He Himself declares a few days later, "With desire I have desired to eat this passover with you before I suffer" (Luke 22:15), and later still, just previous to His arrest, "Behold, the hour is at hand [Greek: near], and the Son of man is betrayed into the hands of sinners" (Matthew 26:45). The phrase "is at hand" always denotes proximity and never total arrival.[27]

It appears that Jesus was referring to preservation rather than to deliverance, with regard to the hour of His death. Thus John 12:27 provides an example (parallel in many respects with Revelation 3:10) in the Johannine literature where the meaning of *ek* is position outside the object of the preposition.

Hebrews 5:7. A second example of *ek* indicating outside position is found in Hebrews 5:7, in which the Lord is said to have prayed "to the One [who was] able *to save* Him *from death*" (*sōzein . . . ek thanaton*). The description of His prayer as being made "with loud crying and tears," and the reference to the Father as "able to save Him from death," indicates that the Gethsemane prayer is in view (Matt. 26:39; cf. Mark 14:36; Luke 22:42). This connection is significant for the present discussion, since, as Hewitt points out, "If the prayer which Christ offered *with strong crying and tears* was a prayer to be saved 'out of' death, it cannot easily be reconciled with another request made in Gethsemane: 'Father, if thou be willing, remove this cup from me' (Luke 22:42)."[28] In order to reconcile Hebrews 5:7 with the Gospel accounts, which stress preservation from death and not resurrection out of death, *ek* must have the idea of position outside its object rather than emergence from the object.[29]

James 5:20. This passage presents yet another use of *sōzō* with *ek*, where the meaning of the preposition is "outside position." James writes, "He who turns a sinner from the error of his way *will save* his *soul from death*" (*sōzei...ek thanaton*). This sinner is defined, in 5:19, as a brother who has strayed from the truth he once held (either doctrinal or moral) and who needs to be turned back (*epistrephō*) to his former direction of life. The most natural way of understanding the context is to see this sinner as a true believer who has embraced erroneous doctrine or practice. The death in 5:20, then, must be physical death. Wessel comments, "Since the New Testament teaches the security of the believer in Christ, it is best to take the reference to death as physical death. The early church believed and taught that persistence in sin could cause premature physical death (cf. 1 Cor. 11:30)."[30] This interpretation is supported by the context of 5:15-16, where sin is linked with the loss of physical health. If physical death is in view in James 5:20, then *ek* cannot mean "out from within." Instead it must mean "position outside" its object.

This study of *ek* throughout its linguistic history, and especially its usage in the New Testament, has shown that the preposition may sometimes indicate "outside position" (whereas at other times it means removal "out from within"). In relation to the interpretation of *tēreō ek* in Revelation 3:10, this finding establishes the pre-tribulational position as a bona fide grammatical possibility. To understand *tēreō ek* as indicating preservation in an outside position is well within the bounds of the linguistic history and usage of *ek*.[31]

John 17:15. In order to determine the most probable meaning of *tēreō ek* in Revelation 3:10, its usage in John 17:15 must be considered. This is the only other occurrence of *tēreō* with *ek* in either biblical or classical Greek.[32] It is significant that both verses are Johannine and in both cases Jesus speaks the words. Hence much can be learned from John 17:15 about the meaning of *tēreō ek* in Revelation 3:10.

John 17:15 begins with a negative petition using *airō* and *ek*. Jesus uses these words to express His prayer that the disciples not be physically removed from the earth. Removal would be one way of preserving them spiritually in His absence, but it would violate their commission as witnesses (cf. John 15:27). It is significant that in the case of *airō* with *ek*, the idea of motion in the verb naturally lends itself to the idea of taking (*ek*), in the sense of motion out from within (cf. *oi erchomenoi ek*, Rev. 7:14). This points up the necessity of considering the verb and the preposition together, and not simply isolating the components of the expression. The context is also an important factor in deciding the exact force of the phrase. The disciples were in the world (17:11), so *ek* must mean "out from within" in John 17:15a.

In 17:15b the Lord contrasts (using *alla*) His first petition with a petition using *tēreō* and *ek* for preservation from the evil one.[33] Gundry asks, "How then can *tēreō ek* [in Rev. 3: 10] refer to the rapture or to the results of the rapture, when in its only other occurrence the phrase opposes an expression [*airō ek*] which would perfectly describe the rapture?"[34] The answer lies in the combined effect of the verb and the preposition in the context—factors which Gundry tends to overlook.

Regarding the context, the disciples were in the world physically. This combined with the idea of motion in *airō*, demands that *airō ek* in John 17:15a be understood as removal out from within. However, John 17:15b *describes an entirely different situation.* The disciples were *not* in the evil one spiritually when Jesus prayed. This, combined with the fact that *tēreō* demands not the idea of motion but rather the idea of preservation, indicates that *tēreō ek* in John 17:15b be understood as preservation in an outside position.[35] This is in line with the pretribulational understanding of Revelation 3:10: Just as the disciples were not in the evil one, so the Philadelphians were not in the hour of testing, and the promise is that Jesus Christ will keep them outside that hour.

Gundry interprets John 17:15b as a prayer for the preservation of the disciples *in* the moral sphere of Satan, since they are to be left in the world (John 17:15a).[36] However, both the immediate context and John's other writings argue against this interpretation. In the context of John 17:11-16, the idea of "keeping" is related to salvation and the possession of eternal life, not preservation from the moral assaults of Satan. The issue is the keeping of salvation (i.e., the perseverance of the saints), not progression in sanctification, which is taken up in 17:17.

First John 5:18-19 also stands against Gundry's premise. In 1 John 5:18, the evil one does not *touch* (*aptō*) the one who has been born of God, because the One who was born of God (Jesus Christ) *keeps* (*tēreō*, cf. John 17:11) him. In 1 John 5:19 the apostle wrote, "We know that we are of God, and the whole world lies in the power of the evil one." Gundry's interpretation of John 17:15b, as preservation in the moral sphere of Satan, does not square with the Johannine emphasis on the separation of believers from the spiritual realm of the evil one.

Thus the idea in John 17:15b is not the moral sphere of the evil one (i.e., the world system), as Gundry and most posttribulationists suppose, but the spiritual realm of the evil one (i.e., spiritual death). The disciples were not in Satan's realm spiritually, and Christ prays, using *tēreō ek*, that the Father would keep them so. Hence *tēreō ek* in John 17:15 is an expression for preservation in an outside position. Applied to Revelation 3:10, this evidence indicates that the pretribulational position is not only possible but probable.

Revelation 3:10 may then be paraphrased, "Because you have held fast the word which tells of My perseverance, I also will preserve you in a position outside the hour of testing" (NASB). This paraphrase points up an important nuance of meaning that must be recognized. *Tēreō ek* in Revelation 3:10 does not describe the rapture as such. Instead, it describes the position and status of the church during the hour of testing. It describes the results of the rapture, not the rapture itself. Revelation 3:10 does not state directly how the church will be preserved outside the hour of testing. However, the remainder of the verse indicates that the proper logical deduction is preservation by means of a pretribulational rapture of the church.

The Meaning of "The Hour of Testing"

The Meaning of "The Hour"

The object of the preposition *ek* in Revelation 3:10 is "the hour of testing" (*tēs ōras tou peirasmou*). The preservation promised the Philadelphians is in relation to a *specific period of time.* This is indicated by the inclusion of *tēs* as an article of previous reference. Jesus is speaking of *the* well-known hour of testing, which is a reference to the expected time of trouble, the Tribulation period, before the return of Messiah (Deut. 4:26-31; Isa. 13:6-13; 17:4-11; Jer. 30:4-11; Ezek. 20:33-38; Dan. 9:27; 12:1; Zech. 14:1-4; Matt. 24:9-31).[37] This period is graphically portrayed in Revelation 6–18 (cf. "the great tribulation," 7:14; and "the hour of His judgment," 14:7).[38]

In relation to the rapture question, it is significant that the Philadelphian church is here promised preservation outside the *time period* of the Tribulation. The combination (*ek tēs ōras*) thwarts the posttribulation view of the church being kept from trials while on earth during the hour of testing. As Thiessen notes, the promise "holds out exemption from the period of trial, not only from the trial during that period."[39] Ryrie comments, "It is impossible to conceive of being in the location where something is happening and being exempt from the time of the happening."[40]

Gundry attempts to "undercut stress on the term 'hour'" in three ways.[41] First, he claims that the hour will elapse in heaven as well as on earth. But the verse claims that this hour is coming on the *oikoumēnē* ("inhabited earth") and thus is related to the earthly time continuum. This was certainly John's perspective.

Second, Gundry claims that "the hour of testing" does not emphasize a period of time, but rather the trials during that period. Although Delling notes this possibility in his article on *ōra*, he gives Revelation 3:10 as an example of *ōra* in the general sense of " 'the divinely appointed time' for the actualization [*sic*] of apocalyptic happenings."[42] Gundry's view errs in failing to square with the use of the definite article *tēs* which indicates that a well-known hour (fixed in length by Dan. 9:27) is in view. A careful evaluation of the evidence seems to prove all the more that both time and event are inextricably linked.

Third, Gundry notes that in Jeremiah 30:7 (LXX, 37:7) Israel is given a similar promise of being saved from (*sōzō apo* with *apo* in the Septuagint) the "time of Jacob's trouble" (cf. "hour of testing"). Even though *apo* denotes separation more strongly than *ek*, Israel is preserved within the time of trouble not outside it. Gundry concludes his argument by stating, "If a pretribulational rapture was not or will not be required for deliverance from the time of Jacob's distress, neither will a pretribulational rapture be required for preservation from the hour of testing."[43]

This appears to be a strong argument until one considers the context of Jeremiah 30:7. Jeremiah 30:5-6 indicates that the nation is already in the great day of trouble when salvation comes. This is confirmed in Matthew 24, where the Jews are told to flee the persecution of the one who desecrates the temple, and in Revelation 12, where the dragon persecutes the woman and her offspring. From this trouble, the nation is promised rescue in Jeremiah 30:7. Thus the promises are different and not comparable. Israel is promised rescue within the time of trouble,[44] the church is promised preservation from the hour of testing. Only the latter case demands rapture from earth to heaven.

The Scope of "The Hour"

The qualifying phrase, "which is about to come upon the whole inhabited earth," further describes the hour as imminent and worldwide in its impact. *Tēs mellousēs erchesthai* goes beyond conveying future tense. It carries a note of imminency, as indicated by *erchomai tachu*, which begins Revelation 3:11. Both the coming of the hour and the coming of the Lord are imminent. This connection indicates a relationship between the promise of "keeping" in 3:10 and the coming of the Lord in 3:11. There will be preservation outside the imminent hour of testing for the Philadelphian church when the Lord comes. This, in turn, indicates that although *tēreō ek* in 3:10 does not refer directly to the rapture of the church, rapture as the means of preservation is a proper deduction from the context.

"The whole inhabited earth" will be overtaken by this hour (cf. Rev. 2:10, where local persecution is in view). Since the church is to be preserved outside a period of time that encompasses the whole world, preservation by a pretribulation rapture is again seen to be a logical inference from the context. Only a rapture to heaven removes the church from the earth and its time continuum.[45]

The Purpose of "The Hour"

"To test those who dwell upon the earth" gives the purpose of the coming hour. In both secular and biblical Greek *peirazō* has the root idea of a test that is applied in order to expose the true character of someone.[46] Usually *peirazō* denotes negative intent: to test in order to break down, to demonstrate failure.[47] Hence the hour of testing will come on the whole world, with the specific purpose of putting earth-dwellers to the test, which will demonstrate their utter failure before God. In other words, the Tribulation period will provide condemning evidence for the judgments the Lord will carry out when He returns to the earth (cf. Matt. 25; Rev. 19:19-21; 20:4).

According to Johnson, *tous katoikountas epi tēs gēs* corresponds to the Hebrew idiom—*yošbēy hāareṣ* which, in Isaiah 24:1,5,6; 26:9, becomes a technical term for people on the earth during the time of Jacob's trouble.[48] The term is not all-inclusive, since in each of its seven other uses in Revelation the reference is to unbelievers, and both pretribulationists and posttribulationists agree that there will be many saints in the Tribulation period. The question is whether these saints are the preserved church (which is unlikely since many are martyred), or people who come to salvation during the Tribulation and are martyred for their faith. In Revelation 13:8 and 17:8 an earth-dweller is further defined as one "whose name has not been written in the book of life from the foundation of the world." These are the nonelect of the Tribulation period, and as a result they worship the beast (cf. Rev. 13:8,14). On these earth-dwellers will come judgments that have the purpose of openly demonstrating their absolute and utter depravity (cf. Rev. 6:15-17; 9:20-21; 16:21). McClain notes, "In that hour the physical judgments will generally fall upon saved and unsaved alike."[49] But the special objects of testing and wrath will be the earth-dwellers.

Conclusion

In seeking a solution to the pretribulational/posttribulational debate over the nature of the preservation promised the church in Revelation 3:10, the preposition *ek* was traced throughout its history in order to establish the fact that *ek* may at times indicate "outside position" as well as at other times indicating motion "out from within." This brought the pretribulational interpretation of Revelation 3:10 within the realm of possibility. In addition, John 17:15—

the only other occurrence of *tēreō ek* in either biblical or classical Greek—was studied. Pretribulationists and posttribulationists alike note the similarity in meaning between John 17:15 and Revelation 3:10. Hence when it was determined that *tēreō ek* in the context of John 17:15 demanded the idea of preservation outside the evil one, this had the effect of making outside preservation the preferred (or most probable) interpretation of Revelation 3:10.

The preservation promised in Revelation 3:10 is in relation to a specific, well-known hour of trial, the future seven-year Tribulation, which is to precede Messiah's return and which is described in detail in Revelation 6–18. Revelation 3:10 teaches that the coming of this hour is imminent, that it is worldwide in its scope, and that the purpose of the hour is to put the ungodly earth-dwellers of the Tribulation period to the test to reveal evidence of their wickedness in preparation for the Lord's judgments when He returns to the earth.

Although Revelation 3:10 describes the result of the rapture (i.e., the position and status of the church during the Tribulation), and not the rapture itself, the details of the hour of testing just mentioned establish the pretribulation rapture as the most logical deduction from this verse. The promise of preservation is from a period of time that will envelop the whole world. Only a pretribulation rapture would remove the church completely from the earth and its time continuum. Thus the pretribulation rapture is found to be a proper logical deduction from the data found in Revelation 3:10.

Arnold G. Fruchtenbaum

Is There
a Pre-Wrath Rapture?

_____*OVERVIEW*

How biblically accurate and valid is the recently developed "pre-wrath rapture" theory? In this essay the author briefly follows and critiques the major pre-wrath rapture publication in a chapter by chapter approach. This review challenges the pre-wrath theory showing its major biblical inconsistencies and theological weaknesses. The author demonstrates that when carefully analyzed, the pre-wrath theory fails to uphold sound doctrine and solid biblical exposition.

*M*arvin Rosenthal's recent work, *The Pre-Wrath Rapture of the Church* (Thomas Nelson, 1990), has created considerable confusion and concern among evangelicals engaged in eschatological dialogue. The purpose of this essay is to review and critique Rosenthal's major points.[1] His book has a double-edged approach. First, it attacks pretribulationism. Second, it defends a new view of the timing of the rapture, which is, as the title implies, the pre-wrath rapture of the church.

The concept "pre-wrath" is neither ideal nor unique, for in reality *all* rapture views are pre-wrath views. Pretribulationism, midtribulationism, and posttribulationism all have the rapture occurring before God pours out His wrath. The disagreement in these views is *when*, in the seventieth week of Daniel, the wrath of God begins? The more correct description of Rosenthal's view would be the "three-quarter tribulation" view. According to Rosenthal, the rapture occurs somewhere between the middle and the end of the Tribulation; or, as he would prefer to call it, the seventieth week of Daniel.

Rosenthal's Pre-Wrath Position

The book's tone is aggressive, as the author feels he has to demolish pretribulationism. In the early pages, Rosenthal recounts his struggle with abandoning pretribulationism and the development of his new view. It is in his third chapter, "The Options of 'When' Laid Out," that he presents the basis of his position. He writes:

The basic theses of this book are simple:

1. The rapture of the church will occur immediately prior to the beginning of the Day of the Lord.

2. The Day of the Lord commences sometime within the second half of Daniel's seventieth week.

3. The cosmic disturbances associated with the sixth seal will signal the approach of the Day of the Lord.

4. The Day of the Lord will begin with the opening of the seventh seal (Rev. 8:1).

Everything else will be presented as confirmation of those theses.

The Olivet discourse (Matt. 2-25) will be a central text. It is the author's contention that the Olivet discourse is Jewish in character, sequential in progression, logical in argument, parallel to the seals of Revelation 6 in nature, covers the seventieth week of Daniel in scope, answers the dual question concerning the Lord's coming and the end of the age posed by the disciples (which was the catalyst for the Lord's teaching), and encompasses both the rapture and the return of Christ within its borders. It will also be demonstrated that the seventieth week of Daniel has three major, distinct, and identifiable periods of time: the "beginning of sorrows," the Great Tribulation, and the Day of the Lord—all found in the Olivet discourse (pp. 60-61).

Absolutely essential to Rosenthal's view are the following points: First, the "Day of the Lord" does not encompass the whole seven years but only the last quarter or so. Second, the Tribulation does not encompass all seven years; and also, that the "Great Tribulation" (which some, but not all pretribulationists apply to the second three-and-a-half years) does not encompass all of the three-and-a-half years, but only about a quarter (the final quarter) of the seven years, or about half of the second half of this period. Third, the seventieth week of Daniel is not comprised of two equal halves, but of three distinct periods: the "beginning of sorrows" (the whole of the first half); the Great Tribulation (the third quarter); and the Day of the Lord (the fourth quarter). Fourth, the rapture will take place between the third and fourth quarters. Fifth, the sixth seal, the seven trumpet judgments, and the seven bowl judgments all take place in the last quarter of the Tribulation.

Rosenthal then tries to fit Scripture into the mold presented in this chapter. The validity of this position will be critiqued as the review continues. But, as a preliminary observation, Rosenthal's view will totally collapse if certain crucial points are made, i.e., if it can be shown that 1) the Day of the Lord covers more than just the last quarter of the seven years; 2) that the Bible views the seven years as being two parts, not three parts; 3) that the wrath of God is not limited to the fourth quarter of the seven years; and 4) that the seven trumpet and the seven bowl judgments cover a greater period of time than the last quarter of the seven years. Rosenthal brings in corollary evidence, such as the seven churches and the "last trump," which he forces into his scheme; and these, too, will be critiqued

How Long Is the Tribulation?

In the chapter, "And What of the Tribulation Period?" Rosenthal tries to do away with some commonly accepted terminology. His points are that the seven years should not be called the Tribulation, and that the Tribulation begins only in the middle of the seven years. He cites passages in the Olivet discourse where the term "tribulation" is used and concludes, "Of the four times the Lord spoke of *tribulation* in a prophetic context, He was speaking of the Great Tribulation which begins in the middle of Daniel's seventieth week—precisely three-and-one-half years into it" (p. 105).

However, Rosenthal ignores Matthew 24:9, which he places in a prophetic context, and which he places in the first half of the seven years. That verse uses "tribulation" in reference to the first half of the seven years! Rosenthal contradicts himself, and one wonders whether he merely missed seeing the word in Matthew 24:9, or if he deliberately chose to ignore it because it devastates his argument in this chapter. Was this only an oversight? With as much work as he does on Matthew 24, it seems unlikely that he merely missed it Rosenthal betrays himself when he writes:

> If the seventieth week is the Tribulation period, or "the time of wrath," and God's people are exempt from "wrath," the matter is settled. But such an argument is both unbiblical and illogical and cannot be allowed to stand.... The use of the phrase *tribulation period* (coined by men but not justified in the Bible)

creates, at the very least, a built-in bias for pretribulationism (pp. 106-07).

There you have it! Rosenthal does not like the term "tribulation" used for the first three-and-a-half years, for it automatically
creates a bias for pretribulationism. But Matthew 24:9 *does* use it for
the first half. Furthermore, he states that the term "tribulation
period" is a term "coined by men but not justified in the Bible," and
the reason he does not like it is because it has a "built-in bias for
pretribulationism."

Rosenthal does not want to make the first half of the seven years
part of the Tribulation, or Great Tribulation, but only "the beginning
of sorrows." He tries to parallel Matthew 24:4-8 with the first five
seals of Revelation 6, but there are three problems here. First, the
similarities are quite superficial and the differences outnumber the
similarities. Nowhere in Matthew does it mention a destruction of
humanity, and there is no mention of martyred saints. Revelation
does not mention the fact of many deceivers, while Matthew does
not mention the Antichrist. There are other dissimilarities as well.
Second, even if there were a greater level of similarities, it would
not prove his point since similarity does not mean sameness, and a
more exact linguistic correlation than found in the two texts is necessary to prove sameness. Third, Rosenthal has not actually proved
that verses 4-8 are part of the seven years. He merely assumes it to
be true and cites pretribulationists who agree with him. But verses
4-8 can also refer to prophetic events preceding the seven years,
with the seven years only beginning at verse 9. Rosenthal builds his
three-fold division of the seven years on a tenuous foundation.

The Tribulation and the Wrath of God

To claim, as Rosenthal does, that the first five seals are not the
wrath of God but only the wrath of man is to try to force his position
on the text. The fact is that all seven seals are broken by Christ; the
first five seals are as much a part of "the wrath of the Lamb" as are
the last two. Furthermore, the four horsemen of the apocalypse in
the first four seal judgments are initiated by the four living creatures; so these judgments do not only concern "man's activity under
the controlling influence of Satan." To claim that these seals are
only describing the wrath of men goes contrary to the context, since

all the seal judgments originate in heaven. In fact, the very damage that they do is described in the Old Testament as resulting from the wrath of God. For example, the seal judgments mention four things: death by sword (Rev. 6:7-8); famine (6:5-6,8); wild animals (6:8); pestilence and plague (6:8). Ezekiel 14:21 states:

> For thus saith the LORD Jehovah: How much more when I send my four sore judgments upon Jerusalem, the sword, and the famine, and the evil beasts, and the pestilence, to cut off from it man and beast! (ASV).

While all four things could be said to be what man does to man, it is clearly God who sends all four. The wrath of man may be involved, but not to the exclusion of the wrath of God. That these four things all result from the wrath of God is clearly stated in Ezekiel 14:19. Other references to God sending these four things as part of divine judgment include:

- Sword: Leviticus 26:25; Deuteronomy 28:22,25-26; 32:25; 2 Chronicles 29:8-9; 36:16-17; Jeremiah 15:2-3; 16:4; 19:7; 44:12-13; Ezekiel 5:12,17; 6:11-12; 7:14-15; 33:27; 38:19.

- Famine: Leviticus 26:26; Deuteronomy 11:17; 28:23-24, 38-42; 32:24; Jeremiah 15:2; 16:4; 19:9; Ezekiel 4:16-17; 5:12,17; 6:11-12; 7:14-15.

- Wild Animals: Leviticus 26:26; Deuteronomy 32:24; Jeremiah 15:3; 16:4; Ezekiel 5:17; 33:2; 39:4.

- Pestilence: Leviticus 26:25; Numbers 11:33; 16:46; 25:6-11; Deuteronomy 28:21-22,27,35,59-61; Jeremiah 15:2; 21:6-7; 44:12-13; Ezekiel 15:12,16-17; 6:11-12; 7:14-15; 38:22.

To claim so dogmatically, as Rosenthal does, that the first five seals have nothing to do with the wrath of God is to: 1) ignore the Bible's own statements on the matter; 2) force one's preconceived view on the passage; and 3) set up an artificial dichotomy, that if it is the wrath of God it is a direct judgment, but if it comes through human agency it is not divine judgment. Nothing is further from the truth. In Revelation 17:16-18, John says it is God who divinely judges the harlot of Babylon, but this destruction is done by human agency.

As all the above references clearly show, the things in the first five seals are all part of the wrath of God. To put the rapture any time after the fifth or sixth seals would *not* be a pre-wrath rapture.

How Long Is the Great Tribulation?

As Rosenthal does not want the term "tribulation" applied to the first half of the seven years, he does not want it applied to *all* of the second half either, but only to the third quarter (pp. 108-10). This is a good example of reading one's position into the text. Rosenthal sees the second half as containing two distinct parts: the Great Tribulation and the Day of the Lord. Therefore, the Tribulation is not the entire second half but only the third quarter. Since the seven years must last a full seven years and since the second half must last a full three-and-a-half years, it is the Great Tribulation that is shortened, making it only about 21 months long, more or less. As far as the book of Revelation is concerned, there is not much space for the Great Tribulation, and it all must be limited to the time of the fifth and sixth seals only.

However, that is not the only option, or even the best option for the meaning of Matthew 24:22 and Mark 13:20. The context of that verse (Matt. 24:15-22; Mark 13:14-20) is dealing with the persecution of the Jews, instigated by the "abomination of desolation" at the mid-point of the seven years; and Matthew 24:15 reminds the hearer that it is the same one spoken of by Daniel the prophet (Dan. 9:27; 12:11). This persecution of the Jews will be worse than anything they have ever suffered in the past, and never will they suffer anything like this again. In fact, if God did not at some point put a stop to this persecution, no Jews would survive.

God will bring the period of persecution to a stop. What is being "shortened" is the persecution period, so as to allow the Jews to survive. But how long is this period of Jewish persecution to last? Is it only 21 months? Is it only one quarter: the third quarter of the seven years? On the contrary, the period of persecution of the Jews, which is the context of Matthew 24:15-22 and Mark 13:14-20, is exactly three-and-one-half years, the second half of the seven years.

This is twice stated in Daniel (9:27; 12:5-7), and it is Daniel who gave the beginning point of the persecution as being the abomination of desolation. It is this very point that Jesus picked up (Matt. 24:15; Mark 13:14) and gave as a sign for the Jews to flee the land. The book of Revelation also gives the timing of Jewish persecution as being three-and-one-half years (12:6, 13-14), even specifying that it will be exactly 1260 days.

Obviously, the period of Jewish persecution is not being "shortened," and neither is the rest of the Great Tribulation being "shortened," since in the Olivet discourse the two are contemporaneous. So, what is being "shortened"? As Rosenthal himself noted in the above quotation, the word can also have the meaning of "cut short." That is the meaning here. In other words, the period of Jewish persecution and the period of "great tribulation" for the Jews will be suddenly cut short in the sense that it will not be allowed to continue even one day beyond its allotted time. God will allow the Antichrist to persecute Jews for exactly 1260 days and not one second beyond that. Once the last second comes, it will be suddenly cut short for the sake of Jewish survival. In fact, Mark's Greek tense (13:20) speaks of this shortening as already having taken place, as an accomplished fact. There is no exegetical requirement to make the shortening mean that the persecution will last for a shorter time than three-and-a-half years. Nothing in the passage indicates that the term "shortening" actually means less than three-and-a-half years. Only Rosenthal's preconceived need to divide the second half into two parts introduces an unnatural meaning to the text.

How Many Comings?

Not only has Rosenthal failed to prove that the term "tribulation" cannot be used for the first half of the seven years, he has also failed to prove that the term is limited to the third quarter and is not applicable to the fourth quarter. Using the term "tribulation" for the whole seven years is not without biblical justification, as Rosenthal claims (p. 103). He criticizes pretribulationism for requiring another coming of Jesus before the seven years commence, and he insists that "evidence for such an event is simply nonexistent." However, he seems to have a blind spot in that his system requires the very same concept. According to that section, the rapture takes place at the three-quarter point, and the return of Christ takes place at the end of the fourth quarter. *Regardless of the semantics Rosenthal may use, his system requires the rapture and the second coming to be two separate events, separated by a period of time. The only disagreement between pretribulationism and Rosenthal's three-quarter tribulationism is how much time there actually is in between the two events.*

Bashing Straw Men

It is Rosenthal himself who states that the shortening of the Great Tribulation is crucial to his position (pp. 110-11), and much of his system stands or falls on this one point. After assuming his position to be absolutely proven, he then forces a view on pretribulationism and does exactly what he claimed he would not do: use a straw man argument. According to Rosenthal, since pretribulationists fail to see the Great Tribulation as not extending to the end of the seven years, "they are logically forced to place the sixth seal at the end of the seventieth week in their interpretation of Matthew 24:22, if they are consistent, and are then faced with the unsolvable dilemma of what to do with the trumpet and bowl judgments of the book of Revelation which arise out of the opening of the seventh seal." This reviewer, a pretribulationist, never knew he had such a position!

Rosenthal then resorts to self-aggrandizement and claims that a proper understanding of the book of Revelation has escaped Bible students "to this very hour" (p. 112). The implication is that only his view will unlock the mystery of the book. But this reviewer has not had any trouble understanding Revelation or teaching it. There is very basic and substantial agreement among pretribulationists as to the meaning of the book of Revelation. The book is not a mystery!

How Long Is the Day of the Lord?

In chapter 9, entitled "And Then the Day of the Lord," Rosenthal argues against the common view that the term "Day of the Lord" includes the millennium. Many have assumed this view based on the common use in the Old Testament of the phrase "in that day," which speaks of both the Tribulation and the millennium. Many have assumed that "in that day" is equivalent to the "Day of the Lord," and so include both the 7 and the 1000 years in it. While it is true that "in that day" includes both a time of judgment (tribulation) and a time of blessing (millennium), the same is not true of the "Day of the Lord," which in every context is always judgment and is never found in a millennial context. Blessings, however, could be found in the context of judgment, but these are not millennial blessings. The "Day of the Lord" does not include the millennium, and on this point Rosenthal is correct.

However, Rosenthal does make a major blunder, showing he is not always careful with the text, when he states, "The prophets... spoke of the Day of the Lord with the definite article—they knew of only one such event" (p. 129). In none of the appearances of the term in the Hebrew Bible, is it used with the definite article. He is obviously relying only on an English translation; yet he uses this as evidence of his own position. Even if the definite article was there, it would not, by itself, prove his point, for the use of the definite article in Hebrew and Greek—or in English, for that matter—never means that there is only one thing which this term could refer to. Rosenthal is guilty of a linguistic flaw.

However, he wants to limit the "Day of the Lord" to the last quarter of the seven years, insisting that it cannot be applied to the whole seven years, or even to that which he calls the Great Tribulation: the third quarter. But the facts are the Day of the Lord cannot be limited only to the last quarter; it actually covers the whole seven-year period. How the Day of Jehovah affects the Gentiles is detailed in Isaiah 2:12-22; 13:6-16; Ezekiel 30:1-9; Joel 1:15-20; Obadiah 1:10-20; Zephaniah 1:14-18; and 2 Peter 3:10-12. How the Day of Jehovah affects Israel is given in Ezekiel 13:1-7; Joel 2:1-11; 3:14-17; Amos 5:18-20; and Zephaniah 1:7-13. It is mere assumption to limit all this to the last quarter.

The Last Trump

Later in the same chapter, Rosenthal focuses on "the last trump" (pp. 131-32). This is a point Rosenthal comes back to in a later chapter. Here, he defines "the last trump" as being "the final outpouring of God's wrath." But, in neither passage on the rapture (1 Cor. 15:50-58; 1 Thess. 4:13-18), where the trumpet is mentioned, is it connected with God's wrath. While the trumpets of Revelation are connected with God's judgment, even Rosenthal does not try to connect "the last trump" with the seventh trumpet of

Revelation, as midtribulationists and posttribulationists often do. Rather, he makes "the last trump" to include "a comprehensive whole," which includes the seventh seal, the seven trumpets, and the seven bowls. Here again, he is reading his position into the text. The seventh seal, the seven trumpets, and the seven bowls are events that will take a great number of months to complete (the fifth trumpet judgment alone lasts for five months). But "the last trump" is quite instantaneous; it is "in a moment," to use Paul's own words. There is no exegetical basis for connecting "the last trump" with the long, drawn out process of the seventh seal, the seven trumpets, and the seven bowls. Nor is there any reason to assume that the trumpet at the rapture is connected with the final outpouring of God's wrath. No wrath is mentioned in either passage. Furthermore, the trumpet is used in strictly blessing contexts as well. According to Isaiah 27:12-13, it will be the sound of a great trumpet that will signal the final regathering and restoration of regenerate Israel. Here is another example where Rosenthal interprets a passage based on the assumption that his view is proved and, therefore, it is read into the passage.

Cosmic Disturbance

In chapter 10, "Cosmic Disturbance," the author again deals with the Day of the Lord. How important the issue is to him is made clear in the opening statement:

> The issue developed in this chapter is crucial. It deals with a main artery leading directly to the heart of the rapture issue. It will be demonstrated that if the Day of the Lord does not start at the beginning of the seventieth week of Daniel, pretribulation rapturism is fatally flawed. It is not a matter of a hole in the dike that can be plugged—it is a veritable flood that cannot be averted. If, on the other hand, as the thesis of this book contends, the Day of the Lord starts with the opening of the seventh seal, then it will be seen that the church must enter the seventieth week of Daniel, there to experience the testing and then deliverance by rapture before the Day of the Lord begins. (p. 137)

One need not take Rosenthal's bold statement too seriously. Pretribulationism does not stand or fall upon the issue of when the

Day of the Lord actually begins in relation to the seven years. Rosenthal states the issue in such either/or terms because he is looking for evidence of his position. In this chapter, he again uses straw man arguments. He also tends to make a view that is held by some pretribulationists as being germane to the system, which it need not be. The following is one example:

> The vast majority of pretribulational writers believe
> that the Day of the Lord will begin with the rapture of
> the church—that it will encompass the entire seven-
> tieth week and beyond. (p. 138)

True; some do. But some do not. The reviewer does not start the Day of the Lord with the rapture but with the signing of the seven-year covenant. Nor does he place the Day of the Lord beyond the seven years. However, neither position actually effects pretribulationism, though Rosenthal obviously wishes that it did.

The straw man approach is Rosenthal's insistence that pretribulationists have to have the rapture take place just before, or at the start of, Daniels seventieth week. Some pretribulationists have taught this, but many have not; and that has never been this reviewer's position. Rosenthal is simply trying to force a position on all pretribulationists. One should note that Rosenthal does not provide a single passage that actually says that the Day of the Lord immediately follows the rapture. His evidences are all based either on analogy or presupposition, not on exegesis.

The analogy Rosenthal uses is that of Noah and Lot. In the day that Lot left Sodom the city was destroyed; and in the day that Noah entered into the ark, the flood came. Rosenthal states: "Noah entered the ark, then the judgment began—on the same day." The statement is correct for Lot, and the text does teach that Sodom was destroyed the same day Lot left Sodom. But, the statement is *not* true in reference to Noah. Luke 17:27 simply states "that Noah entered into the ark, and the flood came, and destroyed them all." There is nothing Jesus said that implies that the judgment came "on the same day" that Noah entered the ark. In fact, Genesis 7:10 states that the waters of the flood began seven days *after* Noah entered the ark, and then continued forty days. The flood did not come the same day that Noah entered the ark, nor was all flesh destroyed in that day. So, Rosenthal's own analogy breaks down. Just as there was a period of time between Noah entering the ark and the start of the rain, so there can also be a period of time between the rapture and the start of the seven years.

Rosenthal's concluding statement, "Deliverance of the righteous immediately precedes judgment of the wicked" (p. 140), is a fallacy. His comment that "to postulate a period of time between rapture (deliverance) and wrath (judgment) is to contradict the Scriptures," (p. 140) is patently untrue, and *none* of the passages he cites prove this bold assertion. Rosenthal intends to assert this so as to prove pretribulationism wrong and his own view right. He wants to insist that pretribulationism requires that the rapture take place immediately before, or at the beginning of, the seven years. This is *not* a biblical, theological, or exegetical necessity for pretribulationism.

Now, what about the first six seals? Rosenthal insists that they are not part of the wrath of God or part of the judgment of God; they only show what men do to men. It is hard to escape the conclusion that Rosenthal must do all kinds of exegetical gymnastics to deny that the seals are a divine judgment of God.

Rosenthal claims that right through the first five seals God is inactive, and that what happens only happens because of His permissive will, not His active will. One must ignore the obvious to conclude this and, when the obvious does become apparent, to place a smoke screen between God's active and permissive will. The fact is, Jesus Christ has exactly the *same* relationship to the first five seals as He does to the last two. It is Christ who is opening all seven seals. To claim that Christ is passive in the first five and active in the last two is only to presuppose one's position in the text. It is not exegetically sound. Christ opens all seven seals and all have negative consequences on earth. They are all judgments. A more proper biblical distinction is to say that sometimes God judges directly (flood; overthrow of Sodom), and sometimes indirectly (Egypt; Babylonia), but that He is active in both types, responsible for both types, and that both types are the judgments of God and evidences of His wrath.

Rosenthal's evidence against the first five as being judgments of God focuses on the first and fifth seals. The first seal, he argues, represents the Antichrist. Then he states: "To attribute the emergence of the Antichrist to God is obviously preposterous." But is it? Who is responsible for placing kings and rulers on earthly thrones?

According to Daniel, it is God who rules over the kingdoms of men and appoints human rule "to whomever He will" (Dan. 4:25; 5:17, 21). Furthermore, it is God who raises up even "the basest of men" at times. It was God who appointed Nebuchadnezzar to punish Israel. Sennecherib the Assyrian was merely a tool in God's hand to punish Israel (Isa. 10:5). Jesus told Pilate that his authority was given to him "from above." Pilate used that authority to execute Jesus.

The Habakkuk Model

Actually, Rosenthal's dilemma has already been settled by Habakkuk. After the prophet complains to God about Judah's sinfulness (1:2-4), God answered that He was doing a marvel, for He will raise up the Babylonians to punish Israel (1:5-11). This was not a passive work of God, or even merely something that happened by His permissive will. God is viewed as very active (1:5) in bringing about the Babylonian destruction of Judah. But now Habakkuk has a new problem (apparently the same as Rosenthal's). How could God use a people as sinful as the Babylonians to punish a less sinful people (1:12–2:1)? God's answer was that when Babylon has accomplished His will upon Israel, then He will punish Babylon (2:2-20). There is no theological or biblical problem with viewing the emergence of the Antichrist as a judgment of God. Once the Antichrist has accomplished God's purpose in relation to Israel and the Gentiles, the Antichrist will also be judged. All this shows that Rosenthal is merely assuming a problem that is not really there. God once even sent a demon to trouble Saul (1 Sam. 16:14). Just as Sennecherib and Nebuchadnezzar were raised up by God to be instruments of divine judgment, so is the Antichrist.

Rosenthal's argument that if God is responsible for the emergence of the Antichrist then "God alone must take direct responsibility for a counterfeit religious system," is flawed logic. God created Satan, but He cannot be held directly responsible for Satan's fall and his counterfeit system. Closer to the issue at hand is that even though God did bring the Assyrian and Babylonian monarchs to their positions, that does not make Him directly responsible for their idolatry.

A simple, honest look at Revelation 6, without preconceived notions, clearly shows that all the seals are divine judgments from

God. Thus the judgment of God is already present in the first half of the seven years—the place where Rosenthal himself puts the first five seals.

When Does the Day of the Lord Begin?

The point Rosenthal is trying to make throughout the chapter is that a major cosmic disturbance is predicted to take place *before* the Day of the Lord. If the Day of the Lord starts at the beginning of the seven years, then the cosmic disturbance must take place before the seven years and this, in turn, destroys the doctrine of imminency, and that, in turn, destroys pretribulationism. But this is all wishful thinking in which Rosenthal makes both a logical and an exegetical mistake.

First, as to his exegetical error, Rosenthal lumps all mentioned cosmic disturbances into one, ignoring the timing given in the text. For example, the Isaiah 13:9-10 and Joel 3:14-15 passages clearly take place *within* the Day of the Lord, as even a casual reading of the text will show. Joel 2:30-31 describes cosmic disturbances *before* the Day of the Lord. In the prophetic scheme of things, there are several cosmic disturbances. Rosenthal cites one, Revelation 6:12-13, in connection with the seventh seal. But there are also cosmic disturbances in connection with the fourth trumpet (8:12), the fifth trumpet (8:10-11), the seventh bowl (16:17-21), and so on. There are several cosmic disturbances throughout the end times, not just one. Rosennthal needs to reduce all prophesied cosmic disturbances into one for his view to hold; a pretribulationist does not.

Second, as to his logical error, Rosenthal insists that if a pretribulationist starts the Day of the Lord at the beginning of the seven years, then one cosmic disturbance must take place before the seven years; and just as soon as you have something before the seven years, you have destroyed imminency and, with it, pretribulationism. Hence, this whole argument rests on the erroneous assumption that pretribulationism requires the rapture to occur just before, or right at the start of, the seven years. This, again, is a straw man argument. As has been shown before, this is what Rosenthal wants all pretribulationists to believe, but it is patently untrue. This reviewer believes the following two points: the rapture will occur before the seven years; and, a major cosmic disturbance will come before the seven years. However, it is impossible to know which will come first. Imminency is not destroyed and neither, for that matter, is pretribulationism.

Rosenthal has not succeeded in showing that the Day of the Lord is limited to the last quarter. One can hold that all seven years are the Day of the Lord, but there will be a cosmic disturbance before and even during it. The sixth seal does portray a cosmic disturbance, but nowhere does it say that it is that cosmic disturbance which kicks off the Day of the Lord. It is Rosenthal's system which requires that identification and correlation, not exegesis. For Rosenthal's system to stand, it is crucial to begin the Day of the Lord with both Revelation 8:1 and the seventh seal. However, *nothing* in the text states that that is when the Day of the Lord begins. With Old Testament predictions about the Day of the Lord already being found in chapter 6, it is best to begin the Day of the Lord in 6:1.

The Day of His Wrath

In chapter 12, "The Day of His Wrath," Rosenthal again works on the presupposition that the wrath of God and the Day of the Lord are synonymous terms. But they are not. There is already present a wrath of God revealed against the ungodliness and unrighteousness of men (Rom. 1:18), yet we are not in the Day of the Lord. To make the Day of the Lord and the wrath of God exactly the same is only a presupposition, not a clearly stated biblical fact.

Rosenthal then deals with the aorist tense and correctly states that it can be used either for a past or future event and, for that matter, a present event. Ultimately, context determines what the aorist tense means in a given place. Because many pretribulationists view the aorist of Revelation 6:17 as describing past events, relating to all the preceding seals—or, at least, concerning the events of the sixth seal—Rosenthal objects, since the aorist does not *have* to mean that. He is correct: it does not *have* to mean that. But, Rosenthal then insists that it should be taken as a future tense, in reference to the seventh seal and all that it contains: the trumpets and the bowls. It *could* mean that. But, again, it does not have to. As Rosenthal admits, "it can refer to either a past action or an event still future." Rosenthal, grammatically speaking, has no more basis to take it as a future event than pretribulationists have to take it as a past event. What Rosenthal then does is cite examples from where it is found with the future meaning. However, all this proves is that in those passages it is to be understood as a future tense. This is not proof-positive that it has a future meaning in Revelation 6:17. One could cite passages elsewhere, where it has a past meaning (Rev. 5:7; 7:13; 8:3; 11:18; 17:1,10; 21:9), but that is not proof-positive of a past meaning in Revelation 6:17. It is best to go with the context, especially the *immediate* context, and see if it indicates how best to take the aorist.

It should be noted that the future use of the aorist is rare, and normally it refers to a past act. There is no grammatical or contextual reason to make the usage in Revelation 6:17 future. It is only a theological necessity for Rosenthal. The context does not favor a future meaning. Rosenthal insists that the wrath is a reference to the seventh seal, which does not come until Revelation 8:1, some distance away. Between 6:17 and 8:1, the 17 verses of chapter 7 intervene. The seventh seal is not in the immediate context. Those speaking the text of 6:17 are, in context, responding to the cosmic convulsions of verses 12-14, for it is the events of the sixth seal that cause the unbelieving world to flee to the mountains and cry that the wrath of God is come. So the context favors a past and not a future reference. While the *wrath* of 6:17 may not refer to all the preceding seals (though it may), it at least refers to the events of the sixth seal. While grammatically the aorist tense is inconclusive for either view, context favors the past view and the pretribulational view. The context shows that during the judgments of the first four seals humanity did not recognize it as coming from God, but with the fifth seal they do recognize it as coming from God, and not just the first seal but all five seals so far.

It is correct, as Rosenthal claims, that there is no *grammatical* reason to make the aorist tense of the sixth seal retroactive; but neither is there a *grammatical* reason to make it future. But there is another grammatical reason to make it past. In the Greek text, the word for "come" is not only an aorist, but it is in the indicative mood. According to Greek grammarians, such as Dana and Mantey, this always refers to a past and not to a future event. Rosenthal would have done well to check all references where this word is found just in the Greek of Revelation. It is found a total of 11 other times: 5:7; 7:13; 8:3; 11:18; 14:7,15; 17:1,10; 18:10; 19:7; 21:9. In all these examples the word is used of a past event or a present event. Not once is it used of a future event. Rosenthal is forced to make the Greek of 6:17 the exception to the rule. But, this is *not* a result of exegesis. It is clearly a theological necessity for Rosenthal's view. This is interpreting a verse based on one's own preconceived theology.

The answer to Rosenthal's question: "If God's wrath begins with the first seal, as pretribulationism normally asserts, why do men not flee from God's wrath until after the sixth seal is opened...?" (p. 169) is quite simple. While the first five seals are judgments of God, these judgments come through human agencies, and so the unbelieving world does not discern them to be from God. But the sixth seal results in cosmic convulsions, in which it will be obvious to everyone that no human agency is involved, and so they flee. Rosenthal's argument is easily answered. Yet, Rosenthal continues to strain himself when he writes:

> ...in the phrase, "the great day of his wrath is come; and who shall be able to stand?" John is undeniably alluding to Malachi 3:2. The prophet Malachi wrote, "But who may abide the day of his coming? And who shall stand when he appeareth?" In Revelation 6:17 what John calls "the great day of his wrath," Malachi calls the "day of his coming" and "when he appeareth." Therefore, the expressions *the day of the Lord, coming*, and *appearance* are tied together and used interchangeably in anticipation of the opening of the seventh seal. Since the "coming" is intimately associated with the Day of the Lord, it is impossible to have the Day of the Lord commence within the seventieth week and the Lord's coming for the church be pretribulational. (p. 170)

One should again note Rosenthal's presuppositions in the word "undeniably." It is *undeniable* that Revelation 6:17 is an allusion to Malachi 3:2! But is it? First of all, John is quoting what unbelievers will be saying, *the wrath of God is come*, and it stretches credulity that the unbelievers of Revelation 6:17, responding to the cosmic events of the sixth seal, are consciously alluding to Malachi 3:2. That assumes an awful lot of knowledge on the part of Gentile unbelievers! Second, there is little, if any, linguistic similarity between the two passages. Revelation is speaking of a process and a period of time in which divine judgments are poured out—whether the entire seven years or just the first 21 months. But Malachi is speaking of the actual day of the second coming. For Rosenthal to use this as an argument against pretribulationism is extremely weak.

Wrath in Revelation

Rosenthal next focuses on how the word "wrath" is used in Revelation (pp. 171-72). He again operates on the basis of assumptions, and he also misses an important observation as to what the "wrath" is. The assumption is that the "wrath" of Revelation 6:16-17 is a reference to the seventh seal, but contextually it is best taken with the sixth seal, with a question mark as to whether it also includes the first five seals. Another assumption is that the Day-of-the-Lord wrath begins in Revelation 6:17, but that passage does not mention the Day of the Lord, and Rosenthal only reads his theology into it.

So what has Rosenthal actually proved, and what has he failed to observe? First, he states that the word "wrath" is not found before Revelation 6:16-17. This is true. But who in this passage is actually identifying the sixth (or, as Rosenthal prefers, the seventh) seal as being the wrath of God? It is not God, nor an angel, nor even John. It is the unbelievers, and John is quoting the conclusion of unbelievers, which may, or may not, be correct. Much of Rosenthal's position is based on the words spoken by these unbelievers in Revelation 6:16-17. If what the unbelievers conclude here is truly the Word of God, then what about the conclusion of the unbelievers in Revelation 13:4? Second, when the wrath of God is identified by John, angels, or God, it never identifies any of the seal judgments as wrath, nor even the first six trumpet judgments. As mentioned earlier, the usage of "wrath" in Revelation is far more limited than even Rosenthal makes it, for it is used *only* of the bowl judgments and the seventh trumpet, which contains the seven bowl judgments. Rosenthal's own listing of the passages on page 172 shows this to be true. Every usage of "wrath" in Revelation is in reference to the bowl judgments. The only exception is Revelation 6:16-17, which quotes the conclusion of unbelievers; but that conclusion is not affirmed by John, angels, or God. When John, angels, or God uses the term "wrath," it is only of the bowl judgments, which Rosenthal, by a strained exegesis of Daniel 12:11, limits to the last 30 days.

On page 173, he writes "none of the seals are angelically induced. The reason is clear: the seals are not God's wrath." Here is yet another presupposition: the wrath of God must be "angelically induced." There is simply no such biblical statement. The wrath of God on Israel in Luke 21:23 was not angelically induced but carried out by human agency: the Romans. Although Rosenthal claims here that "the seals are not God's wrath," he earlier claimed that the seventh seal is; and that seal, like the first six, is opened by Christ. Again, only the bowl judgments are actually called "wrath" in Revelation. The seals may not be angelically induced, but they are induced by Christ, which is far more direct.

Chapter 13 is titled, "The 144,000 and a Great Multitude No Man Could Number." By this chapter, Rosenthal has built up and compounded a number of assumptions to hold his "unassailable" superstructure.

The first assumption is that the first five seals cover the entire first half of the seven years. However, there is nothing in the text that even implies that. In fact, the book of Revelation itself clearly indicates when the second half begins. As Rosenthal himself believes, it is the "abomination of desolation" that marks the middle of the seven years. This involves the Gentile takeover of the temple compound. That takeover is described in Revelation 11:1-2. The second half in Revelation begins only in chapter 11, and Revelation chapters 11–14 describe midtribulational events, concluding with the bowl judgments (Rev. 15–16) in the second half. But because the middle point begins only with Revelation 11:1, this puts not only the first four seals but all of the seal judgments and the first six trumpets into the first half.

The second assumption is that the Great Tribulation begins with the fifth seal, but there is nothing in the context of the fifth seal that indicates this. For Rosenthal, the Great Tribulation is the first part of the second half. But, again, following Revelation's own chronology, the second half begins with chapter 11. Rosenthal's basis is the usage of the term in Matthew 24:21, which follows the abomination of desolation in 24:15. However, Matthew 24:15 corresponds to Revelation 11:12, and both kick off the second three-and-one-half years. The "persecution" of in Matthew 24 follows the abomination, and the "persecution" spoken of in the fifth seal precedes it. The two passages do not speak of the same persecutions but two distinct ones. The persecution spoken of Matthew 24 is against the Jews, something Rosenthal himself believes and teaches. The persecution of the fifth seal saints is that of believers in general, and nothing in the text or context of Revelation 6 implies that it is a persecution of Jews. Later, Revelation 12 does speak of persecution of Jews, and that persecution of Revelation 12 follows the Gentile takeover of Jerusalem and the temple in chapter 11, just as in Matthew 24. It is Revelation 11–12, then, that corresponds with Matthew 24:15-28, not Revelation 6. The persecution of the fifth seal saints corresponds with the persecution of believers found in Matthew 24:9-10, which precedes the midpoint, which itself only begins in Matthew 24:15. This puts the fifth seal in the first half.

The third assumption is that the fifth seal saints are martyred because they would not bow to the Antichrist. Again, there is nothing in the context of the fifth seal to indicate this. To be sure, they are martyred for their faith. But the text does not say that it was specifically for refusing to bow down to the Antichrist. The self-proclamation of deity by the Antichrist takes place at the time of the abomination of desolation (Matthew 24:15; 2 Thess. 2:4), which, as Rosenthal asserts, happens at the midpoint of the seven years. In Revelation, that midpoint begins with chapter 11, when the temple is taken over by Gentiles for 42 months (the second three-and-one-half years). The Antichrist then proceeds to remove all opposition by killing the two witnesses (chapter 11) and by persecuting the Jews (chapter 12). He then proclaims himself to be God and sets up his image (chapter 13). Only those saints in and subsequent to chapter 13 are being killed for refusing to accept the Antichrist. The saints of chapter 6 come well before this, for those saints are part of the fifth seal, while those of chapter 13 follow the second trumpet (chapter 11). Rosenthal is doing exactly what he accuses pretribulationists of doing: trying to "grandfather clause" the events of Revelation 11–13 to come before the sixth seal of Revelation 6, and this with a lot less exegetical validity. Is it possible to know who is killing the fifth seal saints if it is not the Antichrist? The Antichrist is not the only one persecuting the saints in the seven years. Revelation 17 provides further details on how the Antichrist takes over world religion and political control.

Using typical Old Testament imagery, John pictures a great harlot—in the Old Testament, a symbol of a false religious system—who rules over the world, at least in a religious sense (17:1,15). Verses 16-17 state two things. First, all other political rulers turn their authority over to the Antichrist. Second, the Antichrist and the other kings then destroy whatever system the harlot represents. In this way, the Antichrist destroys both political and religious opposition to himself. Now, the political and religious rule of the Antichrist takes place during the second half of the seven years (Revelation 13:5), as Rosenthal himself teaches. The harlot is destroyed in the middle of the seven years, and then the Antichrist rules for the second half This also means that the worldwide religious rule of the harlot must be during the first half of the seven years. The religious system of the first half is represented as the harlot. She is destroyed in the middle, and the religious system of the second half is the worship of the Antichrist. Not only does the Antichrist persecute believers (during the second half), this religious system of the harlot also persecutes the saints (17:6); so this persecution must be during the first half, which is when the fifth seal saints are martyred. The fifth seal saints, then, were not killed by the Antichrist in the second half but by the harlot in the first half. This simple solution is in keeping with the chronology of Revelation itself.

The fourth assumption is that the sixth seal announces the wrath of God which comes with the seventh seal. This point has already been discussed. *It is important to emphasize how much of Rosenthal's view is based on his assumptions rather than on exegesis.* Rosenthal insists that there is no other way to understand this if one is honest and a lover of God's Word. But as this critique is trying to show, these are not the only ways, nor even the best ways, of explaining these texts.

The 144,000 Witnesses

On pages 181-82, Rosenthal turns to the issue of the 144,000 and more presuppositions come forth. He again insists that angels must be involved in the wrath of God. Since the first five seals did not involve angels, they would not be part of the wrath of God. Therefore, the wrath can only begin with the sixth seal. There is simply no basis for such a presupposition. The simple use of a concordance will show that when God poured out His wrath in history, angels were not always involved. The citing of 2 Thessalonians 1:7-8 proves nothing, as it is speaking of the second coming when He will come with His angels. That angels have been used, and will be used, to pour out God's judgment, is not the issue. The issue is: Are angels *always* involved in the wrath of God? The answer is *no*!

As to the issue of the rapture's timing, Rosenthal insists that the 144,000 must be sealed before God can pour out His wrath. Since the wrath of God begins with the seventh seal, the 144,000 are sealed between the sixth and seventh seals. One cannot be sure exactly how this relates to the rapture's timing. If the rapture takes place with the seventh seal, and if the 144,000 are sealed between the sixth and seventh seals, then the 144,000 would leave the earth in the rapture. But Rosenthal has them on earth throughout the wrath of God, for they are "sealed for protection from that wrath." This is just one of several inconsistencies and contradictions.

The Great Multitude

Rosenthal next goes on to deal with the great multitude of Revelation 7 which he identifies as the church (pp. 183-85). His opening statement is that the "identification of this great multitude in heaven is of importance," because this great multitude is the church. If this can be substantiated, he has proved his point. In fact, within the book of Revelation, this would be the only place where the church is seen in heaven, following Rosenthal's short Great Tribulation, which these saints have "come out from." If it can be shown that these are church saints, his point is largely proven. If not, then Rosenthal has lost his best evidence. He seems to sense the weakness of his position in a footnote. After admitting that the identification of the great multitude is important, a footnote seems to deny it:

> The identity of the "great multitude" of Revelation 7 is not crucial to the prewrath rapture. The biblical evidence, however, strongly favors identifying them as the raptured church in heaven before the Day of the Lord commences (p. 304).

But the fact is, the identity of the "great multitude" *is* crucial to his argument. Within the book of Revelation, this is pretty much all he has!

Another point is ignored by Rosenthal. If this great multitude is the church, then, of necessity, this is only a partial rapture, something Rosenthal himself does not espouse. Verses 13-17 state that these saints came out of the Great Tribulation. This would exclude all church saints who have died since Acts 2, or who will die before the Great Tribulation. This shows that the great multitude simply cannot be the church, the whole body of Christ. Rosenthal ignores such details in the text.

The Last Trump

Rosenthal's sweeping statement in chapter 14 that "pretribulation rapturists do not make strong appeal to Paul's statement that the rapture will occur before the last trump to support their position," (pp. 189-90) should not be taken seriously. Anyone well-versed in pretribulationism knows that the statement is both untrue and unfair. Rosenthal avoids the trap that both midtribulationists and post-tribulationalists fall into by being careful not to connect "the last trump" with the seventh trumpet of Revelation; the Corinthians, after all, would have no knowledge of the book of Revelation. As he correctly observes, "The Corinthians had to understand the significance of the phrase 'at the last trump' without any knowledge of the book of Revelation, which had not yet been written" (pp. 190-91). Rosenthal's identification is not of a specific trumpet sound, but to a more general trumpet that includes all seven trumpets and seven bowls; but he must of necessity prove it from a passage outside of Revelation. His definition of the last trump is: "The last trump will be nothing more, nothing less, and nothing different than the final, climactic, eschatological outpouring of the wrath of God" (p. 193).

Rosenthal, again, does not identify the last trump with the seventh trumpet, but he generalizes it as a collective of all the seven trumpets and bowls combined in the seventh seal. His "last trump" is really a period of 21 months, rather than a specific point of time which signals the rapture. To reach this conclusion, Rosenthal makes the trumpet of Joel 2:1, 1 Corinthians 15:52, 1 Thessalonians 4:16, and the seven trumpets of Revelation 8–9 all the same "last trump." Would anyone arrive at such a conclusion if he did not approach all these texts with a preconceived theology? This is an impossible conclusion purely on exegetical grounds. Another point, which should not be missed, is that the author insists that the rapture takes place with the breaking of the seventh seal. If so, why then is the rapture not mentioned here?

The Coming and the End

In chapter 16, titled "The Coming and the End," Rosenthal begins a semantic approach in which he is merely playing word games. His argument is that the second coming is a "comprehensive whole," and that this composite whole includes "the rapture of the church, the outpouring of God's wrath during the Day of the Lord, and Christ's physical return in glory" (pp. 221-22). He says that the pretribulation rapture requires two comings, while his own view requires only one. This is pure foolishness and completely illogical. What Rosenthal says about his own view can be claimed by both midtribulationists and pretribulationists. If the rapture takes place at the three-quarter point, and if this rapture is followed by a period of time (Rosenthal's Day of the Lord), and if this period of time is followed by "Christ's physical return" to the earth, then this view has the same number of appearances of Christ as the mid- and pretribulationist views. The only difference is the actual amount of time between "the rapture of the church" and "Christ's physical return in glory."

In reference to 1 Thessalonians 5:2, Rosenthal put forth an argument that is a product of shallow exegesis, and again requires a presupposition of the position in order to be true. He states: "The apostle Paul warned the Thessalonians that the Lord's coming (*parousia*) would be as 'a thief in the night'" (p. 224). From this statement, he goes on to claim that while Paul teaches that the *parousia* (the second coming) will catch the unbelievers by surprise, it will not catch the believers by surprise. He then gives what he thinks is a blow to pretribulationism. If the rapture is both pretribulational and imminent, then this *parousia* "will, of an absolute necessity, return as 'a thief in the night' even for the believers."

His treatment and exegesis of the text borders on sloppiness, reading into it words and concepts which are not there and ignoring the actual wording that is there. Nowhere in 1 Thessalonians 5:2 does Paul mention the *parousia*, although a reader would think otherwise based on Rosenthal's wording. Paul is not saying that the *parousia* will overtake the unbeliever as a thief in the night, but that the Day of the Lord will overtake them like that. Paul dealt with the rapture in 4:13-18, and he introduced a new subject in 5:1, as the Greek *peri de* construction shows. That new subject is the Day of the Lord, or the Tribulation, and that day will overtake the unbeliever. The passage then states that it will not overtake the believers, though Rosenthal ignores the reason why. The reason is given in 5:9: God appointed the believer "not unto wrath." In context, the "wrath" of 5:9 is the Day of the Lord in 5:2. Because the wrath of God is not for the believer, the believer is removed before the Day of the Lord occurs. The means of the believer's removal is by the rapture of 4:13-18. This fits quite well with pretribulationism, and it is in keeping with what the subject of 5:1-11 is: not the *parousia*, but the Day of the Lord.

In chapter 17, titled "Kept From the Hour," Rosenthal states why people of all rapture views have been wrong until he came along:

> However, because commentators have not generally understood that there are *three* sections to the seventieth week—the beginning birth pangs, the Great Tribulation, and the Day of the Lord—they have, in the view of this author, made a fundamental error (p. 233).

Rosenthal's "fundamental error" is the failure to recognize the fact that the seventieth week of Daniel has three, and not two, divisions. It is assumed that *all* leading biblical, theological, and Greek scholars from *all* other rapture views have missed something so simple. Yet there is a good reason why all three schools of thought have missed it: it is simply not there! Whenever the timing of the rapture is spoken of, it is always in two parts, not three. Either the whole seven years is spoken of, or only a half of the period is spoken of, but never a quarter. The first reference, Daniel 9:27, speaks of all seven years and divides it into two equal parts rather than three. All other time references are always of the first or second half. Daniel and Revelation use phrases such as: "Time, times and half a time;" "42 months;" and "1,260 days." These are all equivalent to three-and-a-half years, either the first half or the second half. There is never any reference to 21 months or 630 days. The point is that there is no exegetical validation for dividing the seventieth week into three parts. This is not required by exegesis, only by Rosenthal's view.

The Day of Jehovah

Part of Rosenthal's scheme is to distinguish between the Great Tribulation and the Day of the Lord. However, a comparison of the Scriptures on the "Great Tribulation" and the "Day of Jehovah" shows that these are not separate time frames, but that they all refer to the same thing. The key is to compare the Scriptures that describe a period of time which is unparalleled and worse than any other time in human history, past or future. The first passage is Jeremiah 30:7

> Alas! for that day is great, so that none is like it: it is even the time of Jacob's trouble (ASV).

Jeremiah's "time of Jacob's trouble" is a day so "great, so that none is like it." The second passage is Daniel 12:1:

> And at that time shall Michael stand up, the great prince who standeth for the children of thy people; and there shall be a time of trouble, such as never was since there was a nation even to that same time (ASV).

Daniel is speaking of the "time of trouble" that is to fall upon the Jewish people. Concerning this time of trouble, he states "such as never was since there was a nation even to that same time." The third passage is Joel 2:1-2:

> Blow ye the trumpet in Zion, and sound an alarm in my holy mountain; let all the inhabitants of the land tremble: for the day of Jehovah cometh, for it is nigh at hand; a day of darkness and gloominess, a day of clouds and thick darkness, as the dawn spread upon the mountains; a great people and a strong; there hath not been ever the like, neither shall be any more after them, even to the years of many generations (ASV).

Here, Joel is describing the "day of Jehovah," and he describes it as, "there hath not been ever the like, neither shall be any more after them, even to the years of many generations." The fourth passage is Matthew 24:21:

> ...for then shall be great tribulation, such as hath not
> been from the beginning of the world until now, no,
> nor ever shall be.

Jesus is clearly speaking of the "Great Tribulation," of which He says, "such as hath not been from the beginning of the world until now, no, nor ever shall be."

All four spoke of a day, or period, which is unparalleled and unique in all of time, both past and future. It is obvious that there can only be one worst and unparalleled time, and so all four men were speaking of the same time. Joel called it "the Day of Jehovah"; Jesus called it the "Great Tribulation"; Jeremiah called it "the time of Jacob's trouble" [the Hebrew word for "trouble" was translated by the Septuagint (LXX) with the Greek word used by the New Testament for "tribulation"]; Daniel called it "a time of trouble," which is also translated by the LXX by the same Greek word. Furthermore, Daniel, in context, is detailing further the seventieth week of Daniel, especially the second half (12:5-7). All of this shows that the terms "Day of the Lord," "great tribulation," "time of trouble," and "time of Jacob's trouble" all refer to the same period of time, and are not distinctive "time zones" in that span of time. What Joel says about the Day of the Lord, Jesus says about the Great Tribulation. There is no exegetical justification for distinguishing the Great Tribulation from the Day of Jehovah, and even less so to make the seventieth week of Daniel three different periods rather than the obvious two periods found in the Scriptures.

Revelation 3:10

What about the key passage of Revelation 3:10? Rosenthal deals with the crucial verse of Revelation 3:10, but interprets it entirely on the presupposition that his view is already true (pp. 237-40). In doing so, he accuses others of failing to use the literal hermeneutic, even though he does exactly what he accuses others of doing. Rosenthal accuses all those who make the promise of Revelation 3:10 a general promise of being guilty of interpreting "the Scriptures non-literally." Yet Rosenthal himself ignores a strict literal interpretation. He insists that the promise of 3:10 is made only to the church of Philadelphia and declares that "no such exemption is promised to the other six churches." But what is the church of Philadelphia? If Rosenthal follows a strictly literal approach, he would have to limit the promise to the believers living at that time in the city of Philadelphia in Asia Minor, or modern-day Turkey. That church has long since disappeared; a visitor would be hard pressed to find an evangelical church in Philadelphia today. Revelation 3:10 can no longer be fulfilled to the church of Philadelphia, for it is no longer there. But Rosenthal does not follow literal interpretation. He interprets the promise of 3:10 to those believers who "faithfully endured during the adversity of the first three and one half years." This, of course, hardly limits the promise to the church of Philadelphia and would easily include members of the other six churches that have faithfully endured adversity. Those believers in this definition, Rosenthal states, "are exemplified by the church of Philadelphia." However, this, too, is taking the passage "nonliterally," and one must be absolutely blind not to notice the self-contradiction within such few paragraphs.

What Rosenthal is trying hard to do is to avoid the obvious implication of 3:10: that the church is somehow exempt from "the hour of trial" which is about to fall upon the whole earth, as detailed in chapters 6–18 of Revelation, a section where the church is not mentioned even once, in spite of its frequent mention in the first three chapters.

Why This View Now?

In chapter 19, "The Prewrath Rapture: Why This View Now?" Rosenthal answers by viewing himself as being part of the fulfillment of the Daniel 12:4 prophecy that knowledge will be increased in the last days. He forwards his view as a fulfillment of that prophecy (pp. 276-78). In this same chapter (pp. 267-68), he argues his view of the rapture from Daniel 12:1-3. But there is no rapture there; furthermore, Daniel is clearly speaking of Israel and not the church. The resurrection is, in fact, of the Old Testament saints and not the church saints.

Catalyst for Holy Living?

The final chapter is titled, "The Prewrath Rapture: Catalyst for Holy Living." Here, Rosenthal tries to show that his view will produce holy living and spiritual maturity for future adversity in a way superior to that of pretribulationism. Such an assertion is yet to be proven and is purely subjective. This reviewer's observations of pretribulationists and their holy living and spiritual maturity in the face of adversity has been, for him, unmatched by others. They have greatly influenced his own spiritual growth and also stirred a deep interest for greater knowledge of God's Word. In this chapter, Rosenthal again uses a straw man argument by a false definition of imminency:

> Perhaps here is the ultimate error of pretribulation rapturism. It holds out the false hope of *imminent* rapture,...A careful appeal to verses said to teach imminency (no prophesied events must occur before the Rapture)...(p. 282).

Again, imminency does *not* mean that "no prophesied events must occur before the rapture." Imminency means that no prophesied event *must* be fulfilled before the rapture, although the possibility does exist. The reestablishment of Israel in 1948 was a prophesied event; imminency means that this event did not have to come before the rapture, although nothing ruled out the possibility. Imminency means that the rapture could have come either before or after 1948. There may even be other pretribulational prophesies that will be fulfilled before the rapture. On the other hand, they may not. That is the meaning of imminency, rather than what Rosenthal wants it to mean.

Conclusion

The rapture is indeed pre-wrath, but in order to be that it must also be pretribulational. This review has not dealt with every issue raised by Rosenthal, but it has dealt with his major arguments. For them to stand, many of the others merely presuppose that the view is true. Rosenthal has labeled pretribulationism as "wrong or inconsistent" (p. 33); "facing impossible-to-resolve problems" (p. 197); having "insurmountable exegetical" difficulties (p. 147); not to mention being "calamitous," and that it could cause "a spiritual catastrophe" and "a satanically planned sneak attack" (pp. 281-82). This review has attempted to show that such descriptive epitaphs are far from true. Rosenthal has also described his own view as being one of "simplicity, clarity, logic" and "the fruit of an unstrained, clear, unified, and normative interpretation of the Word of God" (p. 31). Its evidence is "strong and compelling, the reason clear and logical" (p. 67); and is "unstrained and biblically accurate" (p. 194). As this reviewer has shown, merely saying so does not make it so, and Rosenthal's work is not as intimidating as he seems to think.

This work is the latest in a long line of attacks by various sources on pretribulationism. As pretribulationism survived all the others, it will much easier survive this one. It is pretribulationism that is "not built upon sand" and which "has the Word of God to sustain it." That is why it has survived all previous attacks, and why it will survive this one.

20

Robert L. Thomas

A Critique of Progressive Dispensational Hermeneutics

_____*OVERVIEW*

How does a new form of dispensationalism, which calls itself "Progressive Dispensationalism," interpret Scripture? Is this new interpretative approach a help or hindrance in its support of the pretribulational rapture? The author of this essay identifies crucial differences between traditional dispensational literalism and the more subjective aspects of progressive dispensationalism. See why the author believes that the hermeneutics of progressive dispensationalism will lead to an undermining of pretribulationalism.

A recent development related to the pretribulational rapture has come from a relatively new movement calling
itself "Progressive Dispensationalism" (hereafter usually designated "PD"). For the most part, progressive dispensationalists
believe in a rapture prior to the future seven-year Tribulation, but
they do so in a rather tentative fashion.[1] Their system could dis-
pense with this doctrine without altering their position significantly.

A closer look at PD will clarify why its adherents do not hold
the pretrib view to be crucial. The name "Progressive Dispensationalism" derives from the proclivity of its adherents to see
themselves in the lineage of dispensational theology, and from the
understanding that dispensations are not different arrangements
between God and the human race but successive arrangements in the
progressive revelation and accomplishment of redemption.[2] An
attempt at defining PD must remain vague for the time being
because progressive dispensationalists themselves are still trying to
define it. The title of a recent book, *Dispensationalism, Israel, and
the Church: The Search for Definition* (1993), reflects the uncertainty of those within the movement about definition.

Lineage and Mediating Stance
of Progressive Dispensationalism

The leaders in the movement[3] view themselves and their sup-
porters as taking a further step in the continuing development
of dispensational theology.[4] For example, Bock sees himself as
combining two elements, one from what he calls Scofieldian
dispensationalism and the other from so-called essentialist dispensationalism, into his system.[5] Advocates of PD, in other words, see
themselves in the lineage of dispensational theology.

Yet they do so knowing that they are moving toward theological
systems that are nondispensational. Saucy's quest is for a mediating

position between traditional dispensationalism and nondispensationalism.[6] In this quest, however, some of his PD associates have gone far enough to suggest to outside observers that a nondispensational orientation is in their systems.[7] Bock admits the closeness of his views regarding a present kingdom to those of George Ladd's historic premillennialism—a system adverse to dispensationalism—though claiming a distinction regarding the future kingdom.[8] In fact, the desire for cordial relations with theologians of other systems appears to be a primary motivation behind the emergence of PD.

Hermeneutical Self-Assessment
of Progressive Dispensationalism

With PD's desire for cordial relations has come a hermeneutical shift away from literal interpretation—also call the grammatical-historical method—which has been one of the ongoing hallmarks of dispensationalism.[9] In late twentieth-century writings, advocates of this developing theological perspective have shifted in the direction of nondispensational systems by adopting some of the same hermeneutical practices as found in these other systems. For whatever reason, proponents of PD sometimes call their hermeneutics by the name "grammatical-historical," but they mean something quite different by the phrase. Blaising and Bock confirm this difference:

> Evangelical grammatical-historical interpretation was...
> broadening in the mid-twentieth century to include
> the field of biblical theology. Grammatical analysis
> expanded to include developments in literary study,
> particularly in the study of genre, or literary form, and
> rhetorical structure. Historical interpretation came to
> include a reference to the historical and cultural con-
> text of individual literary pieces for their overall
> interpretation. And by the late 1980s, evangelicals
> became more aware of the problem of the inter-
> preter's historical context and traditional preunder-
> standing of the text being interpreted. These develop-
> ments...have opened up new vistas for discussion
> which were not considered by earlier interpreters,
> including classical and many revised dispensational-
> ists. These are developments which have led to what
> is now called "progressive dispensationalism."[10]

So the hermeneutics of PD represent a significant discontinuity in their alleged lineage of dispensationalism. The recent and more sophisticated "grammatical-historical" interpretation does not lead to dispensationalism, in its traditional sense, but to PD.[11]

Blaising and Bock see the continued use of "grammatical-historical" in its traditional sense as running the risk of anachronism,[12] presumably because their analysis of consensus is that *all* agree on the new principles of interpretation.[13] This appraisal of current views on hermeneutics is open to serious question. No such unanimity in favor of new interpretive approaches exists. Even if it did, who is guilty of anachronism? Is it not those who have taken traditional terminology and read into it new connotations?

Recent additions that differentiate the hermeneutics of PD from traditional dispensational hermeneutics include rhetorical and literary matters, the history of interpretation, the matter of tradition, and the historical context of the interpreter.[14] The method advocates consideration of the problem of historical distance between the text and the interpreter, the role of the interpreter's preunderstanding, and methodological applications of the hermeneutical spiral.[15] In fact, Blaising and Bock in at least one place call the approach by the name "historical-grammatical-literary-theological,"[16] which, of course, is more sophisticated and therefore quite different from simple grammatical-historical hermeneutics. It emphasizes the subjective element in its reasoning and hence is more provisional in its conclusions.[17]

This is not the appropriate forum for evaluating recent developments in hermeneutics as a whole—the trends to which these authors refer[18]—but it is appropriate to compare perspectives regarding several of the new hermeneutical principles with traditional grammatical-historical hermeneutics. For purposes of comparison, Milton S. Terry and Bernard Ramm will furnish principles pertaining to traditional grammatical-historical interpretation in the following discussion.[19]

Comparing Old and New
Hermeneutical Maxims

The following rules of interpretation will illustrate the acknowledged difference in approach to Scripture between PD and dispensationalism. They compare grammatical-historical-literary-theological interpretation with grammatical-historical interpretation.

The Function of the Interpreter

One principle that conspicuously distinguishes the two systems of interpretation relates to the interpreter's role. Traditionally, the interpreter has sought to suppress his own viewpoints regarding what he thinks the passage should mean, so as to allow the exegetical evidence from the passage under investigation to speak for itself. Terry writes:

> In the systematic presentation, therefore, of any scriptural doctrine, we are always to make a discriminating use of sound hermeneutical principles. We must not study them in the light of modern systems of divinity, but should aim rather to place ourselves in the position of the sacred writers, and study to obtain the impression their words would naturally have made upon the minds of the first readers.... Still less should we allow ourselves to be influenced by any presumptions of what the Scriptures ought to teach.... All such presumptions are uncalled for and prejudicial.[20]

> He [the interpreter] must have an intuition of nature and of human life by which to put himself in the place of the biblical writers and see and feel as they did.... He must not allow himself to be influenced by hidden meanings, and spiritualizing processes, and plausible conjectures.... Such a discriminating judgment may be trained and strengthened, and no pains should be spared to render it a safe and reliable habit of the mind.[21]

Ramm puts the principle this way:

> It is very difficult for any person to approach the Holy Scriptures free from prejudices and assumptions which distort the text. The danger of having a set theological system is that in the interpretation of Scripture the system tends to govern the interpretation rather than the interpretation correcting the system.... Calvin said that the Holy Scripture is not a tennis ball that we

may bounce around at will. Rather it is the Word of
God whose teachings must be learned by the most
impartial and objective study of the text.[22]

The hermeneutics of PD are a bold contrast to this principle of
seeking objectivity through repression of one's biases. Its relevant
principle advocates the inclusion of one's preunderstanding in the
interpretive process as a starting point. Leaders in the movement
pointedly advocate allowing one's biblical theology, and other elements of preunderstanding, to influence interpretive conclusions.
Blaising and Bock note this in a number of places, and they affirm it
as a proper evangelical procedure of interpretation.[23] For example,
Bock's preunderstanding in coming to Scripture includes the assumption that a New Testament appearance of several elements of
an Old Testament promise constitutes an initial or partial fulfillment
of that promise as a whole.[24] This foregone conclusion with which
he initiates his research is what ultimately leads him to conclude that
Christ is presently ruling from the Davidic throne in heaven.

In the words of Blaising and Bock, "Each of us has our own
way of seeing, a grid for understanding, that impacts what we expect
to see in the text, the questions we ask of it, and thus the answers we
get."[25] They apparently agree with McCartney and Clayton that
preunderstanding, not interpretive methodology, determines the end
result of interpretation.[26] This, of course, differs radically from the
quest of traditional hermeneutics for objectivity in hermeneutical
investigations.

Though not as specific as Blaising and Bock, Saucy apparently
shares this view of the hermeneutical role of preunderstanding. He
writes, "The fact that earthly human ministry still has significance
after the finality of Christ's coming leads to a second truth with
hermeneutical implications. The application of Christ's fulfillment
of the eschatological promises is progressive."[27] In coming to the
New Testament, he assumes that it contains a progressive unfolding
of the dispensations rather than seeing the church as a parenthesis.
This, of course, colors his interpretation of many aspects of revelation regarding the church.

Quite clearly, the issue of preunderstanding distinguishes the
hermeneutics of PD from principles of traditional grammatical-
historical interpretation.

The Historical Dimension

Another contrast between the two approaches lies in an understanding of the meaning of "historical" in the expression "grammatical-historical." Traditionally, the historical dimension in interpretation has referred to the historical setting of the text's origin, as Terry describes:

> The interpreter should, therefore, endeavour to take himself from the present, and to transport himself into the historical position of his author, look through his eyes, note his surroundings, feel with his heart, and catch his emotion. Herein we note the import of the term grammatico-*historical* interpretation.[28]

He states further, "Subject and predicate and subordinate clauses must be closely analyzed, and the whole document, book, or epistle, should be viewed, as far as possible from the author's historical standpoint."[29] In support of history's importance, Ramm writes, "Some interaction with the culture and history of a book of Holy Scripture is mandatory."[30] And "the interpreter must know *Biblical history.*...Every event has its historical referent in that all biblical events occur in a stream of history."[31]

Bock, on the other hand, advocates a multilayered reading of the text, which results in a "complementary" reading (or meaning) that adds to the original meaning as determined by the text's original setting. The "complementary" perspective views the text from the standpoint of later events, not the events connected with the text's origin.[32] He also proposes a third layer of reading, that of the entire biblical canon.[33] In essence, he sees three possible interpretations of a single text, only one of which pertains to the text's original historical setting. He refers to his method as a historical-grammatical-literary reading of the text.[34] He notes that "such a hermeneutic produces layers of sense and specificity for a text, as the interpreter moves from considering the near context to more distant ones."[35]

By thus ignoring the way the original historical setting "freezes" the meaning of a text, Bock concludes that the meaning of any given passage is not static but dynamic. It is ever changing through the addition of new meanings.[36] In principle, Saucy indicates the same perspective Though acknowledging that Jesus' sermon on the mount in its original utterance had pre-Christian Judaism as its target,[37] he views the sermon as directly applicable to the church.[38] This can be true only if that portion of Scripture at some point received additional connotations that were not part of its original historical utterance. Adapting Saucy's words from another setting, this amounts to "a bending [of the text] that would have been quite foreign to the original readers [i.e., listeners]."[39]

For PD hermeneutics, "historical" has apparently come to incorporate not just the situation of the original text, but also the ongoing conditions throughout the history of the interpretation of that text.[40] According to traditional hermeneutical principles, such a "bending" is impossible because the historical dimension fixes the meaning of a given passage and does not allow it to keep gaining new senses as it comes into new settings.

The "Single-Meaning" Principle

Closely related to the dimension that (according to the traditional method) fixes the meaning of a text in relation to its original historical surroundings, is the guiding principle that a given text has one meaning and one meaning only. Terry states the principle thus: "A fundamental principle in grammatico-historical exposition is that the words and sentences can have but one significance in one and the same connection. The moment we neglect this principle we drift out upon a sea of uncertainty and conjecture."[41]

Ramm states it in another way: "But here we must remember the old adage: 'Interpretation is one, application is many.' This means that there is only one meaning to a passage of Scripture which is determined by careful study."[42]

The PD position, however, is to refrain from limiting a passage to a single meaning, and to allow for later complementary additions in meaning, which of necessity alter the original sense conveyed by the passage.[43] These later alterations are in view when Blaising and Bock write, "There also is such a thing as complementary aspects of meaning, where an additional angle on the text reveals an additional element of its message or a fresh way of relating the parts of a text's message."[44] In part, Bock admits this characteristic of his hermeneutics:

> Does the expansion of meaning entail a change of meaning?... This is an important question for those concerned about consistency within interpretation. The answer is both yes and no. On the one hand, to add to the revelation of a promise is to introduce "change" to it through addition.[45]

He tries to justify this change by calling it revelatory progress but whatever the attempted justification, the fact remains that change is present.[46] This contrasts with the denial by traditional grammatical-historical hermeneutics of the possibility of a passage as having multiple meanings.

Saucy also practices the hermeneutics of multiple meanings Acknowledging the reference of "seed" in Gen. 12:7 to the physical posterity of Abraham, he assigns the term an additional meaning by including Jews and Gentiles who follow Abraham's pattern of faith.[47] He finds that an original meaning of Psalm 110 received added meaning through Peter's sermon at Pentecost.[48] This leads him to assign two meanings to the Old Testament throne of David one a throne in heaven and the other a throne on earth.[49]

In other instances, however, he strongly opposes a reinterpretation of the Old Testament, when it comes to equating the church with the new Israel.[50] Yet this is precisely what he has done in instances when necessary to fit his PD system. One wonders why he does not treat these passages as he does Hosea 1:9-10; 2:23, and make them an application of Old Testament passages rather than an added interpretation of them.[51]

To theorize that the apostles assigned additional meanings to Old Testament texts, as Saucy does,[52] cannot qualify as grammatical-historical interpretation, because in numerous cases the meanings they added to the Old Testament were beyond the reach of human recipients of these Old Testament Scriptures. Yes, God knew all along that the passages would ultimately attain these added nuances, but the additions were unavailable to human interpreters until the time of the New Testament spokesmen and writers.[53] It is an example of anachronistic hermeneutics to read New Testament revelation back into the context of the Old Testament under the banner of grammatical-historical methodology. This method limits a passage to one meaning and one meaning only

The Issue of Sensus Plenior *(Fuller Meaning)*

The issue of whether to assign a fuller sense to a passage than grammatical-historical examination warrants is not too remote from the issue of the principle of single meaning. The practice of doing so has characterized Roman Catholicism for centuries,[54] and amounts to an allegorical rather than a literal method of interpretation. Terry strongly repudiates this practice: "He [the systematic expounder of Scripture] must not import into the text of Scripture the ideas of later times, or build upon any words or passages a dogma which they do not legitimately teach."[55] Recently Protestant evangelicals have begun advocating the incorporation of this "fuller meaning" too.[56] Remarks in the earlier discussion of "historical dimension" and "single meaning" reflect the disharmony of *sensus plenior* (fuller meaning) with traditional grammatical-historical interpretation.

Facing the issue of "fuller meaning," PD comes down clearly on the side of incorporating it into hermeneutical methodology. Its delineation of "complementary hermeneutics," as described above, is clearly of this nature. Blaising and Bock explicitly refuse to limit textual meaning to a reproduction of what the author meant.[57] Regarding this issue they state, "These texts have a message that extends beyond the original settings in which they were given. Something about what they say lives on."[58] They deny the well-known maxim of "one interpretation, many applications," referring to later applications as added meanings that accrue to various biblical texts.[59] This opinion is in essence none other than an advocacy of *sensus plenior* (fuller meaning), when they refer to a meaning beyond that determined by the historical circumstances of the text's origin.[60] When referring to the possibility of a later revelation expanding of previous revelation, one means an addition to the original text,[61] and it is tantamount to assigning a meaning beyond that yielded through grammatical-historical study.

In his expansion of the meaning of "seed" in Gen. 12:7,[62] Saucy follows the same pattern of assigning a fuller meaning than called for by traditional hermeneutics. He also points out that Peter's preaching in Acts 2 added something to the meaning of Psalm 110, which was unrecognized in earlier interpretations.[63] All such interpretations of PD, of which there are many, fall into the category of historical-grammatical-literary-theological hermeneutics and are a distinguishing mark of this new system.

Saucy, on the other hand, sometimes takes New Testament uses of the Old Testament not as fulfillments, but as new applications of the Old Testament. He summarizes an extended discussion of how Hebrews uses the Old Testament in these words: "In this connection it is important to recognize that the purpose of the writer to the Hebrews is not to give us an interpretation of Old Testament prophecy. The book is rather 'a word of exhortation' (13:22)...."[64] He also notes:

> The Scriptures frequently reveal different applications of similar language without implying a change in identity. The fact that the same phrase about God's son being called out of Egypt applies to both Israel and Christ does not make these objects identical (cf. Hos. 11:1 and Matt. 2:15).[65]

This principle of seeing the New Testament use of the Old Testament as applications rather than as interpretations is more in accord with grammatical-historical practices. The fact that the added meanings supplied in the New Testament did not become discernible until provided by inspired New Testament writings means that the authority for such interpretations derives from the New Testament citation, not from the Old Testament passages themselves. This being the case, the support for PD vanishes when evaluated by grammatical and historical criteria. Of course, God knew from eternity past that fuller meanings would eventually emerge, but so far as human beings were concerned, such meanings were nonexistent until the time that New Testament apostles and prophets disclosed them.

The Importance of Thoroughness

The expression "hermeneutical hopscotch" describes a final characteristic of PD hermeneutics. Hopscotch is a game in which players choose which squares they want to hop into and avoid stepping in the squares that would lose the game for them. PD hermeneutical procedures resemble this game through a selective use of passages seemingly in support of their system—avoiding others that do not—and through selective comments regarding the passages they cite. The following illustrates this.

Traditional grammatical-historical exegesis refrains from such passage selectivity. Ramm warns against the danger of *apparent* cross references, i.e., places where a word or words may be the same in two passages, but when equating the two misrepresents the meaning of one or both passages.[66] The practice to which this warning applies is remarkably close to Bock's treatment of the words "light" and "sit" in some of Luke's writings.[67] He builds major doctrinal conclusions on the repetitions of these words in contexts that differ considerably. Another instance of selectivity, this time of a thematic type, is Bock's survey of Luke's gospel and Acts to prove that Christ's promised kingdom rule presently exists. He selects scattered passages in the two books that allegedly prove his point, but omits those that are destructive to his theory, such as Luke 8:10, where Christ, through His use of "mysteries," indicates He is talking about a kingdom unforeseen in the Old Testament.[68]

Traditional grammatical-historical exegesis also refrains from making only selective comments regarding texts that are crucial to the point to be proven. Careful study of a passage is the way to obtain the one and only meaning of that passage.[69] Progressive dispensationalists do not exhibit "careful study" in their handling of critical texts. Regarding Romans 16:25-27, the three principal spokesmen fail to acknowledge another interpretation of the passage that refutes their use of it.[70] They consistently interpret "the Scriptures of the prophets" (lit., "the prophetic scriptures") (16:26) as referring to the Old Testament. They conclude on the basis of this assumption that "the mystery which has been kept secret for long ages past" (16:25) was made known in the Old Testament. Nowhere in their major writings on the subject do they show an awareness that another very viable interpretation of "the Scriptures of the prophets" exists, i.e., that it refers to the utterances and/or writings of New Testament prophets.[71] This latter meaning would negate the conclusion they draw from the passage. Thorough-going grammatical-historical interpretation does not condone this kind of superficial treatment of texts, particularly when they are critical to support a doctrine being propounded.

In the matter of hermeneutical hopscotch, then, lies another distinction between grammatical-historical interpretation and PD methodology. The five principles, of which this is the last, are not all that distinguish the two approaches, but they are sufficient to illustrate that significant differences exist.

The Bottom Line

The difference in hermeneutical methodology summarized above explains why PD is less clear-cut in its support of a pretribulational rapture and several other long-standing distinctives of dispensationalism. It is not the purpose of this essay to raise the question of how proper it is to apply the name "dispensational" to the new theological system. The discussion above has only sought to clarify wherein lies the basic difference between dispensationalism and PD.

By now it is evident, from the self-assessment of progressive dispensationalists and from the comparison of illustrative hermeneutical principles, that a choice between the two amounts to a choice between two systems of interpretation. If one endorses recent trends in evangelical hermeneutics, that person may easily fit into the PD camp, or perhaps even into a theological system that is decidedly nondispensational. On the other hand, a choice of grammatical-historical interpretation must lead to dispensational conclusions.

In the latter case, a consideration of the hermeneutics of PD is beneficial in sharpening an appreciation for some of the finer points of the traditional method. Positive lessons from above comparisons include the importance of interpretive objectivity, of a passage's historical and cultural background, of limiting each passage to a single meaning, of avoiding the temptation to assign a "fuller meaning," and of thoroughness in letting each passage have its complete contribution to the totality of biblical revelation. Practicing these lessons will have a stabilizing and building effect in the growth of Christ's body.

Twelve Reasons Why This Could Be the Terminal Generation

_____*OVERVIEW* ·

Are we only a few years away from the second advent of Jesus Christ? Many believe that we are. Without saying that we are, the author provides 12 reasons why he thinks this generation could be living on the verge of Christ's return. Since Christ's first coming, Israel has been reconstituted as a nation, in 1948. This begins to set the stage for the conditions which the Bible indicates will take place in the last days. The author believes that this makes many other signs significant, when taken together. However, because the rapture will occur at least seven years before the second coming, all must be prepared, through belief in the gospel, for Christ's any-moment return.

*F*or 2000 years, Christians have believed Jesus Christ would return to this earth, physically, in his "second coming," in their generation. Even though Our Lord knew the church would not see that return for two millennia, He wanted each generation to live as though He could come at any time for motivational purposes. Our Lord knew He would "go into a far country. and after a great while... return and demand an accounting," as He taught in His parables. He knew that routine living was an enemy to spiritual motivation in a physical universe. So He presented His second coming in such a way that Christians would be motivated to so live as though He would interrupt their lives and return before their natural life span had ended.

The apostles and first century church almost universally expected His return in their lifetime, which is why they were so motivated to live holy lives and so dedicated to evangelism and reaching the world for Christ. The second and third century churches similarly expected His return, even in the face of unbelievable persecution. They were so evangelistic they literally turned the world upside down, and by the fourth century they saw the Roman empire embrace Christianity as the dominant faith. In later centuries, as the Bible was withdrawn from the people, the truth about the second coming waned, as did the fires of evangelism. After the Protestant Reformation, the translating of the Bible into the mother tongue of the people, and the printing press, which made the Bible available to the common people, the study of prophecy and the second coming resumed. After all, one third of the Bible is prophecy, so if you study the whole Bible you study prophecy. Since the second coming is mentioned more than any other subject in Scripture, except for the doctrine of salvation, it is understandable that prophetic teaching, followed by evangelism, missions, and holy living would return. Historically, that is exactly what happened during the last three centuries—as the Bible had its greatest distribution.

Watching for "Signs"

It is only natural that Bible-taught Christians, excited about Christ's return, would be interested in "signs" of His coming. Even the disciples, once they realized Jesus would soon leave, asked, "What shall be the Sign of your coming?" which they obviously equated with "the end of the age" (Matt. 24:3). The fact that the Lord did not rebuke the disciples for their question tells us that it was a legitimate one. It is equally legitimate today. That many wild speculators have sensationalized signs, and so brought confusion to the church, should not prohibit us from using them at all. It should make us more careful in "rightly dividing the Word of Truth." So we do not add to the confusion. Neither should we rob the church of legitimate motivation for holy living, evangelism, and missionary vision, by refusing to face the fact that there are many events today that constitute seeming fulfillment of certain prophecies.

We should, however, avoid speculations that go beyond the intent of Scripture, and not make them mean more than is indicated. Certainly we should avoid date-setting. The 1988 experience of the now discredited Edgar Whisenant, and the 1994 date setting of Harold Camping, do nothing to build confidence in the soon coming of Christ. Instead, they disillusion many. Any time a person sets a specific date we know he is wrong. According to our Lord's statement in Matthew 24:36, we cannot know "the day or the hour." However, in the same passage, He allows us to see indications that would lead us to believe "it is near, even at the doors."

It is my contention that, while we cannot say dogmatically that Jesus will return in our generation, we can say that our generation has more legitimate reasons for believing it than any previous generation. Consider the following 12 reasons carefully. No one of them is conclusive in itself, though number two comes close. But considered together, these 12 reasons for expecting the Savior to "shout from heaven" and rapture his church in our generation, should affect the way we live.

There Are More Fulfilled Signs
Today Than in Any Previous Age

A whole book could be written on the signs of our Lord's return that have already been fulfilled. In fact, I have written such a book,

The Beginning of the End, where I list 12 signs. Other students of prophecy have found more. The 12 I see as most specific are listed below with their Scripture text.

1) *World War I:* Matthew 24:1-8. Actually, there are 4 parts to this one sign: a world war started by one nation, joined by the kingdoms of the world, followed by famines, pestilences, and earthquakes in several places at the same time. This century has already been the most barbaric century in history, killing a record number of souls in two world wars and with the spread of communism. In excess of 180 million lives, more than all the wars of history put together, have been lost. In addition, over 5000 lives have been lost in earthquakes, famines, and pestilence in this generation.

2) *The Regathering of Israel:* Ezekiel 36–37. This is such a significant sign it shall be dealt with separately.

3) *The Rise of Russia and Her Allies in Preparation of Fulfilling:* Ezekiel 38–39. Only in this century (since 1917) has Russia been anything like a dominant player on the world scene. This is a compelling sign worthy of individual study. Not only is Russia depicted clearly by Ezekiel to rise as a political threat in the last days, but her allies—the Arab nations—and her enemy—Israel—are named.

4) *The Increase in Travel and Knowledge:* Daniel 12:4. This is the "information age." Who can doubt the prophet's prediction of "running to and fro on the earth"?

5) *The Capital and Labor Conflicts:* James 5:1-6. These have produced revolutionary changes in labor and management during this century.

6) *Scoffers Have Come:* 2 Peter 3:1-2. This is a sign of the "last days." Scoffers dominate the most influential agencies of all countries today, even our own. They control media, entertainment, education, and, for the most part, government. They are "willfully ignorant" and "walk after their own lusts," as predicted.

7) *The Current Moral Breakdown in Society:* 2 Timothy 3:1-5. The 18 trends of moral breakdown during the last days are read almost every day in the newspapers.

8) *A Rise in Lawlessness:* 2 Thessalonians 2:7-10.

9) *A Rise in Occultism and Cults:* 1 Timothy 4:1-5. There have always been cults and demon activity, but nothing in modern history is like today, and it is increasing.

10) *Apostasy:* 1 Timothy 4:1. The liberalism and rejection of the faith that has shipwrecked so many souls in this century had its roots in the last century, as whole denominations departed from their original beliefs in the deity of Jesus Christ and other doctrines.

11) *The Rise of Mystery Babylon, the Ecumenical Church:* Revelation 17. Ever since the pagan practices of Babylon and other heathen religions began creeping into the church of Rome (mid fourth and fifth century), faithful Bible teachers have identified the church of Rome as the harlot riding the "beast" of government in Revelation 17. Today we even have evangelical leaders making attempts to reconcile with Rome, Babylon, a most dangerous trend, but to be expected in the light of the prophecy of Revelation.

12) *The One World Government:* Daniel 2. Many saw the establishment of the United Nations, in 1945, as a giant step in fulfilling the long-recognized prophecy of a one world government in the end times. The World Trade Organization (NAFTA) recently passed into law, the federating of the countries of Europe into the "United States of Europe." The World Trade Organization could well be fulfillment of the move toward a one-world government, just as Daniel prophesied.

A case can be made that each of the above events, or common trends of our day, are signs of our Lord's return, but as stated earlier, that in itself is a subject worthy of a book. It is significant to point out, here, that they all occurred in this century, and that they are working inexorably toward a climax that could well culminate in our generation. Together, they give us a basis for concluding that this generation has more reason to believe that Christ could come in our lifetime than at any time before it. Below we will expand on these ideas and look at others as well.

Israel's Regathering: The "Super Sign" of Christ's Return

Israel is a miracle nation. It was born by a miracle, it lived by a miracle, and it has been preserved by the miraculous hand of God all through history. That after 1500 years without a homeland this dispersed people could be gathered back into the holy land in this century, and recognized as an official nation in 1948, is itself a miracle. Historians tell us that no other nationality has been able to survive extinction after 500 years of being removed from its homeland. Yet, scattered as they were to all the world, with the signing of

the Balfore Treaty in 1917, the miracle nation that we today call
Israel began. They came from all over the world, until the handful of
Jews in the holy land at the time of World War I, had grown until,
today, there are almost five million Jews in that land, testifying that
God keeps His Word.

A careful reading of Ezekiel 37 shows that God predicted a very
gradual regathering of this seemingly dead nation. The prophet pictured the nation as in the "valley of dry bones," which, after the
signal of the Lord, began coming together, "bone to its bone" ...
then the "sinews, flesh," ... then the ... "skin," and finally the
"breath" (world recognition in 1948). There is no doubt that the dry
bones were the nation of Israel, for verse 11 says, "Son of man,
these bones are the whole house of Israel." Even though they
thought, "Our bones are dry, our hope is lost and we ourselves are
cut off!" God has brought them back into their land. It is a miracle!

Now all that is needed is for God to pour out His Spirit, so the
nation can experience the spiritual revival that is predicted for her in
verses 12-15 and other passages. But that is yet future. It is expected
to occur during the Tribulation period, under the preaching of the
144,000 Jewish witnesses described in Revelation 7.

What is significant, here, is, this "super sign," as the editor of
this book, prophecy scholar Tommy Ice, terms it. It all started in
1917, with the fulfillment of the sign our Lord gave His disciples in
Matthew 24:6-7: World War I, followed by unprecedented "famines, pestilences, and earthquakes in various places." Notice, "wars
and rumors of wars" were not the sign. Man's history is filled with
war after war, but Jesus said, "See that you are not troubled; for all
these things must come to pass, but the end is not yet." The sign was
not wars, but a most significant war, which was World War I, with
its accompanying phenomena of famines, pestilences, and earthquakes. Out of the fulfillment of this sign, Israel started going back
into the land, leading many prophecy scholars to conclude that
God's prophetic clock began ticking again. Personally, I look on that
period, 1917–1948, as God winding His clock. It was set in motion
when president Harry Truman pushed through the United Nations
the vote to recognize Israel as a nation and she rose up from the
valley of dry bones and began to "live."

When you add to that fulfilled prophecy the next two chapters
of Ezekiel, 38–39, which foretell the amazing story of how Russia
and her Arab allies will (as Gog and Magog, Rosh and the prince of

Rosh) go down against the mountains of Israel and be destroyed supernaturally by God, you are faced with the remarkable fact that it too began in 1917. That is when Russia became a mainstream player in the world of nations. Just 100 years ago, Russia was such a backward nation that it couldn't even best the newly emerging nation of Japan in 1905. Yet for decades Russia has been a dominant force on the world scene. And it is today a mortal enemy of Israel, just as the Bible predicted!

The Middle East:
Focus of World Attention

Has it ever seemed unusual to you that the focus of world attention is continually on the little nation of Israel? Even today they only have five million people in the land, plus Arabs, Palestinians, Syrians, and Jordanians. At one place the country is only eight miles wide, and it has all kinds of survival problems. Yet almost every night on the evening news, billions of people focus their attention on that tiny spot of land that God gave Abraham for a homeland, for the nation He would raise up through Abraham and his wife Sarah.

To put this in perspective, think of the country of Singapore When I visited missionaries there some years back, one of them told me that Singapore was the center of world population. He said, "If you draw a two thousand mile wide circle around Singapore, you will encompass fifty percent of the world's population!" But how often do the happenings in that area of 50 percent of the world's population ever hit our evening news? Yet Israel is on the evening news regularly.

Why? Because God predicted, in those most important prophecies in Ezekiel 37–39, that Israel, Russia, and the Arab hordes would be the principle focus of world attention in the last days. It is significant that that was not the case in the last century or in the 19 centuries before it.

The Potential
of Nuclear or Other Holocausts

For the first time in human history man has the potential of destroying himself from the face of the earth. Most scientists' greatest fear is that a nuclear device could be set off and cause a chain reaction that could obliterate the planet. *Psychology Today* magazine featured a cover design showing the typical mushroom like cloud of a nuclear explosion, titled "Children Growing Up with the Fear of Never Growing Up." Disarmament agents in education and media use this threat to advance their cause of universal disarmament, which only intensifies the fear, particularly among young school children, causing many in their youth to adopt the hedonistic lifestyle.

Christians do not share that concern. The Bible forecasts that Christ will come back and rapture His church at a time of enormous population. He will not only take many to be with Him to His Father's house, but He will leave behind multitudes more to go through the Tribulation. This world will one day be destroyed, but it will be destroyed by God, not man, after the return of Christ for His church.

Former president Ronald Reagan is quoted as saying, "We see around us today the marks of a terrible dilemma, predictions of doomsday. Those predictions carry weight because of the existence of nuclear weapons, and the constant threat of global war...so much so that no president, no congress, no parliament can spend a day entirely free of this threat." Not only do they fear rogue nations, which would threaten other more civilized nations to surrender to them to avoid nuclear holocaust, making world domination by another Joe Stalin-type possible, there is always the threat of nuclear proliferation by some terrorist group which, if they could develop a delivery system, would blackmail cities or countries with annihilation.

That possibility is not as farfetched as some people think. Recently, a news report indicated that a nuclear device had been developed that could fit into a briefcase. It is just a matter of time before this frightening scenario from science fiction becomes reality.

Nuclear weapons or explosives are not the only technological threat to mankind today. Dr. George Wald, Nobel prize-winning scientist, and biology department head at Harvard University, is quoted as saying, "I think human life is threatened as never before in the history of this planet. Not by one peril, but by many. They are all working together coming to a head about the same time. And the time lies very close to the year 2000. I am one of those scientists who find it hard to see how the human race is to bring itself much past the year 2000." French biologist, Dr. Jacques Monod, is only slightly more optimistic, "I don't see how we can survive much later than 2050."

My point is not to suggest that these doomsday prophecies will come to fulfillment in our lifetime, or before Christ returns. As we have seen, they most assuredly will not. My point is, since Christ is going to return to a populated earth He will have to return soon or some man or nation will try to destroy humankind. The threatened, or possible, nuclear holocaust, that is conceivable in our generation points to a soon coming of Christ before such an event occurs.

Worldwide Gospel Preaching
by the Year 2000

One of our Lord's well-known promises about the end of the age is found in Matthew 24:14, "And this gospel of the kingdom will be preached in all the world as a witness to all the nations, and then the end will come." Most prophecy scholars locate this worldwide preaching of the gospel during the Tribulation period. It is assumed this will be done under the ministry of the 144,000, in Revelation 7, who reach a "multitude that no man can number from every tongue, tribe and nation" (v. 9). That means it will be fulfilled *after the rapture* of the church.

The point is, we are coming close to preaching the gospel to all the world in the very near future! At the 1992 National Convention of Religious Broadcasters, the heads of three worldwide Christian shortwave radio ministries shared their current decade evangelistic tragedy. The presidents of Far Eastern Broadcasting ministries, HCJB in Quito, Equador, and Trans-World Radio, which covers Europe, have launched a plan to take the gospel via short wave radio to the entire world "by the year 2000"! They represent the three largest radio networks in the world. My friend Bill Bright, whose vision has stirred my heart for over 40 years, announced that Campus Crusade For Christ International has a plan to "help reach the world for Christ by the year 2000." Other mission agencies have similar target dates.

While we know this prophecy will be fulfilled during the Tribulation, the fact that so many effective groups are working for the same target date, at a time when such an effort is technologically possible, does indeed suggest the coming of Christ for His church may soon be at hand. Also, there is the movings of the Holy Spirit throughout the world. As I read the *International World Religion Report,* which comes to my desk twice a month, I am amazed at the moving of the Holy Spirit in leading millions of souls to the Savior—all over the world. Since the fall of the Soviet Union, just five years ago, God is opening many doors for gospel preaching which have been closed for over 70 years. Consequently, we hear of millions of people making decisions for Christ. South America too has seen millions of its people come to faith in Christ.

During the Reagan years, when communists tried to overpower the young democracies of Central America, all five countries elected conservative presidents who were either professing Christians or favorable to Christianity. On one of my visits to his country, one of those presidents said to me that it was "the evangelicals that got me elected." The number of Christians had grown fourfold in his country, and it is they who went to the polls and elected him over his communist opponent. The same is true of the other countries. It can be accurately said that the amazing soul harvest in Central and South America in the last two decades is what saved those regions from going communist. Similar soul harvests are reported throughout the world, from Africa to China.

It is safe to say that Matthew 24:14 will soon be fulfilled, which means, the coming of Christ could be at hand.

The New World Order

One of the signs of the end is that the governments of the world will relinquish their sovereignty to one federal head, to become the international world leader of the future. Unknown to many in the world, there are already secret societies and organizations working tirelessly to make that come to pass soon. During the past few years, shocking revelations have confirmed that, indeed, for over 200 years, many influential leaders of some of the most powerful countries of the world are committed to ushering in the one-world government.

So much has been said about secret orders like the Illuminati, founded in 1776, the Skull and Bones of Yale, founded in 1856, the Order at Oxford in 1904, the Club of Rome, The Fabian Society, the Bildeburgers. Others, are not secret, like the influential Council on Foreign Relations, founded in 1921, which established the Trilateral Commission in 1973. What is important about these organizations is that whenever their membership comes to light it includes the elitists who control government, banking, education, and media in their countries. Few Christians are ever found in such groups which often reveal a hostility to our Judeo-Christian culture and values.

Another thing these groups have in common, is that they are all working in one way or another for a world government. Some think it is Satanically inspired. Even if that can't be proven, the point is, when Satan does prepare the world for uniting under one master controller, he will probably use a system of interlocking secret organizations that seek to control the economy, the religion, and the media of the world. With this power he will be able to control the most powerful world governmental leaders.

NAFTA and the GATT world trade treaties, passed recently, are the result of such organizations, who believe they must unite the world commercially to make them so interdependent that they can merge the world into one constitution, judicial system, and government. Already plans have been made to divide the world into three currencies, the Japanese yen for the Orient, the German mark for Europe, and the U.S. dollar for the Americas. This is to be the first step toward a one-world currency—controlled by one panel or one person. A somewhat recent suggestion by one of the most powerful elite insiders, who controls several of these groups, is that they divide the world into ten regions, appoint a ruler over each, with a seat on the ruling council of the world (the expanded UN security council?). Who can say that the world is not already on the fast track toward a one-world government, which could be consummated in this or the next generation?

The Mark of the Beast— Technology Already Here

One of the best known prophecies of the Tribulation is that the "beast" or world leader popularly called the Antichrist, will have the ability to put his mark, "666," on the forehead and hand of the people. To buy or sell during that period, you will need that mark. For the first time in 2000 years, it is now technologically possible to enforce such a system. Micro chips have already been invented that can be placed in the fatty tissue behind the ear, or in other places of the body, which could provide computer tracking. We are all familiar with the scanner at the check-out counter of most stores. All it would take is a computer program that required the "666" number on peoples' accounts, or hands, in order for them to "buy or sell." Mark of the beast technology is already here!

Revelation-Type Plagues
Already Exist

One of the frightening events of the Tribulation period is the many plagues that will strike the people, in God's attempt to get them to repent of their sins and turn to Him. The two witnesses have the power to put plagues on their enemies, at the same time that the plagues of the trumpet and vial judgments occur. Although we do not know the extent of those plagues, we do know that the people who contract them will suffer so unbearably that they will begin to die.

Even without knowing the medical details of these plagues, we can already identify AIDS and STDS, or Sexually Transmitted Diseases, having similar types of effects on people. Four decades ago, the medical profession thought it had eliminated sexually transmitted diseases. Unfortunately they have returned with a vengeance. Penicillin and antibiotics worked for a while, but the diseases developed stronger strains, too powerful for drugs to contain, and today they are worse than before.

AIDS is one of the most frightening diseases of our times, particularly for the sexually promiscuous. Once it is contracted it is fatal. It spreads like wildfire and no cure seems to be on the horizon. In 1981, the United States reported its first case. Since then cases have reached into the millions. Experts predict it will infect ten million people by the year 2000, and that is probably underestimated. AIDS in Africa, the most tragically hit by AIDS, will soon reach 50 percent of the population, unless a cure is found. I am not saying AIDS is the fulfillment of Revelation, just that we already have that type of plague on our hands, and the most advanced scientific laboratories of our day can do nothing to halt it.

It is instructive that these diseases have hit in the last decade, along with the many other events typical of the last days.

Unprecedented Earthquakes and Natural Disasters

An increase in earthquakes, even multiple and enormous earthquakes, was predicted by both our Lord in Matthew 24:7, and also by the apostle John in the book of Revelation, for the time of the end. Because of their frightening and uncontrolled intensity, earthquakes have always been considered a sign of God's judgment, at least since His destruction of Sodom and Gomorrah because of their sinful lifestyle.

For our purposes, I wish to call attention to the fact that something unusual is going on in nature during the 1990s. Some of the most disastrous "natural" catastrophes have occurred in both intensity and numbers. For example, killer earthquakes were very rare for centuries, numbering perhaps one each decade. Notice in the following chart how they have increased during the past five decades, according to the U.S. Geological society:

- 1940–1949: 4
- 1950–1959: 9
- 1960–1969: 13
- 1970–1979: 56
- 1980–1989: 74

What has seismologists concerned is the obvious increase in killer earthquakes during the last five decades. Each decade has seen an increased number of earthquakes over the decade before it. The period between 1990–94 has already exceeded the number of killer quakes in the decade before it. I am writing this one day after the 7.2 quake in Kobe, Japan, which destroyed over 5000 lives and injured tens of thousands. This is thought to be the worst earthquake to hit Japan in almost 50 years. There have been frightening quakes in Africa, Ethiopia, Pakistan, Tibet, the Philippians, and of course San Francisco and Los Angeles, which toppled freeway bridges, leaving at least 57 dead. It is obvious that earthquakes are increasing with each passing decade. Something unusual is transpiring with planet Earth!

One seismologist at the Scripps Research Center in LaJolla, California, said, "It is almost as though the earth's plates are gyrating in anticipation of the world's greatest earthquake." Whether that is the one described in Revelation 6, 11, or 18, is yet to be determined. But who can doubt that we are seeing the very fulfillment of earthquake phenomenon that could be preparing the earth for the coming judgments of God as foretold for the Tribulation?

In 1993, a news report indicated there were other worldwide problems of nature:

- South Africa experienced wide-spread crop failures...floods...
- Bangladesh—nearly half under water, 316 people killed, 6 million homeless...
- 2100 people die in flooding in Southeast Asia...
- 1100 flood victims in Himalayan kingdom of Nepal..
- 700 die in floods in India..

In our own country, in one year we experienced hurricane Andrew in Florida, which destroyed 40,000 homes at a cost of over $20 billion. In March, 50 inches of snow paralyzed the East, causing Washington D.C. to close down. Floods hit the Mississippi valley at a cost of $20 billion. Early in 1995, torrential rains hit northern California and devastated a whole region. But it is not limited to America. Hailstones the size of tennis balls bombarded France, and torrential rains created what they called a "black rainstorm alert" in Hong Kong.

The proportions of these unnatural phenomenon can be seen in the fact that one of the world's oldest and most stable insurance companies, Lloyds of London, has had to pay so many claims of late it is on the verge of bankruptcy.

All this, and more is expected, at a time when all these other events indicate Christians today have very good reason to believe their Lord could come soon, to take them to their Father's house. Yet there is more.

The Potential Collapse of Russia

For centuries prophetic scholars have been convinced that "Rosh and the Chief prince of Rosh" mean that Russia and those who control will lead the march of the Arab world down to the mountains of Israel, where God will show Himself powerful to all the world by destroying their armies according to Ezekiel 38–39. Not only the etymology of the names leads us to identify this chief antagonist as Russia, but her location in "the uttermost part of the North," clearly means Russia, which is located north of Israel (38:6).

The problem is, for the past five years, ever since the fall of the Berlin Wall and the break-up of the old Soviet Union, the nation of Russia has been on shaky ground. First, their leader was the charismatic Boris Yeltsin, but his vice of alcoholism has all but rendered him ineffective. The economy of the country is in shambles as they refused to adopt full scale free enterprise but retained enough of the socialist policies that have stultified the economy. The country is in worse shape today than when it enjoyed freedom for the first time in 70 years. The unstable government makes it vulnerable to a takeover by the hard-line communists, who are just waiting in the wings to be brought back into control.

At risk is the peace of the world, because Russia and her independent satellite countries still have over 30,000 nuclear missiles pointed at the West. And one important factor should be remembered, Russia still maintains a close relationship with the Arab world. Actually, 55 million of her 250 million people are Arabs, plus their allies in the middle east, all of whom hate Israel.

My point is, Russia is in precarious straits. She could have a revolution, become a dictatorship, or just collapse under her own bureaucratic weight and become a fifth-rate power. Her army is really not the fearful monster it was once pictured to be, since it is obvious she failed miserably in Afghanistan, and as I am writing, is proving to be a paper tiger in her takeover of the little independent country of Chechnya.

It does not seem that time is on Russia's side. If she is going to be the major power that Ezekiel forecasts her to be, she had better make her move soon, or she won't be able to. Which means, if Russia is to go down against Israel, she had better do it soon!

This Generation Has the Capability of Fulfilling the Amazing Feat of Revelation 11:9

During the first three-and-a-half years of the Tribulation, the two supernatural witnesses, probably Moses and Elijah, will return to assist the children of Israel against their enemies. They will have power to "shut heaven so that no rain falls," they preach for 1260 days, and they have power over waters to "turn them to blood, and to strike the earth with all plagues" (v. 6). When they finish their testimony they are so hated that people kill them and leave their bodies lying in the street for three days. Verse 9 says, "Those from the peoples, tribes, tongues, and nations (a description of the whole world) will see their dead bodies three and a half days."

Technologically, this has never been possible before. Today, however, people with televisions see bodies lying in the streets on the evening news. Just a decade ago that would have been impossible. But when the U.S. troops went into Panama in 1989, it was seen in 55 countries of the world. The expulsion of Iraq from Kuwait and the bombing of Israel during the Gulf War was seen nightly in 109 countries. By 1993, CNN claimed to be in over 200 countries of the world daily, and still growing.

This is the first generation to see the possible fulfillment of that end-time prophecy.

The Year-Day Theory of the Jews and Early Christians

The oldest theory about when Christ would come back to this earth was taught by some rabbis even before Jesus' birth. Since they accepted the Old Testament, many of the early Christians also espoused it. Basically, they believed that since the Lord created the earth, sun, moon, stars, and man in six days, and then rested for a day, and since one day is as "a thousand years," as God reckons time, then Christ will come back around the year 2000. They teach that since there were about 4000 years prior to Christ and about 2000 since his birth, what better fulfillment of the "day of rest" (or 1000 years) than His glorious coming back to earth to set up 1000 years of millennial "rest," when the world will experience peace, and blessing, without war.

Now I am not suggesting that we adopt the theory. I do not find it specifically taught in Scripture. I only suggest it here because it is the oldest of theories, and if true, it would culminate in our generation. The exact number of years from Adam to the death of Christ may be off by several years. So, too, the actual dating system since Christ's death and resurrection, which was not assigned until at least six centuries after the fact. Consequently, the actual date of the year 2000 may be off 4 to 40 years, or more.

The point is not that the year 2000 is the year. I doubt that it is. The point is, it is well within the "season," or generation. Our generation.

Jesus Christ may not come in this generation, no one really knows! Of that we can be definite! However, our generation has more reason to believe His coming *could* be during our lifetime than any other generation before us. For that reason we should "number our days" and live each one in the light that He may come at any time.

Don't Forget to Subtract Seven Years

If you are tempted to use this theory of the early church, remember that that is all it is—a theory. Do not forget, we have been talking about Jesus' glorious appearing. There are no signs for the rapture. All signs of the Lord's return relate to His glorious appearing. Therefore, you must subtract at least the seven-year Tribulation period when thinking about the rapture. Consequently, don't be surprised if you realize it is later than you think! Christ could indeed come today, or tomorrow, or soon.

The big question is, are you ready? If you have never repented of your sins and by faith in Jesus' resurrection invited Him into your heart, please do so immediately. It would be tragic to know what you do and and yet be like 61 percent of the American population who indicated to the 1994 *U.S. News and World Report* pollsters that they believed Christ will return to this earth—but that they are not ready for Him. (Only 38 percent of the population profess a "born again" experience.) May I suggest that if you have any doubt, that you invite Jesus Christ into your heart. Consider saying a prayer similar to the following:

Dear God:

I am a sinner! I believe Jesus Christ died on the cross for my sins and rose the third day. I wish to repent of my sins and do confess them to you, and to ask that you forgive me and save me. I give myself completely to you. Amen.

If that is your need, make it your sincere prayer and trust God for your salvation. Believe the Scripture that says, "Whosoever shall call on the Name of the Lord shall be saved" (Rom. 10:13).

If you are already a Christian, let me ask you a question: Are you ready for Jesus' return? Oh, I know you will be raptured when He comes, but are you living the kind of life you want Him to find you living when He comes? Are you faithfully serving Him? Are you a regular part of a Bible-believing church? If not, resurrender your life to Him, live pleasing to Him, and do whatever He leads you to do.

Our Lord's final statement in Revelation is still appropriate " 'And behold, I am coming quickly, and My reward is with Me, to give to each one according to his work. I am the Alpha and the Omega, the Beginning and the End, the First and the Last.' Blessed are those who do His commandments, that they may have the right to the tree of life, and may enter in through the gates into the city."

Notes

Chapter One—Back to the Future

1. Merrill C. Tenney, *Interpreting Revelation* (Grand Rapids: Eerdmans, 1957), 136.
2. LeRoy E. Froom, *The Prophetic Faith of Our Fathers*, 4 vols. (Washington, D.C.: Review and Herald, 1948), Vol. II, 506-07.
3. David Chilton, *The Days of Vengeance* (Ft. Worth: Dominion Press, 1987), 43.
4. John F. Walvoord, *Armageddon, Oil and the Middle East Crisis* (Grand Rapids: Zondervan, 1974, 1976, 1990), 21-22.
5. Cited in David A. Rausch, *Zionism Within Early American Fundamentalism, 1878-1918: A Convergence of Two Traditions* (New York: The Edwin Mellen Press, 1979), 117.
6. John F. Walvoord, *Israel in Prophecy* (Grand Rapids: Zondervan, 1962), 129.

Chapter Two—Major Rapture Terms and Passages

1. Marvin R. Vincent, *Word Studies in the New Testament*, vol. 4 (McLean, VA: MacDonald Publishing Co., 1888), 41.
2. Fritz Reinecker, Cleon Rogers, *Linguistic Key to the Greek New Testament* (Grand Rapids: Zondervan Publishing House, 1980), 599.
3. Albert Barnes, *Notes on the New Testament*, vol. 12 (Grand Rapids: Baker Book House, 1983), 56.
4. H. E. Dana, Julius R. Mantey, *A Manual Grammar of the Greek New Testament* (New York: The Macmillan Co., 1957), 172.
5. A. T. Robertson, *Word Pictures in the New Testament*, vol. 4 (Nashville: Broadman Press, 1931), 36.
6. William F. Arndt, F. Wilbur Gingrich, *A Greek-English Lexicon of the New Testament*, 4th ed. (Chicago: University of Chicago Press, 1959), 41.
7. William Hendricksen, *I Thessalonians*, New Testament Commentary (Grand Rapids: Baker Book House, 1990), 128.
8. Alfred Plummer, Arch Robertson, *I Corinthians*, The International Critical Commentary (New York: Charles Scribner's Sons, 1911), 354.
9. Charles John Ellicott, ed., *Ellicott's Commentary on the Whole Bible*, vol. 8 (Grand Rapids: Zondervan Publishing House, 1959), 348.
10. Henry Alford, *Alford's Greek Testament*, vol. 3 (Grand Rapids: Guardian Press, 1976), 609
11. Plummer, Robertson, 354.
12. Ibid.
13. A. T. Robertson, *Word Pictures*, vol. 4, 60
14. Ibid., 61.
15. Albert Barnes, *Notes*, vol. 13, 88.
16. Robertson, *Word Pictures*, vol. 4, 14
17. Hendricksen, 57.
18. Barnes, *Notes*, vol. 12, 18.
19. John Calvin, *Calvin's Commentaries*, vol. 21 (Grand Rapids: Baker Book House, 1989), 279.
20. Leon Morris, *The First and Second Epistles to the Thessalonians* (Grand Rapids: Wm. B Eerdmans Publishing Co., 1979), 146.
21. Robertson, *Word Pictures*, vol. 4, 47.
22. John Walvoord, Roy Zuck, eds., *New Testament, The Bible Knowledge Commentary* (Wheaton. Victor Books, 1984), 543-44.
23. W. Robertson Nicoll, ed., *The Expositor's Greek Testament*, vol. 2 (Grand Rapids: Wm. B Eerdmans Publishing Co., 1988), 940.
24. Plummer, Robertson, 376.
25. Arndt, Gingrich, 38.
26. Henry George Liddell, Robert Scott, comps. *A Greek-English Lexicon* (Oxford: At the Clarendon Press, 1968), 68.
27. Barnes, *Notes*, vol. 11, 319-20
28. Arndt, Gingrich, 176.
29. Alford, 186.
30. Robertson, 547.
31. Alford, 419.
32. Arndt, Gingrich, 176
33. Nicoll, vol. 4, 195.
34. Arndt, Gingrich, 636

35. Walvoord, Zuck, 893
36. Liddell, Scott, 68
37. Ibid., 1117
38. Ibid., 1757
39. Frank Gaebelein, ed., *The Expositor's Bible Commentary,* vol. 11 (Grand Rapids: Zondervan Publishing House, 1984), 148
40. Dana, Mantey, 246.
41. Barnes, *Notes,* vol. 13, 312
42. Robertson, *Word Pictures,* vol. 5, 249
43. Dana, Mantey, 185
44. Alford, 288
45. Ellicott, 84.
46. Hendricksen, 57
47. Liddell, Scott, 467
48. Arndt, Gingrich, 744
49. Alford, 253
50. Gaebelein, 248.
51. Liddell, Scott, 693
52. Marvin R. Vincent, *Word Studies,* vol. 4, 20
53. Morris, 145
54. Robertson, *Word Pictures,* vol. 6, 219
55. Arndt, Gingrich, 657
56. Robertson, *Word Pictures,* vol. 4, 38
57. Arndt, Gingrich, 770.
58. Ibid., 64
59. Robertson, *Word Pictures,* vol. 6, 219
60. Walvoord, Zuck, 893
61. Adolf Deissmann, *Light from the Ancient East* (New York: Doran, 1927), 368
62. Robertson, *Word Pictures,* vol. 5, 249
63. Dana, Mantey, 185
64. Liddell, Scott, 467.
65. Gerhard Kittel, *Theological Dictionary of the New Testament,* vol. 2 (Grand Rapids: Wm. B Eerdmans Publishing Co., 1987), 330
66. Barnes, *Notes,* vol. 13, 89.
67. Ellicott, *Commentary,* vol. 8, 154
68. Robertson, *Word Pictures,* vol. 5, 47
69. Dana, Mantey, 115
70. Vincent, vol. 4, 345
71. Gaebelein, ed., 440-41
72. Dana, Mantey, 147
73. Gaebelein, 285
74. Ibid., 148

Chapter Three—Old Testament Tribulation Terms

1. Cf. Matt. 24:5-28; Mk. 13:5-23; Lk. 21:8-19, 25-28; Rev. 3:10.
2. Cf. 1 Thess. 1:10; 5:1-9; 2 Thess. 1:6-9; 2:3-12; 1 Jn. 2:18; Rev. 6-19; cf. characteristics present throughout "last days," 1 Tim. 4:1-3; 2 Tim. 3:1-9.
3. Cf., e.g., R. J. Bauckham, "The Great Tribulation in the Shepherd of Hermas," *Journal of Theological Studies* 25:1 (April 1974): 27-40.
4. E.g. cf. 2 Bar. 25-30, which gives a detailed description of the Tribulation, states that it is for the punishment of Israel, and places it within the 70 weeks of Daniel. For a complete discussion cf Dale Allison, Jr. "The Great Tribulation in Jewish Literature," in *The End of the Ages Has Come: An Early Interpretation of the Passion and Resurrection of Jesus* (Edinburgh: T. & T Clark, 1987), 5-25
5. For a discussion cf. Joshua Bloch, *On the Apocalyptic in Judaism, Jewish Quarterly Review* Monograph Series, No. II (Philadelphia. The Dropsie College for Hebrew and Cognate Learning, 1952), esp. 23-25, 121-122
6. Dan. 9:27 in Matt. 24:15/Mk. 13:14
7. Jer. 30:6-7 in Matt. 24:8-9/Mk. 13:8; Dan. 12:1; cf. Joel 2:2; in Matt. 24:21/Mk. 13:19
8. Isa. 13:6 in Rev. 6:16-17
9. *Thlipsis* is used both for the expression of the Great Tribulation (Matt. 24:21/Mk. 13:19) and for the eschatological "wrath" [of God], from which believers are promised deliverance (1 Thess

1:10). Other Greek terms for the Tribulation include *peirasmos* ("trial"), as in Rev. 3:10 ("the hour of trial").

10. Even so, as Wenham has observed, the juxtaposition of the A.D. 70 "distress" with the Tribulation context serves to direct the reader's attention from the local disaster to the greater events of the divine intervention, cf. David Wenham, "The Rediscovery of Jesus' Eschatological Discourse," *Gospel Perspectives 4* (Sheffield: JSOT Press, 1984), 137-138. However, contra Wenham, this connection is between past and future, type and antitype.

11. These represent terms or groups of terms used in prophetic judgment contexts regardless of their immediate or ultimate chronological referent.

12. In the Zephaniah passage (vv. 15-16) ten additional terms are paralleled with *yom sarah* as Tribulation terms (see above) as describing various events characterizing the Day of the Lord (v. 14, cf. the judgment section of Rev. 6–19).

13. This term is paralleled by the similar expression *nakriah' avodato* ("His alien/foreign deeds") which enforces the idea that *this* act of judgment is unusual because it is *against* YHWH's people rather than *for* them.

14. The reading of the Qere *shot* is also supported by the Isaiah Scroll from Qumran (*1QIsa*). The literal meaning of the term is "whip," however, with *shotef* ("overflowing") a mixed metaphor would result, therefore the sense is drawn from the action (the wavy motion) or the result (the sting) of a whip. The assonance also indicates this figure of a punishment that comes like a flood.

15. This "day" is qualified especially as YHWH's (Isa. 34:8a; 63:4a [see 62:8]), and God's (Isa. 35:4a; 61:2b).

16. This negative term is paralleled with positive expressions in its various contexts: Isa. 34:8b; 35:4b—*snat sillumim* ("The Year of Repayment"), Isa. 61:2a—*shnat rason* ("The Year of Acceptance"), Isa. 63:4b—*shnat ge'ulah* ("[My] Year of Redemption"). The use of both *yom* ("day") and *shanah* ("year") in these parallels point both to a *definite* time in which this punishment will be enacted, and to the two purposes of the Tribulation judgments: to destroy the domination of the Gentile powers (negative), and to deliver the remnant of the Jewish people (positive).

17. This view is adopted by the school of "realized eschatology." Cf. Dale Allison, Jr., who writes: "Jesus had suffered and died in the great tribulation," *The End of the Ages Has Come: An Early Interpretation of the Passion and Resurrection of Jesus* (Edinburgh: T. & T. Clark, 1985), 3.

18. David Chilton, *The Great Tribulation* (Dominion Press, 1987).

19. The classic dispensational hermeneutic of dual sense or double fulfillment (*contra* the Reformed hermeneutic of single fulfillment based on the principle of *analogia Scriptura*) is better understood in light of progressive revelation and the continuity between motifs that particularize and intensify as they move toward the eschaton. Therefore, we can allow that there is one primary historical meaning/reference in an Old Testament text without excluding a secondary eschatological meaning/reference as the original concept develops and assumes an eschatological character.

20. Cf. Douglas Stuart, "The Sovereign's Day of Conquest," *Bulletin of the American Schools of Oriental Research* 220/221 (December 1975, February 1976): 159-164.

21. Cf. Gerhard von Rad, "The Origin of the Concept of the Day of Yahweh," *Journal of Semitic Studies* 4 (1959): 97-108.

22. Robert B. Chisholm, Jr., "Joel," *The Bible Knowledge Commentary* (Wheaton, IL: Victor Books, 1985) 1:1412.

23. Simon John DeVries, *Yesterday, Today and Tomorrow: Time and History in the Old Testament* (Grand Rapids: Wm. B. Eerdmans Publishing Co., 1975), 341.

24. The following passages apparently include the millennial blessings as part of the "Day of the Lord": Isa. 30:23-25; 35:1-10; Joel 3:18; Zech. 14:6-11.

25. The debate in this case is over the theme of the "Day of the Lord"—whether it is strictly one of divine judgment or also includes the divine blessings that follow, usually introduced by the phrase *yom hahu'* ("that day")? Those who argue for the former contend that the blessings are the *result* of the "Day of the Lord," rather than a part of the "Day of the Lord" itself, i.e., a new order restored by divine justice. They would also argue that "that day" is a more general eschatological referent, and is not necessarily equivalent to the "Day of the Lord." Those who argue for the latter, point to the unbroken succession from judgment to blessing in many texts (e.g., Zech. 14:1-21; Joel 3:9-21) which appear to describe one event with a two-fold nature. As to the form *yom hahu'* ("that day"), Zech. 14:1 is introduced by the phrase *la'donai ... yom* ("a day ... for YHWH"), but the events which describe that day in vv. 2-21 are introduced by *yom*

hahu' ("that day"). In this context, which includes blessings with judgment, the "Day of the Lord" and "that day" are equivalent.

26. Cf. Richard Mayhue, "The Prophet's Watchword: Day of the Lord," *Grace Theological Journal* 6:2 (1985): 231-246 who argues that the "Day of the Lord" properly occurs only at the climatic time of judgment at the end of the Tribulation (2 Thess. 2:2; Rev. 16-18) and at the consummating judgment at the end of the millennium which puts down the final rebellion of unbelief (Rev. 20:7-9) and ushers in the new earth (Rev. 20:10–21:1; 2 Pet. 3:10-13).

27. Cf. Joel 2:1 which states that the day is "near." The statement of uniqueness in v. 2 should not be equated with statements of uniqueness or incomparableness ascribed to the Tribulation period in other texts. While the "Day of the Lord" is the general subject of vv. 1ff, in v. 2 the subject shifts to the invading army which by means of simile is compared with the locust of chapter 1 (cf. 2:25). It is to this army that the ascription of uniqueness applies, rather than to the "Day of the Lord" itself.

28. Cf. H. Hosch, "The Concept of Prophetic Time in the Book of Joel," *Journal of the Evangelical Theological Society*, 15 (1972): 32-38.

29. In the New Testament use of this term some uses are in dispute, e.g., Rev. 1:10 where "on the Day of the Lord" (eschatological) could also mean "on the Lord's day" (ecclesiological). John's vision, however, is of the events surrounding the "Day of the Lord."

30. In the Olivet discourse, the chiastic structure requires an essential identity between the corresponding elements. *Thlipsis* occurs in both divisions, the lesser leading to the greater, just as false prophets lead to the false prophet and the abomination of desolation.

31. This is seen by the use of the constative aorist ("has come") in Rev. 6:17 to indicate that the Tribulation wrath begins with the first five seals and is climaxed in the sixth. A similar use of the aorist passive ("has been finished") in Rev. 15:1 reveals that the Tribulation judgments had been going on and had only now ended. For a discussion of this interpretation cf. Robert Thomas, *Revelation 1–7: An Exegetical Commentary* (Chicago: Moody Press, 1992), 451-452, 458-59.

32. Orthodox Jewish interpreters share the belief of evangelical Christians that eschatology can be traced for the explication of the development of later motifs to the preprophetic period. Hartman, as a representative of this view, contends that "in the age of the Patriarchs, of Moses and Joshua, and of the Judges, and in the first few centuries of the monarchy there is little evidence of true eschatology. Yet the basis of later Israelite eschatology was really laid down in that early age," Louis F. Hartman, "Eschatology: In the Bible," *Encyclopedia Judaica*, 6 (1972), 862.

33. Akkadian historical texts indicate an immediate or remote future time. The cognate Akkadian term, *ina ahrât umi* (from the Sumerian *ina ahriat umi*), often shortened to *ina ahrâti* ("in the future," or "for [all] the future"). In like manner the phrase *be^ah^arit hayamim* can sometimes mean simply "in the future, in time to come" (e.g., Deut. 31:29; cf. *'ah^arit* ("a future," Jer. 29:11). Ugaritic texts have non-temporal meanings such as "then," "last one" or "destiny" or "last person" (remnant or destiny). Aramaic terms, such as *'ah^ari*, found in the Qumran texts, is the closest equivalent to the Hebrew term and refers in the contexts of its two usages to the end of a discourse ("finally"), *4QEnGiants*, or to the latter ("final") portion of Job's life (*11Q Job*). Other Aramaic uses refer to the general future or to the time of death.

34. One such case is the possible eschatological meaning of Akkadian *ahratas in the Enuma elish* epic. In line 133 of Tablet VII we may read: "Into the future [*ahratas*] of mankind, when days have grown old . . ." The problem with the translation is that the relevant line appears in a recitation of the 50 names of Marduk and does not seem to harmonize with its context. One of the names bestowed, which appears in the line preceding, is an appellative of praise in view of vanquishing Tiamat. If the praise is for a past event (chronicled in Tablet IV), how can it be thought of as an eschatological future event in the next line? Nevertheless, Speiser contends that it has a remote future sense and translates: "May he vanquish Tiamat until the days have grown old" (i.e., until the end), *ANET*, 72. The Chicago Assyrian Dictionary (CAD), although noting the difficulty of this line, also opts for a remote future sense.

35. The verb (in the *Pi'el stem* 15 of its 17 appearances) has the meaning of "tarry," "delay," or "defer." The preposition *'achar*, appearing in the plural construct form *'achare* has the temporal meaning of "after or behind." The adjective, *'achar*, sometimes bears the sense of "following, next" (cf. Gen. 17:21), although generally it means simply "other, another." Another adjective *'acharon* has the temporal idea of "future," although its primary meaning is "behind, beyond," with reference to a geographical location which lies beyond or "westerward" (cf. Deut. 11:24). That these uses have the sense "behind," which appears opposite of "what lies ahead" (the future") is not problematic in light of the Hebrew conception of time as Hans Walter Wolff notes: "a man rowing a boat sees where he has been and backs into the

future" (lecture notes as recorded by R. Laird Harris, "*'achar*," *Theological Wordbook of the Old Testament* (*TWOT*) (Chicago: Moody Press, 1980), 1:34.

36. Cf. Horst Seebass, "*'acharit*," *Theological Dictionary of the Old Testament*, ed. by G. J. Botterweck and H. Ringgren (Grand Rapids: Wm. B. Eerdmans Publishing Co., 1974), 1:207.

37. In a similar manner, both the expression *'acharit* ("last") and *qetz* ("end") are used with *hayamim* ("the days") in the Dead Sea Scrolls; with *'acharit hayamim* ("the last days") having the sense of the "messianic time," which comes, in distinction to *qetz* ("end [time]"), comes after the "end" (*qetz*) of wickedness. Examples of usage are: *be'acharit hayamim* (D IV. 4, 10)/*le'ach^arit hayamim* (pHab II. 5; V. 3-6; IX. 6), and *qetz* (D VI. 10, 14; XII. 23; XV. 7, 10; pHab VII. 7, 12)/*qetz 'acharon* (S IV. 16; pHab VII. 7, 12).

38. E.g., G. A. Smith, *The Book of Deuteronomy*, Cambridge Bible for Schools and Colleges (Cambridge: University Press, 1918), 69; J. A. Thompson, "Deuteronomy," *Tyndale Old Testament Commentary* (Downers Grove, IL: Inter-Varsity Press, 1974), 107; Peter Craigie, "The Book of Deuteronomy," *The New International Commentary on the Old Testament* (Grand Rapids: Wm. B. Eerdmans Publishing Co., 1976), 141; Duane L. Christensen, "Deuteronomy 1-11," *Word Biblical Commentary* (Waco: Word Books, 1991), 94.

39. W. J. Schroeder, "Deuteronomy," *Lange's Commentary on the Holy Scriptures* (Grand Rapids: Zondervan Publishing House, 1976) 3:73.

40. C. F. Keil, "Deuteronomy" in *The Pentateuch*, Biblical Commentary on the Old Testament (with F. Delitzsch) (Grand Rapids: Wm. B. Eerdmans Publishing Co., n.d.) 3:313.

41. Merril F. Unger, *Unger's Commentary on the Old Testament* (Chicago: Moody Press, 1981), 1: 240; Jack Deere, "Deuteronomy," *The Bible Knowledge Commentary* (Wheaton, IL: Victor Books, 1985), 270.

42. The reading of the Massoretic Text has as a consequence of Israelite exile the punishment of serving idols. However, the Targum Onkelos renders this as "you shall serve *peoples* who serve idols." Rashi therefore understands that the deliverance from this "tribulation" (v. 30), will be the end of Gentile domination and the restoration of covenantal blessings (v. 31), resulting from Israelite repentance (v. 29), cf. Rashi, "Deuteronomy," *Pentateuch with Targum Onkelos, Haphtorah and Rashi's Commentary* (Jerusalem: Silberman Family, 1973), 27-28.

43. As with the section from Ezek. 36–40, of which this passage is a part, the events *could* have had their fulfillment in the return from exile, but *did not*, and therefore were understood to belong to an apocalyptic scenario at the end of the age.

44. This formula was employed by the apocalypticists of Qumran and in the New Testament where the expression is *ep' eschastou ton chronon* or *kairon*. In most instances *chronos* appears to be used synonymously with *kairos*. Often the term *sunteleia* (from *sunteleo*, "finish, bring to an end") is also used to express this eschatological period. Examples of New Testament passages for the formula are: Matt. 8:29; Mk. 1:15; 10:30; 13:33; Lk. 1:20; 19:44; 21:8; Rom. 3:26; 12:11; 13:11; 1 Cor. 4:5; Gal. 6:9; Eph. 1:10; 5:16; Col. 4:5; 1 Thess. 5:1; 2 Thess. 2:6; 1 Tim. 2:6; 4:1; 6:15; 2 Tim. 3:1; Heb. 9:9; 1 Pet. 1:11; 4:17; 5:6; Rev. 1:3; 11:18; 12:14; 22:10. Hans Kosmala, in his study of the formula: "At the End of the Days," *Annual of the Swedish Theological Institute*, 2 (1963), edited by Hans Kosmala (Leiden: E. J. Brill), 27-37, argued that it is not used consistently to mean "the end time" in the biblical texts, and that the Christian sense of the term differs from the primitive Hebrew concept. However, even if the connotation of the formula should differ between early and later texts, this might be expected since a developmental aspect (assuming progressive revelation) would naturally account for the more definite meaning in the later apocalyptic literature and the New Testament.

45. In three texts (Amos 8:2; Lam. 4:18; Ezek. 7:2,3,6), *qetz* ("end") is employed in the context of the "Day of the Lord," with clearly eschatological intent.

46. For a study of this phrase in Daniel, cf. Gerhard Pfandl, "The Time of the End in the Book of Daniel." *Adventist Theological Society Dissertation Series 1* (Berrin Springs, MI: Adventist Theological Society Publications, 1992), 213-272.

47. S. Lewis Johnson, *The Old Testament in the New: An Argument for Biblical Inspiration* (Grand Rapids: Zondervan Publishing House, 1980), 70.

48. By contrast, Richard M. Davidson sees Christ's temptations in the wilderness (Matt. 4; Lk. 4) as the typological pattern for the Church's experience (1 Cor. 10:5-14), and ultimately of the "hour of temptation" (Rev. 3:10) and the Great Tribulation (Rev. 7:14), cf. chart 4: "The Salvation-Historical Substructure of Biblical Typology" in "The Hermeneutics of Biblical Theology." Unpublished paper, Evangelical Theological Society Annual Meeting (Chicago, November, 1994), 4. However, Christ's temptation was not in terms of the covenantal curses (for He never violated the covenant), and 1 Cor. 10:5-14 is a typological correspondence based on Israel's exodus *experience*, which unlike the covenantal stipulations, is applicable to the Church.

49. For a chart detailing this progressive development see the author's *In Search of Temple Treasures* (Eugene, OR: Harvest House, 1994), 249.
50. Josephus used similar phrases to describe Jewish suffering during their war with Rome (cf. *Wars*, Proem. 4; V. x. 5; VI. ix. 4). George Beasley-Murray also cites Plato (*Republic* 6, 492E) as another example, cf. *A Commentary on Mark Thirteen* (London: Macmillan & Co., 1957), 78 and *Jesus and the Last Days: The Interpretation of the Olivet Discourse* (Peabody, MA: Hendrickson, 1993), 419.
51. Jeremiah also used this figure to apply to other than eschatological distresses (e.g., 4:31; 6:24; 22:23), however, if it applied to lesser times of trouble, it was even more appropriate for the greatest time of trouble.
52. Cf. A. Bauman, *"chil," Theological Dictionary of the Old Testament* (Grand Rapids: Wm. B. Eerdmans Publishing Co., 1980), 4:344-45.
53. The eschatological interpretation of this passage may have influenced the Qumran text 1QH 3:7-10, in which the birth of the community is depicted as occurring at the eschaton after a terrible description of birth pangs (v. 8).
54. The term expresses the idea that Israel, like a mother, was to bring forth the Messiah through the labor pains of childbirth. As such, they would begin at a determined point and increase in intensity until the time of delivery.
55. In Isa. 66:7-9 the figure of birth pangs applied to Israel at its national rebirth (v. 8). This may have served as the principal Old Testament reference for the rabbis in their conception of the Messianic birth pangs. The term as a technical expression is first seen in rabbinic literature in Sahn. 98b and Mek. on Ex. 16:25, where it is attributed to Eliezer, who may be the son of Hyrcanus (c. A.D. 90). Nevertheless, the Jewish concept of the "messianic woes" was already in place by the first century, as revealed by the Greek term ὠδίνων (*odinon*) "birth pangs" used in the New Testament as a Tribulation term (Matt. 24:8; Mk. 13:8).
56. R' Sh'muel Masnuth, *Midrash Daniel* (Jerusalem: I. S. Lange & S. Schwartz, 1968) [Hebrew]. Ten signs of the messianic birth pangs are enumerated in *Sanhedrin 97b* as: (1) the world is either all righteous or all guilty, (2) truth is in short supply, (3) inflation will soar, (4) Israel will have begun to be repopulated according to Ezek. 36:8-12, (5) wise people will be scarce, (6) the Jews will have despaired of Redemption, (7) the young will be contemptuous of the old, (8) scholarship will be rejected, (9) piety will be in disgust, and (10) a growing number of Jews will turn on their own people. Similar statements are given in *Sotah* 9:15 concerning the days of messianic advent, called here "the footprints of the Messiah."
57. R' Solomon ben Yitzchak (Rashi), *Commentary to the Bible* (Jerusalem, 1956) [Hebrew].
58. Other rabbinic literature also presents the concept of the end-time Jewish sufferings in its discussions of false prophets, cf. George W. Buchanan, *Revelation and Redemption: Jewish Documents of Deliverance from the Fall of Jerusalem to the Death of Nachmanides* (Dillsboro, North Carolina: Western North Carolina Press, 1978), 73, 75, 91-105, 150-53, 320-21, 410-11.
59. The same eschatological significance is seen in the use of this term in Jewish apocalyptic literature (cf. *Apocalypse of Abraham* 30:3-8), and at Qumran, where one text foretells the advent of the Messiah in the period of eschatological Tribulation (cf. 1Q 3:7-18).
60. See Gerhard Delling, *"chronos,"* s.v. "Time in Judaism," *Theological Dictionary of the New Testament* (Grand Rapids: Wm. B. Eerdmans Pub. Co., 1974), IX:586. However, he notes that *chronos* is only used by the LXX for '*et* in Jeremiah and then only in addition to Jer. 30:7 (37:7) in Jer. 30:2 (49:8) and 38 (31):1. His argument in part derives from his equation of '*et* with *qez*, which is also translated by *chronos*. However, context must determine usage, and the context of Jer. 30:3-9 contains demonstrably eschatological referents.
61. In v. 8 the Hebrew text reads "*his* yoke," perhaps implying an understood oppressor in the context.
62. The Hebrew noun '*ol* ("yoke") was derived from the verbal idea of *inserting* ('*alal*), i.e., inserting the neck into a restrictive device.
63. Some commentators suggest that the similar wording of Isa. 10:27 was in Jeremiah's mind, but even so, it would not require that Jeremiah intended an immediate historical reference by its use.
64. The restoration phrase is *sub s^ebut* (literally "turn the turning") and indicates a reversal of condition.
65. Cf. the LXX which reads: "they shall no longer serve foreigners."
66. The LXX, however, reads simply "*the* yoke," perhaps as an attempt to circumvent the ambiguity with the suffixes.
67. The presence of these northern and southern tribes is revealed in the make-up of the 144,000 (Rev. 7:4-8), and the distinction between these 144,000 Jewish believers and the rest of the Jewish population may be indicated in Rev. 12:17.

68. The LXX omitted these verses from chapter 30 (which in its arrangement would have been a restatement), and included them only in chapter 46, although chapter 30 appears to be the original context.

69. For justification as to this text applying to the end time see my discussion "Prophetic Postponement in Daniel 9 and Other Texts," chapter 7 in *Issues in Dispensationalism*, eds. J. Master, W. Willis, C. C. Ryrie (Chicago: Moody Press, 1994), 133-65. For my discussion of the citation of Dan. 9:27 in the New Testament see my published dissertation *The Desecration and Restoration of the Temple in the Tanach, Jewish Apocalyptic Literature, and the New Testament* (Ann Arbor, MI: UMI, 1993), 353-411 (Dan. 9:27), 502-10, 563-78, 587-96 (Dan. 9:27 in N.T.).

70. The idiomatic construction *higᵉbbir bᵉrit* ("to strengthen a covenant") may be interpreted as either inaugurating ("making") a new covenant or ratifying ("confirming") an existing covenant. In either sense, the purpose for which the covenant is established—to effect a religio-political accord permitting the rebuilding of the Temple—is the same.

71. The implied personal subject of the verbal clause (cf. personal object "the many") may be either "the Messiah" or "the coming leader" of the previous verse. Since "the coming leader" is the nearer antecedent, it is grammatically preferable.

72. It is the *trouble* in the rebuilt temple, not temple's rebuilding, that is the urgent concern and the basis for warning. Furthermore, under the terms of the covenant, Jerusalem would have the status of a protected place, until the violation of the covenant changed this condition. This change would have been additional motive for writing the words of warning (cf. Matt. 24:16-28; Mk. 13:15-23; Rev. 11:1-2).

73. *Daniel*, The Artscroll Tanach Series (New York: Mesorah Publications, Ltd., 1989), 260.

74. This arrangement is adapted from the chiastic structure diagrams by S. Joseph Kidder, "'This Generation' in Matthew," *Andrews University Seminary Studies* 21:3 (Autumn, 1983), 208-09.

75. John Hartley, s.v. *"sar," Theological Wordbook of the Old Testament* (Chicago: Moody Press, 1980), 2:778.

Chapter Four—The Blessed Hope and the Tribulation in the Apostolic Fathers

1. George Eldon Ladd, *The Blessed Hope* (Grand Rapids: Wm. B. Eerdmans Publishing Co., 1956), 19.
2. Ibid., 20.
3. Ibid., 31.
4. Robert H. Gundry, *The Church and the Tribulation* (Grand Rapids: Zondervan Publishing Co., 1973), 173. For a more recent study that essentially follows Ladd and Gundry see Thomas Lea's "A Survey of the Doctrine of the Return of Christ in the Ante-Nicene Fathers" *Journal of the Evangelical Theological Society*, 29 (June 1986), 163-77.
5. Henry C. Thiessen, *Introductory Lectures in Systematic Theology* (Grand Rapids: Wm. B. Eerdmans Publishing Co., 1949), 477.
6. John F. Walvoord, *The Return of the Lord* (Grand Rapids: Zondervan Publishing House, 1955), 80.
7. John F. Walvoord, *The Rapture Question*, rev. ed. (Grand Rapids: Zondervan Publishing House, 1979), 51.
8. John F. Walvoord, *The Blessed Hope and the Tribulation* (Grand Rapids: Zondervan Publishing House, 1976), 24-25.
9. Ladd, *The Blessed Hope*, 31, and Robert H. Gundry, *The Church and the Tribulation* (Grand Rapids: Zondervan Publishing Co., 1973), 178. For a recent study which reaches the same conclusions see Thomas Lea's "A Survey of the Doctrine of the Return of Christ in the Ante-Nicene Fathers" *Journal of the Evangelical Theological Society*, 29 (June 1986), 163-77.
10. Gundry, *The Church and the Tribulation*, 179.
11. Ladd, *The Blessed Hope*, 31
12. Ibid.
13. Millard J. Erickson, *Contemporary Options in Eschatology* (Grand Rapids: Baker Book House, 1977), 112.
14. Thomas Lea's "A Survey of the Doctrine of the Return of Christ in the Ante-Nicene Fathers" *Journal of the Evangelical Theological Society*, 29 (June 1986), 177.
15. J. Barton Payne, *The Imminent Appearing of Christ* (Grand Rapids: Wm. B. Eerdmans Publishing Co., 1962), 12-19.
16. *I Clement* 23. The two Scripture passages are from Habakkuk 2:3 (cf. Hebrews 10:37) and Malachi 3:1 respectively
17. Ibid., 34
18. Ibid., 35

19. Gundry, *The Church and the Tribulation*, 173
20. Ibid.
21. Ibid., 93-95
22. Ibid., 173
23. Ignatius, *Epistle to the Ephesians* 11
24. Ibid., *Epistle to Polycarp* 1
25. Ibid., 3
26. *The Didache* 10.6. Compare with 1 Corinthians 16:22 and Revelation 22:20. Unless otherwise stated, all patristic quotations in this study are from Alexander Roberts and James Donaldson, eds., *The Ante-Nicene Fathers*, 10 vols. (Grand Rapids: Wm. B. Eerdmans Publishing Co., n.d.), or Philip Schaff and Henry Wace, eds., *Nicene and Post Nicene Fathers*, 14 vols., second series (Grand Rapids: Wm. B. Eerdmans Publishing Co., n.d.)
27. *The Didache* 16.1-2
28. Ibid., 16.2-3
29. Ibid., 16.3-5
30. This very rare expression is difficult to render (see Matt. 24:30). Some have suggested that it speaks of the hole in the heavens through which Christ will descend. Others "derive the word from πέτομαι· 'a being caught up, a flying up, to heaven' " (Johannes Quasten and Joseph C Plumpe, eds., *Ancient Christian Writers*, 42 vols. (New York; Ramsey, NJ: Newman Press, 1946), 6.166). Whatever the expression means, it will be a visible sign of some sort. If it does refer to the rapture of the saints, it is in keeping with the usual practice of the early fathers to associate this event with the second coming with little or no intervening time.
31. *The Didache* 16.6-8. The parallel passage in the *Constitutions of the Holy Apostles* (various dates from early third to mid-fourth century), the compiler of which seems to have used *The Didache* as a source, adds references at this point to the final judgment and the eternal state (Ch. 32).
32. Ladd, *The Blessed Hope*, 20
33. J. Barton Payne comes closer perhaps than any other modern writer to approximating the position of the early fathers on tribulationism. For a presentation of his views, see *The Imminent Appearing of Christ* (Grand Rapids: Wm. B. Eerdmans Publishing Co., 1962). For a valuable analysis of Payne's concepts as they relate to the fathers, see Walvoord, *The Blessed Hope*, 16-17, 21-25
34. Gundry, *The Church and the Tribulation*, 175. Irenaeus' position on the subject will be discussed in its proper place
35. *The Didache* 16.1
36. *The Epistle of Barnabas* 4. Compare this portion of *Barnabas* with *The Didache*, 16.1-3, where there is remarkable similarity. Cf. R. Ludwigson, *A Survey of Bible Prophecy* (Grand Rapids, Zondervan Publishing Co., 1973), 25
37. Victorinus of Petau *Commentary on the Apocalypse* 17.10-11
38. Commodian, *The Instructions of Commodianus* 41, Lactantius, *Of the Manner in Which the Persecutors Died* 2
39. Justin Martyr, *Dialogue with Trypho* 110. In the early church there seemed to be a perpetuation of the Thessalonian error that the Day of the Lord had already come (2 Thess. 2:2). However, unlike the Thessalonian congregation, the fathers clearly understood that the "lawless one" must be revealed (2 Thess. 2:8-9) before the coming of Christ. Barnabas seems to believe that the "lawless one" is already here, while the Didachist speaks in the future tense. But this does not necessarily contradict Barnabas' position. The Didachist is merely recounting what Scripture says about the last days. He says nothing specifically about where the church is in that outline of end-time events.
40. See Ignatius, *Epistle to the Ephesians* 9; *Epistle to the Trallians* 10-11
41. *The Didache* 16.1
42. Walvoord, *The Rapture Question*, 51
43. *The Constitutions of the Holy Apostles* 31 (italics added).
44. *The Didache* 16.5. Walvoord observes that the teaching on the fiery trial, sounding of the trumpet, and the resurrection can all "be harmonized with pretribulationism as it is taught today" (*The Rapture Question*, 53). The point Walvoord makes is that while this is not explicit pretribulationism, neither is an explicit posttribulational position required by the passage.
45. *The Didache* 16.8
46. Ladd, *The Blessed Hope*, 21
47. Gundry, *The Church and the Tribulation*, 175 (of course Gundry assumes a posttribulational interpretation of Matt. 24:31); *The Didache* 9 and 10. Stated mathematically, Gundry's line of

reasoning is that since the Didachist calls for the church (x) to be gathered from the "four winds" (z), and Matthew 24:31 calls for the "elect" (y) to be gathered from the "four winds" (z), then the church (x) = the elect (y). For if x = z and y = z, then x must equal y because things equal to the same thing must be equal to each other. The problem with Gundry's argument is that the Didachist never introduces the value y, nor does he anywhere suggest that z is to be understood in the context of Matthew 24. Consequently, Gundry's conclusion is based solely upon basic premises which he has invented and which cannot be demonstrated to have been in the mind of the Didachist.

48. Johannes Quasten and Joseph C. Plumpe, eds., *Ancient Christian Writers*, 42 vols. (New York; Ramsey, NJ: Newman Press, 1946), 6.160 note 60.

49. In chapter 16, Barnabas pictures a temple in ruins. Thus the date of the epistle is variously set between the destruction of the temple in A.D. 70 by Titus and the second destruction during the Barcochba rebellion (ending A.D. 138). The fact that Barnabas then seems to indicate that the temple is being rebuilt in his own day by those who destroyed it (in fulfillment of Isa. 49:17 in the LXX), has led some scholars to look to the building of the temple of Jupiter in Jerusalem during Hadrian's reign (117–138) as the most likely time frame for composition (see Johannes Quasten, *Patrology*, 3 vols. [Westminster, Md.: Christian Classics, Inc., 1983], 1:90-91). Of the two primary texts for this epistle, the *Codex Sinaiticus* (fourth century) and the *Codex Hierosolymitanus* (1056), the former (an older manuscript) omits the reference to the rebuilding of the temple in Barnabas's day (see Roberts and Donaldson, *The Ante-Nicene Fathers*, 1:147, note 13).

50. *The Epistle of Barnabas* 21.

51. Ibid., 4. See the discussion of imminency in *The Didache* for further analysis of the portion of this chapter which parallels that work. For the phrase "The final stumbling-block...approaches," the *Ancient Christian Writers* series has, "The final stumbling block has appeared" (Quasten and Plumpe, *Ancient Christian Writers*, 6.40).

52. Kelly, *Early Christian Doctrines*, 462.

53. See Ladd, *The Blessed Hope*, 22; Gundry, *The Church and the Tribulation*, 173-74; and Erickson, *Contemporary Options*, 149.

54. *The Epistle of Barnabas* 4 (italics added).

55. Ibid., 21.

56. Ibid., 2 and 3.

57. Thiessen, *Introductory Lectures*, 476.

58. Ladd, *The Blessed Hope*, 23-24. Cf. Gundry, *The Church and the Tribulation*, 174-75, and Erickson, *Contemporary Options*, 129.

59. *The Shepherd of Hermas* 3.9.7.

60. Ibid., 1.3.8.

61. This paragraph is the substance of 1.4.1.

62. *The Shepherd of Hermas* 1.4.2.

63. Ibid.

64. Ibid., 1.4.3 (emphasis added).

65. Thiessen, *Introductory Lectures*, 476. Cf. Henry C. Thiessen, "Will the Church Pass Through the Tribulation?" *Bibliotheca Sacra* 92 (April 1935):196.

66. Ladd, *The Blessed Hope*, 23.

67. *The Shepherd of Hermas* 1.4.2.

68. Thiessen, "Will the Church Pass Through the Tribulation?" 196.

69. *The Shepherd of Hermas* 1.2.2.

70. Ladd, *The Blessed Hope*, 23-24.

71. *The Shepherd of Hermas* 1.2.3.

72. Ibid., 1.4.3. The concept of purification through persecution is one which will be encountered in later writers.

73. Ibid., 3.9.18.

74. Ibid., 1.4.3.

75. See, for example, Clement of Rome, *1 Clement* 23, 34-35; Ignatius, *Epistle to Polycarp* 1 and 3; *The Didache* 16.1; *The Shepherd of Hermas* 3.5, 7 and 26; *The Epistle of Barnabas* 21. For fathers of the second century see Tertullian, *Apology* 21, and Cyprian, *The Treatises of Cyprian* I.27. There are expressions of imminency even in those who expect certain events to occur before the end, as in Hippolytus, *On Christ and Antichrist* 5; and Lactantius, *The Divine Institutes* 25.

76. Walvoord, *The Rapture Question*, 50-54.

77. Millard J. Erickson, who is himself a posttribulationist, says "To be sure, the premillennialism of the church's first centuries may have included belief in a pretribulational rapture of the

church..." But he avers elsewhere that "While there are in the writings of the early fathers seeds from which the doctrine of the pretribulational rapture could be developed, it is difficult to find in them an unequivocal statement of the type of imminency usually believed in by pretribulationists" (*Contemporary Options in Eschatology* [Grand Rapids: Baker Book House, 1977], 112, 131). This in essence is all that we are arguing for. We do not say that the early fathers were pretribulationists in the modern sense, only that the seeds were indeed there but were crushed under the allegorist's foot before they could sprout and bear early fruit.

78. See *The Didache* 16; Irenaeus, *Against Heresies* 5.29.1; Tertullian, *On the Resurrection of the Flesh* 41, and Victorinus *Commentary on the Apocalypse* 12.1 and 15.1.

79. For examples of the language of escape see *The Shepherd of Hermas* 1.4.2-3; Hippolytus, *Appendix to Works* 32 and 35; and Lactantius, *The Epitome of the Divine Institutes* 71.

80. See, for example, Ignatius, *Epistle to the Romans* 4; Irenaeus, *Against Heresies* 5.28.2; and *The Shepherd of Hermas* 1.4.3.

81. Among these are *The Epistle of Barnabas* 4; Irenaeus, *Against Heresies* 5.30.2; Hippolytus, *Treatise on Christ and Antichrist* 28-29; Tertullian, *On the Resurrection of the Flesh* 24-25; and Lactantius, *The Divine Institutes* 7.25.

82. See *The Epistle of Barnabas* 4. That Barnabas understood the fourth beast of Daniel 7:7-8 to be the Roman empire is certain. But what he thought of the ten-three-one horn scenario we do not know. The single horn was of course the evil one to come in the end (the Roman empire). And perhaps he held the others to represent minor kingdoms already subdued by Rome. In any case, as patristic scholar J. N. D. Kelly points out, "Barnabas is satisfied that the scandal of the last days is actually upon us..." (*Early Christian Doctrines*, rev. ed. [New York: Harper and Row. Publishers, 1978], 462).

83. See Irenaeus, *Against Heresies* 5.29.1 and 5.30.2.

84. Tertullian, *The Shows, or De Spectaculis* 30.

85. Lactantius, *The Divine Institutes* 25 (italics added).

86. Obviously Hippolytus' chronology made the imminent return of Christ impossible in his day. By his reckoning, some 250 years remained before the allotted 6000 years of man were to expire (*Fragments from Commentaries*, "On Daniel," 2.4-6).

87. Some of the fathers, Hippolytus, Tertullian, Lactantius, and others, clearly have posttribulational elements in their views concerning the end-times. But we have been unable to find an instance of the unequivocal classic posttribulationism taught today. Walvoord's assessment of the fathers' views on the tribulation is essentially correct. He says, "The preponderance of evidence seems to support the concept that the early church did not clearly hold to a rapture as preceding the end-time tribulation period. Most of the early church fathers who wrote on the subject at all considered themselves already in the great tribulation. Accordingly Payne, as well as most other posttribulationists, takes the position that it is self-evident that pretribulationism as it is taught today was unheard of in the early centuries of the church. Consequently the viewpoint of the early church fathers is regarded by practically all posttribulationists, whether adherents of the classic view or not, as a major argument in favor of posttribulationism. However, the fact that most posttribulationists today do not accept the doctrine of imminency as the early church held it diminishes the force of their argument against pretribulationism" (*The Blessed Hope*, 1976, 24).

88. Walvoord, *The Blessed Hope and the Tribulation*, 25.

89. Erickson, *Contemporary Options*, 131.

Chapter Five—A Pretrib Rapture Statement in the Early Medieval Church

1. Grant R. Jeffrey, *Final Warning* (Toronto: Frontier Research Publications, 1995).

2. George Eldon Ladd, *The Blessed Hope: A Biblical Study of the Second Advent and the Rapture* (Grand Rapids: Wm. B. Eerdmans Publishing Co., 1956), 31.

3. John L. Bray, *The Origin of the Pre-Tribulation Rapture Teaching* (Lakeland, FL: John L. Bray Ministry, 1980), 30-31.

4. Dave MacPherson, *The Incredible Cover-Up* (Medford, OR: Omega Publications, 1975), 156.

5. *On the Last Times, the Antichrist and the End of the World* by Ephraem the Syrian or Pseudo-Ephraem—around A.D. 373.

6. Bray, 30.

7. Paul J. Alexander, *The Byzantine Apocalyptic Tradition* (Berkeley: University of California Press, 1985), 210-11.

8. C. P. Caspari, ed., *Briefe, Abhandlungen und Predigten aus den zwei letzten Jahrhunderten des kirchlichen Altertums und dem Anfang des Mittelaters*, Christiania, 1890.

9. Alexander, 210-11.

10. William E. Bell, "A Critical Evaluation of the Pretribulation Rapture Doctrine in Christian Eschatology" (Ph.D. diss., New York University, 1967), 27.
11. Ibid., 26-27.

Chapter Six—J. N. Darby's Early Years

1. See John Nelson Darby, *Letters of J. N. Darby* (London: Stow Hill Bible and Tract Depot, n.d.; reprint, Sunbury, Pa.: Believers Bookshelf, 1971), 1:73, 205, 431, 451, and 524. An excellent recent biography on Darby is by Max S. Weremchuk, *John Nelson Darby: A Biography* (Neptune, N.J.: Loizeaux Brothers, 1992), 256.
2. W.G. Turner, *John Nelson Darby* (London: C. A. Hammond, 1944), 12.
3. Stuart O. Seanoir, personal letter, Dublin, Ireland, 26 January 1989. Mr. Seanoir is an assistant librarian in the Manuscripts Department at Trinity College, Dublin. He took this information from the *Alumni Dublinenses*.
4. See Darby, *Letters*, 2:310.
5. Ibid., 3:297.
6. Turner, *Darby*, 13-15.
7. Ibid., 16.
8. John Nelson Darby, *The Collected Writings of J. N. Darby (CW)*, ed. William Kelly, new ed. (London: G. Morrish, n.d.; reprint, Sunbury, Pa.: Believers Bookshelf, 1971), 20:288. (Pagination in the new edition is different from the original.)
9. John Howard Goddard, "The Contribution of John Nelson Darby to Soteriology, Ecclesiology, and Eschatology" (Th.D. diss., Dallas Theological Seminary, 1948), 15-16.
10. Darby, *CW*, 1:36.
11. William Blair Neatby, *A History of the Plymouth Brethren* (London: Hodder and Stoughton, 1901), 15.
12. Darby, *CW*, 1:1.
13. Ibid., 1:1-19.
14. See Darby, *Letters*, 1:344; 3:298.
15. Ibid., 3:298-99.
16. Ibid., 3:299.
17. Darby, *CW*, 1:20-35.
18. Larry Vance Crutchfield, "The Doctrine of Ages and Dispensations as Found in the Published Works of John Nelson Darby (1800-1882)" (Ph.D. diss., Drew University, 1985), 10.
19. Darby, *CW*, 2:1-31.
20. Ibid., 2:32.
21. Ibid., 2:31.
22. Ibid., 2:27.
23. Neatby, *History*, 20. Compare, however, Darby's own statement: "When I left it [the Establishment], I published the tract on 'The Nature and Unity of the Church of Christ'" (*CW*, 1:36). This tract is dated 1828.
24. Darby, *CW*, 1:37.
25. Darby, *Letters*, 1:344.
26. Ibid., 3:298-99.
27. Darby, *CW*, 2:1-31.
28. Ibid., 2:32.
29. Ibid., 2:7-9.
30. Ibid., 2:9.
31. Ibid., 2:4.
32. Ibid., 2:18.
33. Ibid., 2:40.
34. Ibid., 2:23.
35. See Richard Graves, *A Sermon Preached in St. Andrew's Church, Dublin, on Sunday, 21st April, 1811. I Aid of the London Society for Promoting Christianity Amongst the Jews* (Dublin: J. Jones, 1811), 38, 40; John in F. C. Harrison, *The Second Coming: Popular Millenarianism (1780-1850)* (New Brunswick, N.J.: Rutgers University Press, 1979), 78; and D. N. Hempton, "Evangelicalism and Eschatology," *Journal of Ecclesiastical History* 31 (April 1980): 182-83. On the little horn of Daniel 7, even Darby remarked, "Napoleon may serve to give us an idea of this state of things" (*CW*, 5:147; cf. 11:386-87).
36. John in F. C. Harrison, *The Second Coming: Popular Millenarianism (1780-1850)* (New Brunswick, N.J.: Rutgers University Press, 1979), 6-14.
37. Hempton, "Evangelicalism and Eschatology," 182.

38. See Ernest R. Sandeen, *The Roots of Fundamentalism: British and American Millenarianism 1800-1930* (Chicago: The University of Chicago Press, 1970), 18-21.
39. Ibid., 20-21.
40. Ibid., 32.
41. See Neatby, *History*, 39; and Harold H. Rowdon, *The Origins of the Brethren, 1825-1850* (London: Pickering and Inglis, 1967), 87.
42. See Erich Geldbach, *Christliche Versammlung und Heilsgeschichte bei John Nelson Darby*, 2d ed. (Solingen: Herm. Weck Sohn, 1972), 26-27.
43. Darby, *Letters*, 1:5-7; Neatby, *History*, 39; and Sandeen, *Roots*, 38.
44. See Turner, *Darby*, 34.
45. Darby, *Letters*, 1:5-7.
46. Sandeen, *Roots*, 36.
47. Darby, *Letters*, 1:6-7.
48. Ibid., 1:7.
49. For a modern historicist approach, see Oral Collins, "Premillennial Historicism," *Henceforth* 11 (Fall 1982-Winter 1983): 29; and the "two-books-in-one" booklet by Edward C. Whisenant, *On Borrowed Time [and] 88 Reasons Why the Rapture Could Be In 1988* (Nashville, TN: World Bible Society, 1988).
50. See John Nelson Darby, *Synopsis of the Books of the Bible*, new ed. (London: G. Morrish, n.d.; reprint, London: Stow Hill Bible Tract Depot, 1965), 5:371-72.
51. Darby, *Letters*, 1:7.
52. Ibid., 1:58. See also Darby's article, "What Saints Will be in the Tribulation?" (*CW*, 11:110-17).
53. Darby, *Letters*, 1:7.
54. Sandeen, *Roots*, 36-37.
55. Ibid., 37.
56. For a different opinion, see Sandeen, *Roots*, 37-38.
57. Darby, *Letters*, 1:7.
58. Ibid., 1:330.
59. Sandeen, *Roots*, 38.
60. Ibid., 64.
61. Darby, *Letters*, 3:299. See also *Letters*, 1:345, written in 1863.
62. Rowdon, *Origins*, 96-97.
63. Darby, *Letters*, 1:58.
64. Darby, *CW*, 14:68. See also Darby, *Letters*, 3:259; *CW*, 2:166.
65. See Robert Gundry, *The Church and the Tribulation* (Grand Rapids: Zondervan Publishing House, 1973), 186-87; and Crutchfield, "The Doctrine of Ages and Dispensations," 35.
66. See Charles C. Ryrie, "The Origins of Dispensationalism," in *Dispensationalism Today* (Chicago: Moody Press, 1965), 65-85; Ralph Franklin Porter, "The Historical Development of the Doctrine of the Distinction Between Israel and the Church" (Th.M. thesis, Dallas Theological Seminary, 1969); and Max Allen Wiley, "Historical Antecedents of Dispensationalism" (Th.M. thesis, Dallas Theological Seminary, 1960).
67. For an opposing opinion, see Larry Vance Crutchfield, "Rudiments of Dispensationalism in the Ante-Nicene Period—Part 1: Israel and the Church in the Ante-Nicene Fathers," *BSac* 144 (July-September 1987): 254-76.
68. Owen Chadwick, *The Victorian Church*, 3d ed. (London: Adam and Charles Black, 1971), 1:6.
69. Darby, *CW*, 18:146, 156.
70. Ibid., 1:33.
71. See Harold H. Rowdon, "Secession from the Established Church in the Early Nineteenth Century," *Vox Evangelica* 3 (1964): 76-78; and Larry Edward Dixon, "The Pneumatology of John Nelson Darby (1880-1882)" (Ph.D. diss., Drew University, 1985), 24-30.
72. Sandeen, *Roots*, 90.
73. W. MacNeile Dixon, *Trinity College, Dublin* (London: F. E. Robinson and Co., 1902), 234.
74. Ibid., xii.
75. Ibid.
76. Ibid., 131.
77. *The Whole Works of Richard Graves, D.D.*, compiled with a Memoir by his son, Richard Hasting Graves, 2d ed., vol. 1, *Memoir—Essay on the Apostles and Evangelists* (Dublin: William Curry, Jun. and Co., 1840), lxxvii.
78. Dixon, *Trinity College*, 186.
79. Ibid., 185.

80. Graves, *Works*, 1:liv.
81. Dixon, *Trinity College*, 194.
82. Ibid., 123, 186. See also Graves, *Works*, 1:xcviii.
83. Richard Graves, *The First Praelection, Delivered as Professor of Divinity* (Dublin: Graisberry and Campbell, 1815), 8. This address has appended to it the regulations for the annual examination of graduates and a list of recommended books to prepare students.
84. "Assemblies of Brethren," *Ecumenical Review* 24 (April 1972): 132-33.
85. Darby, *CW*, 6:205-6.
86. Darby was a moderate Calvinist (see Darby, *CW*, 1:252-53). Graves was an avowed Arminian (see Graves, *Works*, 1:cxlix).
87. Graves, *Works*, 1:xxxi.
88. Richard Graves, *A Sermon Preached in St. Andrew's Church, Dublin, on Sunday, 21st April, 1811. In Aid of the London Society for Promoting Christianity Amongst the Jews* (Dublin: J. Jones, 1811).
89. Stuart O. Seanoir, personal letter, Dublin, Ireland, 26 January 1989; and Dixon, *Trinity College*, 232.
90. Dixon, *Trinity College*, 259.
91. Geldbach, *Christliche Versammlung*, 9.
92. Graves, *Works*, 2:390-92.
93. See Hempton, "Evangelicalism and Eschatology," 185.
94. Sandeen, *Roots*, 38.
95. Richard Watson, *A Biblical and Theological Dictionary* (New York: T. Mason and G. Lane, 1840), 241 (emphasis added).
96. J. Addison Alexander, review of *The Valley of Vision: or the Dry Bones of Israel Revived. An Attempted Proof (from Ezekiel 37:1-14 of the Restoration and Conversion of the Jews* by George Bush, *The Biblical Repertory and Princeton Review* 16 (1844): 380.
97. See Dixon, *Trinity College*, 27, 30.
98. See James R. Payton, Jr., "The Emergence of Postmillennialism in English Puritanism," *Journal of Christian Reconstruction* 6 (Summer 1979): 87-106.
99. Peter Toon, "The Question of Jewish Immigration," in *Puritans, the Millennium and the Future of Israel: Puritan Eschatology 1600 to 1660*, ed. Peter Toon (Cambridge, England: James Clark and Co., 1970), 119.
100. Sandeen, *Roots*, 4.
101. J. Van Den Berg, "Appendix III: The eschatological expectation of seventeenth-century Dutch Protestantism with regard to the Jewish people," in *Puritans*, 141 (emphasis added)
102. Ibid., 148.
103. Ibid., 141.
104. Graves, *Works*, 2:438
105. Graves, *Sermon*, 37
106. Graves, *Works*, 2:435.
107. Alexander Keith, *Evidence of the Truth of the Christian Religion, Derived from the Literal Fulfillment of Prophecy*, 6th ed. (New York: J. J. Harper, 1832).
108. Leslie Stephen and Sydney Lee, eds., *The Dictionary of National Biography* (Oxford: Oxford University Press, 1922), s.v. "Keith, Alexander (1791-1880)," by George Clement Boase
109. Keith, *Evidence*, 83
110. Ibid., 109.
111. Graves, *Works*, 2:407
112. Ibid., 2:421. Other passages Graves used to defend the restoration of Israel are Isa. 11:10-11, 14:23; 18:8; 30:18; 35:10; 43:13-16; 47:5,6,11; 54:7-11; 60:8-12; 61:1-8; Jer. 23:5-8; 46:28; and Ezek. 29:15. (See *Sermon*, 30.)
113. Keith, *Evidence*, 78.
114. Graves, *Works*, 2:399
115. Ibid., 2:435.
116. Ibid., 2:420.
117. Graves, *Sermon*, 35. Graves followed Buchanan's *Christian Researches* (226), which said that "Mr. Lee, a scholar of enlarged views, who published a tract called 'Israel Redux,' in the year 1677, has calculated, from the prophecies of Daniel and the Apocalypse, that in the year 1811 the times of happiness to Israel should begin" (*Works*, 2:433).
118. Graves, *Sermon*, 49-50
119. Ibid., 52.
120. Graves, *Works*, 2:399. See also his *Sermon*, 54. Kik quoted H. Witsius' *Economy of the Covenants* (3:352f), written in 1775, in which Witsius laid out a similar scenario. (See Kik, *An Eschatology of Victory*, 8.)

121. See, for example, J. Dwight Pentecost, *Things to Come* (Grand Rapids: Dunham Publishing Co., 1958), 214, 238; and Alva J. McClain, *The Greatness of the Kingdom* (Winona Lake, IN· BMH Books, 1959), 458

122. Graves, *Sermon*, 37

123. Graves, *Works*, 2:420

124. Graves, *Sermon*, 52.

125. Graves, *Works*, 2:360-61, 436

126. Ibid., 2:437 (emphasis added)

127. Ibid., 2:436

128. Graves put Secker on the recommended reading list for theology students. See Graves, *First Praelection*, 35

129. Thomas Secker, *Lectures on the Catechism of the Church of England*, 3d ed. (London: John and Francis Rivington, 1771), 110

130. Ibid

131. Watson, *A Biblical and Theological Dictionary*, 241. While Watson rejected this conclusion, he declared that it was "common with divines" to speak in such terms

132. Darby *CW* 2:35

Chapter Seven—The Rapture and the Return

1. John Feinberg, "Arguing for the Rapture: Who Must Prove What and How?" paper presented to the Pre-Trib Research Center; quoted by Thomas Ice, in "Why the Rapture and the Second Coming are Distinct Events," *Pre-Trib Answers to Post-Trib Questions* (Aug.-Sept. 1994), 2

2. Millard Erickson, *Christian Theology* (Grand Rapids: Baker Book House, 1985), 1186.

3. Thomas Ice, "Why the Rapture and Second Coming are Distinct Events," in *Pre-Trib Answers to Post-Trib Questions* (Aug.-Sept 1994), 2

4. Ibid., 3

5. Cf. Robert Gundry *The Church and the Tribulation* (Grand Rapids: Zondervan, 1973), 85-86

6. C.F. Hogg and W.E. Vine *The Epistles to the Thessalonians* (London: Exeter Press, 1929), 144

7. Ibid., 242

8. George Milligan, *St. Paul's Epistles to the Thessalonians* (Old Tappan, NY: Revell, 1908), vol. 2 96 Cf. also A.T. Robertson, *Word Pictures in the New Testament* (Grand Rapids Baker, 1931 reprint), vol. IV. 47 He also notes that it refers to the rapture in 2 Thess. 2:1

9 Cf. W.S. LaSor, *The Truth About Armageddon* (Grand Rapids: Baker Book House, 1982), 120-134; and G.E. Ladd, *The Blessed Hope* (Grand Rapids: Eerdmans, 1956), 71-104.

10. These may be found in an expanded version in Edward Hindson, *End Times & the New World Order* (Wheaton· Victor Books, 1991), 164-67

Chapter Nine—Arguing for the Rapture: Who Must Prove What and How?

1. See Douglas J. Moo "The Case for the Posttribulation Rapture Position," in Gleason Archer, Paul Feinberg, Douglas Moo, *The Rapture· Pre- Mid-, or Post-Tribulational?* (Grand Rapids Zondervan, 1984), 169-211.

2. See Paul D Feinberg, "The Case For The Pretribulation Rapture Position," in Gleason Archer, Paul Feinberg, Douglas Moo, *The Rapture· Pre-, Mid-, or Post-Tribulational?* (Grand Rapids. Zondervan, 1984), 45-86

3. See Gleason L. Archer, "The Case For The Mid-Seventieth-Week Rapture Position," in Gleason Archer, Paul Feinberg, Douglas Moo, *The Rapture: Pre-, Mid-, or Post Tribulational?* (Grand Rapids: Zondervan, 1984), 113- 45

4. There were three stages to the Semitic wedding. The first was the betrothal. This might happen even when the husband and wife-to-be were children. In the eyes of the Mosaic law, the two were legally married. Second, there eventually came the day when man and woman could actually begin to live together as husband and wife. On that day, the groom went from his home to the home of the bride, and took her to his home. When they arrived at his home, they celebrated with the marriage feast (the third stage in the process). As this relates to Christ and the church, the marriage would be initially "contracted" by Christ's payment on Calvary for the sins of the church. The taking of the bride to the home of the groom would occur at the rapture, and then the wedding feast would be celebrated in heaven as we see it occurring in Revelation 19

5. For further handling of the similarities and dissimilarities of rapture and second advent passages, see Feinberg, 80-86.

6. Robert Gundry, *The Church and the Tribulation* (Grand Rapids: Zondervan, 1973), 82

7. Ibid., 137, 164, 166-67.
8. Ibid., 24.
9. Ibid., 135.
10. Ibid., 164.
11. See, for example, J. Oliver Buswell, A *Systematic Theology of the Christian Religion* (Grand Rapids: Zondervan, 1962), 2:397.
12. See Archer in Archer, Feinberg, Moo, 142-44. For responses to this view see Feinberg in same work, 149-50.
13. Any midtrib who associates the last trump of the rapture with the trumpet of Matt. 24:31 will have another problem. As already noted, Matt. 24:31 speaks about events at the end of the Tribulation. So, if the last trump for the rapture is blown at the middle of the Tribulation as midtribs say, then it can't be the same as the trump of Matt. 24:31, since that occurs at the end of the Tribulation.
14. Gundry, 49.
15. Ibid., 48.
16. For further amplification of some of these arguments, plus other arguments supportive of the pretribulational position, see Feinberg, 45-86.

Chapter Ten—Literal Interpretaion
1. Martin E. Marty, "Literalism" in *Bible Review*, vol. x, no. 2, April 1994:42-43.
2. Ibid, 42. See further James Barr, *Fundamentalism* (Philadelphia: Westminster, 1978): 191-207.
3. David H. Kelsey, *The Uses of Scripture in Recent Theology* (Philadelphia: Fortress Press, 1975), 14-31.
4. Wayne Grudem "Scripture's Self-Attestation and the Problem of Formulating a Doctrine of Scripture" in *Scripture and Truth*, eds. D. A. Carson and John D. Woodbridge (Grand Rapids: Zondervan Publishing House, 1983), 19-64.
5. Robert H. Bork, *The Tempting of America* (New York: Simon and Schuster, Inc., 1990).
6. Leland Ryken, *Words of Delight* (Grand Rapids: Baker Book House, 1987).
7. E. D. Hirsch, *Validity in Interpretation* (New Haven, CT: Yale University Press, 1973).
8. John S. Feinberg, "Truth: Relationship of Theories of Truth to Hermeneutics," in *Hermeneutics, Inerrancy and the Bible*, eds. Earl D. Radmacher and Robert D. Preus (Grand Rapids: Zondervan, 1984), 1-50; and Mortimer Adler, *How to Read a Book,* (New York: Simon and Schuster, 1960).
9. David L. Cooper, *The World's Greatest Library Graphically Illustrated* (Los Angeles: Biblical Research Society, 1970), 11. Emphasis mine.
10. Hirsch, *Validity in Interpretation.*
11. This particular problem is chosen to illustrate the importance of certain Old Testament prophecies. While there is typological prophecy, there is also direct, predictive prophecy. To read them as historical types when in fact they are predictions is to lose the truth of the passage.
12. Franz Delitzsch, *The Psalms*, vol. 1 (Grand Rapids: Wm. B. Eerdmans Publishing Co., 1871), 64-78.
13. G. B. Caird, *The Language and Imagery of the Bible* (Philadelphia: The Westminster Press, 1980), 131.
14. Marty, 42.
15. D. A. Carson and John D. Woodbridge, *Hermeneutics, Authority, and Canon* (Grand Rapids: Zondervan, 1986); and Earl D. Radmacher and Robert D. Preus, *Hermeneutics, Inerrancy and the Bible* (Grand Rapids: Zondervan, 1984). A number of articles discuss historicity. Gleason L. Archer, *Encyclopedia of Bible Difficulties* (Grand Rapids: Zondervan, 1982).
16. Karen Armstrong, *A History of God* (New York: Knopf, 1993).
17. D. A. Carson, "Recent Developments in the Doctrine of Scripture," in *Hermeneutics, Authority and Canon,* 1-48.
18. Thomas D. Ice, "Dispensational Hermeneutics" in *Issues in Hermeneutics*, eds. Willis and Master (Chicago: Moody Press, 1994), 35.
19. This untenable treatment of the text is illustrated in a conversation between an imagined critic and reader:

> A reader of Isaiah 9:6 wonders aloud about the meaning of the text: "Who is this king?"
> The critic responds, "In Isaiah's time, it meant Solomon, the Son of David."
> In a follow-up question: "Did it only mean Solomon?"
> "Well, yes, Solomon was the historic king that matched the words of the text most closely. This is what it meant.

"But then the times changed and Jesus was born. And with the events surrounding his birth, new facts appeared and the words took on a new and different meaning."

Then the reader became even more confused. "How can it mean both Solomon and Christ? Which does the text mean? Does it mean Solomon *or* Christ?"

The critic then seeks to explain. "Solomon is a *type* of Christ."

But the reader then puzzled over what the *type* might be. "Solomon is 'mighty god' in the sense that he is powerful like God among other kings.

"Christ is Mighty God in the sense that He is God, Himself."

So the one sense is not a type of the other sense but involves two textually distinct senses. And the same words are treated as though they were an equivocal statement. The reader then wonders if there is any way out of our problem. There is! The same sense is meant in both the historic and in the prophetic reading. In the historic reading it meant more than any historic king and so held out prophetic hope for the future. In the futuristic reading, the language matches Christ and Christ alone in its full force. Christ is the One about whom Isaiah spoke and that in a single sense.

20. Marty, 42.
21. Ibid.

Chapter Eleven—The Doctrine of Imminency

1. John F. Walvoord, *The Rapture Question*, revised and enlarged ed. (Grand Rapids: Zondervan Publishing House, 1979), 51.
2. Philip Schaff, ed., *A Select Library of the Ante-Nicene Fathers*, reprint (Grand Rapids: Wm. B. Eerdmans Publishing Co., 1978), vvi:382.
3. Adolph Harnack, "Millennium," *Encyclopedia Britannica* (ninth ed.), XVI, 314.
4. Jesse Forest Silver, *The Lord's Return* (New York: Fleming H. Revell Co., 1914), 62-63.
5. Cited by Richard R. Reiter, "A History of the Development of the Rapture Positions," in *The Rapture: Pre-, Mid-, or Post-Tribulational?* Archer, Feinberg, Moo, and Reiter (Grand Rapids: Zondervan Publishing House, 1984), 12.
6. Ibid., 22.
7. J. Barton Payne, *The Imminent Appearing of Christ* (Grand Rapids: Wm. B. Eerdmans Publishing Co., 1962).
8. Robert Cameron, *Scripture Truth About the Lord's Return* (New York: Fleming H. Revell Co., 1922), 21-69.
9. Gerald B. Stanton, *Kept from the Hour*, revised and enlarged ed. (Haysville, NC: Schoettle Publishing Co., 1991), 108-37.
10. Marvin Rosenthal, *The Pre-wrath Rapture of the Church* (Nashville: Thomas Nelson Publishers, 1990), 18.
11. For a critque by the author, see *Kept from the Hour*, 374-400 and "A Review of *The Pre-Wrath Rapture of the Church*," *Bibliotheca Sacra* 148 (Jan-Mar 1991): 90-112.
12. Rosenthal, 54, 150, 158-59, 174, 197, 282.
13. George N. H. Peters, *The Theocratic Kingdom*, 3 vol. reprint ed. (Grand Rapids: Kregel Publications, 1952) quoted by Chafer, *Systematic Theology*, IV: 270-75.
14. John Wesley, cited by Silver, 162.
15. The above quotations of Crippen, Luther, Calvin, and Latimer come from I.M. Haldeman, *The History of the Doctrine of Our Lord's Return*, and are cited by Chafer, *Systematic Theology*, IV: 275-79.
16. See Stanton, *Kept from the Hour*, 221-22 for additional discussion on this early and important quotation.
17. Ibid., 119.

Chapter Twelve—Are the Church and the Rapture in Matthew 24?

1. Francis Wright Beare, *The Gospel According to Matthew* (San Francisco: Harper & Row, Publishers, 1981), 463. Cf. Alan Hugh M'Neile, *The Gospel According to St. Matthew* (New York: MacMillan & Co., 1955), 343.
2. J. C. Fenton, *Saint Matthew* (Philadelphia: The Westminster Press, 1963), 379-80.
3. Robert H. Mounce, *Matthew* (Peabody, MA.: Hendricksen Publishers, 1985), 221.
4. J. Marcellus Kik, *Matthew Twenty-four, An Exposition* (Swengel, PA.: Bible Truth Depot, n.d.), 9. Cf. Joseph Addison Alexander, *The Gospel According to Matthew* (Grand Rapids: Baker Book House, 1980 [Reprint], 452-53; John A. Broadus, *Commentary on the Gospel of Matthew* (Philadelphia: The American Baptist Publication Society, 1886), 479-90; Michael Green, *Matthew for Today* (Dallas: Word Publishing, 1988), 234-35; G. Campbell Morgan, *The Gospel According to Matthew* (New York: Fleming H. Revell Company, 1929), 286.

5. Ibid., 65.
6. William Hendriksen, *Exposition of the Gospel According to Matthew* (Grand Rapids: Baker Book House, 1973), 847.
7. R. V. G. Tasker, *The Gospel According to St. Matthew* (Grand Rapids: Wm. B. Eerdmans Publishing Co., 1961), 224-28. Cf. Richard B. Gardner, *Matthew* (Scottsdale, PA: Herald Press, 1991), 342; Robert H. Smith, *Matthew* (Minneapolis: Augsburg Publishing House, 1989), 284-85.
8. John F. Walvoord, *The Blessed Hope and the Tribulation* (Grand Rapids: Zondervan Publishing House, 1976), 11-69.
9. John F. Walvoord, *The Rapture Question* (Grand Rapids: Zondervan Publishing House, 1979), 131-45. Cf. Gerald B. Stanton, *Kept from the Hour* (Miami Springs, FL: Schoettle Publishing Co., 1991), 316-400.
10. Robert H. Gundry, *The Church and the Tribulation* (Grand Rapids: Zondervan Publishing House, 1973).
11. Bruce A. Ware, " Is the Church in View in Matthew 24-25?" *Bibliotheca Sacra* 138 (April-June 1981): 158-72.
12. Gundry, 131.
13. Ibid.
14. Ibid., 131-32.
15. Ibid., 132-33.
16. Ibid., 132.
17. E. Schuyler English, *Studies in the Gospel According to Matthew* (New York: Our Hope Publications, 1935), 170; A. C. Gaebelein, *The Gospel of Matthew* (Neptune, N.J.: Loizeaux Brothers, 1910), 2:165, 174-77; W. Kelly, *The Lord's Prophecy on Olivet in Matthew XXIV, XXV* (London: T. Weston, 1903), 6-7; J. Dwight Pentecost, *Things to Come* (Findlay, OH: Dunham Publishing Co., 1958), 267; Charles Caldwell Ryrie, *The Ryrie Study Bible* (Chicago: Moody Press, 1976), 1489; John F. Walvoord, *Matthew: Thy Kingdom Come* (Chicago: Moody Press, 1974), 182.
18. Others have noted the close relationship of the three questions. Cf. Broadus, 482; Alexander Balmain Bruce, "The Synoptic Gospels," *The Expositor's Greek Testament*. W. Robertson Nicoll, ed. (Grand Rapids: Wm. B. Eerdmans Publishing Co., 1910), 1:289; G. Campbell Morgan, *The Gospel According to Matthew* (New York: Fleming H. Revell Company, 1929), 281, 283.
19. Mounce calls the Mount of Olives, "a setting connected with apocalyptic expectations; cf. Zech 14:4." 222.
20. *BAG*, s.v. Παρουσία, 635; A. Oepke, s.v., Αρουσία, *TDNT*, 5:860.
21. Colin Brown, ed., *The New International Dictionary of New Testament Theology* (Grand Rapids: Zondervan Publishing House, 1971), 2:899, s.v. Παρουσία.
22. Gundry, 133.
23. Ibid.
24. David Hill, *The Gospel of Matthew* (London: Marshall, Morgan and Scott, 1972), 321.
25. Ware, 170.
26. Gundry, 135.
27. Ibid.
28. Ibid., 137-39.
29. Ibid., 135.
30. Walvoord, *The Rapture Question*, 187.
31. Gundry, 137.
32. Ibid., 138.
33. Ibid., 137.
34. Ibid., 137-38.
35. Ibid., 138.
36. BAG, s.v. Παραλαμβάνω, 624.
37. English, 179-80; Charles Lee Feinberg, *Israel in the Last Days: The Olivet Discourse* (Altenda, CA: Emeth Publications, 1953), 27; Gaebelein, 216-17; Mounce, 229; Stanley D. Toussaint, *Behold the King* (Portland: Multnomah Press, 1980), 281; Warren W. Wiersbe, *Meet Your King* (Wheaton: Victor Books, 1980), 178; Walvoord, *The Rapture Question*, 188-90.
38. Marvin Rosenthal, *The Pre-Wrath Rapture of the Church* (Nashville: Thomas Nelson Publishers, 1990).
39. Ibid., 150-53.
40. Ibid., 141-42, 145.

41. Ibid., 182.
42. Ibid., 142.
43. Ibid., 218-19.
44. Ibid., 219, cf. 229-30.
45. Ibid., 222.
46. Ibid.
47. Ibid., 223.
48. Ibid., 284.
49. Ibid., 108-09.
50. Ibid., 206.

Chapter Fourteen—'Apostasia' in 2 Thessalonians 2:3

1. Henry Alford, "The Second Epistle to the Thessalonians," *The Greek Testament*, Vol. III: Galatians-Philemon (Chicago: Moody Press, 1959), 289.
2. τί ἐστιν ἡ ἀποστασίὰ αὐτὸν καλεῖ τὸν ἀντίχριστον ἀποστασίαν.
3. ἀποστασία τουτεστι ὁ Ἀντίξπιστος," quoted from John Eadie, *Commentary on St. Paul's Second Epistle to the Thessalonians*, reprint (Minneapolis: James & Klock Christian Publishing Co., [1877], 1977), 266.
4. *diemque judicii non esse venturum, nisi ille prior venerit, quem refugam vocat*, quoted from *De Civitate Dei*, lib. vol. VII, 958, *Opera*, Gaume, Paris.
5. James Moffatt, *The Expositor's Greek Testament*, vol. 4: 2 Thessalonians, W. Robertson Nicoll, ed. (Grand Rapids: Eerdmans, n.d.), 48.
6. D. Edmond Hiebert, *The Thessalonian Epistles* (Chicago: Moody, 1971), 305. Brackets mine.
7. Donald G. Bloesch, *Essentials of Evangelical Theology*, vol. 2 (San Francisco: Harper & Row, 1978), 182.
8. E.g., see reference to 2 Thess. 2:3 for the following: Charles R. Erdman, *The Epistles of Paul to the Thessalonians* (Philadelphia: Westminster, 1935); Harold J. Ockenga, *The Church in God. Expository Values in Thessalonians* (Westwood, NJ: Revell, 1956); William Hendriksen, "Exposition of I and II Thessalonians," in *New Testament Commentary* (Grand Rapids: Baker, 1955); A. J. Mason "The Epistles of Paul the Apostle to the Thessalonians," in Ellicott's *Commentary on the Whole Bible*, vol. 8, reprint (Grand Rapids: Eerdmans, 1952); John Calvin, *Commentary on the Second Epistle to the Thessalonians*, reprint (Grand Rapids: Baker, 1979).
9. E.g., Marvin Rosenthal, *The Pre-Wrath Rapture of the Church* (Nashville: Thomas Nelson, 1990), 198.
10. F. F. Bruce, "1 and 2 Thessalonians" in *Word Biblical Commentary* (Waco, TX: Word Books, 1982), 167; and I. Howard Marshall, *1 and 2 Thessalonians* (Grand Rapids: Eerdmans, 1983), 189.
11. Charles C. Ryrie, *Dispensationalism Today* (Chicago: Moody, 1965), 151.
12. Louis Berkhof, *Systematic Theology* (Grand Rapids: Eerdmans, 1941), 718.
13. Rosenthal, 198.
14. Ibid., 207. Paul Karleen, *The Pre-Wrath Rapture of the Church: Is It Biblical?* (Langhorne, PA: BF Press, 1991), 198, interacting with Rosenthal, notes that the Greek word *apostasia* is used by Luke in Acts 21:21 "in reference to Jews who were complaining that Paul had told them to 'turn away from' Moses, i.e., the Law." Then he quotes Rosenthal, "When Paul used the word *apostasy* in 2 Thessalonians 2:3, he did so in exactly the same way as Dr. Luke. He was speaking of the Jews who, during the seventieth week of Daniel, will totally abandon the God of their fathers and their messianic hope in favor of a . . . false messiah. . . ." 198. Karleen agrees that Luke *could* be using apostasia the same way but there is no support in the text of Acts. Karleen notes that Rosenthal contrasts his view with pretributionalists who believe that "Paul was speaking of believers in this age who will apostatize before the Rapture and the beginning of the seventieth week."
15. James E. Frame, "A Critical and Exegetical Commentary on the Epistles of St. Paul to the Thessalonians," in *The International Critical Commentary* (New York: Scribner, 1912), 251.
16. C. F. Hogg and W. E. Vine, *The Epistles to the Thessalonians*, reprint (Grand Rapids: Kregel, 1959), 247.
17. Lewis Sperry Chafer, *Systematic Theology*, Vol. VI (Dallas: Dallas Seminary Press, 1948), 86.
18. Ibid., Vol IV, 353.
19. A. T. Robertson, "The Epistles of Paul" in *Word Pictures in the New Testament* (Nashville: Broadman Press, 1931), 49.
20. A. L. Moore, ed., *1 & II Thessalonians* (London: Marshall, Morgan & Scott, 1969), 100-01.
21. Marshall, 189.

22. Morris, 127.
23. David Williams, *1 & 2 Thessalonians* (*New International Bible Commentary Series*, vol. 12 (Peabody, MA: Hendrickson Publishers, 1992), 124. Also see Bruce, 166: ἀποστασία, "the rebellion" a Hellenistic formation, corresponding to classical ἀποστασία, denotes either political rebellion (as in Josephus, *Vita* 43, of the Jewish revolt against Rome) or religious defection (as in Acts 21:21, of abandonment of Moses' law). Since the reference here is to a world-wide rebellion against divine authority at the end of the age, the ideas of political revolt and religious apostasy are combined."
24. Bruce, 167.
25. See Richard R. Reiter, "A History of the Development of the Rapture Positions," in Gleason Archer, Paul Feinberg, Douglas Moo, *The Rapture: Pre-, Mid-, or Post Tribulational?* (Grand Rapids: Zondervan, 1984), 32.
26. Stanley Ellisen, *A Biography of a Great Planet* (Wheaton: Tyndale, 1975), 121.
27. Gordon R. Lewis, "Biblical Evidence for Pretribulationism," *Bibliotheca Sacra*, vol. 125, no. 499 (1968), 218.
28. See appendix A at the end of the chapter.
29. Ibid.
30. Henry George Liddell and Henry Scott, *A Greek-English Lexicon*, revised with a Supplement [1968] by Sir Henry Stuart Jones and Roderick McKenzie (Oxford, Eng.: Oxford University Press, 1940), 218.
31. G. W. H. Lampe, *A Patristic Greek Lexicon* (Oxford: Clarendon Press, 1961), 208.
32. This is not absolutely clear since a Greek-English Septuagint translates the word "revolt." *The Septuagint Version of the Old Testament and Apocrypha* (Grand Rapids: Zondervan Publishing House, 1975), 142.
33. 2 Chronicles 29:19: καὶ πάντα τὰ σκεύη, ἃ ἐμίανεν Αχαζ ὁ βασιλεὺς ἐν τῇ βασιλείᾳ αὐτοῦ ἐν τῇ ἀποστασίᾳ αὐτοῦ, ἡτοιμάκαμεν καὶ ἡγνίκαμεν, ἰδού ἐστιν ἐναντίον τοῦ θυσιαστηρίου κυρίου. (And all the vessels, which king Achaz polluted in his reign in his *apostasy*, we have prepared and purified, behold, they are before the altar of the Lord); 2 Chronicles 33:19: προσευχῆς αὐτοῦ, καὶ ὡς ἐπήκουσεν αὐτοῦ, καὶ πᾶσαι αἱ ἁμαρτίαι αὐτοῦ καὶ αἱ ἀποστάσεις αὐτοῦ καὶ οἱ τόποι, ἐφ᾽ οἷς ᾠκοδόμησεν τὰ ὑψηλὰ καὶ ἔστησεν ἐκεῖ ἄλση καὶ γλυπτὰ πρὸ τοῦ ἐπιστρέψαι, ἰδοὺ γέγραπται ἐπὶ τῶν λόγων τῶν ὁρώντων. (And his prayer, and his entreaty, and all his sin, and his *trespass*, and the places in which he had built high places and made stand the Asherim and the graven images before he was humbled, behold, they are written in the Matters of the Seers); Jeremiah 2:19: παιδεύσει σε ἡ ἀποστασία σου, καὶ ἡ κακία σου ἐλέγξει σε· καὶ γνῶθι καὶ ἰδὲ ὅτι πικρόν σοι τὸ καταλιπεῖν σε ἐμέ, λέγει κύριος ὁ θεός σου· καὶ οὐκ εὐδόκησα ἐπὶ σοί, λέγει κύριος ὁ θεός σου. (Your own evil shall teach you, and your *apostasies* shall reprove you. Know, then, and see that is evil and bitter your forsaking Yahweh your God; and My fear is not in you declares the Lord Yahweh of Hosts).
34. 1 Maccabees 2:15: Καὶ ἦλθον οἱ παρὰ τοῦ βασιλέως οἱ καταναγκάζοντες τὴν ἀποστασίαν εἰς Μωδεῖν τὴν πόλιν, ἵνα θυσιάσωσιν. (In the meanwhile, the king's officers, such as compelled the people to *revolt*, came into the city Modin, to make them sacrifice.)
35. I was led to this idea by an unpublished paper by Stanley Ellisen, 141-42.
36. See appendix B.
37. Chafer, Ibid., 86-87.
38. *Our Hope* (June 1950), 720.
39. J. Oliver Buswell, *A Systematic Theology of the Christian Religion* (Grand Rapids, Zondervan, 1962), 392.
40. John Walvoord, *The Blessed Hope and the Tribulation* (Grand Rapids, Zondervan, 1976), 125.
41. Ibid.
42. Ibid.
43. Ibid. Brackets mine.
44. Robert Gundry, *The Church and the Tribulation* (Grand Rapids, Zondervan, 1973), 115.
45. Ibid.
46. Ibid., 115-16.
47. Since he has included cognates in the other portions of his review of the subject, one wonders why they would not be included at this point.
48. James H. Moulton and George Milligan, *The Vocabulary of the Greek Testament* (Grand Rapids, Eerdmans, 1930), 98.

ἀλόγως ἀπέστητε μὴ ἄραντες τὸ σῶμα τοῦ ἀδελφοῦ ὑμῶν ὦτα ἀφεστηκότα.

ἐμπλεκείς τέ μοι οὐκ ἀπέστη εἰ μὴ ἠνάηκασε κτλ

49. Gerhard Kittel, ed., *Theological Dictionary of the New Testament*, trans. Geoffrey W. Bromiley (Grand Rapids: Eerdmans, 1969), 512.
50. See Susan Foh, "What Is the Woman's Desire," *Westminster Theological Journal*, vol. 37 (Spring 1975):380-81
51. Gundry, 116
52. Gundry, 116.
53. Gundry, 116-17
54. Gundry, 117
55. E. Schuyler English, *Re-Thinking the Rapture* (Neptune, NJ: Loizeaux Brothers, 1954), 67-69 and Kenneth S. Wuest, *Prophetic Light in the Present Darkness* (Grand Rapids: Eerdmans 1956), 57
56. Gundry, 117.
57. Bruce agrees with Gundry on this, against English: "English argues that the article ἡ marks the ἀποστασία out as something about which the readers were already informed; true: they had been informed about it by Paul when he was with them (v. 5)." Bruce, 167.
58. Ibid., 117-18
59. Though not adopting the view that *apostasia* refers to the rapture, both John Eadie and O. H Ludwig recognize that *apostasia* and the revelation of the man of sin are two separate events, the *apostasia* being that which precipitates the revelation of the man of sin. This is in contrast to I. Howard Marshall, who views the two events as really a complex, or one.

   "The 'falling away,' therefore, is not the result of the appearance of the Man of Sin, but the antecedent... Thus ἀποστασία, so signalized by the article ἡ, is something distinct, something so far familiar to them, and on which they had enjoyed previous instruction." "The καί of the following clause has something of a consecutive force—marking its clause as the result of the previous one." Eadie, 266: "The falling-away from the Faith stands in a causal connection with the appearance of Antichrist. 2 Thess. 2:3: 'unless there be a revolt first, and the man of sin be revealed, the son of perdition.'" O. H. Ludwig, *Fundamentals of Catholic Dogma*, 487; "His next sentence forms an anacolouthon in the Greek. Literally it runs *for unless the rebellion comes first...* RSV has correctly given the sense by interpolating the words *that day will not come* "

   "Two related elements must occur first. The first is described as *the rebellion*, literally the apostasy. Paul says nothing to elucidate the word, unless we are to assume that it is more narrowly defined by the second element, the revealing of *the man of lawlessness*. Although various commentators think that two consecutive events are in mind, it seems more probable that one complex event is in mind. (The RSV rendering makes it clear that *first* refers to the relation of both events to the day of the Lord)." Marshall, 188.
60. J. Dwight Pentecost, *Our Hope* (June 1950), 728.

Chapter Fifteen—2 Thessalonians 2 and the Rapture

1. Robert H. Gundry, *The Church and the Tribulation* (Grand Rapids: Zondervan, 1973). See also Doug Moo, "The Case for the Posttribulation Rapture Position" in *The Rapture: Pre-, Mid-, or Posttribulational?* Gleason Archer, et al. (Grand Rapids: Zondervan, 1984), 186-90.
2. Ibid., 100-11, especially 105-06.
3. Ibid., 113.
4. Ibid., 114.
5. Ibid., 134-35. See also Moo, 190-96.
6. Ibid.
7. Ibid., 113-14.
8. Robert L. Thomas "Second Thessalonians" in *EBC* (Grand Rapids: Zondervan, 1978), 319.
9. Gundry, 105.
10. Robert L. Thomas, "First Thessalonians' in *EBC* (Grand Rapids: Zondervan, 1978), 280.
11. For a fuller discussion see, Paul D. Feinberg, "Response to Doug Moo" in *Rapture: Pre-, Mid-, or Posttribulational?* Gleason Archer, et al. (Grand Rapids: Zondervan, 1984), 226-27.
12. For a fuller discussion see Ibid., 229-31.
13. Ibid., 224-26
14. Gundry, 135-36
15. Ibid., 118. See also Moo, 187-190
16. I have included an appendix on this issue. I set out my reasons for thinking that a physical departure and thus a rapture is not the correct interpretation of this verse.
17. See Gundry's fine discussion of the options, 122-26.
18. See both Gundry 126-28; and Feinberg, 228-29.

19. See E. Schuyler English, *Re-Thinking the Rapture* (Travelers Rest, SC: Southern Bible Book House, 1954), 67-71; and Kenneth S. Wuest, "The Rapture—Precisely When?" *Bib Sac* 114 (1957): 63-67.
20. *Ibychus, Thesaurus Linguae Graecae,* The Regents of the University of California, Packard Humanity Institute, 1992, Listone.
21. This point was made to me by my colleague Douglas Moo.
22. This point was made to me by Ron Nickelson, presently a Ph.D. student in New Testament at Trinity Evangelical Divinity School, Deerfield, IL.

Chapter Sixteen—Chronology and Sequential Structure of John's Revelation

1. Greg K. Beale, "The Influence of Daniel upon the Structure and Theology of John's Apocalypse," *Journal of the Evangelical Theological Society* (1984): 413-23.
2. Ibid., 415.
3. Jan Lambrecht, "A Structuration of Revelation 4, 1-22, 5," in *L' Apocalypse johannique et l'Apocalyptique dans le Nouveau Testament* BETL 53 (Louvain: Leuven University Press, 1980), 79.
4. Robert L. Thomas, "John's Apocalyptic Outline," *Bibliotheca Sacra* 123 (1966): 334-41.
5. John M. Court, *Myth and History in the Book of Revelation* (Atlanta: John Knox, 1979), 43.
6. Ibid., 48.
7. Bornkamm (1937), 132-49. Bornkamm only maintains recapitulation for the trumpet and bowl septets and not the seals.
8. Robert Mounce, *The Book of Revelation* NICNT (Grand Rapids: Eerdmans, 1977), 46. See also Lambrecht (1980), 95-99. Lambrecht cites Revelation 7:1-17; 10:1–11:13; 12:1–14:20 as examples. He uses the term "intercalations," and suggests they have a delaying function but do not disturb the structure or flow of the narrative.
9. Merrill C. Tenny, *Interpreting Revelation* (Grand Rapids: Eerdmans, 1957), 74-80.
10. Dale Ralph Davis, "The Relationship between the Seals, Trumpets, and Bowls in the Book of Revelation," *Journal of the Evangelical Theological Society* 16 (1973): 150.
11. See Gary Cohen, *Understanding Revelation* (Chicago: Moody, 1978), 86-94 for a complete analysis of succession within the septets.
12. See G. R. Beasley-Murray, *The Book of Revelation* NCB (London: Marshall, Morgan, Scott, 1974), 87-88; and Lambrecht (1980), 93.
13. Ugo, Vanni, *La struttura letteraria dell' Apocalisse Aloisiana* 8 (Rome: Herder, 1971), 123-33, 163-66.
14. Davis (1973), 150.
15. R. H. Charles, *A Critical and Exegetical Commentary on the Revelation of St. John,* 2 vols. ICC (New York: Charles Scribner's Sons, 1920), 1:158-59; J. M. Ford, *Revelation: Introduction, Translation and Commentary* AB 38 (Garden City: Doubleday, 1975), 104; Mathias Rissi, "The Rider on the White Horse," *Interpretation* 18 (1964): 407-418; John M. Court (1979), 49-81; J. P. M. Sweet, *Revelation* (Philadelphia: Westminster, 1979), 52-54; A. Wilkenhauser, *Die Offenbarung des Johannes ubersetzt und erklart* Regensburger Neues Testament 9 (Regensburg: Frederick Pustet, 1947).
16. Zane C. Hodges, "The First Horseman of the Apocalypse," *Bibliotheca Sacra* 119 (1962): 324. See also J. S. Considine, "The Rider on the White Horse," *Catholic Biblical Quarterly* 6 (1944): 406-22, and Pierre Prigent, *L'Apocalypse De Saint Jean* Commentaire du Nouveau Testament 14 (Lausanne: Delachaux et Niestle, 1981), 107-10.
17. Hodges, Ibid., 324-34.
18. J. P. M. Sweet, *Revelation* (Philadelphia: Westminster, 1979), 52-54.
19. Rissi, 413-18. See also Martin Rist and Lynn Harold Hough, *The Revelation of St. John the Divine* IB 12 (New York: Abingdon, 1957), 81.
20. Rissi, 415-16.
21. BAGD s.v. "δηνάριον," 179.
22. Adela Yarbro Collins, *The Apocalypse* (Wilmington: Glazier, 1979), 45-46.
23. Court (1979), 65.
24. BAGD s.v. "θηρίον," 361.
25. BAGD s.v. "θάνατος," 350-51.
26. Paul S. Minear, *I Saw a New Earth* (Washington: Corpus Books, 1968), 261, notes this phrase is used 11 times in four visions.
27. Charles (1920), 1:184. He cites as examples: Ps. 114:2; 1 Enoch 62:16; 108:12; 2 Enoch 22:8. See also George B. Caird, *A Commentary on the Revelation of St. John the Divine* (New York: Harper and Row, 1984), 86.

28. Richard Bauckham, "The Eschatological Earthquake in the Apocalypse of John," *Novum Testamentum* 19 (1977): 224-33.
29. BAGD s.v. "τότε," 823.
30. Charles, (1920), 1:181.
31. See John A. McLean, *The Seventieth Week of Daniel 9:27 as a Literary Key for Understanding the Structure of the Apocalypse of John* (Ph.D. dissertation, University of Michigan, 1990), 213-47 for a complete development of the relationship of Revelation 7–19 to the synoptics.
32. See K. Hanhart, "The Four Beasts of Daniel's Vision in the Night in the Light of Rev. 13:2," *New Testament Studies* 27 (1980), 576-83 for various interpretations concerning this beast.
33. Πόλεμος (war), ἔθνος (nation), σεισμός (an earthquake), ψευδοπροφήτης (false-prophet), βδέλυγμα (abomination), are examples of themes which are unique to the synoptics and Apocalypse within the New Testament corpus.
34. Marvin Rosenthal, *The Pre-Wrath Rapture of the Church* (Nashville: Thomas Nelson Publishers, 1990).
35. The purpose of this chapter is to examine structural problems with the pre-wrath rapture theory. See the article "Another Look at Rosenthal's 'Pre-Wrath Rapture'" by this author in *Bibliotheca Sacra*: 592:387-398 for an exegetical critique of this view.
36. See Rosenthal, 163-80, where he suggests the translation "is come—it is about to occur." I do not deny that ἦλθεν can have a futuristic aspect (see Rev. 19:7), but not in this context. See Rev. 5:7; 7:13; 8:3; 11:18; 17:1, 10; 18:10; 21:9 where ἦλθεν used in contexts that show the reaction of people to events that have already occurred.
37. Ibid., 103, 105. Italics are his but the bold face is added for emphasis.
38. Ibid., 109, 110.
39. Ibid., 117.
40. Ibid., 18. He places the rapture at Rev. 8:1.
41. Ibid., 143.
42. See Richard Bauckham, "The Eschatological Earthquake in the Apocalypse of John," *Novum Testamentum* 19 (1977): 224-33 for further discussion.
43. Rosenthal, 146. See also his charts on 147, 276.
44. Ibid., 193-94.
45. Ibid., 194.
46. For a complete discussion, see John A. McLean, *The Seventieth Week of Daniel 9:27 as a Literary Key for Understanding the Structure of the Apocalypse of John* (Ph.D. dissertation, University of Michigan, 1990).
47. Gleason Archer, *The Rapture Pre-, Mid-, or Post-Tribulational?* (Grand Rapids: Zondervan, 1984), 142. This placement of the rapture in this text is also followed by Robert Gundry, *The Church and the Tribulation* (Grand Rapids: Zondervan, 1979) for his posttribulational viewpoint. The writer will not give any exegetical criticism of this view since such comments have been offered by Paul Feinberg in the same book, 147-58.
48. Ibid., 143.
49. Ibid.
50. J. Oliver Buswell, Jr., *A Systematic Theology of the Christian Church* (Grand Rapids: Zondervan, 1962), 2:397.
51. Douglas Moo in Archer, et al., *The Rapture Pre-, Mid-, or Post-tribulational?* (Grand Rapids: Zondervan, 1984), 198.
52. The writer will not give any exegetical criticism of this view since such comments have been already offered by Paul Feinberg in the same book, 223-32.
53. Ibid., 204.
54. Gundry, 75.

Chapter Eighteen—The Rapture in Revelation 3:10
1. Robert H. Gundry, *The Church and the Tribulation* (Grand Rapids: Zondervan Publishing House 1973), 54.
2. Gundry claims that "where a situation of danger is in view, τηρέω means to *guard,*" and that "throughout the LXX and the NT τηρέω always occurs for protection within the sphere of danger..." (Gundry, *The Church and the Tribulation,* 58). Although "to guard" does not differ much from "to protect," Gundry's second statement is questionable. In 2 Peter 2:9 and Jude 21, for example, the idea of protection within the sphere of danger is inappropriate.
3. Ibid., 80.
4. John A. Sproule, "A Revised Review of *The Church and the Tribulation* by Robert H. Gundry" (paper delivered at the Postgraduate Seminar in New Testament Theology, Grace Theological Seminary, Winona Lake, IN, May 15, 1974), 32 (italics his).

5. Gundry's comment that "were the Church absent from the hour of testing keeping would not be necessary" (Gundry, *The Church and the Tribulation*, 58) looks at the situation from a post-tribulational viewpoint within the tribulation where keeping seems necessary. There is also the viewpoint of the Philadelphians prior to the hour of testing. To them, protection from that hour definitely necessitated some form of keeping. In relation to a worldwide judgment, it would seem that keeping in heaven would be a necessity.

6. A. T. Robertson, *A Grammar of the Greek New Testament in the Light of Historical Research*, 4th ed. (New York: George H. Doran Co., 1923), 596.

7. Alexander Reese, *The Approaching Advent of Christ: An Examination of the Teaching of J. N. Darby and His Followers* (London: Marshall, Morgan, & Scott, 1937), 205.

8. As Ladd puts it, "This verse neither asserts that the Rapture is to occur before the Tribulation, nor does its interpretation require us to think that such a removal is intended" (George Eldon Ladd, *The Blessed Hope* [Grand Rapids: Wm. B. Eerdmans Publishing Co., 1956], 86).

9. Cf. E. Schuyler English, *Re-Thinking the Rapture: An Examination of What the Scriptures Teach as to the Time of the Translation of the Church in Relation to the Tribulation* (Travelers Rest, SC: Southern Bible Book House, 1954), 89.

10. Gundry, *The Church and the Tribulation*, 55-56.

11. Ibid., 59.

12. Henry George Liddell and Robert Scott, *An IntermediateGreek-English Lexicon* (Oxford: Clarendon Press, 1968), 498-99.

13. Homer, *The Iliad* 2.14.130 (italics added).

14. Cf. ἐκ καπνοῦ "out of the smoke" (Homer, *The Odyssey* 2.19.7); εν μέσου κατῆσατο, "stood aside" (Herodotus 2.3.83).

15. Gundry, *The Church and the Tribulation*, 55.

16. Old Testament citations are based on the Masoretic text. Variations in the Septuagint are indicated in parentheses.

17. Joseph Henry Thayer, *A Greek-English Lexicon of the New Testament* (Grand Rapids: Zondervan Publishing House, 1962), 142. Cf. *Theological Dictionary of the New Testament*, s.v. "τηρέω," by Harold Riesenfeld, 8: 151.

18. Preservation in an outside position is also found in Psalm 12:8 (Septuagint, 11:7) using διατηρέω with ἀπό. Thus ἐκ in the Septuagint is capable of the idea of separation normally found in ἀπό.

19. Also compare ἐκκλίνω with ἐκ in Proverbs 1:5 and ἀνέχω with ἐκ in Amos 4:7.

20. Edwin A. Abbott, *From Letter to Spirit: An Attempt to Reach Through Varying Voices the Abiding Word*, Diatessarica, part 6 (London: Adam & Charles Black, 1903), 311. In the Septuagint the reference is Psalm 58:1-2.

21. Josephus, *Jewish Anitquities*, 4.2.1 (italics added). Cf. ῥύουαι ἐκ in *Antiquities* 12.10.5; 13.6.3.

22. In a similar context of keeping from idols, 1 John 5:21 employs τηρέω with ἀπό, indicating that, as in the Septuagint, ἐκ and ἀπό are difficult to distinguish as to meaning in the New Testament. Both may mean "separation from." (Compare John 17: 15 with James 1:27; Mark 1:10 with Matthew 3:16; and 1 Thessalonians 1:10 with Romans 5:9.)

23. In addition to the verbal constructions with ἐκ, the nonverbal expression ελεύθερο...ἐκ πάντων ("free from all") in 1 Corinthians 9:19 seems to use ἐκ in a way that indicates a position outside its object.

24. Smith notes a further correlation with Revelation 3:10. "It is significant that Jesus is the speaker and John the writer just as is the case in the Revelation [3:10] text, and that in each case mention is made of a coming hour of suffering. In all probability, therefore, the meaning of the phrase from *the* hour is similar in both instances" (J.B. Smith, *A Revelation of Jesus Christ: A Commentary on the Book of Revelation*, ed. J. Otis Yoder [Scottdale, PA: Herald Press, 1961], 331).

25. William F. Arndt and F. Wilbur Gingrich, *A Greek-English Lexicon of the New Testament and Other Early Christian Literature* (Chicago: University of Chicago Press, 1957), 805-06.

26. Robertson, *A Grammar of the Greek New Testament*, p. 598.

27. Smith, *A Revelation of Jesus Christ*, 331.

28. Thomas Hewitt, "The Epistle to the Hebrews: An Introduction and Commentary," *Tyndale New Testament Commentaries* (Grand Rapids: Wm. B. Eerdmans Publishing Co., 1960), 99-100.

29. Both Bruce and Lenski are correct in answering the question of how the Lord's prayers were answered since He went to the cross in spite of His prayers. "While Gethsemane provides 'the most telling illustration' of our author's words, they have a more general reference to the whole course of our Lord's humiliation and passion" (F. F. Bruce, "The Epistle to the Hebrews: The English Text with Introduction, Exposition and Notes," *New International Commentary on the*

New Testament [Grand Rapids: Wm. B. Eerdmans Publishing Co., 1964, 100]. "Jesus prayed for deliverance from death only with an 'if: 'if it be possible' (Matt. 26:39); 'if this cup may not pass away from me, except I drink it' (v. 42). The real burden of his prayer was: 'Nevertheless, not what I will, but what thou wilt' (Mark 14:36). So also Matt. 26:39, 42, 'thy will be done,' and this prayer of Jesus was fully and truly granted" (R. C. H. Lenski, *The Interpretation of the Epistle to the Hebrews and the Epistle of James* [Minneapolis: Augsburg Publishing House, 1943], 164).

30. Walter W. Wessel, "The Epistle of James," in *The Wycliffe Bible Commentary*, eds. Charles F. Pfeiffer and Everett F. Harrison (Chicago: Moody Press, 1962), 1439.

31. As Morris puts it: " 'Keep thee from (ἐκ) the hour of temptation' might mean 'keep thee from undergoing the trial' or 'keep thee right through the trial.' The Greek is capable of either meaning" (Leon Morris, "The Revelation of St. John: An Introduction and Commentary," *Tyndale New Testament Commentaries* [Grand Rapids: Wm. B. Eerdmans Publishing Co. 1969], 80). Cf. Henry Alford, *The Greek Testament: with a Critically Revised Text, a Digest of Various Readings, Marginal References to Verbal and Idiomatic Usage, Prolegomena, and a Critical and Exegetical Commentary*, rev. Everett F. Harrison, 4 vols., vol. 4: *Hebrews-Revelation* (Chicago: Moody Press, 1958), 585; James Moffatt, "The Revelation of St. John the Divine," in *The Expositor's Greek Testament*, ed. W. Robertson Nicoll, 5 vols. (London: Hodder & Stoughton, 1900-10), 5 (1910):368.

32. *Theological Dictionary of the New Testament*, s.v. "τηρέω" by Harald Riesenfeld, 8:142.

33. Although τοῦ πονηροῦ may be either masculine or neuter, it is most likely masculine and a reference to Satan, according to Johannine usage, (cf. John 12:31; 14:30; 16:11; 1 John 2:13-14; 3:12; 5:18-19).

34. Gundry, *The Church and the Tribulation*, 59.

35. Evidently, combining τηρέω with ἐκ modifies the meaning of the preposition from the primary meaning of motion out from within to the secondary meaning of outside position (S. Lewis Johnson, Jr., class notes in 228 The Revelation, Dallas Theological Seminary, Fall 1976).

36. Gundry, *The Church and the Tribulation*, 59.

37. For evidence that πειρασμός was associated with θλῖψις in the New Testament, compare Luke 8:13 with Matthew 13:21 and Mark 4:17.

38. Mounce thinks that the hour is "three and a half years of rule by Antichrist in Revelation 13:5-10. In fact, all the judgments from 6:1 onward relate to this final hour of trial" (Robert H. Mounce, "The Book of Revelation," *New International Commentary on the New Testament* [Grand Rapids: Wm. B. Eerdmans Publishing Co., 1977, 119]. However, it seems better in the light of the seventieth week concept of Daniel 9:27 to see the hour as a seven year period of time. Cf. Henry C. Thiessen, "Will the Church Pass through the Tribulation?" *Bibliotheca Sacra* 92 (January-March 1935):45-50.

39. Henry C. Thiessen, "Will the Church Pass through the Tribulation?" *Bibliotheca Sacra* 92 (April-June 1935):202-03.

40. Charles Caldwell Ryrie, *A Survey of Bible Doctrine* (Chicago: Moody Press, 1972), 170.

41. Gundry, *The Church and the Tribulation*, 60.

42. *Theological Dictionary of the New Testament*, s.v. "ὥρα," by Gerhard Delling, 9:677.

43. Gundry, *The Church and the Tribulation*, 60.

44. That it is possible for ἀπό to indicate prior existence in its object (as ἐκ normally does) is demonstrated by its use in Psalm 69:14 (Septuagint, 68:14) and Psalm 140:1, 4 (Septuagint, 139:1,4). According to Turner, in both the Septuagint and the New Testament ἀπό encroaches on ἐκ (James Hope Moulton, *A Grammar of New Testament Greek*, 4 vols. [Edinburgh: T. & T. Clark, 1906-76], vol. 3 [1963]; *Syntax*, by Nigel Turner, 250-51).

45. Some posttribulationists insist that οἰκουμένη limits the hour of testing to the Roman world of John's day. Bell writes, "The seemingly universal terms are used elsewhere in the New Testament to mean the civilized world of that day, i.e. the Roman Empire.... The several empire-wide persecutions of Christians could easily satisfy the universal terminology" (William Everett Bell, Jr., "A Critical Evaluation of the Pretribulation Rapture Doctrine in Christian Eschatology" [Ph.D. diss., New York University, 1967], 304). But as Johnston notes, οἰκουμένη may have a very wide reference.... Sometimes it is synonymous with αἰών and κόσμος ....Hence, *oecumenē* may mean also mankind as a whole..." (George Johnston, "Οἰκουμένη and Κόσμος in the New Testament," *New Testament Studies* 10 [April 1964:353). This is exemplified by the use of οἰκουμένη in Matthew 24:14 and Acts 17:31. Commenting on the use of οἰκουμένη in the Matthew passage, Michel writes, "It is certainly not to be linked here with political imperial style. The reference is simply to the glad message which is for all

nations and the whole earth" *(Theological Dictionary of the New Testament,* s.v. *"ἡ οἰκουμένης"* by Otto Michel, 5:158). In both Acts 17:31 and Revelation 3:10 οἰκουμένη is set in an eschatological context that also seems to demand the widest possible reference.

Furthermore, the next phrase in Revelation 3:10 τοὺς κατοικοῦντας ἐπί τῆς γῆς (."those who dwell upon the earth"), is used only pejoratively in Revelation (cf. 6: 10; 8:13; 11:10; 13:8, 14; 17:8), thus indicating that unbelievers are designated by the phrase. This is fatal to Bell's view because, as Brown points out. "If the enemies of the Christian religion are to be affected...by the 'hour of trial,' it is clear that the author cannot be thinking of a persecution directed against Christians" (Schuyler Brown, " 'The Hour of Trial' (Rev. 3:10)," *Journal of Biblical Literature* 85 [Summer 1966]:310).

46. Cf. *Theological Dictionary of the New Testament.* s.v. "πεῖπα κτλ" by Heinrich Seesemann, 6:23; and Thayer, *A Greek-English Lexicon of the New Testament,* 646.
47. Richard Chenevix Trench, *Synonyms of the New Testament* (New York: Redfield, 1854), 281. Cf. *Theological Dictionary of the New Testament,* s.v. "πει–πα κτλ" 6:23.
48. Johnson, class notes.
49. Alva J. McClain, *The Greatness of the Kingdom* (Grand Rapids: Zondervan Publishing House, 1959), 465.

Chapter Nineteen—Is There a Pre-wrath Rapture?
1. This essay is a condensed version of a 75-page work, "A Review of *The Pre-Wrath Rapture of the Church* by Marvin Rosenthal"published by and available from Ariel Ministries, P.O. Box 3723, Tustin, CA 92681.

Chapter Twenty—A Critique of Progressive Dispensational Hermeneutics
1. E.g., Robert L. Saucy, *The Case for Progressive Dispensationalism: The Interface Between Dispensational & Non-Dispensational Theology* (Grand Rapids: Zondervan, 1993), 8-9; Craig A. Blaising and Darrell L. Bock, *Progressive Dispensationalism* (Wheaton: Victor, 1993), 317 n. 15; cf. Walter A. Elwell, "Dispensationalists of the Third Kind," *Christianity Today* 38 no. 10 (September 12, 1994): 28.
2. Blaising and Bock, *Progressive Dispensationalism,* 48.
3. For purposes of this chapter, Craig A. Blaising, Darrell L. Bock, and Robert L. Saucy— sometimes called "the father of Progressive Dispensationalism"—will receive major attention because of their key leadership roles among progressive dispensationalists.
4. E.g., Craig A. Blaising, "Dispensationalism: The Search for Definition," *Dispensationalism, Israel, and the Church: The Search for Definition,* eds. Craig A. Blaising and Darrell L. Bock (Grand Rapids: Zondervan, 1992), 16-34; Saucy, *Progressive Dispensationalism,* 9.
5. Darrell L. Bock, "The Son of David and the Saints' Task: The Hermeneutics of Initial Fulfillment," *Bibliotheca Sacra* 150, no. 600 (October-December 1993): 442.
6. Robert L. Saucy, "The Church as the Mystery of God," *Dispensationalism, Israel, and the Church:* eds. Blaising and Bock, 150; idem, *Progressive Dispensationalism,* 9, 29.
7. E.g., Elwell, "Dispensationalists of the Third Kind," 28.
8. Darrell L. Bock, "Current Messianic Activity and OT Davidic Promise: Dispensationalism, Hermeneutics, and NT Fulfillment," *Trinity Journal* 15NS (1994): 70 n. 29; cf. Elwell, "Dispensationalists of the Third Kind," 28.
9. See Charles Caldwell Ryrie, *Dispensationalism Today* (Chicago: Moody, 1965), 20, 45-46, 86-90; J. Dwight Pentecost, *Things to Come* (Findlay, OH: Dunham, 1958), 11-12, 33, 60-61; Thomas D. Ice, "Dispensational Hermeneutics," *Issues in Dispensationalism,* Wesley R. Willis and John R. Master, gen. eds. (Chicago: Moody, 1994), 32. Ice points out the error of Poythress and Blaising in attributing a spiritualized hermeneutics to early dispensationalists such as Darby and Scofield. Dispensationalism has always practiced a literal method of interpretation (Ice, "Dispensational Hermeneutics," 37-38).
10. Blaising and Bock, *Progressive Dispensationalism,* 35-36.
11. Ibid., 36.
12. Ibid., 37.
13. Ibid., 58, 77
14. Ibid., 52.
15. Blaising, "Dispensationalism: The Search," 30.
16. Blaising and Bock, *Progressive Dispensationalism,* 77.
17. Ibid., 83.
18. The *Journal of the Evangelical Theological Society* plans to publish my partial evaluation of recent developments in evangelical hermeneutics in one of its forthcoming issues (in 1995 or 1996). The title of the article is "Current Hermeneutical Trends: Clarification or Obfuscation?"

19. Milton S. Terry, *Biblical Hermeneutics*, 2nd ed. (Grand Rapids: Zondervan, n.d.); Bernard Ramm, *Protestant Biblical Interpretation, A Textbook of Hermeneutics*, 3rd. rev. ed. (Grand Rapids: Baker, 1970).
20. Terry, *Biblical Hermeneutics*, 595 [emphasis in original]
21. Ibid., 152-53
22. Ramm, *Protestant Biblical Interpretation*, 115-16. Ramm also quotes Luther to emphasize this point: "The best teacher is the one who does not bring his meaning into the Scripture but gets his meaning from Scripture" (Ibid., 115, citing Farrar, *History of Interpretation*, 475).
23. E.g., Craig A. Blaising and Darrell L. Bock, "Dispensationalism, Israel, and the Church Assessment and Dialogue," *Dispensationalism, Israel, and the Church*, eds. Blaising and Bock, 380; Blaising and Bock, *Progressive Dispensationalism*, 58-61.
24. Bock, "Current Messianic Activity," 72
25. Blaising and Bock, *Progressive Dispensationalism*, 59.
26. Dan McCartney and Charles Clayton, *Let the Reader Understand, A Guide to Interpreting and Applying the Bible* (Wheaton, IL: Victor, 1994), 65; cf. Millard J. Erickson, *Evangelical Interpretation, Perspectives on Hermeneutical Issues* (Grand Rapids: Baker, 1993), 88
27. Saucy, *Progressive Dispensationalism*, 32.
28. Terry, *Biblical Hermeneutics*, 231 [emphasis in original].
29. Ibid., 205
30. Ramm, *Protestant Biblical Interpretation*, 150
31. Ibid., 154 [emphasis in original].
32. Bock, "The Son of David," 445
33. Ibid., 445 n 9. Blaising and Bock elsewhere call the three levels of reading the historical-exegetical, the biblical-theological, and the canonical-systematic (Blaising and Bock, *Progressive Dispensationalism*, 100-01)
34. Bock, "The Son of David," 447.
35. Ibid.
36. Bock, "Current Messianic Activity,' 71, cf. Blaising and Bock, *Progressive Dispensationalism*, 64
37. Saucy, *Progressive Dispensationalism*, 87 (see also n. 24)
38. Ibid., 18
39. Ibid., 235.
40. Blaising and Bock, *Progressive Dispensationalism*, 29-30
41. Terry, *Biblical Hermeneutics*, 205
42. Ramm, *Protestant Biblical Interpretation*, 113.
43. Blaising and Bock, "Dispensationalism, Israel, and the Church, 392-93
44. Blaising and Bock, *Progressive Dispensationalism*, 68.
45. Bock, "Current Messianic Activity," 71.
46. Ibid. Progress in divine revelation is quite apparent in tracing through the books of the Old and New Testaments chronologically, but "progress" in the sense only of adding to what has already been revealed, not in any sense of a change of previous revelation. To change the substance of something already written is not "progress"; it is an "alteration" or "change' that raises questions about the credibility of the text's original meaning
47. Saucy, *Progressive Dispensationalism*, 42-43
48. Ibid., 71.
49. Ibid., 72
50. E.g., ibid., 134, 211.
51. Cf. ibid., 205-06
52. Ibid., 33
53. Saucy himself illustrates the difference between divine and human perspectives in his defense of the validity of an offer of the kingdom to Israel prior to the prophesied cross of Christ: "We suggest that the solution lies in the same realm as other problems related to the sovereign decree of God for history and the responsible actions of mankind. The idea that God could offer humankind a real choice and opportunity, knowing all the while that humankind would fail (and, in fact, having decreed a plan on the basis of that failure), is expressed in other passages of Scripture. In Eden, humankind was given a genuine opportunity to choose holiness, yet Scripture indicates that God's plan already included the sacrifice of Christ 'from the creation of the world' (Rev 13:8; cf. Acts 2:23; 4:28). Thus in this instance, a similar unanswerable question as that related to the offer of the kingdom might be posed: What would have happened to the death of Christ if Adam and Eve had not sinned?" (Ibid., 92). The analogy holds here too: the humanly discernible meaning of these Old Testament passages was limited to the single

connotation determined by grammatical and historical factors, the additional divine nuance being reserved for later New Testament revelation to humans. The answer to the question, "What would have happened to the added meanings if the NT writers had never penned new meanings to OT passages?" is also unanswerable. Would the meanings have remained unknown to men?

54. Ramm, *Protestant Biblical Interpretation*, 40-42.
55. Terry, *Biblical Hermeneutics*, 583.
56. E.g., McCartney and Clayton, *Let the Reader*, 162, 164; cf. William W. Klein, Craig L. Blomberg, and Robert L. Hubbard, Jr. *Introduction to Biblical Interpretation* (Dallas: Word, 1993), 139, 145-50; Moisés Silva, *An Introduction to Biblical Hermeneutics, The Search for Meaning*, coauthored with Walter C. Kaiser (Grand Rapids: Zondervan, 1994), 267.
57. Blaising and Bock, *Progressive Dispensationalism*, 64.
58. Ibid.
59. Ibid.; cf. also ibid., 65-68.
60. Bock elsewhere denies that this hermeneutical principle amounts to *sensus plenior* or spiritualizing interpretation, choosing to refer to it as "pattern" fulfillment or typological-prophetic fulfillment ("Current Messianic Activity," 69; cf. Blaising and Bock, *Progressive Dispensationalism*, 102-04). Whatever name one applies to the practice, it still violates the strict standards of a consistent grammatical-historical interpretation
61. Bock, "The Son of David," 446.
62. Saucy, *Progressive Dispensationalism*, 49
63. Ibid., 71.
64. Ibid., 56.
65. Ibid., 206.
66. Ramm, *Protestant Biblical Interpretation*, 140-41. Terry also warns, "... We must avoid the danger of overstepping in this matter [i.e., the matter of using cross-references too carelessly]" (Terry, *Biblical Hermeneutics*, 222), and "There may be a likeness of sentiment without any real parallelism [i.e., in regard to verbal parallels between separate passages]" (ibid., 223)
67. Bock, "The Son of David," 447-48, 451-52.
68. Cf. ibid., 449-54.
69. Ramm, *Protestant Biblical Interpretation*, 113.
70. Cf. Blaising and Bock, "Dispensationalism, Israel, and the Church," 393 n. 8; Bock, "The Son of David," 456 n. 26; idem, "Current Messianic Activity," 84; Saucy, "The Church as the Mystery," 144.
71. Cf. Frederic Louis Godet, *Commentary on Romans* (1977 reprint, Grand Rapids: Kregel, 1883), 504-05; James M. Stifler, *The Epistle to the Romans* (Chicago: Moody, 1960), 254-55

Glossary

The terms listed below occur throughout the book. The definitions given are broad and intended to help the non-theological reader.

Abomination of desolation—The Antichrist's desecration of the holy of holies in the third temple, in the middle of the Tribulation

Apocalyptic—Adj., prophetic; n., prophetic literature.

Amillennialism—The second coming of Christ is the final event of history and there is no earthly millennial kingdom.

Covenant theology—A system of theology that interprets Scripture from the perspective of salvation covenants between God and humanity.

Critical method—Approach to Scripture historically rooted in liberalism, which interprets the Bible primarily as literature, rejecting its inspiration and inerrancy, dismissing a literal interpretation of biblical prophecy.

Dispensationalism—A system of theology that interprets Scripture literally and from the perspective of God's interaction with humanity through successive ages.

Eschatology—The study of end times.

Exegetical—Pertaining to the study of Scripture from the original languages.

Futurist—The belief that major prophetic events are yet future.

Hermeneutic—One's method of interpreting literature, especially Scripture.

Historicism—The belief that major prophetic events are being fulfilled during the current church age.

Idealism—The belief that the timing of major prophetic events are undetermined.

Majority Greek Text—An edition of the Greek New Testament as the text found in most existing manuscripts.

Midtribulationism—A type of premillennialism in which the rapture will occur in the middle of the seven year Tribulation.

Millennium—The future 1000-year messianic-kingdom reign of Christ on earth

Olivet discourse—Christ's prophetic sermon which is found in the following passages: Matthew 24–25; Mark 13; Luke 17:22-37: 21:5-38

Postmillennialism—The belief that the second coming of Christ is prior to the millennium

Posttribulationism—A type of premillennialism in which the rapture will occur after the seven-year Tribulation.

Premillennialism—The belief that the second coming of Christ follows the millennium.

Preterist—The belief that most major prophetic events have already been fulfilled in history.

Pretribulationism—A type of premillennialism in which the rapture will occur before the seven-year Tribulation.

Pre-wrath rapture theory—A type of premillennialism in which the rapture will occur approximately three-fourths of the way through the seven-year Tribulation.

Progressive dispensationalism—A recent form of dispensationalism which emphasizes the present spiritual reign of Christ on David's throne.

Rapture—The coming of the Lord to meet the church in the air.

Septuagint—An ancient Greek translation of the Hebrew Old Testament.

Textus Receptus—An edition of the Greek New Testament from the sixteenth century used in the translation of the King James version.

Tribulation—The seven-year period also known as the seventieth week of Daniel

About the
Editors and Contributors

Malcom O. Couch, Th.D., Ph.D., is founder and dean of Tyndale Theological Seminary and Tyndale Biblical Institute in Texas.

Larry V. Crutchfield, M. Phil., Ph.D., is a mentor for Faraston Theological Seminary and a free-lance writer living in Colorado.

Timothy J. Demy, M.A., Th.D., is a military chaplain living in Washington, D.C, and editor.

Floyd S. Elmore, Th.M., Th.D., is an associate professor of Bible at Cedarville College in Ohio.

John S. Feinberg, Th.M., Ph.D., is associate professor of Bible and Systematic Theology at Trinity Evangelical Divinity School in Illinois.

Paul D. Feinberg, M.A., Th.D., is professor of Bible and Systematic Theology at Trinity Evangelical Divinity School in Illinois.

Arnold G. Fruchtenbaum, Th.M., Ph. D., is founder and director of Ariel Ministries in California.

Robert G. Gromacki, Th.M., Th.D., is distinguished professor of Bible and Greek at Cedarville College in Ohio.

Edward E. Hindson, Th.D., D.Phil., is vice-president of *There's Hope!* in Atlanta, Georgia, and is distinguished visiting professor at Liberty University in Virginia.

H. Wayne House, J.D., Th.D, is a visiting professor of Theology at various institutions and a free-lance writer living in Oregon.

Thomas D. Ice, B.A., Th.M., is executive director of the Pre-Trib Research Center in Washington, D.C, and an editor and contributor.

Grant R. Jeffrey is an internationally recognized Bible teacher and bestselling author living in Toronto, Canada.

Elliott E. Johnson, Th.M., Th.D., is professor of Bible Exposition at Dallas Theological Seminary.

Tim F. LaHaye, D.Min., D.D., is a bestselling author and the director of Family Life Seminars in Washington, D.C.

John A. McLean, Th.M., Ph.D., is president of Michigan Theological Seminary.

J. Dwight Pentecost, Th.M., Th.D., is distinguished professor emeritus at Dallas Theological Seminary.

J. Randall Price, Th.M., Ph.D., is founder and director of World of the Bible Ministries in Texas.

Charles C. Ryrie, Th.D., Ph.D., is professor emeritus at Dallas Theological Seminary and adjunct professor at Philadelphia College of Bible.

Gerald B. Stanton, Th.M., Th.D., is president of Ambassadors International in Florida.

Robert L. Thomas, Th.M., Th.D., is professor of New Testament Language and Literature at The Master's Seminary in California.

Stanley D. Toussaint, Th.M., Th.D., is professor emeritus at Dallas Theological Seminary.

Jeffrey L. Townsend, B.A., Th.M., is pastor of Woodland Park Community Church in Colorado.

John F. Walvoord, Th.D., D.D., is chancellor and professor emeritus at Dallas Theological Seminary.

Other Good
Harvest House Reading

READY TO REBUILD
by *Thomas Ice and Randall Price*

A fast-moving overview of contemporary events which indicate that a significant move to rebuild the Temple is gaining momentum in Israel. Important pictures and charts.

HOW TO STUDY BIBLE PROPHECY FOR YOURSELF
by *Tim LaHaye*

This excellent book provides fascinating study helps and charts that will make personal Bible study more interesting and exciting. A three-year program is outlined for a good working knowledge of the Bible.

IN SEARCH OF TEMPLE TREASURES
by *J. Randall Price*

The product of years of research and interviews with religious leaders and archaeologists in Israel, this book takes readers on a treasure hunt through the world of the past, with a look toward the prophetic world to come.

THE MASTER PLAN
by *David R. Reagan*
A riveting tour of the prophets and prophecy contained in the Bible, laying a foundation for a fuller understanding of Scriptures relating to the end times. A balanced and thoughtful approach.